ARTISTIC IMPRESSIONS:
FIGURE SKATING, MASCULINITY, AN .... OF SPORT

In contemporary North America, figure skating ranks among the most 'feminine' of sports, and few boys take it up for fear of being labelled effeminate or gay. Yet figure skating was once an exclusively male pastime – women did not skate in significant numbers until the late 1800s, at least a century after the founding of the first skating club. Only in the 1930s did figure skating begin to acquire its feminine image.

Artistic Impressions is the first history to trace figure skating's striking transformation from gentlemen's art to 'girls' sport.' With a focus on masculinity, Mary Louise Adams examines how skating's evolving gender identity has been reflected on the ice and in the media, looking at rules, technique, and style and at ongoing debates about the place of 'art' in sport. Uncovering the little-known history of skating, *Artistic Impressions* shows how ideas about sport, gender, and sexuality have combined to limit the forms of physical expression available to men.

MARY LOUISE ADAMS is an associate professor in the School of Kinesiology and Health Studies and the Department of Sociology at Queen's University.

MARY LOUISE ADAMS

Artistic Impressions

Figure Skating, Masculinity, and the Limits of Sport

UNIVERSITY OF TORONTO PRESS
Toronto Buffalo London

Reprinted 2012

ISBN 978-1-4426-4318-5 (cloth)
ISBN 978-1-4426-1171-9 (paper)

Printed on acid-free paper.

Library and Archives Canada Cataloguing in Publication

Adams, Mary Louise, 1960–
Artistic impressions : figure skating, masculinity, and the limits of sport /
Mary Louise Adams.

Includes bibliographical references and index.
ISBN 978-1-4426-4318-5 (bound). – ISBN 978-1-4426-1171-9 (pbk.)

1. Figure skating – History.   2. Figure skating – Social aspects.
3. Masculinity in sports.   I. Title.

GV850.4.A33 2011   796.91'2081   C2010-907148-4

This book has been published with the help of a grant from the Canadian
Federation for the Humanities and Social Sciences, through the Aid to
Scholarly Publications Program, using funds provided by the Social
Sciences and Humanities Research Council of Canada.

University of Toronto Press acknowledges the financial assistance to its
publishing program of the Canada Council for the Arts and the Ontario
Arts Council.

University of Toronto Press acknowledges the financial support of the
Government of Canada through the Canada Book Fund for its publishing
activities.

Contents

Illustrations follow page 172

Acknowledgments

This book has been very long in the making. Its first iteration was a course paper for a graduate seminar with Roger Simon at the Ontario Institute for Studies in Education almost twenty years ago. After turning the essay into a few conference presentations and a short article, I thought I was done. I wrote a dissertation on another subject, started teaching, changed cities and jobs, and worked on other things, but through all that the questions about figure skating kept coming back. Eventually I gave in. The story was too compelling to be left untold. And so, what started as a fairly straightforward analysis of contemporary men's skating evolved into a broad historical project that spanned more than two centuries and several national contexts. I would not have been able to complete this work without a tremendous amount of practical and moral support.

I was very fortunate to receive financial and other forms of institutional support as I carried out my research. Long-term, single-author projects on cultural topics like the gender history of figure skating are not very close to the top of the current research policy agenda in Canada. One worries that, in the future, researchers who want to pursue such work will have to struggle to follow their intellectual inclinations. I want to acknowledge the many scholars, professional societies, and faculty associations that have been working hard to make sure that curiosity-based (non-applied) humanities research and the scholars who undertake it continue to thrive in the Canadian university environment.

Funding for this project was provided by the Social Sciences and Humanities Research Council of Canada, a Queen's University Chancellor's Research Award, two grants from the Queen's University Advisory Research Committee, and a University Research Grant from the Faculty of Social Sciences at Carleton University. I conducted most of my primary archival research during the course of a year-long sabbatical that allowed me time away from my teaching position at Queen's University. A second six-month sabbatical, spent as Visiting Scholar in the Centre for Women's Studies in Education at the University of Toronto, provided time and space for writing.

I am indebted to a number of colleagues and friends who have read portions of the manuscript and offered thoughtful feedback that has made the final product much better than it otherwise might have been: Hart Cantelon, Karen Dubinsky, Samantha King, Mary McDonald, Eric Mykhalovskiy, and Geoff Smith. William Bridel and Eleanor Mac-Donald both read the entire manuscript – a huge task for which I am especially grateful. My old comrade Bob Gardner gave me an excellent critique of the original paper out of which this book grew. British skating historian Dennis Bird read early drafts of two chapters and offered useful advice and careful criticism. I regret that I was not able to send him a copy of the completed book before he passed away. His 1979 history of the National Skating Association of Great Britain still stands as the best institutional history of the sport. I am also very appreciative of the careful reading of the manuscript – not once but twice! – by the two anonymous reviewers engaged by the University of Toronto Press. Their comments and constructive criticisms have improved this work considerably. Any remaining weaknesses persist despite their diligent efforts to make this a better book.

Over the years I have received all manner of practical assistance from friends, friends of friends, relatives, and acquaintances. Patricia Chafe – a consultant to the International Skating Union – explained skating's new scoring system to me. She also helped me to understand the way that gender inequalities have been built right into it. My former skating teacher Fred Hawryliw agreed to be interviewed in the very early days of the project. Historians Gertrude Pfister, Doug Brown, and Paul Deslandes all responded to queries and offered sources. Nicole LaViolette and the late Alan Berube forwarded newspaper clippings as I was getting started. Barbara Adams and Julie Guard collected newspapers for me. Barbara Adams, Bob Gardner, Cathy Humphreys, Helen Humphreys, and Eric Mykhalovskiy made tapes of televised skating competitions. Paul Renwick shared with me his wonderful unpublished Master's research paper on skating in New York City in the nineteenth century. Debi Brock passed on a collection of old skating publications that had been collected by a neighbour who used to be a professional skater.

My understanding of contemporary skating has been much improved by conversations with William Bridel, who provided significant support to the project in terms of research assistance and an extensive insider knowledge of the sport. He has also made the last stages of the project much more fun. The late Susan Shea contributed her fabulous library skills as the big version of the project was getting off the ground. Alana Hermiston did an excellent job during weeks of archival and other research work in Ottawa. Special thanks are also due to Alana's father Ian Hermiston, who is a stellar and very generous clipper and taper. The final stages of the project would never have been completed without the careful help of Martyn Clark. The other Queen's University students who have assisted with this work are Kristi Allain, Michele Donnelly, Tamara Ferguson, Leanne Findlay, Audrey Giles, Tiff Mochinsky, Alissa Overend, Shannon Smith, and Anne Warner. Former Queen's student Mark Falcous helped me track down sources in England.

Many of the German translations that appear in this book were provided by Christine Reisinger and Ruba Turjman. Christine also provided excellent research assistance and many diversions in Vienna. At some point during the course of the project, it became clear that I was going to have to learn at least some German myself. Jorica Perryman and Jill Scott kindly let me sit in on their undergraduate classes in the Department of German at Queen's. A language training grant from the DAAD, the Deutscher Akademischer Austausch Dienst, made possible further study at the Goethe Institute in Berlin. Petra Fachinger has been a huge support, providing assistance and encouragement, supplying me with German-language resources, connecting me with tutors, and helping me with my own shaky translations.

When I was an undergraduate my fantasy of the academic life involved a lot of reading – on topics of my own choosing – at big tables in quiet rooms full of books. I got to do a lot of that over the course of this project. My research was made possible by the collections and work of archivists and librarians at: the archives of Skate Canada, where I had excellent assistance from Emery Leger and Natalie Park; the World Figure Skating Museum and Archives, especially Karen Cover; Library and Archives Canada; the British Library; the National Library of Scotland; the Austrian National Library; and the German National Library. I would not have been able to work at the British Library had Frances

Humphreys not introduced me to her old friend Anne Seagrim. Thanks are due to Anne for the exceptional hospitality that made a research trip to London a great adventure. Research in Vienna would have been neither possible nor so enjoyable without the friendship of Marlene Rodrigues, Christine Reisinger, Bernadette Haller, and, especially, Ines Rieder, who facilitated a little bit of everything – housing, language, research, and fun. The incredible luck of running across Ines in Vienna – after having last seen her more than a decade earlier in Toronto – was a happy coincidence that has been a great bonus of working on this book.

When I began to study figure skating, I was a historian of sexuality. Somewhere between then and now I found an intellectual home in the cultural studies of sport and the body. For making this shift I have been rewarded with fantastic colleagues. I first crossed paths with Samantha King when she too was working on a paper about figure skating. When she joined our department at Queen's, several years later, a colleague joked that we should set up a figure skating research group in recognition of the fact that the department was now home to the greatest concentration of skating researchers in the world. There was no centre, of course. But I have been fortunate to have collaborated with Sammi in many other ways both inside and outside the department, academically and otherwise, and she has been an important influence on my thinking. Her friendship has made life at work and, more importantly, away from work a lot richer.

Thanks to current and former colleagues in what is now called the School of Kinesiology and Health Studies at Queen's University for taking a chance on a social historian who was just starting to get interested in sport and for making the department so collegial. Thanks especially to my colleagues in the sociocultural field from whom I have learned so much: Rob Beamish, Hart Cantelon, Samantha King, Elaine Power, and Geoff Smith. Thanks also to successive department heads, all of whom have supported this lengthy project and all of whom were kind enough not to ask when it was going to be completed: Joan Stevenson, Janice Deakin, Jean Côté, and Pat Costigan. In the broader world of sport sociology, thanks to feminist colleagues and friends – Judy Davidson, Michelle Helstein, Kathy Jamieson, Mary McDonald, and Geneviève Rail – who are a constant source of analysis, advice, and good humour. Thanks also to Brian Pronger, whose early encouragement made this project seem like a good idea and whose insistence on going dancing at conferences made sport sociology seem a lot more fun. For many years of friendship that has helped to keep university life in perspective, I am grateful to Kingston friends Susan Belyea, Elizabeth Christie, Karen Dubinsky, Stevenson Fergus, Paul Kelley, Susan Lord, Kip Pegley, and Jon Sargent. Thanks are also due to my friend and former skating coach Dale Ashworth and the long-standing group of adult figure skaters with whom I have been sharing the 'pretty art' and some of the ideas in this book for years.

Thank you to my old friend Becki Ross who was in the right place at the right time to help this book find its way to the desk of University of Toronto Press editor Len Husband. Thanks to Len for taking seriously a not-quite finished manuscript and making sure it actually turned into a book, to copy-editor John St James for improving the text, and to Doug Richmond for his persistence and patience with the cover. I am also grateful to Jeffrey Buttle, who allowed the Press to use the wonderful photograph of him that appears on the cover.

Thanks to my sister, Barbara Adams, and to the friends who have been providing the right mix of sustained support and distraction for, well, quite a long time: Craig Dale, Helen Humphreys, the late Hazel Humphreys, Bruce Martin, Eric Mykhalovskiy, Daintry Norman, Todd Sherman, Barb Wisnoski. As I have worked through the last not-always-pretty stages of completing this book I have been immensely thankful to have had the intellectual, emotional, and practical support of my partner Eleanor MacDonald, whose insight and clear thinking made the process and the book better. Finally, I am incredibly grateful that my parents – my mother Betty Adams, who passed away in the middle of this project, and my father, Donald Adams – thought it would be a good thing for my sister and brother and I to learn how to figure skate and that they had the resources to make that happen. Those early lessons fostered the love for the sport that grounds this book.

Sections of this book were originally published in other publications. An early version of chapter 4 was published as 'The Manly History of a Girls' Sport: Gender, Class and the Development of Nineteenth-Century Figure Skating,' *International Journal for the History of Sport* 24, no. 7 (July 2007), 872–93, published by Taylor & Francis. A section of chapter 5 was included as part of 'Freezing Social Relations: Artificial Ice and the Social History of Skating,' in *Sites of Sport: Spaces, Place, Experience*, edited by Patricia Vertinsky and John Bales (London: Routledge, 2004), 57–72. Sections of chapter 6 previously appeared as 'From Mixed-Sex Sport to Sport for Girls: The Feminization of Figure

Skating,' *Sport in History* 30, no. 2 (June 2010), 218–41, published by Taylor & Francis. Discussions on male dancers that appear in chapters 3, 7, and 8 appeared previously in the article '"Death to the Prancing Prince": Effeminacy, Sport Discourses and the Salvation of Men's Dancing,' *Body and Society* 11, no. 4 (December 2005), 63–86, published by (at that time) Sage.

ARTISTIC IMPRESSIONS:
FIGURE SKATING, MASCULINITY, AND THE LIMITS OF SPORT

1 Introduction

When rivalry between the world's best men's figure skaters – sex addict-
ed, improvisational Chazz Michael Michaels and germophobic, precise
Jimmy MacElroy – breaks into a fight on the awards platform, they're
banned from the event for life. Three years later, desire for a gold medal
and a careful reading of the rules lead them to compete as skating's first
male-male pair.[1]

Cue the incredulous laughter. In the 2007 Hollywood comedy *Blades
of Glory*, comedian Will Ferrell stars as Chazz Michael Michaels, a
paunchy rocker and self-declared sex addict who fancies himself the
bad boy of figure skating. The winner of an 'adult film award,' he's a
'leather-clad Lothario' and a rough-edged anomaly in his sport. His
foil, played by Jon Heder, is the younger, prettier Jimmy MacElroy, a
former child prodigy who takes to the ice in full peacock regalia, furl-
ing and unfurling his royal blue arms, ruffling his feathers and flashing
his sequins. The two men come together like oil and water as they set
out to transform themselves into a competitive team. The improbability
of Chazz being a skater and the greater improbability of two straight
men (yes, Jimmy is straight) wanting to compete as a pair in one of
the world's most heterosexual sporting events, account for much of the
humour in what is, surprisingly, a very funny film. Much is made of
the contradiction between Chazz's exaggerated virility and the popular
stereotype of male skaters as effeminate and/or gay. Indeed, the promise of a good gay joke, inherent in the film's concept but admirably
resisted by the filmmakers, is surely one of the reasons *Blades of Glory*
rose immediately to the top of the *Variety* box office chart.[2]

In contemporary North America, the fit between figure skating and mainstream masculinity is not an easy one. This book is an attempt to make sense of their fraught relationship. What makes men's figure skating seem so incompatible with popular definitions of manliness? What inspires skating's lingering reputation, confirmed by the premise and the reception of *Blades of Glory*, as an effeminate sport suited primarily for sissies and gay men? Why do so few men and boys figure skate? Any boy raised in North America could give quick answers to such questions: Figure skating is not like other sports. Its costumes and music make it arty and dance-like and, therefore, more appropriate for girls than boys, just like ballet.

By virtue of choosing a so-called feminine sport, male figure skaters are often assumed to be effeminate themselves. In a culture in which effeminacy is the primary and most stereotypical signifier of male homosexuality, this means they are also often assumed to be gay. For many boys, gay and straight, three decades of gay rights victories and the increasing assimilation of queer people into mainstream culture have done little to make 'gay' a word with which they would want to be associated. In this book I use figure skating as a heuristic device to help me understand better the social context in which that fear of association persists. I am particularly concerned with sport as an important lens through which many boys and men make sense of themselves and the gendered world around them. *Artistic Impressions* is an attempt to decipher the persistent devaluing of effeminacy in mainstream contemporary North America and the special contribution sport makes in this regard.

When I began this project my starting point was the common sense 'fact' that figure skating is the quintessential 'girls' sport,' and thus boys and men who skate are put in an awkward position. As a sociologist who favours historical methods I should have known better: this starting point was exactly that which needed to be explained. In the more than four decades that I have been involved in skating, I have known it as a sport heavily dominated by girls and women. So I was surprised to learn that in much of Europe and North America the type of skating that evolved into figure skating was, in its earliest days, the almost-exclusive pursuit of upper-class men. Women did not start skating in significant numbers until the 1860s, more than a century after the world's first skating club was founded by a group of privileged men in Edinburgh, Scotland. It was not until the 1930s and 1940s, after several decades during which men and women participated in the sport on relatively equal terms – they actually competed against each other in some events – that figure skating started to be seen as a 'feminine' sport. How did the gendered meanings of skating come to shift so dramatically? What made possible the transformation of skating from a gentlemanly art to the so-called girls' sport we are familiar with today? This book attempts to answer these questions for academics and for skaters and skating fans interested in the history and gender politics of our sport. While I have tried to construct a text that might speak to both of these audiences, there will inevitably be portions that speak more to one than the other. I've tried to explain both skating terminology and sociological concepts in relatively accessible language – a task much easier for the skating than the sociology. But non-academic readers may still want to move quickly through (or past!) those parts of the book (including some parts of this introduction) that veer away from explicit discussions of skating and skaters. Still, as I hope will become clear, if one really wants to understand skating as a social phenomenon, one needs to move a surprising distance from what actually takes place on the ice.

Artistic Impressions analyses the history and the implications of the feminization of figure skating. It looks at figure skating in an attempt to historicize discourses of masculinity in the present day, especially the prejudices about effeminacy that hold figure skating outside the bounds of mainstream manliness. Why is it that male figure skaters, once considered fine specimens of manhood, are so often now perceived to be fey and are deprecated for their failure to meet masculine norms? How is it that behaviours once considered unremarkable and appropriate are now read as signs of gender transgression and sexual non-conformity? Under what conditions was it once acceptable for a man to leave an artistic impression or, without fear of ridicule, to make a conscious effort to comport his body with beauty and grace? Why is it – and more's the pity – that so few men want to, or feel able to, do so today?

The history of men's skating is, in part, a history of the relationship between effeminacy and dominant versions of masculinity. It is a history of the ways that effeminacy, as a marginalized social category, is produced through and against other versions of being a man that are culturally promoted and validated. As the narratives in this book demonstrate, this relationship is shaped by discourses of sexuality, class, race, and nation. Three decades of social history, critical race theory, and feminist theory have made clear the impossibility of understanding gender separate from other social categories. As early as the 1970s, feminist activists in the United States were talking about the convergence of race, gender, and class and the political necessity of addressing them as interdependent.[3] In the 1980s, feminists of colour in North America and Britain published work demonstrating the inseparability of race, gender, and class in the formation of both personal experience and broader social structures.[4] Such arguments are at the root of what is called intersectional analysis, an approach to scholarship that seeks out the interdependencies and interconnections among the different social relations through which identities, institutions, and social practices are constituted and through which power is exercised.[5] In later chapters it will become clear, for instance, that in England the acceptability of men's skating in the 1800s was a question not just of a generic masculinity but of a very particular upper- and, by the end of the century, upper-middle-class masculinity that would not have been viewed quite so congenially had it been expressed by either lower-middle-class or working-class men. In this example, class and gender came together to confirm for men who skated their elevated status, and thus skating, like other elite leisure pursuits, contributed to the broader cultural and political marginalization of those men who did not have the time or the resources to devote to such an esoteric physical skill, men who did not have the economic or cultural capital that would have enabled them to join a skating club.

The specific upper-class masculinity that shaped nineteenth-century English figure skating stemmed from a racialized world view that saw elegant activities like skating as symbols of 'civilized society,' an idealized community of interests that was seen as the exclusive domain of privileged white Europeans. Such ideas – and the activities and pastimes through which they were expressed – helped to justify and to bolster the imperialist projects being engineered around the globe by the class inhabited by men who skated. Needless to say, the building of an empire was no task for the effeminate; those to whom such a task was entrusted would have been loath to participate in any pursuit that might have had fey associations. Figure skating, at that point in time, among this particular group of men, had none, as I will show in chapters 4 and 5. Over the course of the nineteenth century, figure skating's masculine status was protected by stylistic changes that helped skaters conform to shifting definitions of manliness. In the 1820s and 1830s, skating had been full of expressive arm movements and dramatic poses. Had this expressive style persisted into the 1860s and 1870s, skaters would have found themselves on the wrong side of the gendered boundary that was emerging between sport and art, between manliness and effeminacy. The emergence of an unembellished and rigid style of movement kept the gender reputations of Victorian gentleman skaters intact in a context of imperial, capitalist expansion in which the middle class was rising to prominence and middle-class notions of respectability and restraint were gaining influence over the way upper-class people expressed themselves.

I have had two primary aims in writing this book: first, to understand how figure skating, once a manly pursuit, came to be overwritten by notions of effeminacy and, second, to consider the practical and ideological implications of that conjunction and what it might tell us about the broader politics of gender and sexuality today. To this end I contextualize my own reading of recent men's skating with a somewhat idiosyncratic history of the sport. *Artistic Impressions* is not a general history of figure skating; rather it is a history that prioritizes gender – masculinity in particular – in both idea and practice, while recognizing that gender cannot be understood apart from the other discursive formations, like class and race, through which it is constituted.

The history of skating makes two contributions to the study of sport more generally. First, it forces us to go beyond standard feminist criticism of gendered sport categories to demonstrate the social processes through which the notions of 'feminine-appropriate' and 'male-appropriate' sports have been produced and made to adhere differently at different times to particular forms of physical activity. Even in academic work, gendered sport categories are too often taken for granted. *Artistic Impressions* shows that such categories are not inevitable or unavoidable, or intrinsic to certain sports, but are, rather, social phenomena produced and reproduced through the ideologically motivated actions of people in particular historical and cultural contexts.

Second, a history of figure skating suggests the value of adding a historical dimension to studies of sport that are concerned with queer issues or that draw on queer theories. Over the past decade there has been a tremendous increase in research and writing in the field of queer sport studies, very little of which has adopted a historical perspective. One of the effects of the overwhelming orientation of this body of work to the present is that its primary categories of analysis – forms of gender and sexual identity and gender and sexual norms – seem stable and fixed. A historical perspective can help show the ways that such categories take shape, how they are both accepted and refused, how they change over time. In attending to the historical social processes through which adjectives like effeminate, gay, or transgender come to have meaning, researchers confirm one of the central tenets of queer theory: sexuality is fluid, and identities which attempt to fix it are the result of social and political processes which might best be understood as struggles over meaning.

The analysis that follows relies on an understanding of gender categories as fully embedded in and constituted by the exigencies of normative heterosexualities. With the term 'normative heterosexualities' I refer not just to heterosexuality as a sexual orientation, but to the social and cultural processes through which particular forms of heterosexuality are constantly reproduced as the norm and as 'normal' while other forms of heterosexuality and non-heterosexual identities are produced as abnormal, deviant, and definitely not the ideal. The process of normalization is key to relations of domination and marginalization; it has a powerful effect on how people understand themselves and the people around them. 'As a concept, normalization draws our attention to discourses and practices that produce subjects who are "normal," who live "normality," and, most importantly, who find it hard to imagine anything different ... As a form of social regulation, normalization defines and limits the choices that are available to us ... The point is not that we simply try to meet social norms, it's that we *want* to.'[6]

The French philosopher and social theorist Michel Foucault explains how such processes of normalization are routes for the circulation of power. Distinctions like those between normal and abnormal, legitimate and illegitimate, are expressions of power that determine the boundaries between social inclusion and exclusion. Foucault's great insight was that such processes are not simply repressive; we do not strive to meet definitions of normality because we are being forced to by more powerful individuals or by institutions; rather, we are encouraged to meet these definitions in myriad ways and when we do so we are rewarded. It's this productive aspect of power, as it works at the level of the individual that, Foucault says, is fundamental to the organization of modern societies.[7] In a frequently quoted passage Foucault writes, 'In thinking of the mechanisms of power, I am thinking ... of its capillary form of existence, the point where power reaches into the very grain of individuals, touches their bodies and inserts itself into their actions and attitudes, their discourses, learning processes and everyday lives.'[8] What he is trying to get us to think about here is a notion of power that is not just something that represses us – that prohibits or stops us from doing things; rather, it is something that works through us and produces us as particular kinds of individuals. When we feel bad because we are not satisfied with what our bodies look like, that is an effect of power. But it is also an effect of power when we have been working hard at the gym and we are happy with what we see in the mirror. In our society there are rewards for being fit and slim. The average person understands normative body ideals and wants to meet them. No one actually forces us to do this – we do this ourselves. In Foucault's view, this is how power works.

Among the norms that feel most important to our sense of who we are and to the sense that others make of us, are those related to sexuality and gender. During the late nineteenth and early twentieth centuries, as many historians have shown, sexuality came to be seen as fundamental to personality and identity, as the basis upon which a person's normality or lack thereof might be determined.[9] During the same period, the 'proper' alignment of bodies, genders, and desires came to be seen as key to this determination.[10] Male bodies should behave in masculine ways, they should desire female bodies, and female bodies should be inhabited by feminine personalities. It's an equation that has been widely challenged and discredited by feminist, transgender, and queer activists and scholars.[11] The goal of a project like *Artistic Impressions* and of the many others motivated by a similar politic is to contribute in some way to the future unintelligibility of this equation. Although I focus my analysis in this book most often on gender, it is always with the full appreciation that heterosexuality gives the binary organization of gender its meaning and stability in mainstream Western cultures. What becomes clear in the narratives I piece together here is that skating's effeminate reputation depends on a chain of meaning that privileges one among the many possible ways that bodies, sex, gender, and sexuality could be linked.

As a piece of research, *Artistic Impressions* has clear links to other work that might fall under the banner of queer sport studies. Certainly it was motivated by my own interest in and concern about mainstream understandings of queerness and their effects as they are produced and circulated in discourses and practices related to sport. As Samantha King and Heather Sykes have both pointed out in their recent and useful review articles, queer studies of sport and studies of queer sport make up a growing field.[12] There are two major themes in this literature, each of which has been approached from a number of theoretical perspectives. The first investigates the experiences of athletes who are variously identified as lesbian, gay, queer, transgender, or transsexual, in both mainstream and queer sport organizations. The second looks at sport as a cultural site permeated by discourses about gender and sexuality. Research in this vein looks at the contribution sport makes to homophobia, to binary understandings of gender, to the marginalization of people who express non-normative sexual or gender identities; and at the contribution made by sport to a persistently heteronormative culture. It's this second strand of work to which I hope to contribute with this book. This is not, therefore, a book about gay skaters. Instead, it is a book that tries to look historically at what is now the routine association of gayness with men's figure skating. This association persists whether male skaters are gay or not.

Some readers may be disappointed that women receive far less attention here than do men or that there is almost no discussion of ice dance or pairs figure skating. These disciplines have their own fascinating gender arrangements and deserve far more consideration and analysis than I could offer here. Historians may take issue with my uneven chronology and the rather loose geographic boundaries that I have used to contain my narrative. But my goal has not been to excavate the complete story of men's skating in a particular place or time period; instead, I have engaged with both historical and contemporary sources to help make sense of the views about men's skating that we encounter here in Canada in rinks, on television, in our daily newspapers, and in everyday conversations. The historical material I rely on in this book provides me with a way of putting the present into context and, more importantly, of considering how the present might have been different.

Figure Skating as an Object of Study

This book makes no claims for figure skating as any kind of major cultural phenomenon. Even in Canada, the nation with the largest national figure skating organization and a consistently large skating audience, it is a sport of relatively modest status in terms of participation and media attention. Although a regular fixture on winter sport broadcast schedules, figure skating stands with sports such as tennis, track and field, and skiing, all of which attract devoted fans and casual viewers but sit well behind the major professional men's team sports in terms of mass appeal. National skating championships and big international events receive coverage in newspapers and on television. But it is hard to find a figure skating magazine on general newsstands, and only the most successful international competitors have any kind of name recognition. In the North American sport hierarchy, hard-hitting, aggressive team activities pursued by men occupy the highest rungs, and to these sports and the athletes who participate in them accrue the highest status, the greatest profits, and the most media coverage. In a ranking system that places games like football and ice hockey at the top, skating occupies, at best, a middle rung. It is not surprising then that the existing literature, popular and academic, on figure skating is not large.

Before the 1994 attack on Nancy Kerrigan perpetrated by the husband of Tonya Harding, the popular skating literature consisted almost exclusively of instructional manuals and books about famous skaters. But the brief figure skating craze that followed that sensationalized event sent publishers scurrying to add skating titles to their catalogues. Among these were glossy coffee table books, biographies and autobiographies of famous and not-so-famous skaters, how-to books, and journalistic accounts of the skating world. Only a few of these books attempted to go beyond the question of who won what to look at some of the historical and cultural issues that have shaped the sport.[13]

A more specialized literature, directed at an audience of skating insiders and/or particularly ardent fans, has existed since the mid-nineteenth century. Many of these books are textbooks or documentary histories of skating clubs or of national and international skating organizations. Specific historical themes are considered in texts like Richard and Lois Stephenson's hand-coloured history of skating costume, Lynn Copley-Graves's detailed and thorough history of ice dancing, or Duncan Thomson and Lynn Gladstone-Millar's book about an eighteenth-century portrait, 'The Reverend Robert Walker Skating on Duddingston Loch,' perhaps the most famous painting in the history of Scottish art.[14] Such specialized titles might suggest that the sport has been well served by a range of histories, but to my knowledge there exist only two book-length general histories of the sport in English. The first, *Ice Skating: A History* by Nigel Brown, is an overview of skating from pre-history to the mid-twentieth century, and has been cited by practically everyone who has written about skating since the book appeared in 1959. The second, *Figure Skating: A History* by James Hines, published in 2006 with the collaboration of the World Figure Skating Museum in the United States, is a gorgeous and impressive updating of Brown's project, with a heavy focus on champions and competitions. A third historical overview was published in German in 1994: *Stilwandel im Eiskunstlauf, Eine Ästhetik und Kulturgeschichte* [Style Transformation in Figure Skating, an Aesthetic and Cultural History] by Matthias Hampe is more analytical than the English texts and draws on a larger range of sources. While still attuned to champions and competitions, Hampe discusses these through an explicit focus on aesthetic trends in the sport. These three historical texts all provide useful descriptive chronologies of skating and they helped immeasurably as I conducted the present study. However, none of them takes up any of the major conceptual themes – gender, sexuality, race, class, nationalism, the body, commodification – that have grounded scholarly attempts to understand other sports in their broader cultural context, especially their tight relationship with power. Conversely, the sport literature that addresses these conceptual themes has only rarely considered figure skating.[15]

For the most part, scholarly research on figure skating has been located in the sciences. Psychologists, for instance, have written on eating disorders among female skaters.[16] Biomechanists have looked at forces involved in the take-offs and landings of jumps.[17] Researchers in sports medicine have looked at the prevention of injuries.[18] Motor learning specialists have looked at practice and training techniques through which elite figure skaters become 'expert performers.'[19] Nutritionists have looked at the dietary needs of competitive skaters.[20] Statisticians have written on figure skating's scoring systems.[21] By contrast, researchers in the humanities and social sciences have written very little.

When figure skating does receive mention in sport sociology or history texts, it often functions as the emblematic example of a problematic 'girls' sport.' For instance, in discussions of women's traditionally limited athletic options, figure skating has been called upon to represent the narrow feminine norms that once restricted girls to aesthetically pleasing sports that did not involve contact with other competitors and that precluded obvious demonstrations of strength.[22] Invoked in this way, figure skating seems like a sport that few female athletes would choose unless forced to by restricted options. Certainly the aesthetic elements that make figure skating different from traditional male sports are never presented as something that might be attractive to athletically minded women or men. Current research on women and sport is far more likely to focus on women in traditionally defined masculine sports than traditionally defined feminine sports. And thus sport research does not yet help us to understand the fact that, despite now having access to the majority of sports previously off limits to them, many women and girls still choose to put their athletic energies into figure skating. One could say that the lingering tendency of girls to want to express their athleticism as they wear pretty costumes and perform to music is evidence of a kind of false consciousness, of the pernicious power of restrictive gender norms. But one could also say that there is something about figure skating that gives some girls a pleasure they cannot find with soccer or rugby or softball. It is the argument of this book that whatever that pleasure is, it should be validated and made more widely available, not just to girls and women but to boys and men too.

Of the sociological and historical work that purposefully engages with figure skating, about half addresses issues concerning women skaters and/or the representation of femininity in the sport, including a number of pieces on Tonya Harding.[23] Cynthia Baughman's 1995 anthology *Women on Ice*, a feminist response to the Kerrigan/Harding spectacle, is the best and most accessible example of this category of work. The remaining sociocultural literature in English is an eclectic mix of projects that, taken as a whole, presents a somewhat unusual view of skating. In this small collection of literature one finds articles on: a controversy over judging and a rather unsporting rivalry that occurred during the first Olympic figure skating competition;[24] the early days of figure skating as a pastime for men;[25] psychoanalysis and figure skating (a piece motivated by a skating text written by the famous psychoanalyst Ernest Jones);[26] issues of amateurism in the career of Barbara Ann Scott in the late 1940s;[27] issues of femininity in media coverage of Barbara Ann Scott;[28] media representations of masculinity in men's skating;[29] the cultural and political context of Skate the Dream, a skating show and benefit for HIV research organized in memory of Canadian ice dancer Rob McCall;[30] human rights for young figure skaters;[31] and the pleasures of recreational skating.[32] It is a tiny body of work for a sport that is constantly steeped in controversy and that is full of peculiar cultural elements, as even the most untutored spectators inevitably notice.

Two recent full-length studies have finally subjected figure skating to more intensive scrutiny. In her ethnographic research on Canadian figure skating, anthropologist Karen McGarry interviewed coaches, skaters, officials, sponsors, and parents. She spent time in practice rinks and at competitions to look at the way that the production of figure skating as spectacle contributes to the project of Canadian identity-formation.[33] Ellyn Kestnbaum's *Culture on Ice*, published in 2003, is a broad-ranging treatment of figure skating as a semiotic phenomenon, that is, as a phenomenon through which meanings are produced.[34] Kestnbaum articulates her deep knowledge of the sport to the more scholarly preoccupations that emerge from her location in the field of performance studies. What is unique about her contribution is her detailed analysis of specific skating performances. Kestnbaum and McGarry both look across skating disciplines and make a clear case for figure skating as a useful object of study for scholars interested in the relationship between sport and power.

So why has figure skating not generated a greater level of scholarly attention? I think the primary reason is that its reputation as a sport for girls relegates it to the status of a secondary sport in a cultural and political context where men's professional teams dominate both popular and scholarly interest. For many years research in the field of sports studies was most often written by men, many of whom wrote about the sports to which they had strong personal connections, that is, the team and individual sports they had pursued in their own younger days or those with which they had engaged as spectators. Even now, the writing of sport history continues to be dominated by men, a fact not unrelated to the concerns and issues that are considered worthy of attention in the field.[35] We see evidence of this with the continuing and long-standing prominence of articles about men's sports in the most well-read English-language journals.[36] The two most prominent English-language sport sociology journals are more balanced in terms of the gender of their contributors,[37] yet sociologists focus significantly more on those sports traditionally defined as masculine than on those traditionally defined as feminine. This is the case even when the research is about female athletes. Indeed, much of the work in feminist sport studies has been dedicated to advocating for and documenting the participation of women in sports previously reserved for men. Scholars who write about women's sport seem not to be interested in figure skating, perhaps seeing it as too much in keeping with feminine norms and as an activity that is almost inherently oppressive to girls. Scholars who write about men's sports may fail to see figure skating as interesting or important because relatively few men are involved in it.

A second reason for skating's thin presence in the literature is the fact that it has only recently been subject to the large-scale commercialization and media coverage that is the focus of much social science research on sport. This too, I would argue, is related to its late-twentieth-century status as a girls' sport. Figure skating began to appear regularly on television in the 1960s with coverage of the Olympic Games and the world championships. In the 1980s and the early 1990s professional televised skating events began to extend the shelf life of skaters' careers, keeping some athletes in the public eye long after their retirement from amateur competition. It was only in 1995 that the International Skating Union (ISU) augmented what until that point had been a thin international competitive calendar by launching a grand prix series. The series has given the ISU and national skating organizations new opportunities to sell broadcast rights and to make competitive skating more visible during the autumn and winter months before the world championships.

For a brief period following the Kerrigan/Harding incident, figure skating assumed a relatively large presence on television. Professional and made-for-television competitions appeared frequently on broadcast schedules. As sports agent Michael Rosenberg put it, 'skating was always a B-plus sport ... But the '88 Olympics took it to an A sport. The Tonya and Nancy incident took it to a triple-A sport in one whack of the knee ... Twelve months went by with eighty hours of skating shown on network TV – not eight hours, eighty hours.'[38] It is surely no coincidence that the macho elements of men's figure skating were in full flower during this time. But overexposure led to the wane of skating's popularity, and within a decade of the Harding attack, the amount of skating coverage on television had dropped significantly. The sports that have the most media exposure are those that command the most economic power. These are the same sports that generate the most interest on the part of academics. Scholars are not so different from journalists in that they turn their focus to the most culturally and economically important objects – sometimes in a bid to get closer to power, sometimes in a bid to expose it. In either case, they help to firm up the prominence of such sports and thereby contribute to the marginalization of others.

The third reason that figure skating may not have inspired much research in sport studies is the fact that it does not fit easily into popular definitions of sport. While most often promoted as a sport, figure skating is also part art. Moreover, to a much greater extent than most sports, it is dressed up and sold as entertainment. While other sports are certainly packaged as entertainment and have distinct professional and 'amateur' elements, few spin off into completely non-competitive spectator events like Holiday on Ice or Disney on Ice. When baseball or tennis are presented as commercial entertainment, it tends to be the packaging of the game that changes rather than the game itself. For skaters who perform in the big touring ice shows there is no game. If there is no game, can the skaters still be athletes?

For scholars interested in sport as a distinct form of cultural expression, figure skating's hybridity might seem to threaten or to complicate unnecessarily the focus on sport as a distinct cultural field that they want to develop in their work. Yet, I would argue that figure skating's complex discursive positioning provides scholars with a wonderful opportunity to study the limits of contemporary sport discourses and the way that they are constituted through their opposition to other non-sport realms of physical activity. In figure skating we see sport at its most self-conscious. Figure skating must constantly work to assert its identity as a sport in a context where the boundaries between sport, art, and entertainment seem always to be threatening to blur. The fact that people involved in skating put so much effort into asserting this sporting identity – to the detriment of others they could take on as alternatives – demonstrates forcefully the cultural value that accrues to sport, no small reason for which is its assumed relationship to masculinity.

Studying Gendered Sports

Sociologist R.W. Connell argues that 'sport has come to be the leading definer of masculinity in mass culture,'[39] and sport scholars who look at gender have certainly taken seriously the importance of sport in contributing to gender hierarchies and to the maintenance of male supremacy. The masculinities produced in professional men's team sports or in marquee events like the Tour de France are often venerated in popular culture, and so one studies them in part to learn about prevailing masculine ideals and the contribution of sport to them. Much research on masculinity in sport tends to deal with aggressive, unquestionably 'manly' sports like rugby or boxing or hockey. Many scholars consider these sports from a position of concern about their social implications, especially the way they contribute to and reflect notions of masculinity that can be physically and emotionally damaging to both men and women.[40] These are the sports that confirm the now commonplace assertion that sport is, in a fundamental and historical sense, a masculine domain. But if sport is a masculine domain, what are we to make of those sports – like figure skating – which seem not very manly at all? What are we to make of sports that attract very few men or of the men who participate in them? Scholars who are interested in the workings of ideology and discourse – in systems of cultural meaning and the ways that power circulates through these – argue that such contradictions are precisely the points at which power becomes most evident. And, as we have learned from any number of social theorists, they are the points at which ideologies are most vulnerable to being challenged or changed, for which reason they are important objects of study.

Literary critic Alan Sinfield calls such points faultlines,[41] feminist critic Mary Poovey calls them 'border cases.' In her study on gender ideologies in nineteenth-century England, they were the instances that had 'the potential to expose the artificiality of the binary logic' that structured Victorian gender relations.[42] Border cases allow us to see the ideological inconsistencies that come about as the exigencies of power rather than the exigencies of 'natural' logic prevail. So, for instance, we see the way that male figure skaters, despite their tremendous athletic skill, despite their strength and endurance, their ability to take huge physical risks – characteristics routinely taken as evidence of virility in other sports performed by men (and sometimes those performed by women as well, much to the chagrin of generations of female athletes) – often do not get the respect they feel they deserve as athletes or, in some quarters, as men. Illogically, the ideological links between masculinity and athletic prowess do not apply to figure skaters as they apply to men who compete in baseball or karate or rowing. Men's figure skating is a border case. It helps to make it possible for us to see the soft spots in ideological constructions of masculinity, a necessary first step in imagining how that ideology might be transformed.

Women athletes present the most obvious and cumbersome border case in the ideological formation through which sport is linked to masculinity. Until recent decades, as feminist scholars have shown, women who participated seriously in sport were greeted with incredulity and alarm.[43] It was claimed that their interest in athletic skills was symptomatic of their mannish dispositions, the failure of their femininity, their propensity to lesbianism. The restrictions placed on women's involvement in sport and the disparaging comments that accompanied it, were discursive strategies that helped to keep the ideological connections between sport and masculinity intact. The invention of the category of 'feminine sports' served the same purpose. The link between masculinity and sport could be stronger if women were not actually permitted to engage in sport on the same terms as men. For instance, as women were steered towards and men were directed away from aesthetic sports, it came to appear as if the qualities demanded by these sports – expressiveness, stylishness – were feminine qualities by simple virtue of the fact that male athletes competing in typical male sports were unlikely to be called upon to display them (which is not to say they never did).

Women were similarly steered to participate in sports that highlighted so-called feminine qualities like flexibility, balance, and agility. These are qualities that all athletes require, but they do not draw the kind of attention that accrues to more stereotypically masculine qualities like speed and strength. The division of sport by sex helped to obscure the fact that all athletes, male or female, in 'masculine' or 'feminine' sports, require a complex set of skills that cannot be broken down on the basis of sex. The segregation of women's athletic aspirations and their allegedly sex-specific athletic skills, along with the fact that women were kept from playing men's games, meant that male athletes could compete free of challenges to their own claims of athletic superiority.

This book addresses the category of 'feminine sport' as an ideological construct that has helped to preserve the illusion that there is something essentially, naturally, unavoidably masculine about sport. There exists very little substantive research on so-called feminine sports and research on men in feminine sports is especially rare.[44] Even feminist writers tend to give these sports little attention, perhaps seeing them, not unjustly, as evidence of ideologies and practices that do not allow girls and women to express their athleticism in the same manner as men do. What gets lost in this analysis is the fact that boys and men also face limits in how they might express themselves athletically.

The category of feminine sport is often taken for granted, much as I took it for granted when I began this project. *Of course*, figure skating is a girls' sport; it has music and costumes and demands some kind of emotional expression. *Of course*, synchronized swimming is a girls' sport; it too is judged on aesthetic criteria. Of course nothing. In both cases, the sports have complex gender histories; they were, in different ways, originally seen as appropriate for and were performed by men.[45] Historian Susan Cahn writes similarly of artistic gymnastics.[46] These sports were not founded as feminine sports; they *became* feminine sports. There is nothing inevitable or natural about their current status as inappropriate for boys.

It is worth remembering that sports are highly codified and structured forms of physical activity that have been designed by people. The meanings that accrue to them – in terms of race, gender, national identity, sexuality, class – are not inherent in the physical activities upon which the sports depend; they are attributed to them by people in accord with views of the world produced in specific historical and cultural circumstances. Certain ways of organizing and playing sports and of performing the skills on which they rely have emerged as the 'best' ways or the most 'natural' ways through a process in which other possible ways of organizing, playing, or performing have been marginalized.[47] For instance, in an article that discusses the history of women's ski jumping, Jason Laurendeau and Carly Adams note that in nineteenth-century Scandinavia, women and men both participated in ski-jumping on a local level, often in the same competitions.[48] But as the sport became more structured, with governing bodies, codified rules, and international competitions, ski-jump officials began to promote the sport as more 'natural' for men and too dangerous for women. (Would a man's bones be less likely to break during a fall?) On the advice of medical experts, women were banned and ski jumping became a masculine sport, a turn of events that precluded the possibility of a man having to lose to a woman in an important national or international competition. At the turn of the twentieth century, it seems that the 'best' way to ski jump was in a male body. And so it remained until the turn of the twenty-first century, when women jumpers had finally exerted enough pressure on the Fédération Internationale de Ski to be able to compete internationally – the first women's world championship was held in 2009. But the International Olympic Committee (IOC) has yet to agree to add events for women jumpers. In the face of such intransigence, an international group of women ski jumpers went to court to try to force their sport onto the schedule of the 2010 Winter Olympic Games in Vancouver. While their court case was not successful, the publicity their work has garnered has done a lot to change the gendered meanings that accrue to their sport.

In the case of ski jumping, the dated gender ideologies that continue to shape the sport seem obvious. The position taken by the IOC is not just out of step with the current IOC equity policy, but also with changing gender norms in Western cultures. As Laurendeau and Adams have noted, the IOC has excluded the women ski jumpers on the basis of rules that the organization has waived in order to include other sports, like ski-cross.[49] Looking at this example, it seems clear that women are being kept from the sport through an active process of marginalization. Processes of marginalization permit particular ways of organizing sports to come to be dominant. They are not always as easy for us to see as they are here. When sports – or other cultural institutions – are organized in accord with widespread mainstream values, with what Italian Marxist Antonio Gramsci called 'common sense,' it can be harder to see that a process of marginalization has taken or is taking place. In the 1950s, for instance, it would have been harder than it is today to see the inequity of women's exclusion from ski jumping. The gender ideologies of the time would have made a male-only event seem normal and, more important, would have made changing it difficult to imagine.

One of the tasks of the sport sociologist or the sport historian is to lay bare such processes of marginalization, that is, to investigate the ways that sports are shaped by social relations through which power circulates. How is it that sports have come to look as they do and not like something else? How is it that certain meanings, and not others, accrue to them? And how do those meanings influence the ways that different kinds of people understand the potential of their own bodies or the bodies of others, the sense they make of themselves and the world around them?

Effeminacy and Sport

Artistic Impressions is an effort to piece together the story of how men's figure skating came to mean effeminacy and, then, to consider how anxieties about skating's effeminate reputation have influenced the recent history of the sport. The point of the exercise is not simply to learn about skating, which even skaters would have to admit is not terribly important in the grand scheme of things, but to learn about the assumed tight conflation of male bodies, masculine gender, and heterosexuality that limits the ways that men and boys can experience, move, and display their bodies and, more important, the ways they can see themselves and their place in the world around them. As writers in many fields have repeatedly shown, the fear of being called a sissy, of being thought effeminate, a term often, but not always conflated with gayness, constrains the lives of boys and men in myriad ways. The social imperative of gender conformity combined with misogyny gives the term sissy its considerable weight, making it a powerful mechanism for policing the bounds of 'normal' masculinity.[50]

Effeminacy, it must be said, is not understood here as a 'natural' quality exhibited by particular kinds of boys or men. Nor do I use the term to refer to a list of physical traits or behavioural characteristics, to any set of essential attributes that define the effeminate male. Effeminacy is a social construct that is constituted in relation to normative versions of masculinity and femininity; it only exists to the extent that these categories are seen as being distinct and opposed to each other. Without a notion that femininity is qualitatively different than masculinity, there could be no effeminacy or male femininity, there would simply be a range of ways of living in a male body. Gender categories form a classificatory system that organizes daily life in myriad ways. They are vehicles through which we understand and judge aspects of human experience. To say that they are not 'natural' or biological is not to trivialize their effects. Social relations of gender are among the most powerful influences on large social formations and on individual lives, a fact to which anyone who tries to express a non-normative gender identity can attest.

I've spent a lot of time considering how to represent the concept of effeminacy in this project. For some people the term is so loaded with pejorative connotations that it is too tainted to use.[51] It has too many links to medical and other regulatory discourses to operate as a simple descriptive term or to be recuperated for progressive ends. My use of the term here, obviously, is not meant to reproduce normalizing gender classifications. The intent is, simply, to use a term that some men do find useful to refer to their sense of their own gender and to situate it in a context in which it is valued. As Joon Oluchi Lee has put it, in an article about his 'feminine boyhood,' his 'castrated boyhood,' as he calls it, the heteronormative world hates effeminate boys.[52] In the face of that hate, they need more cultural space. Attempts to shift the meanings that might be taken from the word are an obvious, if tiny, place to start.

I could have chosen to use the term 'male femininity' instead of effeminacy. As a concept, male femininity points to the fact that genders are social phenomena, not biological ones, and it reminds us that femininities can be and are performed by people who were not born into female bodies. This is a useful lesson. And yet, the term 'male femininity' still seems to have embedded in it the notion of crossing, of switching, of moving between opposite genders; it seems to intensify the binary that makes gender so problematic in the first place. Effeminacy, to my mind, suggests a different kind of movement analogy, an extension or a stretching, a sliding of the feminine into masculinity. Given its history, over the last century, as an adjective applied to men, to people who have male bodies, it suggests more pointedly than the term male femininity does that all men have the potential to slide towards femininity. To me, male femininity seems to refer to something unique and bounded, to the few brave souls willing to risk social sanction for betraying the side and venturing into unknown territory. At the risk of essentializing the relationship between gender identities and bodies, I want to argue for effeminacy as a kind of alternative masculinity rather than an alternative femininity. Strategically, this makes effeminacy something other forms of masculinity might change into. And many of them badly need to change.

North American schoolyards, playgrounds, and sport fields are primary sites for the policing of effeminate appearance and behaviours. The taunt of sissy is levelled forcefully at boys whom other children perceive to be effeminate and/or queer, as a means of humiliating them and ostracizing them from the collectivity of the appropriately boyish and heterosexual. It is also used to feminize and belittle boys who exhibit a range of physical, cultural, or social differences – fat boys, Jewish or Muslim or Hindu boys, Asian boys, disabled boys, boys whom children from dominant groups want to subordinate. But it is not just marginalized boys who get called sissy. The term is sometimes used by coaches of male sports teams as a way of humiliating their players in, presumably, the hopes of eliciting better performances.[53] The term can also be directed at boys who are perceived to have crossed the gender boundaries established by their peer groups. These boundaries are easily transgressed. A boy might wear the wrong clothes, have the wrong haircut, or be seen to enjoy the wrong kind of games, sports, or music or, heaven forbid, he might like to read. He might cry. He might show affection to his mother in public. He might make friends with girls. He might figure skate or do ballet. In these cases, the taunt of sissy is used to warn boys that they are approaching the limits of what's considered proper and, indeed, to remind them that such limits exist and that they are under constant surveillance and need to act accordingly.

Insults are not the only threat faced by boys who are identified as sissies. More serious forms of harassment and bullying, sometimes to the point of physical violence, can also plague their school years. Interestingly, for the purposes of this project, education researchers have noted that some boys who fear being labelled sissies consciously develop their athletic skills as a means of protecting themselves. For instance, in a British study focused on primary-school children, Emma Renold looked at the way high-achieving boys negotiated the feminized label of 'good student.' Renold found that some boys saw sport as 'status-enhancing' and they used their athletic prowess to reduce their experiences of bullying.[54] Sporting ability is a currency that boys can exchange among themselves as they establish gendered hierarchies of belonging and exclusion. However, as we learn from skaters, not just any type of sporting ability will do in the complex accounting system through which gender categories are organized and evaluated.

But what of the boys who actually cannot or who do not want to play sport? What of boys whose bodies appear effeminate to other children? Considerable anecdotal and scholarly evidence points towards the fact that, for large numbers of fey boys, childhood and adolescence is a torment.[55] Other students, and sometimes teachers as well, are very good at enforcing gender conformity in schools,[56] while parents and siblings may do the same at home. Indeed, some parents are so concerned about their children's non-conforming gender displays that they seek out psychiatrists or psychologists to get help correcting their sons' 'problems.'[57] Kenneth Zucker, a psychologist who works at a gender identity clinic in Toronto, writes that for the most part parents bring children to gender clinics 'because they don't want their kid to be gay.'[58]

According to the *Diagnostic and Statistical Manual* (DSM) of the American Psychiatric Association, the official diagnosis for a boy whose gender identity and gendered behaviour is seen to be incongruent with his male body is Gender Identity Disorder (GID) in Childhood. The diagnosis is also applied to girls, although less often; a separate category of GID is applied to adults. As a medical concept, GID was originally formulated around the idea of cross-gender identification, which suggests that there are two clearly distinct ways of living in this world – masculine and feminine – and that each should line up neatly with the appropriate set of genitals. If conventional understandings of gender and sex were more open to notions of fluidity, if there were more cultural space for people exhibiting a range of gender identifications, if children were simply allowed to follow their inclinations, the possibility of a disordered gender identity would be meaningless.

So what does cross-gender identification look like for boys? It looks quite similar to the definition of sissy that operates on playgrounds. One would think that a diagnosis of GID would *require* the 'repeatedly stated desire to be, or insistence' that a child 'is, the other sex,' but this is just the first of five criteria of which only four need to be present for a diagnosis that is meant to confirm 'a strong and persistent cross-gender identification.' The other four include:

(2) in boys, preference for cross-dressing or simulating female attire; in girls, insistence on wearing only stereotypical masculine clothing
(3) strong and persistent preferences for cross-sex roles in make-believe play or persistent fantasies of being the other sex
(4) intense desire to participate in the stereotypical games and pastimes of the other sex
(5) strong preference for playmates of the other sex[59]

The DSM-IV-TR – the revised fourth edition published in 2000 – gives examples of what these criteria might look like in practice: 'Stereotypical female-type dolls, such as Barbie, are often their favorite toys, and girls are their preferred playmates. When playing "house," these boys role-play female figures, most commonly "mother roles," and often are quite preoccupied with female fantasy figures. They avoid rough-and-tumble play and competitive sports and have little interest in cars and trucks or other nonaggressive but stereotypical boys' toys.' The DSM states: 'In children, the disturbance is manifested by any of the following: in boys, assertion that his penis or testes are disgusting or will disappear or assertion that it would be better not to have a penis, *or* aversion toward rough-and-tumble play and rejection of male stereotypical toys, games, and activities' [emphasis added].[60]

The diagnosis is not supposed to apply to the kind of non-conforming behaviour that is known as tomboyishness in girls or sissyness in boys; rather, it is only to be applied to cases where the child exhibits marked distress or disturbance. But what would the actual root of that distress be? The behaviours and their associated feelings or the response a child receives for them? In emphasizing non-stereotypical gender behaviours as elements of the diagnosis, rather than the stereotypes that might make the experience of those behaviours distressing, the DSM implicitly pathologizes the child rather than the narrow cultural norms that make his or her life difficult. And it is the behaviour that then becomes the focus of treatment. There is no recognition in the list of diagnostic criteria that definitions of masculinity and femininity are cultural and that they change, that what is an appropriately male activity in one era may not be in another, or that what are considered boys' interests and games in one culture could be seen as girly somewhere else.

It is still relatively uncommon for parents to accept and nurture effeminacy in a son. But, even parents who do not want to change a boy into a more manly specimen will likely have grave worries about the reception he will receive in the world outside his home. Certainly, he will encounter few men upon whom he could model himself. He will see only the most stereotypical representations of effeminacy in film, on television, or in sport. As Daniel Harris writes, 'The media are allergic to effeminacy, as are the other most powerful professions in the country. Would a corporation, for instance, hire an effeminate C.E.O ...? Would a criminal hire an effeminate lawyer to defend him in court ...?'[61]

Sport makes a special contribution to the marginalization and subordination of effeminacy on individual and cultural levels. It does not need to do so. As queer sports theorist Brian Pronger has long argued, sport could encourage a much greater diversity of bodily practices performed in more diverse ways.[62] It could be a cultural resource that allows people to enjoy any or all styles of movement that bring them pleasure. It could be a way of motivating people to challenge the stereotypical gender expectations that they face in other aspects of their lives, as it is beginning to be for some girls and women who now have access to traditionally masculine sports like wrestling or rugby. Surely, boys and men could benefit from the same kind of exploration of non-stereotypical activities.

This book has been motivated by a belief that we would do well to encourage more effeminacy in our culture. It is an attempt to argue, on feminist grounds, for a culture with ample space for effeminate boys and men, a culture that refuses to enforce gender conformity. Such a culture would refuse to privilege masculinity at the expense of femininity or to see masculinity and femininity as resources to be parcelled out to two distinctly different types of creatures. A culture that was able to recognize and accept effeminacy would be a culture in which people would suffer far less over something as trivial as whether they played with the 'right' kinds of toys, wore the 'right' kinds of clothes, or enjoyed the 'right' sports.

About This Book

Artistic Impressions is a gender history of figure skating motivated by present-day concerns about the relationship of sport to mainstream understandings of gender and sexuality. The main empirical contribution of the book is the historical material which documents the transformation of figure skating from a gentlemanly art to a sport that is currently seen as primarily suitable for girls and women and, therefore, a sport that would only appeal to effeminate boys or men. This historical material is bookended by discussions of the gendered meanings produced in figure skating today and of the effects of those meanings.

In chapter 2 I present the issue that prompted this study. In the 1990s there was a pronounced effort to change the image of men's skating. A cohort of male skaters, including Elvis Stojko of Canada, Philippe Candeloro of France, and Michael Weiss of the United States, performed with a self-consciousness about masculinity that had not previously been visible in the sport. For doing so they were celebrated by the press for having changed the face of figure skating, for making it more appealing to men – a claim for which there is little supportive evidence. I have come to think of this brief period in the history of men's skating as the sport's 'macho turn.' In the overall history of skating, it was as unusual as it was short-lived. My discussion in chapter 2 describes this macho turn and some of its effects, and puts these into the broader context of gender relations in late-twentieth-century North America.

In chapter 3 I discuss figure skating's reputation as a sport for girls, sissies, and queers – the backdrop and motivation for the effort to construct a new masculine image for skating and male skaters. I offer evidence to suggest how and why figure skating is currently perceived to be a 'feminine sport' in North America and I show some of the ways that skating fits into broader discursive formations in which sport, gender, and sexuality are intertwined. The chapter demonstrates that the meanings that accrue to figure skating are inevitably constituted through discourses of femininity, even when those discourses are being refused or refuted, as they frequently are by some male skaters.

In chapters 4, 5, and 6 I construct a narrative that covers almost two hundred years of skating history. My goal with these chapters has been to understand how skating evolved from an almost exclusively male pastime to a so-called feminine sport. In each of these chapters the impossibility of separating an analysis of gender from an analysis of class becomes clear. And central to the analysis of class that emerges here is the inseparability of class formation from processes of racialization; the maintenance and reproduction of class status and privilege are tightly entwined with the production of whiteness. Chapter 4 addresses the early history of the type of skating that would, eventually, turn into figure skating. This is a story of skating as an upper-class male pastime. I look at the actual skating itself, the different styles men created in different national contexts, what skaters looked like, the ways they moved their bodies over the ice. In chapter 5, I talk about women's entry into skating and how women were accommodated (or not) as skating came to be organized in exclusive clubs that were powerful signifiers of privilege and class position. This is the context in which skating, an artistic and expressive form of physical activity, was forced into the shape of a competitive sport in the late 1800s. Chapter 6 picks up the narrative in the early twentieth century, during a period when figure skating was relatively gender balanced, with women and men skating together on the same ice, practising the same technical feats and, often, competing against each other in the same events. But as the chapter progresses, I describe the processes through which this gender balance was lost and figure skating came to be a sport in which girls were the primary participants. I argue that two main factors contributed to the feminization of skating: (1) the popularity and prominence of three-time Olympic champion Sonja Henie, who introduced skating to a mass audience in a series of Hollywood films in the 1930s and 1940s; and (2) women's technical dominance in the sport in the late 1920s and early 1930s. By the end of the Second World War skating was firmly positioned as a girls' sport and skating officials launched a decades-long effort to make their sport more attractive to men.

One of the reasons why many boys and men would never consider pursuing figure skating is the fact that the sport has an artistic dimension. Skaters cannot just jump high or skate quickly; they need also to consider what they look like as they do so. More than anything else, the aesthetic component of skating puts it off limits for many boys and men. Chapter 7 looks at long-standing debates within the skating community about the prominence given to skating's artistic and sporting elements. The chapter argues that at different times the debate has been shaped primarily by discourses of class (motivating proponents of skating as art) or discourses of gender (motivating proponents of skating as sport). In both cases, struggles over skating's identity have been struggles over status and privilege, and have always been struggles over the reputations of men.

Finally, chapter 8 looks at the way that anxieties over figure skating's effeminate reputation have been institutionalized in the organization and performance of the sport, shaping how both men and women are able to perform. In this chapter I argue that the rigid notions of gender we see represented in skating – in terms of costumes, music, movement – demonstrate the limitations of sport discourses for expanding what it means to be a woman or a man in mainstream North America.

2 Tough Guys? Figure Skating's Macho Moment

In February 2009 the *Globe and Mail* newspaper reported on a soon-to-be-launched promotional campaign for Skate Canada, the national governing body. The front-page headline announced: 'Figure Skating Gets Tough: Skate Canada Seeks to Rebrand Sport by Playing Up Its Risks and Athleticism.' Skate Canada officials claimed the campaign was not about masculinity, but was part of a 'wholesale rebranding of the sport's image.'[1] Male skaters presented a different line to the press. In an interview with the *Wall Street Journal*, Vaughn Chipeur, a member of Canada's national figure skating team, suggested that the aim of the campaign might be a bit more pointed, 'We have to find ways to show the masculinity.'[2] It seems not everyone thought this was such a good idea. One entry to the popular gay sports website Outsports.com reads:

> Why doesn't [S]kate Canada try to butch up interior decorating and male hairdressers too? This [campaign] is geared at kids who won't enter figure skating because that is a 'fairy' sport, cheered on by their dads. It is a case of [S]kate Canada saying they can't beat homophobia, homophobia is keeping new male skaters away from the sport, so we have to distance ourselves from everything gay.[3]

Criticism of the proposed campaign came from two directions: first, from gay organizations whose members worried about what seemed like a capitulation to macho stereotypes and a disavowal of gay skaters by skating insiders; and, second, from fans who worried that the unique artistic aspects of their sport might be watered down. In the end, the so-called tough campaign was never launched. William Thompson, CEO of Skate Canada, posted a message on Skate Canada's home page in which he said that the press had misunderstood a simple effort to highlight the athletic difficulty of the sport. 'This was in no way to diminish the artistry,' Thompson wrote, instead the intention had been to 'remind viewers of the levels of fitness, mental training and commitment required to be an elite figure skater. This messaging was NOT even intended for the men's event. In fact, our feeling was that often the athleticism of the women was being overlooked.' Thompson then went on to say that while the word 'tough' had been used by the organization's marketing director in an interview, she had intended it only as a synonym for 'difficult.' It was the reporter who drew the connection between 'tough' and 'macho' and then 'made the assumption that it was aimed at the men's event.'[4]

What Thompson does not acknowledge is that whether intentional or not, any public appeal to athleticism, no matter whom it serves (such appeals are often used by dancers), goes to work in a culture where the athletic often trumps the artistic and where these two categories are heavily gendered and not equally valued. Were this not the case, the female athletes in non-artistic sports who feel the need to assert their femininity would no longer need to do so, and ballet schools and skating clubs would be overrun with little boys. And Skate Canada marketers would have felt equally inspired to highlight their skaters' complex artistic skills along with their athleticism as they tried to increase the size of their television audience in the approach to the 2010 Vancouver Winter Olympics. Whether Skate Canada intended to promote masculinity along with athleticism, it is inevitable that, given the overlap between these two terms in popular culture, others would have assumed that they had.

Figure skating is a highly – perhaps the most highly – gendered sport. It is one of only a few competitive athletic activities that do little to validate the masculinities of their male competitors. Indeed, skating so contravenes the gendered identities produced in more stereotypically 'masculine' sports that male skaters routinely face harassment and ridicule for pursuing it. For this reason, skating officials and coaches struggle to attract young boys to the sport and to keep them involved. Since at least the 1940s, concerned members of the skating community have put considerable effort into reframing popular images of men's skating in order to make the sport more attractive to boys and men, a project with which they have had little success. In particular, they have tried to play up the athletic at the expense of the artistic aspects of men's skating, as it is the emphasis on artistic expression, especially in the North American cultural climate, that makes the sport seem too feminine and therefore too 'gay' to attract bona fide masculine interest.

In repeated attempts to portray skating as a tough, physically demand-ing athletic endeavour rather than an art, skating officials, skaters, and coaches have tried to restrict the meanings that can be taken from skat-ing, to make it clearly intelligible from within the traditionally mascu-line language of sport. What was unique about the recent comments by Skate Canada officials was the attempt to include women in this proc-ess. Historically, as will become evident in later chapters, debates over skating's image have been almost exclusively about men.

The Macho Turn

In the late 1980s and early 1990s, faced with the seeming intransigence of skating's feminine reputation, some skaters and, to a much great-er extent, those who promoted and commented upon them, adopted a new strategy to broaden the appeal of the sport to boys and men. Instead of trying to reframe the sport itself, they focused instead on par-ticular skaters. It was a move that could be read as tacit acknowledg-ment that the gender discourses through which skating is positioned as feminine are too powerful to be overturned – far easier to paint an indi-vidual skater as manly than to shift the reputation of the entire sport.

This new discursive tactic emerged after the 1988 Calgary Winter Olympics. The Games received a tremendous amount of coverage on North American television networks. The exposure increased the audi-ence for figure skating and made some Canadian and American skat-ers household names in their own countries. Capitalizing on the sport's new popularity, skating officials, marketers, agents, and journalists worked hard to keep top male skaters in the public eye. In this context, media coverage of men's skating highlighted virility as much as tech-nique. Some male skaters designed their programs to do the same. Last-ing about fifteen years, from the late 1980s through the early 2000s, this heavy emphasis on stereotypical masculinity – the macho turn – was unprecedented. In this chapter I try to make sense of this short phase in the gender history of the sport, putting it into a broader historical and social context, and situating it on the North American gender landscape at the end of the twentieth century. The late 1980s and the early 1990s were still a time of intense media panic over AIDS in North America. It was the era of Reagan, Mulroney, and Thatcher conservatism, of Rambo and the Terminator. It was a time of backlash against the gains achieved by feminists. There was much in the culture that would have facilitated a heightened concern with masculinity in a sport like figure skating.

The unusualness of the macho period in men's figure skating is what motivated this project. While it is not the main focus of the book, it was the sociological and historical puzzle of this period that was the starting point for my research. In a sport that has been concerned about men's image for decades, the macho trend stands out in figure skating's history for the almost cartoonish way that manliness was emphasized on the ice and in the press. When I first saw the exaggerated performances of masculinity that came to be common in the 1990s, I was surprised and, then, put off. What was more surprising – and more annoying – was the enthusiasm they generated among sports journalists and broadcasters. In the approval directed towards the most macho skaters one could sense strong undertones of misogyny and homophobia and an implicit derision of those skaters whose masculinities were not so heavily marked. I read the praise as a contribution to the pervasive disparagement of effeminacy that makes life difficult for boys and men who do not conform to the requirements of normative masculinities. In my view, attempts to give skating a more macho image were augmenting that which could well have been diminished in the culture. Surely the environment in which we live needs not a whit more machoness. Surely men and women alike would be well served by the expansion rather than the contraction of possibilities for how people in male bodies might live their genders. And yet there was figure skating doing its part for masculine hegemony. As a skater, I hated the feel that the tough-guy discourse was bringing to public representations of the sport. As a feminist and a lesbian, I saw in the perceived need to masculinize men's skating the resoluteness of heteronormative ideas about gender. Almost thirty years after the emergence of lesbian and gay liberation movements, in an era when sexual orientation was, in some jurisdictions, starting to gain protection under human rights legislation, it was clear that some men still felt uneasy about the possibility that someone might think them queer. Bad news, this. But a good hook for a sociologist curious about the tenacious pull of gender conformity and about the ways that discourses of sexuality and gender shape who we might be, the ways we might live, and how we feel about them.

In the impulse to give skaters a more macho image one could discern the anxieties that lie beneath dominant versions of the contemporary masculine ideal: the fear of being seen as feminine, the fear of being seen as gay.[5] In their attempts to replace skating's alleged sissies with more macho jocks, insiders to the sport and sympathetic journalists were working hard to produce a recognizably mainstream masculinity in a context where it was widely thought not to exist. Their desire to perform this work says something about contemporary understandings of effeminacy and homosexuality. The strategies they adopted say something about the constructedness of gender and the power of normative ideals.

Scholars interested in the way that gender works in our everyday lives talk, from our different theoretical perspectives, about 'doing gender'[6] or 'constructing gender'[7] or 'performing gender.'[8] The common thread behind these terms is that gender – the collection of traits, behaviours, expectations, and aesthetics that make up the familiar categories of masculinity and femininity – is not inherent in the individual nor in the type of body into which the individual is born. It is a product of specific cultural and historical contexts. For those who reject current gender arrangements, there is a great power in this insight. As an example, we can see how over the past decades in North America and much of Western Europe changing ideas about the appropriateness of certain kinds of physical activity for women have influenced the ways that women actually use their bodies, the ways that they dress, and what they expect for themselves and their daughters. The once common notion that middle-class white women are too delicate to engage in sport or other strenuous activities[9] is no longer tenable. Indeed, in some contemporary contexts, idealized versions of femininity now require middle-class white women to be active and fit and to create for themselves bodies with obvious (but not too obvious) muscle tone.[10] This twenty-first-century feminine ideal would have been unrecognizable to women of earlier generations.

Such new ideas about gender emerge not just as people think them but as they live them, as women and girls, for instance, develop new skills and carry themselves differently than their mothers did, as they work in concrete ways to prepare futures in which their own physical competence is assumed. This is what sociologists mean when they use the term 'doing gender.'[11] Collectively, in our actions, our attitudes, and our desires we contribute to the reproduction and the transformation of the gender norms that are the context of our experiences. Sometimes we engage with gender norms effortlessly; sometimes we are incapable of or unwilling to meet them; sometimes we challenge them overtly to accommodate our own inclinations or desires or, perhaps, to shift the ways people think about what it means to live in a female or a male body. The negotiation of gender norms can be completely unconscious, as when a man sits down and automatically crosses his legs at an angle and in a manner that can be read immediately by onlookers as masculine. But we routinely negotiate gender in conscious ways too, as when female bodybuilders pay serious attention to their makeup and hair, or when male figure skaters choose costumes and choreography to reflect the versions of masculinity with which they would most like to be associated.

I first stumbled across figure skating's new macho man in *Saturday Night*, a monthly Canadian magazine aimed at 'informed' middle-class readers. After a childhood and youth immersed in figure skating, I had been away from the sport, as both participant and spectator, for years. I had been out of the country during the Calgary Olympics. I had missed the 'Battle of the Brians' (Boitano and Orser, the gold and silver medallists), the Battle of the Carmens (Katarina Witt and Debi Thomas, the gold and bronze medallists), and the surprise triumph of Elizabeth Manley (who won silver). And I certainly knew nothing of the less well-known skaters who followed in their famous wakes. So, sometime in the early 1990s, when I picked up an old copy of *Saturday Night* magazine in my dentist's waiting room and started to read a profile of Canadian skater and world champion Kurt Browning, I didn't know who he was or what to make of the story's subhead: 'Kurt Browning's macho ice image has startled the skating world. He may also be on the cutting edge of changes to the sport.'[12] The author's enthusiasm for Browning's alleged 'macho-ness' startled me. I had never seen the words 'macho' and 'skating' in such close proximity. Nor did I understand why this linkage might be presented to me, the reader, as a positive development. Surely, for many fans and many skaters, one of the primary appeals of skating is its difference from the usual array of tough-guy activities available to men who want to express themselves athletically.

The story about Kurt Browning prompted me to start watching skating again. Over the next decade a 'macho ice image' would become a regular feature in some men's skating performances and in reporting on them. While gender concerns have been a constant in the sport since the Second World War, they were magnified by the macho skaters. For just over ten years, gender was *the* story of men's skating. Over the past few years, gender has been on the decline as a central theme in men's skating although it has yet to fade away completely, as we saw with the debates waged over the value and necessity of quadruple jumps in the men's competition at the 2010 Vancouver Olympics.

Between 1989 and 1993 Kurt Browning won four world championship titles and was the first skater to successfully land a quadruple jump in competition. He was also the first in a series of late-twentieth-century skaters whose masculinity was fervently lauded by reporters. One writer ascribed to Browning a 'masculine mystique which set him apart in the world of figure skating.'[13] Almost always referred to as the 'son of a mountain man from Caroline, Alberta,'[14] he was portrayed in the press as a pioneer, a mould-breaker, and an avowed heterosexual. The suggestion was frequently made that he was not like previous male skaters, a point which Browning, to his credit, consistently refused to corroborate.[15] And rightly so. During his amateur career his style of skating certainly did not seem more virile than other men's; to my eye there was nothing expressly macho about it. Indeed, as his career progressed, Browning developed a fluidity of style that permitted him a musical and choreographic range that was decidedly un-macho. But the evolution of his artistic versatility did little to stop sports journalists from identifying him as somehow uniquely masculine among male skaters.

In Browning's case, his macho identity was, for the most part, produced by journalists enamoured with the fact that he had grown up in rural Alberta, the son of a cowboy. Some (not all) of his competitors were more proactive and worked hard to convey an unmistakable virility both on and off the ice. By the mid-1990s, this cohort of men had the macho turn well under way. With their unabashed performances of heterosexual masculinity, skaters like Elvis Stojko of Canada, Philippe Candeloro of France, Steven Cousins of England, and Christopher Bowman and Michael Weiss of the United States captured the interest of mainstream sports journalists, the producers of professional skating shows, and many fans. These skaters packaged their athleticism in an excess of heavily gendered signifiers. Their costumes, music, and choreography evoked manly sensibilities. Like Chazz Michael Michaels in the film *Blades of Glory*, their performance of manhood was anything but subtle: choreography that mimicked sword fights, karate, and race-car driving; interviews and photographs that emphasized girlfriends and masculine hobbies; costumes that represented soldiers, kings, and gladiators. Like Chazz, skating's macho competitors and those who represented them in the press seemed to want to put as much distance as possible between the image they cut and the stereotype of the effeminate male skater. In their exaggerated and clichéd masculine posing, it was hard not to read a fear of being labelled queer.

It is impossible to say exactly why, after decades of having an effeminate reputation, men's figure skating took a pronounced turn towards manliness in the early 1990s. Money, or the promise of money, likely had something to do with it. As skating's popularity increased after the 1988 Calgary Olympics, the sport became more marketable and a mainstream masculinity would have been a far easier sell than an effeminate one as major corporate endorsement opportunities started opening up, for the first time, for male skaters. But I do not think money alone can explain the macho reframing of skating's men.

Skating in the Era of HIV

In the early 1990s, the HIV-related deaths of a number of prominent figure skaters were widely publicized by the media, reinforcing for some people, in the worst possible way, the association between skating and homosexuality. Barely ten years into the AIDS crisis, public understanding of HIV was still thin. In Canadian popular and medical discourses the virus was primarily associated with gay men, drug users, and Haitians or Africans. Discussions of 'high-risk groups' (rather than risky behaviours) were laced with homophobia, racism, and xenophobia. Treatment had only just made it onto the public agenda after tremendous efforts by AIDS activist groups. Mortality rates among people with HIV were high. Despite the continuing construction of AIDS as a 'gay disease,' that is, as someone else's problem, members of the 'general public' expressed high anxiety about HIV.[16] When Canadian ice dancer and Olympic bronze medallist Rob McCall died of HIV-related cancer in 1991, AIDS was still so stigmatized that at least one of his obituaries – in his hometown newspaper, the *Halifax Chronicle Herald* – made no mention of it.[17]

In the autumn of 1992, an article by *New York Times* journalist Filip Bondy was reprinted in newspapers across North America. The headline that appeared over it in my daily newspaper, the Toronto *Globe and Mail*, was 'AIDS-related Deaths Rock the World of Figure Skating.'[18] The article reported that three prominent Canadian skaters – Rob McCall, Brian Pockar, and Shaun McGill – had died in the previous twelve months and that 1976 Olympic champion John Curry had publicly announced that he was HIV-positive. The article's implicit suggestion was that these men were not the only skaters with HIV, just the only ones whose illnesses had been made public. Bondy made a case for skaters not disclosing their HIV-status, writing that a professional skater 'who acknowledges he is gay or admits to being HIV-positive' would fear losing not only his privacy but his livelihood. Skaters depended on short-term contracts for performing, coaching, or choreography and on opportunities for sponsorship or endorsement. Any of these could easily dry up. It was also the case that non-Americans needed to keep their diagnoses secret if they wanted to work in the United States, skating's most lucrative professional market, where immigration legislation required (as it did until 2010) that people with HIV apply for a special waiver in order to enter the country. Perhaps more to the point, in the early 1990s people who were living with AIDS were treated abysmally (as many still are). At that time, not only figure skaters chose to keep their sero-status private.

Bondy's article appeared a few days before 'Skate the Dream,' a memorial for McCall and benefit for AIDS research that had been organized by Brian Orser and Tracy Wilson, McCall's dance partner and now a well-known colour commentator for skating events on television. The Toronto benefit received widespread coverage in the Canadian press. Much of this coverage repeated the list of skaters known to have died of AIDS-related illnesses, reinforcing links between figure skating and HIV and, therefore, figure skating and homosexuality. In the *Globe and Mail*, skating writer Beverley Smith repeated the arguments for skaters not going public with their diagnoses: 'fear of the stigma attached to a disease that attacked the homosexual population first'; fear of losing work; fear of losing endorsements. Like Bondy, Smith tried to balance the notion that skating was a special case in the sports world (why else was it receiving so much attention?) with the contrasting view, represented in the article by a quote from Brian Orser: 'AIDS isn't just a problem in figure skating. It's everywhere.'[19]

A couple of weeks later a more pointed piece appeared in the *Calgary Herald*. Michael Clarkson was not as concerned as Smith and Bondy to show that skating was just like any other sport. Clarkson worked hard to construct figure skating as a special case in terms of AIDS casualties. His article, 'Skating's Spectre,' opened with the claim that 'at least 40 male skaters and coaches in the top ranks of North American figure skating' had already died and at least a dozen others were living with HIV. Clarkson claimed to have spent two months interviewing 125 skating insiders to gather his statistics. 'Of about 100 senior male skaters who competed nationally in Canada over a 10-year period in the 1970s, at least nine contracted HIV or AIDS. That represents about one out of 11 skaters. Health and Welfare Canada estimates that one out of 670 Canadians may be HIV-positive. But those outside high-risk categories have about a one in 10,000 chance of being HIV-positive.'[20] Clarkson's stark comparison set figure skating up as a special case and suggested that skaters who were HIV-positive were members of 'high-risk categories,' a notion that had already been invalidated by public health authorities and HIV educators. It also positioned male skaters as not just outside but well beyond the allegedly low-risk category of the presumably non-gay, non-drug-using, non-African general public. As Samantha King argues in her article 'Consuming Compassion,' a contextual analysis of the televised 'Skate the Dream' benefit, the *Herald* article's 'apparent concern for the figure skating community turns out to be an exercise in reassuring the "low-risk" Canadian public that they are not susceptible to the virus.'[21]

In the stories by Bondy and Smith, the connections among skating, homosexuality, and AIDS were implied; Clarkson made them explicit. He quoted Patrick Dean, an HIV-positive gay man and former ice dancer who believed that there had been 'too much sex among skaters and in the gay community in general.' Clarkson wrote that 1976 Olympic gold medallist John Curry had admitted shame at having contracted HIV through gay sex and had feared that were he to go public with his HIV status, 'people would throw bricks through the window.' The article presents a community that was not just grieving but defensive, and not just on the issue of HIV. It is not entirely clear whether the 'spectre' of Clarkson's title was HIV or gayness itself.

The story of Canadian figure skaters dying of AIDS clearly had legs. It appeared in newspapers in Canada, the United States, and the United Kingdom. In one odd international exchange, the *Montreal Gazette* reprinted an article from the *London Observer* (UK) that, like almost all the articles, opened with references to Canadians McCall, Pockar, and McGill.[22] *People* magazine published an eight-page feature entitled 'Fear on the Ice.'[23] Many in the skating world were troubled by the coverage. Brian Boitano, 1988 Olympic gold medallist, condemned the *Calgary Herald* story as a 'witch-hunt.'[24] In a 1992 radio interview with the Canadian Broadcasting Corporation (CBC), Boitano claimed he did not know any HIV-positive skaters and that most skaters were straight.[25] A columnist in the American figure skating magazine *Tracings* took issue with 'a whole slew of articles ... speculating about what effect aids [*sic*] has had on the skating community.' She wrote: 'Well, this terrible affliction has had exactly the same effect as on any random cross-section of the public or any profession.' She went on to elaborate the position taken by many skating insiders: their sport had been 'selected unfairly to bear the brunt in the way its image used to be perceived as "too sissy" for boys.'[26] The syntax here is a bit shaky, but surely it is no coincidence that sissyness appears in a complaint about the harm a focus on HIV might do to skating's reputation.

Not everyone connected to skating felt the need to deny the impact of AIDS on the sport or to deny that figure skating had suffered a uniquely devastating relationship with HIV as compared to other sports at that time. For instance, Robin Cousins of England, 1980 Olympic men's champion, told the *New York Times* in 1993 that 'AIDS has absolutely affected our sport.' Cousins wanted the International Skating Union to become 'more active in helping people with AIDS in the professional skating community.'[27] If there were other members of the skating community who were also prepared to deal head on with the impact of HIV in the skating community, the 'slew of articles,' did not mention them. In all the stories and interviews on the topic, the only person to express anger at the senseless deaths of such young men was not a skating insider but columnist Steve Simmons of the *Toronto Sun*.[28] The message coming from the skating world was that AIDS was a broad social problem rather than a problem specific to skating, which, while generally not untrue, ignored the fact that there were skaters suffering from that larger social problem – which included not just illness and the stigma of illness but the stigma's antecedent, homophobia – who needed support and validation. As David Dore, then head of the Canadian Figure Skating Association, told Filip Bondy, the organization was busy 'trying to prevent a panic among parents of junior skaters.' Officials and skaters were trying to protect their product. As Bondy put it, the skating world had two tasks: (1) to educate 'its anxious athletes' and (2) to avoid 'the publicity that might damage this theatrical, market-driven sport.'

The grief and anxiety provoked by HIV within the skating world furnished an important part of the context within which skaters, officials, and journalists began to focus heavily on the masculinity – and the heterosexuality – of certain male skaters. In the early 1990s, there were a number of conspicuous cultural currents available to support and encourage those who wanted to interrupt the possibility of men's skating being read as effeminate or gay. Indeed, throughout the 1990s, popular discourses of masculinity were such that it would have been very surprising had a shift in men's skating not taken place. Film critic Susan Jeffords has written about the prominence of 'hard-body' masculinities that emerged in Hollywood film in the 1980s in the context of Reagan-style conservatism.[29] Jeffords writes that action-adventure films, like

Rambo, that became popular during the Reagan era portrayed tough masculine bodies to symbolize a powerful American nation regaining its vigour after its defeat in the war in Vietnam. Images of Reagan himself – chopping wood, riding a horse – emphasized his own physical and political hardness in contrast to the 'softness' of his predecessor, Jimmy Carter, a president who favoured diplomacy over bravado and force. Jeffords writes that 'the Reagan America was to be a strong one, capable of confronting enemies rather than submitting to them, of battling "evil empires" rather than allowing them to flourish, of using its hardened body, its renewed techno-military network, to impose its will on others rather than allow itself to be dictated to.'[30] American sociologist Michael Kimmel writes that 'the manhood regained under Presidents Reagan and Bush [Senior] was the compulsive masculinity of the schoolyard bully defeating weaker foes such as Grenada and Panama, a defensive and restive manhood of men who needed to demonstrate their masculinity at every opportunity.'[31] Both Jeffords and Kimmel show how this version of masculinity circulated not just in policy and politics but also in popular culture: *Rambo*, *The Terminator*, *Lethal Weapon*, *Robocop*, *Die Hard*.

These Hollywood films and their burly white heroes made a distinctly white American conceptualization of masculinity familiar to international audiences. They were part of a cultural context that provided excellent source material for those wanting to portray male skaters in a more manly light. For instance, journalists and other skaters used the nickname The Terminator for the powerful Canadian skater Elvis Stojko. They could have equally called him a tiger or a leopard for his unwavering ability to land on his feet, but the animal image would not have conveyed the same quality of aggression or virility as the reference to Arnold Schwarzenegger. And cats, even big ones, tend to be associated with grace, a quality that macho skaters tried to downplay. Muscular American cultural references were employed not just by the macho skaters but also by those who were, perhaps, looking to add a bit of masculine gravity to their performances. In 1993 Masakazu Kagiyama of Japan, a tall slim skater, chose the theme music from *Rambo II* and *Rambo III* for his long program. The blatant Americanness of this type of music was perhaps part of its value for non-American skaters looking to signify a potent masculinity. Indeed, the widespread international circulation of American cultural references would have made them easily decipherable anywhere elite skaters competed.

Kimmel reminds us that the Reagan-Rambo style of masculinity was formed by what it contained – hard bodies capable of aggressive, confident actions – and by what it rejected – sensitivity, softness.[32] The counter to the hard-bodied tough guy was the 'new man,' the sensitive guy, more familiarly known as 'the wimp.' Similar struggles over popular representations of masculinity – fuelled in great part by the press – were also under way in Britain, where images of sensitive 'new men' were being usurped by far less sensitive 'new lads' in magazines and advertisements and on television.[33] Where the new man was interested in his appearance, talking with women, and the politics of day care, the new lad was interested in things like beer and football that are typically associated with old-style men. Hard masculinity/soft masculinity. Macho/fey. Scholars often talk about the way that gender is relational, meaning that femininity and masculinity only make sense as binary oppositions. Each is, the theory goes, what the other is not. But there is as much variation within these categories as there is between them. The new lad and the new man, the macho and the wimp are caricatures pulled from a whole range of competing ideas about how to live as a man. Not only does the macho guy not obliterate the wimp in any cultural sense, he actually needs the wimp to know himself as bigger, stronger, more powerful. A similar process was at work in skating, where the contrast between the new macho guys and the more 'classical skaters,' as they tended to be called by the press, helped to make the former seem tougher. Had the macho skaters been compared to, for instance, a group of hockey players, their manliness would have seemed much diminished.

While the notion of binary oppositions is useful to help us understand the ways meanings accrue to different identity categories and how these categories work in relationship to each other, it also leaves us with a picture of gender that is far too simple. People express their genders in all sorts of contradictory and complex ways that exceed the descriptive power of a simple opposition like macho/wimp. Few of us, despite good intentions or deep desires, are able to express our genders consistently in just one way. Even those men who most want to exhibit an unequivocal machoness are likely not able to maintain their macho demeanour all the time. And yet, in popular discussions gender is typically presented in broad strokes, the effect of which is to shore up tight boundaries around what might rightly be included in definitions of masculinity and femininity (note the singular), however inadequate such definitions might be to the task of capturing people's actual experiences. In skating, for instance, the too-easy distinction made between the 'tough guys' and the 'artists' made the men who were supposed to fit those categories seem one-dimensional, while it also eclipsed those skaters to whom neither label was applied. Binary oppositions obscure the range of ways people live their genders. The unequal value ascribed to the two terms of the opposition – straight/gay, macho/wimp, masculine/feminine – also makes clear that some ways of living in the world are more valued than others. As sport sociologist Dayna Daniels would put it, gender binaries, however they are expressed, limit our experiences by making it difficult to recognize or validate the fact that everyone, in some manner or another, crosses the gender divide. We would all be much better off, and the power of gender categories to marginalize or exclude would be diminished, if, as Daniels suggests, we could recognize the extent to which all of us are, in various ways, polygendered.[34]

Kimmel argues that physical and emotional toughness has been a constant theme in the production of American masculinities since at least the nineteenth century. Cultural critic Susan Bordo writes that 'to be exposed as "soft" at the core is one of the worst things a man can suffer in this [American] culture.'[35] Historians have written about the way that ideas about emotional and physical strength, moral and bodily muscularity, were also central to the imperialist white masculinities that organized and executed British colonial expansion. They were, for instance, reproduced in and justified the conquest of aboriginal peoples in Australia, New Zealand, and Canada, and they later influenced the organization of the white settler societies that were founded in the wake of such violence. In part, what made such conquest intellectually and morally possible to white British Christians was the attribution of effeminacy to the cultures they were subjugating and their attribution of a well-developed (culturally and physically), superior manliness to themselves. These differently gendered conceptions of physicality were constituted within and helped to perpetuate discourses of racial difference and the racisms that followed from them. As Anne McClintock writes of British representations of imperial efforts in South Africa, 'The white race was figured as the male of the species and the black race as the female.'[36] The gender analogy was key to the production of the colonizers' racial identity. According to Radhika Mohanram, notions of the European liberal male citizen 'were underpinned by the representation of the colonized Other as effete, excessive, unrestrained, and untrustworthy. Faced with its colonial Other in India (and later … in the West Indies …), British masculinity forged itself as white.' She says that this combined process of 'racialization and masculinization' was supported by a range of forms of cultural expression.[37] Among these, sport made a significant contribution at home and in the colonies.

Clearly there is nothing new or uniquely American about men from dominant groups wanting to be seen as strong and powerful rather than soft and expressive. But something does seem to have shifted in the degree to which strength and power were both desired and expressed by American men as the twentieth century came to a close. In the 1999 documentary film *Tough Guise*, popular educator and anti-violence activist Jackson Katz identifies television programs, films, sports, and action toys as cultural forms that were, in the 1990s, exhibiting increasingly intense versions of masculinity.[38] The evidence he presents points to a never-big-enough, over-the-top machoness, an unquenchable desire for size and muscles and the power they are assumed to represent. Katz cites a study by Harvard psychiatrist Harrison Pope, who compared anthropometric measurements of G.I. Joe dolls from the 1960s and the late 1990s. While the older doll had been made proportional to the build of an average man, the biceps of the more recent doll, increased to human scale, would have been 65 centimetres – 15 centimetres bigger than those of home-run-hitting baseball player Mark McGwire,[39] who has long been suspected of having used banned substances to augment his strength. We can see similar evidence of exaggerated male strength in the bodies that play in the spectacle of the National Football League in the United States. According to a 2006 news article, the size of players in the NFL began increasing significantly in the late 1980s. 'From 1920 to 1984,' the article states, 'there were never more than eight players in any season who weighed 300 pounds or more. This year, there were 570 players who weighed 300 or more listed on 2006 NFL training camp rosters, nearly 20 percent of all players.'[40] Tellingly, a ten-year comparison of win-loss records and the average weight of players on each team did not show any correlation between size and winning. The teams that might have looked the most powerful because they were the biggest were not the most successful. So why have coaches continued to favour size? The contradiction here is an ideological soft spot. In popular understandings of masculinity, bigger is supposed to be better and better in football is measured by winning. When big seems to be getting in the way of winning, coaches seem unable to notice. To admit that bigger might, in fact, not be better would challenge the notions of masculinity that underlie the sport and help to keep it popular.

Some writers have argued that the emphasized manliness that was much in evidence in North America in the 1990s was a reaction to changing gender relations and shifting racial economies in the culture as a whole. The increasing visibility of women in all realms of public life, including previous bastions of male exclusivity like sport and the military, and the erosion of economic position for white male workers, who have lost significant ground in the manufacturing sector, have changed the context in which men, and white men in particular, try to express a normative masculinity. As Kimmel says, 'Gender and racial equality often feel like a loss to white men. If "they" gain, "we" lose.'[41] Without a careful definition of who 'they' are – are they bosses and corporations or are they women or immigrants or people of colour or workers in free-trade zones in southeast Asia? – the feelings of frustration behind this equation can lead to potent racism and misogyny. Some men have lost a lot in the global economic restructuring that has changed the nature of work in both rich and poor countries. In the rich countries the loss of manufacturing jobs, the rise of casual and part-time service positions – most often filled by women – and the steady spread of job insecurity in the face of a diminishing social safety net have combined to undermine the self-determination, the control, and the confidence that are generally assumed to be the foundation of a masculine breadwinner identity. Not surprisingly, it makes many men angry. Add to this the anxiety some men feel about the increasing presence of women in the public sphere and the effects of these changes on so-called traditional heterosexual and family relationships and one can see a need for some kind of remedy that might soothe the anxiety. Unfortunately, that remedy has rarely come in the form of concrete material changes to the organization of work, nor has it come in practical efforts to educate men about or prepare them for changing gender relations or shifting demographics of race in their society. It has come instead in the form of popular cultural representations of tough guys, of hard male bodies (mostly but not all white) with washboard abs and massive biceps. And while muscled bodies have played a privileged role in the support of masculine power – making it look like a biological rather than a social and political fact – masculine power has also been represented by forms of clothing that evoke activities related to hunting or war, by big weapons and big cars, by muscular institutions like professional sport and the military. Such representations of strength are compensatory mechanisms that proclaim the potential of masculine power to men who have only limited access to it.

The Rambo era was not a good time for the fey or the frail. But it offered an array of images that a man might draw upon to constitute for himself a more manly presence. While massive action heroes and huge football players were not the only models of masculinity on display in the 1990s, they did much to push dominant masculine norms towards machoness. Even in the gay community, to which some men might have looked for alternative representations of masculinity, a steroid-inspired aesthetic came to have a place of prominence. Some observers have argued that the pumped-up chests and biceps that many gay men struggled to achieve in the 1990s signified a shared bodily response to the grief and fear engendered during the first decade of the AIDS crisis. Others have seen in the pursuit of a hyper-masculine physique a capitulation to ideologies of male supremacy.[42] In this sense the macho turn in figure skating was a product of its times. For those skaters who worried about being perceived as effeminate or gay, of being associated with AIDS or HIV, the symbols available in a testosterone-laden popular culture presented an easy means of challenging skating's fey reputation, they also made it more likely that skaters would feel the need to do so.

Over the past few years, the heavy emphasis on masculinity has become less evident in televised skating coverage and in reports of skating in newspapers and magazines. There are still, as there were prior to the 1990s, people associated with the sport who find the reputation of men's figure skating a problem that needs correcting, as made evident by the suggestion, in 2009, that Skate Canada was going to launch a 'tough campaign.' But, this worry about the image of men's skating is less prominent in performances and interviews than it was a decade ago. Indeed, at the 2010 Olympics, apart from some macho posturing at news conferences, especially on the part of silver medallist Evgeny Plushenko, there was little evidence on the ice of the macho image that a decade earlier had garnered so much attention. Similarly, in 2009, Canadian television coverage of the world championships seemed to suggest that Brian Joubert of France was on his own carrying the torch for the 'tough guys.' In later chapters I will talk about possible reasons we no longer see as much of the exaggerated masculinity in men's skating as we once did. The 'macho turn' that motivated this study appears to have been a short-lived phenomenon. Hopefully, the lingering anxieties about skating's effeminate reputation will, at some point in the very near future, wither as well. In the next chapter I look in more detail at the mainstream gender norms that have given these anxieties their shape.

3 Girls' Sport?

In 1987, the Canadian magazine *Saturday Night* published a profile of figure skater Brian Orser. In a photo shot from above, the skater clasps his hands awkwardly before his bare torso and gazes demurely to the side. Whether owing to the camera angle or cropping, he appears crooked – his head points towards the top left corner of the page. Positioned this way, Orser seems more nervous choirboy than world champion athlete. Yet in 1987 Orser had become the first Canadian man to win the world figure skating championship since 1962. For almost a decade he had owned the triple axel, a jump once believed to be the outside limit of possibility in free skating. However, journalist Richard Wright opens and closes his profile of Orser not with the challenge of the jump or of winning a world title but with the challenge of being a man in figure skating: 'Brian Orser has felt at odds with his world ever since he began to skate nineteen years ago ... Despite his credentials ... Orser has had to wrest grudging respect from a public largely ambivalent about his sport.'[1] Ambivalent seems to be putting it mildly. When Orser was a child, other boys teased him about his skating. When he was older, he was targeted by obscene phone callers, his car tires were slashed, his license plates were stolen. An arena named in his honour was vandalized. 'You won't get away from it,' Orser tells Wright. 'It's always going to be that way for male figure skaters.'[2] Neither Orser nor Wright explains what 'it' is. Wright says simply that more girls than boys take up figure skating and that many people think of skating as a 'girls' sport.' What they think of the boys and men who pursue the sport is left unsaid, but clearly they think something. In what other sport do world champions *expect* to be harassed?

What many people thought in 1987, as many people think now, is that figure skating is a feminine sport. At all but the most elite levels, boys and men who figure skate are outnumbered by girls and women, are presumed to be effeminate and/or gay, and are, often, ridiculed or worse by their peers. Few boys choose to pursue the sport and those who do frequently face questions about their gender and sexual identities. But what exactly is a girls' sport? And what does it allegedly say about a man or a boy who chooses to participate in one? In this chapter I try to make sense of skating's fey reputation and to show some of the ways it fits into broader discursive formations in which sport, gender, and sexuality are intertwined. Using a range of sources (autobiographies, magazine articles, Skate Canada membership statistics), I demonstrate that the meanings that accrue to figure skating are inevitably constituted through discourses of femininity, even when those discourses are being refused or refuted, as they frequently are by some male skaters. This is a discussion that makes clear the centrality of gender to our understandings of sport and, very often, the relevance of sport to our understandings of gender.

Of course, sports are not unique in being gendered activities. What makes them somewhat different from other highly gendered activities – nursing, parliamentary politics, welding, needlework – is their fundamental physicality, the way they seem to have been made possible by the materiality of differently shaped bodies. It's this appearance of inevitability that can make it seem like the difference between so-called masculine and feminine sports is natural. Thus, there seems to be a lot at stake in transgressions of the gender boundaries that divide sports into masculine and feminine categories.

This chapter opens with evidence for the claim that grounds the arguments I make throughout this book, that is, the claim that for almost six decades figure skating has been seen as a sport primarily suited to girls and, therefore, as not quite suited to boys. In a culture that continues to be structured by binary notions of gender and that, therefore, shows little respect for men or boys who engage in activities or behaviours considered to be feminine, figure skating's reputation as a girls' sport marginalizes male skaters. In combination with popular assumptions about the necessary overlap between gender and sexual identities, skating's feminine reputation throws the sexual and gender identities of male skaters into question. The basic argument here is that normative notions of gender and sexuality, and the homophobia and misogyny embedded in them, mean that a boy's choice to take up skating is rarely as unremarkable as would be his choice to take up running or soccer; indeed, it could expose him to harm, as the experiences of Brian Orser suggest.

The popular conviction that athletic experience is a fine way to turn a boy into a man is embedded in the history of Western sports. Scholars have identified sport as a 'male preserve,' as 'male terrain,' as a contributor to male supremacy.[3] How does figure skating fit into this picture? The question prompts us to disaggregate the category 'sport' to consider the way that different kinds of sports, and the athletes who participate in them, are positioned differently in terms of discourses and practices through which power circulates. Here I look at such differences as they are organized around discourses of gender, especially as they are produced through the categorizing of sports by gender. How would we know a so-called girls' sport if we were to see one? How is it that figure skating ends up in this category? In the final section of the chapter, I talk specifically about the artistic aspects of figure skating, as it is these that lead to the association of skating with femininity and that make it hard for male skaters to receive the masculine gender validation most male athletes take for granted. In contemporary North America, the arts, even when packaged with the trappings of a competitive sport, are complicated terrain for boys and men. I argue that it's the disjuncture between 'artistic impressions' and the versions of masculinity that men are typically expected to express through sport that marginalizes men's figure skating and that makes it so hard for many boys to choose to do it.

Saturday Night Takes on Male Skaters

Between 1987 and 1997, three Canadian men stood atop the podium at the world championships. *Saturday Night* magazine ran profiles of each of them when they were at the height of their careers. These three articles are a good introduction to the way that male figure skaters were represented in the popular press at that time.

In his 1987 article about Brian Orser, Richard Wright uses hockey metaphors to bring Orser's story into familiar sporting territory. Hockey is *the* sport in Canada. Mythologized as key to our national identity and lauded as 'our game,' hockey is supposed to provide Canadians with a shared language and a common passion.[4] So when Wright finds the scene at Orser's training rink 'reminiscent of little-league hockey practice in any small-town rink,' minus the 'clatter of hockey sticks and the boom of slapshots,' he positions Orser's sport closer to the cultural mainstream. He does the same as he describes Orser preparing for a triple axel, mentioning the figure skater in the same breath as a legendary player from the National Hockey League: 'He sweeps up-ice like Bobby Orr on a rush ... Just over the blue line, where a winger would start to cut for the net, Orser turns and glides backwards.' It's no coincidence that Wright uses hockey references to frame his discussion of figure skating. In Canada hockey is the ice sport of choice for boys and men. And the hockey ideal is men's hockey played as it is in the National Hockey League. It's a loud, aggressive game where players are rewarded for the ability to give and take hits and to fight 'like men.' European players who excel at skating and puck handling, rather than checking or fighting, encounter derision from some Canadian fans and sports commentators for not being sufficiently masculine, for being soft.[5] While it is too simple to say that the definitions of masculinity that prevail in hockey are those against which all other Canadian male athletes are measured, it is the case that hockey's influence extends well beyond its own boundaries and that discourses about hockey provide a powerful lens through which other sporting masculinities are seen and assessed. When those other sporting masculinities are also performed on the ice by athletes wearing skates, comparisons with hockey are almost unavoidable. As Orser says of the environment in which he grew up, 'If you weren't a hockey player you were teased. I've seen a lot of good talent wasted, young boys who quit – they just couldn't take it.'[6] Writing for Toronto's gay newspaper *Xtra*, Christopher Richards confirms Orser's observations: 'I left figure skating at the age of 12. My reason is best-summed up by a question my step-mother had asked: "Why can't you do the things that other boys do?"'[7]

While clearly impressed by Orser's perseverance and athletic gifts, Wright nevertheless creates an impression of the skater as fragile. Instead of presenting Orser as a fighter for enduring years of harassment, Wright presents him as long-suffering and resigned. What's worse, Wright fails to name the harassment as homophobia (which would have been possible without outing Orser), and so severs the connection between it and its social context, making the problem seem unique to Orser or to figure skating and not part of a broader system of discrimination. In not naming the harassment as homophobia Wright fails to make clear the potential risks Orser faced, and the courage that took, especially during an era when police did not take homophobic violence seriously and when homophobia had yet to be challenged in any significant way through educational campaigns or human-rights legislation.

Wright also conveys weakness in the way he discusses Orser's competitive history. He pays a lot of attention to Orser's reliance on a sport psychologist (something that is now taken for granted, even at much lower levels of sport) and his long string of second-place finishes in world competition. Either of these points could easily have served a narrative of triumph or of adversity overcome – a standard trope of the typical athletic biography. In the summer of 1987 – a few months before the Calgary Olympics – Orser's story was definitely triumphant. Yet Wright and his editors at *Saturday Night* chose not to shape it as such. We read about Orser's 'fine-featured face,' that Orser collected his gold medal at the world championships with 'tears in his eyes,' and that not once but 'several times' Orser told CBC's *The Journal* that his victory was 'special.' Alongside the choirboy photo, the narrative conveys a feeling of fragility or delicacy, qualities not usually celebrated in sports journalism. By the story's end Wright has constructed the world champion and Olympic silver medallist as a nervous, insecure outsider, motivated not by competitive drive, but by victimization. Here is Wright's final take on the skater and the event that will be the culmination of his amateur career: 'Calgary [site of the 1988 Winter Olympic Games] offers opportunity for one last self-affirming victory over all the nay-sayers. When he skates to his starting position in the Saddledome ... there is a special audience he will perform for: a doubting Thomas of a local reporter, a cowardly obscene phone caller, a gang of thieves, and a certain vandal with Orser's stolen license plate gathering dust in his garage.'[8]

In his story about Orser, Wright drew on discursive techniques that are common in the coverage of female athletes. In a frequently cited 1993 study on gendered language in television sports programming, Michael Messner, Margaret Carlisle Duncan, and Kerry Jensen found that the successes and failures of male and female athletes were framed in significantly different ways. Women were more likely than men to be framed as suffering from 'nervousness, lack of confidence, lack of being "comfortable," lack of aggression.' The setbacks suffered by female athletes were often attributed to the women's own shortcomings, as opposed to the setbacks suffered by male athletes, which were often attributed to the 'power, strength, and intelligence of their (male) *opponents*' rather than to any particular weakness of the men themselves. In short, the researchers found that 'men were framed as active agents in control of their destinies, women as reactive objects.'[9] Although it would be more than a decade before Brian Orser was publicly outed as a gay man, homosexuality and skating's effeminate reputation seem to float just below the surface of Wright's article and to have governed the choice of the photograph that portrays the world champion as coy and vulnerable. Photos of male athletes typically represent the physical and social power associated with hegemonic versions of masculinity. There's none of that in the photo of Orser. And that is one of the points the photo and the profile combine to make.

In 1989, *Saturday Night* published a profile of Kurt Browning, the next Canadian man, after Orser, to become the world figure skating champion. There are no bare shoulders in the photo of Browning. Sporting a black beret and a leather jacket, he stares directly into the camera. The article's subheading claims that Browning's 'macho ice image has startled the skating world.'[10] And if that macho image was not entirely obvious to people who had been watching Browning on TV – certainly I didn't notice it myself when I first saw him skate – writer Stephen Hopkins pulls out all the stops to emphasize it in print. Whereas Wright profiled a figure skater, Hopkins profiles a man.

Browning entered the record books as the first skater to land a quadruple jump in competition. But Hopkins, like many other journalists, seems equally impressed by the fact that Browning is the son of an Alberta trail guide. Indeed, the tone of some of the press coverage of Browning leaves the impression that having a cowboy for a dad gave him a distinct advantage as a free skater! Hopkins speculates that Browning might be the first figure skater (in the world? in history?) to have learned to ride a horse at a young age or to have grown up 'milking Jersey cows.' The writer praises Browning as probably 'the most athletic' skater ever, claiming his championship free skating program is 'the most demanding in the history of the sport.' And if such superlatives are not enough to give Browning the kind of athletic credibility that might pass muster with the average guy, Hopkins makes sure readers know that the world champion figure skater was once a good hockey player too.

Hopkins draws on a range of manly stereotypes to distance Browning from the effeminate reputation of his sport. He portrays Browning as a raw athletic talent and paints him as a rugged (read western) individualist. Heck, Browning's so good he doesn't have to 'lift weights or do sit-ups or push-ups.' Browning has no team of experts. He hates routine. He sets his own schedule. He's not afraid to fall. He doesn't need help. A reference to Orser underscores the point: 'Browning ... contrasts dramatically to his predecessor, Orser, who fought an amateur-career-long battle with himself and employed the services of a

Team Canada sport-psychology consultant for his nerves and a rolfer to massage him by way of emotional therapy. Browning uses no psychologists. "I have a massage therapist," he says, "but he fixes my body, not my mind."[11]

In knitting together manly clichés, Hopkins frames Browning as atypical for a figure skater. For his part, Browning gives him a lot to work with:

> Browning glides onto the ice in a black leather jacket, black beret, dark glasses, black denim pants, and a black leather belt with silver studs. He is carrying a chair and sits down on it. As the music starts to pound, he hops into the rhythm. He flings away his beret, then strips to a black muscle shirt, flexing his biceps and deltoids ... He pumps pelvic thrusts. Some women [in the audience] are stomping and whistling ... He sits down, bows his head, and raises his fists. At the end, always, squeals and shrieks rise above thunderous applause.[12]

It seems Browning had at least some investment in challenging the notion that male skaters are effete or gay. Flaunting his 'sinewy' body, he represented as much toughness as was possible with his 5 foot, 7 inch, 140-pound frame. The contrast between Browning and previous champions like Britain's balletic John Curry, Canada's baroque and flamboyant Toller Cranston, or the always 'elegant' Brian Orser, did not go unnoticed in the press. Hopkins, for instance, contrasts the 'earthy, powerful, and sexy' Browning with the 'genteel elegance' of Orser. There is no explicit mention made of either man's sexuality. Yet normative discourses about what constitutes an appropriately heterosexual masculinity would certainly have permitted readers to interpret Hopkins's adjectives here – powerful versus genteel – as signs of differently gendered men with concomitantly different sexual orientations. Hopkins also tells us that Browning's agent thinks the skater will be able to 'accomplish something no other male skating champion has been able to do: make his sport popular with men.'[13]

Commentators pegged Browning as 'The Cowboy' and 'The Crazy Canuck.' He was compared to daredevil Evel Knievel, best known for launching his motorcycle across the Snake River Canyon.[14] *Toronto Star* columnist Jim Proudfoot wrote: 'The guy is a rarity in figure skating, a fighter.'[15] Such journalistic efforts to represent Browning as a 'real man' belie the fact that a male skater's gender and sexual identities are always open to question. The context in which male skaters perform is considered by many observers to be a feminine one and, unless male skaters can prove otherwise, they will be assumed to have been feminized by their immersion in it; they will be assumed to be effeminate, with all the connotations of devalued gender and sexual deviance that that term holds for men. As sports sociologist Garry Smith told Hopkins, Browning may be a celebrity athlete, but he is unlikely to be a true sport hero, 'mainly because of the sport he's in. A lot of people think of it more as an art form than a real sport. Skating is seen as kind of feminine, so to what extent can he really be a hero to guys?'[16] While Browning quickly grew to be a well-known and well-respected sports and television celebrity in Canada – he was awarded both the Lionel Conacher Award as Canadian male athlete of the year and the Lou Marsh Award as Canadian athlete of the year, he appears regularly in skating and other television specials, he provides colour commentary on skating for the Canadian Broadcasting Corporation – he never did become a 'true' sports hero, if that means someone the average young boy might want to emulate. Nor did his successor.

1997. *Saturday Night* publishes a third consideration of figure skating and masculinity in a profile of Elvis Stojko, Browning's heir as world champion and skating tough guy. If sports journalists warmed to Browning, Stojko made them weak in the knees. As a journalist for *Toronto Life* put it, only slightly tongue-in-cheek: 'With the squat brawn of a pug dog and black belt in karate, Stojko brought a hockey mullet, a Japanese taiko drum soundtrack and gold chains into a sport better known for its lip gloss and puffy chemises.'[17] A three-time world men's figure skating champion and a two-time Olympic silver medallist, Stojko nonetheless could not escape mention of his black belt in karate and penchant for dirt bikes. He met all the criteria of the masculine jock. He was the first to land a quad-triple jump combination. He did the biggest tricks with great consistency. He played hurt. He did not stretch his back or arms nor did he point his toes (all of which Browning eventually learned to do). He was not a pretty skater. He was known by the nickname 'The Terminator.' During the 1998 Nagano Winter Olympic Games Stojko was widely and favourably quoted when he said, 'I'm a powerful skater. I'm a masculine skater, not a feminine skater … I don't skate feminine and I'm not going to be that way. I don't have a feminine side.'[18]

On the opening page of the *Saturday Night* article, there is a photo of Stojko, shot from below. He is wearing black skates, black pants, studded black belt, a tight black, short-sleeved T-shirt with lacing across a

V-neck. He wears what appear to be studded black leather cuffs on his wrists. He is smiling and looking into the distance as he stands on top of a low concrete wall. He seems self-contained and imposing – but not nearly as imposing as he does in the full-page picture on the next page. This time the photographer catches him at the climax of a flying, front karate kick. The shot is taken from the side, to highlight the form of his kick. Stojko grimaces with his effort. Again, he is dressed in black with his karate black belt swinging by his hip. The caption reads: 'I'm male. You want to portray that on the ice. I'm not into being gentle and vulnerable and unprotected.'

As with the story about Brian Orser, the Stojko profile provided a pre-Olympic portrait of a skater expected to win a gold medal. Yet, David Staples's article, 'Skating Is No Wussy Sport,' seems more concerned with Stojko's manhood than his skating. Drawing on, in equal parts, misogyny and homophobia, the writer seems to have set himself the contradictory task of validating figure skating as Stojko's sport of choice while distancing him from other skaters and the 'skating establishment.' Staples presents other male skaters, especially Russians, as ballet dancers (the wusses of the title?) on ice. Stojko, by contrast, wants to be the kind of 'guy who would play football … this is not a pussy sport. This takes a lot of effort.'[19]

In Staples's article, Stojko plays frontman for the masculinization of figure skating. While there is a nod to Kurt Browning, who 'started to win over the skating world and many new fans with his gutsy jumping, magic footwork, good looks, and ladies'-man reputation,'[20] Stojko shines as the real champion of manly skating. More important, where Browning fought public perceptions in order to bring male skaters into the mainstream, Stojko, as portrayed by Staples, confronts skating itself. He's presented as the lone macho challenger to an effete skating world that persists in looking for artistry along with the jumps. In order to champion Stojko, Staples supports rather than challenges the notion that figure skating is fey.

In order to present Stojko as a revolutionary, Staples had to ignore other skaters of Stojko's era who also tried to represent a macho masculinity on the ice. For instance, we read nothing about American Christopher Bowman, nicknamed 'Bowman the showman.' One of Bowman's popular exhibition numbers, set to the music of the Rolling Stones, opened and closed with the skater flirting heavily with his female audience, kissing and hugging his way around the rink. There is no mention of French skater Philippe Candeloro, who was known for his inelegant body lines and for competing several years in a row to music from the film *The Godfather*. In one notable exhibition, Candeloro entered the rink from high in the stands, an American flag draped over his bare chest, his fist pumping to the theme music from *Rocky*. It was this performance of heterosexuality about which *Toronto Star* columnist Rosie DiManno commented, with a nod to skating's fey reputation: 'Philippe Candeloro, shirtless. Rosie DiManno, breathless. Hoo boy. Been gone too long if the mere sight of a half-naked Frenchman – and a figure skater at that – can make us go weak at the knees. I mean, this ain't exactly [Toronto Maple Leafs hockey player] Doug Gilmore macho territory.'[21] Staples could have talked about American skater Michael Weiss, who pretty much grew up in the Gold's Gym that his father owns. With the biceps to prove it, Weiss usually chose tight, short-sleeved costumes that showed off his muscles to their best advantage. Broadcasters and sports journalists rarely missed an opportunity to mention his wife and their children. As one critic wrote, 'I heard more about Michael Weiss's wife and kids in seven minutes last week than I've heard about [hockey player] Mario Lemieux's wife and kids in 15 years.'[22] Staples also ignored commercial efforts to market male skaters as heterosexual heartthrobs – *Blade* magazine's 'superhunk' wall calendar and posters, for instance. Stojko and those who supported and represented him were not the first or the only ones trying to refashion the image of their sport or to create uniquely masculine personae on the ice. But the omission of the other 'tough' guy skaters from his story made it easier for Staples to imply that skating was indeed a 'wussy' sport and that Stojko – misunderstood and undervalued – was its underdog masculine saviour.

On-Ice Masculinities: A Diverse Range of Styles

There is a popular assumption in North America (often repeated to me when I mention the subject of this book) that European skaters, especially Russians and other Eastern Europeans, would be less likely to feel the need to express the kind of pronounced masculinity performed by competitors like Stojko or Candeloro. People usually base this assumption on the greater prominence in Russian society of ballet and the other forms of 'high' culture that would be viewed as effete by many North American men. The dominance of Russian skaters in the more theatrical disciplines of pairs and ice dance seems to suggest a national inclination to the expressive and artistic. The performances of a male singles skater like 1994 Olympic champion Alexei Urmanov seem to confirm it. Urmanov's costuming, music choices, and movements often echoed the traditions of the most elaborate classical ballets. Broadcasters contrasted his long lines, graceful arms, and fanciful costumes – at least one of which included chiffon wings and gloves – to the very different presentations made by the 1994 Olympic silver medallist, Elvis Stojko, who skated without discernible attention to line or to the grace of his arms, wearing costumes that would not have been out of place in a Hollywood action film. The contrast between Urmanov and Stojko was striking. Yet Urmanov, affectionately called 'the ruffled one' by his fans, also presented an obvious contrast to the string of Russian men who followed him as Olympic champion – Ilia Kulik, Alexei Yagudin, Evgeny Plushenko – none of whom presented such long lines or such a 'ruffled' image. Among the Russians, as among the entire cohort of male skaters who were performing in the 1990s and early 2000s, there was a range of masculinities on display on the ice. American Paul Wylie (1992 Olympic silver medallist) and Canadians Sébastien Britten (national champion in 1995) and Emanuel Sandhu (who qualified for the Canadian Olympic team in 1998 and won nationals in 2001, 2003, and 2004) are excellent examples of North American skaters who give no evidence of having felt a need to shape their skating according to normative conceptions of gender. Not all male competitors were caught up in concerns about skating's masculine image.

One of the things that sometimes made it hard to see the diversity among male skaters in the era of the macho trend was the tendency of the press here in Canada to focus more on the 'manlier' skaters – which, given the fact that both Browning and Stojko were Canadians *and* world champions, is not surprising – and to use intensely gendered language and images as they talked about men's figure skating competitions as a whole. For example, on the Canadian television network CTV, men's events have been referred to as 'a shootout in the wild wild west'[23]; a 'showdown'[24]; a 'civil war.'[25] The network's opening montage for the broadcast of the men's long program at the 2000 world championships concluded with a graphic of a bomb.[26] It's impossible to imagine such terms or images being applied to a women's event, and they certainly did little to promote the kind of lyrical skating that might have been on display by competitors like Urmanov, Britten, or Wylie. The fact that little effort was made to use language that could accommodate the range of masculinities that were being performed by male skaters meant that, overall, male skaters as a group came across as more uniformly invested in issues of masculinity than they probably were.

Stojko occupied the extreme edge of those men who were looking to recast skating's image. Given his comments to the press, his costumes, his style of skating, it seems he was striving for an unequivocally macho image, in the tradition of Rocky or the Terminator (after whom he was nicknamed). Other male skaters seemed less concerned about adopting a tough mien than they were with simply looking straight. In the not-always-sophisticated movement vocabulary of men's skating, straightness tends to be represented through clichéd versions of cool and sexy. Male skaters shimmy around the ice, snap their fingers to blues, rock and jazz music, and blow kisses to women in the audience. They cock their hips and run their hands through their hair.

In the skating world, a skater who appears to be heterosexual is more likely to achieve success in his career – or that seems to be the assumption skaters make. Like other elite athletes, skaters are commodities, subject to the whims of the market. Over the past two decades, opportunities for a small number of elite skaters have extended far beyond the limits of their 'eligible' careers (as in eligible for Olympic competition, a status that allows monetary rewards but is regulated by the International Skating Union). A skater's success in the professional realm depends on medals won and on the kind of name and face recognition that he or she has built up through media coverage of national and world championships or the Olympics. High-ranking international competitors can move on to tour with professional ice shows, to star in television specials, and to endorse commercial products, although, in stark contrast to other sports, the most lucrative endorsement opportunities in skating have, historically, gone to women.

Popularity, Sponsorship, and Heteronormative Masculinities

Very few North American male skaters have been able to attract the kind of large corporate sponsorships that have become an expected part of the professional careers of elite male athletes in many other sports. Things are different for skaters in Europe. For example, Stéphane Lambiel of Switzerland, who was the world champion in 2005 and 2006, has had contracts with Ford, Swisscom Mobile, and Hublot, a maker of Swiss watches. At the 2006 Olympics, Lambiel lost the gold medal to Evgeny Plushenko of Russia. One year later, Plushenko was, according to the *Denver Post*, 'the most heavily endorsed athlete in a country that covers 11 time zones.'[27]

In North America, Kurt Browning and Elvis Stojko are the only male skaters to have had significant success with endorsement contracts. Browning landed major contracts with non-sport-related companies like Toshiba and Pepsi. Elvis Stojko signed deals with Canon, McCain's, Roots, and a number of other corporations. Browning and Stojko were both presented by the media as uniquely masculine in their sport, they both won multiple world championships, and they both had the good fortune to be competing at the height of figure skating's mainstream popularity *and* after changes to the rules made it possible for 'amateur' skaters to accept sponsorships. No other North American man has been able to match their success at attracting corporate sponsors, although 2010 Olympic champion Evan Lysacek of the United States may prove to be the exception.

Lysacek has deals with Coca-Cola, AT&T, Flexjet (a 'private aviation service'), and Total Gym (a manufacturer of exercise equipment). His website also sports the logos of clothing designer Vera Wang, who designed his Olympic costumes, and the Toyota Sports Centre, a figure skating training facility in California.[28] Skating commentators started playing up Lysacek's marketing potential after he won his first national title in 2007. As an American skating blogger put it, 'some in the media and U.S. Figure Skating feel very comfortable touting Evan Lysacek as the "meat and potatoes" man our sport, apparently, so desperately needs.'[29] Tall and conventionally good looking, Lysacek's timing could not have been better in terms of marketing opportunities. As the reigning world champion in an Olympic year, he was a good bet for an Olympic gold medal. Also important to his ability to attract endorsement contracts was the fact that 2010 was the first time in decades that American women, who are generally among the most hyped athletes of the winter games, headed into the Olympics with no big names among them. Someone needed to fill the media void. The handsome Lysacek, who, as world champion, had already become a feature of celebrity gossip columns, was a promising candidate. Then, after winning the Olympics, Lysacek performed on the popular American television show *Dancing With the Stars*. No doubt his sponsors appreciated the exposure the show gave him – including to audiences unfamiliar with skating.

Some skaters are very strategic about developing an image that will play well in the marketplace, but not all elite skaters package themselves to appeal to a small pool of potential sponsors or tour promoters – or even to judges. Former competitors Toller Cranston and Emanuel Sandhu of Canada and Rudy Galindo of the United States all challenged conventional wisdom by taking aesthetic and political risks with their public images and their skating. More recently, American Johnny Weir – dubbed by some as the Lady Gaga of skating – has competed with a pointed disregard for norms and he has a huge fan base as a consequence. But skaters willing to buck conformity have definitely been in the minority. It is risky to be too different in a judged sport. And a risk to one's competitive career would have consequences for the professional career that could follow it.

To generate commercial appeal, skaters need to capture the attention of a non-specialist audience mostly comprising middle-class white women and girls. In the late 1980s and 1990s, skaters began to take themselves more seriously as entertainers, even as they competed. We saw the increasing influence of mainstream popular culture at competitions. We began to hear less classical music and more movie soundtracks, to see tighter and more revealing costumes, and to see skaters putting a heavier emphasis on engaging the audience. We saw more skaters hamming it up, during and after their programs. It became commonplace for male competitors to hug and kiss their way around the rink as they left the ice, a habit that played well with female spectators, judging by the often enthusiastic screams that greeted the men as they approached the rink boards. Even for skaters who had never won a world or Olympic medal, the right image could ensure a solid professional touring and competitive career. Eight-time British national champion Steven Cousins, for instance, never stood on a world podium, yet he had a tremendously successful professional career, nurtured in part by his reputation as a 'heartthrob.' According to Cousins's own website, *International Figure Skating Magazine* once named him among the 'Top 10 Most Beautiful People in Skating.'[30]

Does a heterosexual image make a skater more marketable? Some skaters have thought so. In 1997 Brian Orser was 'outed' in a 'palimony' suit launched by an ex-boyfriend. Fearing for his career, Orser made an unsuccessful bid to have documents related to the case sealed by the court. In an affidavit presented to the court and later made public, Orser said he had made the request because he thought his career might be 'irreparably harmed' by publicity about the case and about his sexuality.[31] He argued that 'other skaters, both Canadian and American, guard their gayness closely because of the likely impact of public disclosure on their careers.'[32] Whether Orser was simply asserting what seemed to him like common sense or referring to his personal knowledge of decisions made by other closeted skaters we cannot know. He did, however, make specific reference to Brian Pockar, Canadian men's champion from 1978 to 1980 and world bronze medallist in 1982, who, shortly after he came out as a gay man, lost his job as a skating commentator on CTV.[33] Orser would experience no such setback. When the story of his palimony case hit the newspapers, he received a huge outpouring of public sympathy and support. This approval, however, does not seem to have opened the closet door for other skaters. Certainly no other skater supported Orser by coming out in solidarity with him. He remains one of only a handful of openly gay elite skaters.

Sport, especially professional sport, remains complicated terrain for queer people. Very few gay professional athletes have come out while they are still competing in their sport, not wanting to negotiate the discomfort of teammates nor to risk discriminatory treatment from coaches, fans, or competitors. There is some indication that the sports world is loosening up in terms of its acceptance of queer athletes, especially at lower levels of play. Yet the number of high-level athletes who have come out is still so low that Outsports.com – a popular website focusing on gay athletes in mainstream sports and on organized sports in lesbian, gay, and queer communities – still sees the need to maintain a list of openly gay athletes. If athletes were coming out with any frequency, such a list would not only be difficult to maintain, but would cease to be meaningful. At the 2010 Winter Olympics, a hospitality pavilion for lesbian, gay, transgendered, and queer athletes saw little traffic from its intended audience. The organizers of Pride House claim not to have been surprised, given that only a handful of Olympic athletes are able to be out. Their goal in establishing the pavilion, they said, was primarily to open up a dialogue on homophobia in sporting cultures.[34]

The pressure on athletes not to come out comes from a number of directions: teammates, coaches, managers, agents. Agents counsel gay athletes to keep quiet about their sexualities to protect their earning potential and, not coincidentally, the earnings of the agents as well. Tennis players Billie Jean King and Martina Navratilova are perhaps the most famous examples of athletes who suffered financially for being out. Like Orser, King was outed in a palimony suit, after which she estimates that she lost millions of dollars in endorsements.[35] Navratilova, who came out after she received American citizenship in 1981, has said she struggled throughout her playing career to attract endorsement deals despite being the best woman player of her (or, some would argue, any) era. In 2005 Navratilova discussed her 'paucity of endorsements' with the *New York Times* and said her deals had been 'minuscule' relative to those of 'younger [straight] tennis stars like Serena and Venus Williams or soccer's Mia Hamm.' Apparently Navratilova retired from singles play in 1994 'without a single non-equipment endorsement contract.'[36] Ironically, in recent years, well past the height of her career, Navratilova's status as an easily identifiable lesbian icon has led to a number of endorsement deals as major corporations – like Suburu and Under Armour – have begun to target gay consumers and the lucrative 'pink' or gay and lesbian market.[37]

In North America, popular associations of figure skating and gay-ness have definitely had an effect on the marketing potential of male skaters. At the 1988 Winter Olympic Games, Brian Orser won the silver medal behind American Brian Boitano in one of the most heavily promoted events of the Games. At the expense of the other competitors, including a young Kurt Browning, the North American press reduced the men's competition to the 'Battle of the Brians.' The event received huge coverage, and both Orser and Boitano became household names to North American television viewers. Yet, despite huge popular interest in their skating, neither man was able to convert his increased profile into any kind of significant endorsements. By contrast, women's champion Katarina Witt signed with more than a dozen companies over the course of her career, including Diet Coke, Danskin, Ultrawheels, Swatch, and Dupont. Almost twenty years after Calgary she still had a contract with Mercedes-Benz.[38] In an interview on CBC radio in 1993, Brian Boitano's agent Lee Steinberg told the CBC's Peter Gzowski that 'the very connotation that ice skaters tend to be gay, ... in a sense, ruined part of [Boitano's] marketing effort. I sat there with advertising execs who said, well, you know, the widespread perception is that this is a gay person, that won't help much on the market.'[39] It is likely not a coincidence that Olympic champion Evan Lysacek, whose heterosexual romantic life has been documented by *People* magazine[40] and whose looks are regularly remarked upon in the press, is the first male skater in the United States to achieve some marketing success.

Gay Sport?

The irony of figure skating's reputation as a 'gay sport,' is that there are very few openly gay skaters. The 1996 US national champion, Rudy Galindo, is still the only elite skater to have come out publicly during his competitive career. While American skater Johnny Weir is widely assumed to be gay and presents a very queer public image, he remains coy about his sexuality in interviews. Many other skaters have also generated 'is he? or isn't he?' discussions on the Internet. Both skating fan pages and on-line gay discussion boards have contributed a lot of space to such speculation. In few other sports do the sexual orientations or sexual identities of male athletes attract so much attention.

In his autobiography, Galindo says he had a 'generally feminine demeanor' as a child.[41] As a young 'effeminate and flamboyantly dressed' skater he had been assumed to be gay – by spectators and officials – long before he came out.[42] Galindo twice won the US pairs championship with his partner Kristi Yamaguchi. When Yamaguchi dissolved the partnership to focus on the women's event (she became Olympic champion in 1992), Galindo struggled to refashion his own solo career. His story is one of great hardships overcome. In an upper-middle-class white sport, Galindo was an anomaly – an effeminate, working-class, Mexican American. He lost his brother and his coach to AIDS-related illnesses in 1992 and 1993 and his father died of diabetes in 1993. In 1996, after years when it seemed his career would never advance, Galindo won the US men's championship. He followed this victory with a bronze medal at the 1996 world championships. Yet the following season, the United States Figure Skating Association chose not to assign Galindo to the list of competitors for Skate America, a major annual international competition.

Host nations generally send their own national champions to such events. So, why not Galindo? It was not the first time he had been left off the list for Skate America. In 1993 Galindo had been named first alternate, but when another competitor dropped out, he was passed over and the free spot was given to Todd Eldredge, a solid but far less artistic skater than Galindo. As Galindo writes in his autobiography, his coach was 'convinced it had everything to do with the fact that they [officials from the US Figure Skating Association] did not want an effeminate gay man representing the United States at Skate America. It was no secret that the USFSA tried to project an all-American image, one in which the women were feminine, not the men.' Galindo had felt the judges' discomfort with his gender and his sexuality throughout his career. Judges advised his coach that Galindo 'needed to be more masculine.' Among their concerns: his hand positions, which, apparently, they found 'too girlish.'[43]

In an interview published in 2006, openly gay former international skating judge Jon Jackson argues that many of the judges and skating officials who are most concerned that male skaters not appear effeminate are themselves closeted gay men.[44] Their efforts to keep 'girlish' hands out of skating are meant to protect the reputation of their sport and their personal reputations as well. As Jackson says, older coaches and officials were themselves accustomed to having to 'pass,' that is, to having to appear straight, and so would have expected the same from younger skaters. In his tell-all book, *On Edge*, Jackson quotes judges who claimed it was all right for skaters to be gay as 'long as they weren't flamboyant about it.'[45] In other words, it was all right for skaters to be gay as long as no one could tell. The worry that prompts the policing of hand gestures is that the sport would be damaged by too much visible gayness. But what does gayness look like? Skating officials and coaches focused their worries on effeminacy, on non-conforming gender behaviours that fit the stereotypical understandings of gayness that circulate in popular culture. If they could control the level of effeminate behaviour, they might be able to control public perceptions of their sport. As skating journalist Lorrie Kim has written, 'Many of the officials, judges, and skating federations, especially in the U.S., make it clear that they prefer male skaters to look "masculine" and will be harsher on effeminate-looking skaters when it comes to giving marks or desirable competitive assignments.'[46]

Jackson writes that while 'figure skating was the gayest sport in America ... being gay was not so easy there.'[47] Hence the small number of high-profile openly gay skaters. Why don't more male skaters come out? In an article in the gay magazine *The Advocate*, Jon Jackson quotes an unnamed 'international-level skater' who says that skaters worry about being judged fairly. 'Are there going to be repercussions' for coming out? Skaters fear the power of their federations to control their careers. The skater told Jackson, 'Over and over we have been told that the marketability of the sport is hurt if the public thinks figure skaters are gay. No one skater is going to take the risk of being "the one" that jeopardizes that.'[48] Tangled up with the reputation of the sport are sponsorship opportunities for the governing bodies, television ratings and the profits from the selling of broadcast rights that are linked to them, and also the attractiveness of the sport to families looking to get their children involved in something new. But, apart from a sense of responsibility or protectiveness about the sport, some skaters choose not to come out because they don't want to confirm the stereotype that made their childhoods and teenage years difficult. Others just want to guard their privacy. American skater Johnny Weir, whose campy and flamboyant performances and press conferences have fuelled much speculation about his sexuality, seems simply to enjoy being in the middle of controversy. He also, rightly, makes a point of asking journalists whether they ask all skaters questions about whom they sleep with or do they just ask him?

How many male figure skaters are gay? Up until very recently it was not unusual for skaters and officials to claim publicly that skating has the same proportion of gay men as any other sport. Brian Orser did so in a television interview in 1998, shortly after he was 'outed' publicly in the palimony suit, and two years after Galindo came out: 'I'm sure the ratio of gay people, men and women, in figure skating is no different than in any other profession.'[49] Remarkably, in 2002, Rudy Galindo made a similar claim in an article published on *Salon.com*, telling the interviewer that 'almost every figure skater' he has 'ever met is straight.'[50] Lorrie Kim, who for a number of years published a popular website called Rainbow Ice, which advocated for gay skaters and for more openness around sexual identity and less homophobia in the sport, has said that 'unofficial insider estimates' suggest that somewhere between 25 and 50 per cent of male figure skaters are gay.[51] In 2006 Jon Jackson wrote that 'at least seven of the 14 male Olympic figure skating medallists from the past 20 years are known in certain circles to be interested in other men. In fact, in at least five countries the entire men's singles figure skating team is made up of gay men,' although, as he notes, some 'teams' are made up of only one man. In his book Jackson wrote that there are still more straight men than gay men in skating, although the ratio is almost even.[52]

In the end, it is impossible to say how many male figure skaters are gay. But the proportion of gay men in skating is definitely higher – some skating insiders would say much higher – than it is in the general population. It is likely also much higher than in other more mainstream sports for men, especially team sports, which tend not to be perceived as a welcoming or safe environment for gay men – although some recent reports suggest that team sports are far more welcoming to gay people than they once were.[53] In terms of skating, anecdotal evidence and critics like Kim and Jackson do suggest that within the sport, if not in public, gay men are increasingly likely to be out to friends, coaches, and officials. It also seems to be the case that, in Canada at least, skating officials are no longer shying away from acknowledging that gay men do figure skate. In 1993, Matthew Hall, a member of the Canadian national team, came out. Doug Steele, then president of the Canadian Figure Skating Association (the former name of Skate Canada), told the

Village Voice, 'It's not my business to pry into private lives of athletes, and I couldn't tell you whether other skaters are gay or not … I'm not sure that there are a lot of other gay skaters out there to come forward.'[54] Sixteen years later, William Thompson, the CEO of Skate Canada, was quoted as saying that figure skating is one sport 'where you can be openly gay and successful.'[55] His comments are perhaps a little premature, but they are welcome nonetheless, suggesting that skating organizations might finally be warming up to the fact that skating audiences do not need to be protected from the fact of gay people; indeed, they are well ahead of skating officials when it comes to understanding the social changes that have made the broader culture more open to queer people over the past couple of decades. What will be interesting to see is whether increased acceptance of gay men in skating will include a validation of explicitly effeminate skating styles or whether it will be conditional either on effeminate skaters being outstanding technically or on their conforming, as much as possible within the demands of the sport, to mainstream gender norms.

Girls' Sport

While the Toronto *Globe and Mail* once credited Kurt Browning with 'wip[ing] away the stereotype of effeminate male skaters,'[56] figure skating remains well down any list of popular sports for boys. More than fifteen years after Browning's first world championship, skating's girlish reputation persists. Boys who figure skate risk both their gender identities and social standing. Indirect evidence of this may be found at any local figure skating club. At my own club, during the practice sessions for the most advanced skaters, the ratio of girls to boys stands at about ten to one. Many clubs across the country register no male skaters at intermediate or advanced levels. Indeed, over the years, some of the regional sections of Skate Canada have made special efforts to support those boys who do stay in the sport, for instance, by holding 'boys only' seminars, led by elite male skaters.

Skate Canada's membership records show clearly the skewed gender balance that results from figure skating's feminine reputation. Between 1995 and 2005 – the decade following the Kerrigan/Harding incident and the period in which figure skating enjoyed its greatest public exposure and highest popularity – boys and men never accounted for more than 28 per cent of the total number of skaters.[57] But even this low number presents a distorted picture of the actual number of male figure skaters, as the majority are very young boys who will never learn to spin or to do an axel jump. For them, Skate Canada's popular learn-to-skate programs are a short prelude to careers in minor hockey.

Biographies and autobiographies of famous male skaters are full of evidence of what it is like to be a boy in their sport. In his autobiography, Brian Orser recalls, 'I can't say that I never had any hassles from the kids at school. Almost all figure skaters in small towns encounter problems. There was one boy, in particular, who didn't like the idea that I was a figure skater: he would grab hold of me at recess and squeeze me in a headlock. He'd grind his arms into my ears and hold me bent over in the headlock for the entire recess.'[58] Former Canadian and world pairs champion Lloyd Eisler got into fights with other boys in his elementary school at least once a week: 'The confrontations were always over figure skating which just wasn't done by boys in Seaforth back then ... In those days, if a boy figure skated, everyone just assumed he was gay. It was as if something was wrong with you ... why didn't you play hockey? ... I can't remember how many times I heard, "there's that little faggot again going to skate."'[59] Elvis Stojko was called names like 'twinkle toes,' 'fairy,' and 'faggot.' The 'ragging' stopped in grade 10 when Stojko 'grabbed one of the bullies by the collar and pinned him to a locker.'[60] Former Canadian champion Emanuel Sandhu took both ballet and figure skating lessons as a child. He told an interviewer, 'I was constantly hurt by what kids would say' and how they would 'act towards me ... the racial slurs, the teasing and the taunts, jokes and the insults.' His childhood, he says quite simply, was 'difficult.'[61]

The message in all this harassment is that sports are almost unthinkable apart from their attachments to specific definitions of gender. On the one hand, sport choices are seen to reflect gender – which is conflated with sexual orientation. On the other hand, sport choices are thought to shape gender. The logic goes two ways: (1) figure skating attracts feminine boys who are, or who are likely to become, gay, or (2) figure skating makes boys feminine, therefore putting them at risk of becoming gay. In either case, few heterosexual fathers seem willing to risk their son's involvement. While Lloyd Eisler's dad apparently got used to the idea of Lloyd skating, he never liked his son spending time with other male skaters.[62]

It would be a rare father who would express a similar nervousness about his son showing an interest in track and field, baseball, or skiing. Most male athletes find confirmation of their gender and sexual identities in their participation in sport – even golfers, whose sport seems less defined by the desired masculine quality of physical strength than is figure skating. As sociologists and historians have argued, sport is widely understood to be a fine way to turn a boy into a man. Indeed, sporting ability is a primary measure of masculinity in contemporary North American culture.[63] Despite huge increases in the number of female athletes and in the number of sports in which they participate, sport has yet to become a gender-neutral noun; the idea remains potent that sport is *really* a male thing. We see evidence of this in the infant- and toddler-sized sports paraphernalia given far more often to boys than to girls. We see it in the disproportionate coverage of male and female sports on television and in the newspaper, and in the unequal opportunities available to male and female professional athletes, coaches, and sportswriters. And we see it most clearly when we look at the history of sport, and women's ongoing struggle to gain access to gyms, fields, rinks, and the boardrooms of sport organizations.

The history of sport and its relationship to masculinity is a history of social and economic class with roots in the cultural environment that nurtured British imperialism. Historian James Walvin argues that modern sport and its attendant games grew out of the 'cult of manliness' that pervaded both private and state schools in mid-nineteenth-century Britain.[64] For late Victorians, manliness 'stood for neo-Spartan virility as exemplified by stoicism, hardiness, and endurance.'[65] Educators promoted athletic competition to foster in boys these same characteristics. For the upper-class boys who were being groomed to govern the Empire, sport was meant to promote leadership, team play, and courage. For the working-class boys who would one day have to follow their orders, it was meant to promote discipline, obedience, and deference to authority. In both cases, sport was called upon to help turn particular kinds of boys into particular kinds of men, in other words, to prepare boys for the station determined by their class.

In nineteenth-century Britain, the playing fields and sports clubs frequented by middle- and upper-class males were important sites for the consolidation of power and status.[66] In their struggle for hegemony, bourgeois men promoted the manly virtues of discipline and self-regulation as a means of distinguishing themselves from the so-called 'libertinism and idleness of the gentry and the irregularity and sexual license of the working class.'[67] The British model of sport that was exported to Europe and North America and to British colonies around the world encouraged boys and men to regulate themselves physically and emotionally – an opportunity many resisted.[68] Playing sports and games, boys and young men were expected to learn how to conceal and subdue emotion and to grow mentally, physically, and emotionally tough. The anvil of team sports would forge men who would meet the exigencies of Empire and who would not be overshadowed by women or by men of lesser status and power.

By the late 1800s, some British social critics were explicitly promoting sports and other forms of physical exercise as a means of fostering manliness and preventing effeminacy, especially among schoolboys. Such critics argued that harsh exercise and intense competition against other males could keep a boy from growing languid and effete. For instance, in a lecture on manliness given at the London YMCA in 1857, Rev. Hugh Stowell counselled boys not to become 'brutal, effeminate or demoralized' and prescribed a list of manly sports and exercises, including skating, to bring young men the 'bodily hardiness' necessary to guard their nascent manhood.[69] Stowell's concern about effeminacy was not, as it would be today, a veiled concern about homosexuality. Like other gendered categories, effeminacy is a historically specific concept; in the mid-nineteenth century it had yet to become associated with same-sex sexual activity or attractions. In Stowell's time effeminacy signified weakness and softness and was seen as a consequence of boys having spent too much time on the education of the mind at the expense of the body, too much time in the company of women. Effeminacy was thought to mark boys' lack of appropriately masculine influences.[70] Physically demanding activities, like skating, performed with other males would, Stowell suggested, correct the problem.

In the nineteenth-century United States, similar concerns about an increasingly feminized culture led to a similar promotion of sport and physical exercise.[71] As a rural, frontier society was replaced by an urban, industrial capitalist one, men lost the measures of manhood they had found in the taming of the West or, later, in the financial risk-taking required by an emerging entrepreneurial culture. American social observers worried that white middle-class men – tied as they were to offices, unused to physical labour, consuming rather than producing – were growing soft in both body and character. What was worse, in a social system that established separate, gendered spheres of (male) work and (female) domestic life, middle-class boys spent their days in the company of women: mothers, sisters, and teachers. Critics feared that the culture was on the road to emasculation.

According to historian Michael Kimmel, changes in American economic and social structures contributed to new ways of thinking about gender. In the late 1800s, the notion of masculinity replaced that of manhood. Where manhood was seen as something a boy came to express, masculinity was something he had to achieve and, continually, to prove. Manhood contrasted with childhood. It meant that one was 'fully adult, responsible, and autonomous.'[72] Masculinity contrasted with femininity and was a term steeped in social anxiety. A man who could not meet the requirements of this new identity risked being seen as a sissy.[73]

In their concern to distance themselves from sissies (a category that had emerged in the 1890s) and from women, Kimmel writes, middle-class men became obsessed with visual evidence of their manliness. A hard body was one means of demonstrating masculinity.[74] Men grew beards and moustaches and they 'pumped up,' launching a turn-of-the-century sport craze. Organized sport had only become widespread in the United States in the 1860s. But by 1880, the athlete (who was, by definition, male) had already come to represent the 'man of character.' A strong, developed body was taken as visual evidence of a man's willpower and his commitment to achievement and virtue,[75] to the primary values of American middle-class life. While these commitments could be represented by actions and behaviours, they could also be represented by the body itself. The once lean male body ideal started to be replaced by one that was bigger, stronger, more visibly muscular. It was the type of body that clearly marked men's difference from women and from men like sissies, who were thought to lack fortitude.

As we see today from hazing rituals among university athletes, from misogynous and homophobic talk in locker rooms, and from the schoolyard insults thrown at boys who figure skate, anxiety over masculinity and fear of the sissy still play a role in contemporary sporting cultures. Many people continue to understand sport as a device to toughen up young men, and to see athleticism as a central component of virility.[76] Moreover, a hard, masculine body remains culturally important as a symbol of the inevitability of male dominance and superiority. In the final instance, the argument goes, while women may become prime ministers and astronauts, they will never beat men at football or weightlifting or even at golf. This is the discourse that makes an uneasy fit between figure skating and common-sense definitions of sport. What to make of a sport that seems not to be about the 'hardening of men'? If, historically, 'manliness' has been inherent within the definition of sport, is it possible for something dominated by women to be taken seriously as a sport?

Toronto Star sportswriter Jim Proudfoot once wrote about synchronized swimming: 'If it were a legitimate sport ... there'd be a men's division.'[77] Field hockey and equestrianism are good examples of sports that have disproportionately high numbers of female participants, but do not have the same kind of feminine reputation as figure skating does. They suggest that what is at issue with figure skating is not just the number of women involved but the not-quite-manly nature of the activity. Dominated in North America by girls and women for at least the last sixty years, figure skating does not provide the homosocial environment found in traditionally masculine sports, nor does it prop up ideologies that paint athletic ability and physical strength as marks of virility. Although that is exactly what the tough-guy skaters and those who supported them tried to make it do.

Sport Typing

The peculiar idea that some sports are suited for girls while others are suited for boys helps to blunt the contradictions that arise from female-dominated sports like figure skating. While less prevalent than it once was, this binary classification continues to hold sway in some quarters, as we see with the labelling of figure skating as a girls' sport, a linguistic move that not only complicates life for male skaters, but diminishes the achievements of female skaters. There are sports and there are girls' sports – the latter term relegates female physical prowess to a realm of inferiority. Scholars call this process of categorization 'sport typing.' It is a particularly powerful means of communicating ideas about differences between men and women.[78] The physicality of sport can make it seem like the differences between men and women are natural, that they are the product of differently shaped male and female bodies. Indeed, sporting practices produce gendered bodies (think, for example, of the difference between the bodies of male and female gymnasts). In this way, sport helps to maintain a social structure in which men and women are assumed to be fundamentally different types of creatures. Our physical differences come to serve as both justification and template for differences in many realms of life. For instance, the proposition that most men are stronger than most women has served historically to symbolize and justify men's political and economic domination of women. The results of gendered sporting contests – men's and women's sports and men's and women's events in the same sport – advertise and perpetuate the rigid gender binaries that still limit people's everyday lives in North America.

It is axiomatic in contemporary feminist theory that our notions of gender – of masculinity and femininity – are constituted through their difference from each other. The terms are relational, that is, we understand femininity through the ways in which it is not masculinity and vice versa. Feminist theorists refer to the space between masculinity and femininity as gender difference. This space emerges from the social and cultural expectations that keep femininity and masculinity from getting too close to each other and, therefore, from losing their meanings. Gender difference is what makes gender, as a system of meaning and a form of social relations, work. While there is no question that the scope of the difference between women and men has changed significantly over the last few decades, we still confront it repeatedly in our everyday lives, for instance, in gender-specific clothing sections in department stores, in the different aspirations of little girls and little boys, in the different reactions that attend to men and women who behave in aggressive ways, in the assumptions that certain sports are more appropriate for men while others are more appropriate for women.

It almost goes without saying that male-appropriate sports vastly outnumber female-appropriate sports and that included among them are those sports most valued in the culture. Not only does this unequal categorization of sport by sex support a particular understanding of women's (lesser) place in the broader society, it also constitutes a tremendously effective practical barrier to the sport participation of women and girls. Thus, feminist sport researchers and women's sport advocates have been most concerned with expanding access to the male list. Less energy has been spent trying to open up sports on the female list or to understand the relationship of boys and men to them.[79]

In a 1998 study, Suzanne Laberge and Mathieu Albert asked Montreal high school students to write about their perceptions of men who play women's sports (as popularly defined, figure skating among them). Fifty-three per cent of boys in the study did not approve of men's involvement in women's sport. The authors found significant class differences among their respondents, with two-thirds of working-class boys expressing this belief, as compared to slightly less than half of the middle- and upper-class boys. Laberge and Albert suggest that the higher percentage among working-class boys represents the importance of physical strength as literal and symbolic power in communities where cultural or economic power are less accessible. They also noted that there were boys of all class backgrounds among those who argued that women's sports prohibit men from developing their inherent physical strengths and capacities. Some boys claimed that men who participate in women's sports are less virile than men who play men's sports. Others said, quite baldly, that men who did feminine sports were 'queers' or 'fags.'[80] Such ideas have powerful regulatory effects on who plays what.

Boys and girls who pursue 'inappropriate' sports face similar obstacles: limited opportunities to develop and excel; questions about their gender identities and sexual orientation; harassment; and belittlement of their achievements. Yet, while increasing numbers of girls and women participate in so-called men's sports, there has been no comparable change in the numbers of men and boys who take up so-called women's sports. As any six-year-old will tell you, it may be okay for girls to wear jeans, but it is still not okay for boys to wear skirts. As a category, masculinity remains far narrower than femininity in contemporary North American culture. Hence, boys' figure skating is not nearly as cool as girls' rugby nor does it look like it will be any time soon. In a survey of college students, psychologist Sherri Matteo found that while women's participation was evenly divided between masculine' and 'feminine' sports, men had only limited experience with so-called women's sports.[81] A study of elementary and high school students by Brenda Riemer and Michelle Visio showed similar findings. While the list of sports commonly played by girls is expanding to include so-called masculine sports, the researchers saw no parallel effort to expand the list of sports played by boys to include so-called feminine sports.[82] In a study from 2006, Dorothy Schmalz and Deborah Kerstetter argue that the difference in boys' and girls' willingness and/or ability to participate in 'cross-gender'-typed sport is tied to the different levels of stigma they would face for doing so.[83] Simply put, boys and men face higher gender barriers around their sport choices than do girls and women, and they suffer considerable consequences when they transgress them.

Would You Know a Girls' Sport if You Saw One?

What makes something a girls' sport? When asked to distinguish male and female sports, one of the students in Laberge and Albert's study wrote that male sports were about strength and female sports were about beauty.[84] Another student wrote that women's sports were 'finesse sports mostly based on movement. Men's sports are mostly rough, with physical contact and strategy ... Men's sport is contact, strategy, fast thinking.'[85] Figure skating would fit easily into the women's category under both of these descriptions. It also fits the complex classificatory scheme developed in the mid-1960s by physical educator Eleanor Metheny. Her work is an early attempt to detail the characteristics that determine the acceptability or unacceptability of different sports for women.

Today, among some sport scholars, Metheny is known for her contributions to the racial science of athletic performance, a field widely discredited among sport sociologists. In 1939 Metheny conducted anthropometric studies on black and white athletes in a search for the biological basis of racial differences in performance in certain sports.[86] Perhaps because her work on gender differences was completed twenty years later or perhaps because Metheny herself was more sympathetic to questions of gender inequality than to racism, the model she constructed to describe the differences in masculine- and feminine-appropriate sports has nothing to do with biology. Her work implicitly acknowledges that the gender characteristics accommodated by different sports are historically and culturally specific. She also seems to have understood that acceptable forms of movement for both men and women are not just about gender but about the relationship of gender to sexuality, and the relation of both of these to class. Her works suggests that movement norms are circumscribed by what scholars today would call class-specific forms of heterosexuality. These norms are 'what the members of either sex may be or do without impairing their opportunities for finding a mate within their own social classification.'[87] For the most part, sport participation has validated normative male sexual identities (whether male athletes are concerned to claim such identities or not). Yet, historically, it has done the same for women only if they competed in a narrow range of acceptable sports. Throughout the twentieth century, the threat of being seen as 'masculine' or as a lesbian exerted a powerful constraint on the sport participation of many women, both straight and gay.[88] Social critics, parents, and many women themselves perceived sport as a predominantly masculine institution and worried that participation in sport would either reveal or develop a woman's 'abnormal' masculine tendencies. To preclude the possibility of being seen as manly, a woman needed to restrict herself to sports like figure skating that, as 1960 Olympic champion Carol Heiss put it, 'allowed a girl to be athletic and feminine'[89] at the same time.

While they are quite specific to her time, I quote here at length from Metheny's observations. Thankfully, while many of her classifications no longer apply, her effort to try to understand the influence of social and economic class on the gendering of movement is still relevant:

1. It is *not appropriate* for women to engage in contests in which: the resistance of the *opponent* is overcome by bodily contact; the resistance of a *heavy object* is overcome by direct application of bodily force; the body is projected into or through space over long distances or for extended periods of time [as examples, Metheny suggests combat sports, weight-lifting, hammer throw, pole vault, high hurdles, long-distance running races, and all team games, with the exception of volleyball].

2. It *may be appropriate* for women identified in the lower levels of socioeconomic status to engage in contests in which: the resistance of an *object of moderate weight* is overcome by direct application of bodily force; the body is projected into or through space over moderate distances for relatively short periods of time [as examples, Metheny suggests discus, shot put, javelin, shorter-distance running races, low hurdles, long jump, free exercise].

3. It is *wholly appropriate* for women identified with the more favored levels of socioeconomic status to engage in contests in which: the resistance of a *light object* is overcome with a *light implement*; the body is projected into or through space in aesthetically pleasing patterns; the velocity and maneuverability of the body is increased by the use of some manufactured device; a spatial barrier prevents bodily contact with the opponent in face-to-face forms of competition.[90]

At issue in each of the classifications is not just the use, but also the demonstration, of force and strength. As Metheny points out, the most socially acceptable sports for women – 'swimming, diving, skiing, and figure skating, and such non-Olympic events as golf, archery, and bowling' – de-emphasize power in favour of 'grace and skill.' In each of these events, except swimming, the force that is attained is not solely produced by the woman's own body, but comes with the assistance of manufactured objects,[91] maintaining the illusion that women on their own are incapable of developing force. In the case of swimming, the sport's acceptability is governed by aesthetics – the pleasing lines of a body moving through water – rather than the gender-appropriate use of power.

What has changed most since Metheny wrote her essay in 1964 is that women are no longer restricted to participating in a narrow category of 'feminine' sports. We would definitely have to rewrite this model to make it relevant to today's sporting landscape. What remains important is Metheny's underscoring of the centrality of class to the gendering of movement. Contemporary researchers would also say that notions of which sports are suitable for whom are racialized.[92] Nevertheless it is still largely the case that the so-called masculine sports – whether played by women or men – are primarily about contact, strength, and team play; the so-called feminine sports – whether played by women or men – are often individual and emphasize aesthetics and skill rather than the explicit demonstration of power, with netball and, in some contexts, volleyball being notable exceptions. While the sports seen as most suited to men tend to flaunt power, the sports seen as most suited to women tend to conceal it. Even with the help of a 'manufactured device' like the modern figure skate, for instance, a woman still needs considerable power to perform multiple-revolution jumps or to hold the centre on a spin (to keep it in one place rather than travelling across the ice) or, simply, to skate with speed and flow. But the rules of her sport reward her for not showing this power. Skaters do not, for instance, grimace as sprinters or tennis players do when they exert themselves. They do not grunt. They try not to telegraph their big tricks. Jumps that seem to appear out of nowhere receive higher marks than those that come after much visible effort. The point here is not that it does not take power to figure skate, it is that figure skaters are trained to mask their power. And, thus, their use of power is perceived as feminine rather than masculine. Of course the same is true for male skaters; they are feminized by the expectations of the sport. It is the skaters who make their programs look easy, who help spectators to overlook the strength required to perform them, who are supposed to be rewarded with better marks.

Figure skating fits tidily into Metheny's category of wholly appropriate sports for women. Not only does it rely on manufactured devices, that is, skates, but competitors do not confront each other directly. Most important, they emphasize the aesthetic qualities of their movements. Diving and gymnastics are also aesthetic sports, but figure skating, like synchronized swimming, goes further than these. Not only must skaters look good and present their movements in a 'pleasing pattern,' as Metheny puts it, they are also expected to be emotionally engaging. Here the artistic, expressive aspirations of skating make it seem feminine. Where typical male sports use the body in an instrumental fashion, figure skating uses the body as a means to express intangible moods and feelings.

In present-day skating competitions, skaters receive one set of marks for technical elements and one set of marks for what are called program components. The latter category, previously known as 'presentation,' and before that as 'artistic impression,' assumes the presence of spectators. The term 'artistic impression' pointed to the expressiveness of skating, pulling it into the sphere of theatre or dance and away from discourses that construct sport as a rational, scientific pursuit, a purposeful striving for faster, higher, stronger, as demonstrated by quantifiable results and records and numerical measurements. Television sports commentators have long tried to pull it back:

> Browning's Quad jump confirmed his unparalleled athletic talent. According to measurements in Budapest [at the 1988 world championships], after catapulting off his left toe he is airborne for up to .8 of a second, compared to the .75 of a second that Boitano and Orser manage for their biggest leaps. To get around four times and get in and out of the jump, Browning must whirl at a speed of more than 360 revolutions per minute. In other words, he spins as fast as the wheels of a car doing fifty kilometres an hour or of a bike racing at top speed. And on landing he must instantly transfer that whirling torque into straight-ahead horizontal velocity. 'I get off on jumping,' he says.[93]

While my own view is that skating programs are too complicated to be quantified and reduced to statistics, a new scoring scheme was implemented by the ISU in 2004/5 in order to do exactly that. Yet no mathematical formula can capture the entirety of a skating performance. The best ones are designed not simply to showcase elements – although these are clearly important – but to elicit an emotional response in the viewer, in the same way a dance performance would. The best skating programs are meant to move us. In this sense skating spills out of the safely masculine realm of sport into the less manly realm of art.

Art versus Sport

Artistic and sporting pursuits exist at opposite ends of a masculine continuum. While sport tends to confirm the gender and sexual identities of boys and men, art opens these to question. As musicologist Philip

Brett has put it, '*All* musicians, we must remember, are faggots in the parlance of the male locker room.'[94] Stereotypes of the gay artist/dancer/musician are widespread; in North America almost nothing marks a man or a boy as effeminate as does an interest in the arts, and hence males who want to appear straight often shun them.

Choirs and dance schools suffer the same shortage of boys as do figure skating clubs. The late Tom Waddell was an American Olympic decathalete and founder of the Gay Games. After he began studying ballet, at the age of seventeen,

> something became obvious to me right away – that male ballet dancers were effeminate, that they were what most people would describe as faggots. And I thought I just couldn't handle that. It suddenly occurred to me that this was real dangerous territory for me – I'm from a small town and I was totally closeted and very concerned about being male ... I realized I had to do something to protect my image of myself as a male ... so I threw myself into athletics ... I wanted to be viewed as male, otherwise I would be a dancer today.[95]

Dance, music, and skating are difficult territory for men because they use the body not for its own sake, to demonstrate its own capabilities and 'improveability,' as do typical sports; rather, they use it to express feelings, including desire. Brett writes about music: 'Nonverbal, even when linked to words, physically arousing in its function as initiator of dance, and resisting attempts to endow it with, or discern in it, precise meaning, it represents that part of our culture which is constructed as feminine and therefore dangerous.'[96] Skaters, like dancers and musicians, are feminized by masculine ideals that value emotional restraint, rational thought, and instrumental corporealities – ideals at the root of modern sport.

The other commonality linking music, dance, and skating is that they all demand that men perform; they put men *purposefully* on display and, in so doing, they feminize them. The assumption of spectators is central to the design of a figure skating program – this is not the case with running or football or golf. Skaters put their bodies on display for their own sake; if this were not the case, they would dress in plain tights and T-shirts. Of course, all sports have spectators and all athletes are on display as they compete; indeed, much of the pleasure viewers find in sports spectatorship lies in looking at and scrutinizing athletes' bodies. The assessment of an athlete's appearance, however, is not an

integral part of most sports, as it is in skating and the other aesthetically driven, judged sports like gymnastics and diving. As much as anything else, it is the requirement that skaters care about what they look
like that makes skating seem a sport more suited to girls and women.
'Women may dread being surveyed harshly,' writes Susan Bordo. They
may dread 'being seen as too old, too fat, too flat-chested – but men
are not supposed to enjoy being surveyed *period*. It's feminine to be on
display.'[97]

As a generation of feminist art and film critics have pointed out,
Western cultures have been more likely to display women's than men's
bodies. Moreover, when displayed, women's bodies have been more
likely than men's to be presented explicitly as objects of the gaze, maintaining the stereotypical active/passive and masculine/feminine binaries of heterosexuality – although such representational strategies are
changing, as evidenced by new forms of advertising and music video,
and by the popularity of television make-over programs like Queer Eye
for the Straight Guy and magazines like *Men's Health* or *Men's Fitness*.[98]
Nick Trujillo presents an example of this trend in a discussion of how
advertisers exploited not just the athletic skills but also the stereotypically heterosexual physical attractiveness of baseball pitcher Nolan
Ryan in the late 1980s and 1990s in order to sell their products.[99]

In his book *Hard Looks*, Sean Nixon documents a significant shift in
representations of male bodies that started in the late 1980s as a result
of changing commercial practices in the retail fashion industry and in
mainstream magazine publishing.[100] In an attempt to expand consumer
markets, these industries developed and promoted a new category of
male consumer that came to be known as the 'new man.' The new man
was a fellow concerned with image and style, a reader of glossy male
fashion magazines. He was represented in advertisements by models
who were clearly meant to be looked at by other men, both gay and
straight. In these advertisements, men were explicitly represented as
objects of the gaze. They were not playing golf or washing the car or
steering a yacht. They were not oblivious to their audience. They were,
therefore, not like their predecessors. While the status of these models
as objects marked a substantial shift in forms of masculine representation, Nixon argues that we should not take this publishing trend to suggest that bodily conventions changed for the average man on the street.
Indeed, even the publishing industry quickly grew shy of their own
sexually ambivalent (because of being looked at) creation, and the heyday of the 'new man' was short lived. By the early 1990s, publishers of

men's fashion magazines had already begun to reduce the ambivalent sexuality in their imagery so as to reframe the meanings that could be made of their models. It was not long before 'new men' were replaced by 'new lads,' representatives of a more clearly coded heterosexual masculinity. The look at these new lads, says Nixon, was tempered by their heterosexual positioning in relation to women and to signifiers that marked them well within the bounds of dominant masculinity.[101] And then it wasn't long before the new man was back on the scene, his re-entry made possible by the rise of niche marketing. Today, images of men in popular culture represent a whole range of masculine categories, from the new man's offspring to the most traditional patriarch, the various groupings representing distinct markets in a culture where identities are increasingly based on consumptive practices.

Following Nixon, it is important not to confuse the representational strategies used by advertisers to construct a demand for products with the everyday practices or views of men on the street. While media representations are certainly contributing to a shift in the importance men place on their looks, this shift does not sit easily with all men. The whole premise of a show like *Queer Eye for the Straight Guy* was that it remains outside the norm for a heterosexual 'guy' to admit to being concerned about his own appearance or the appearance of other men. In a 2005 study that explored the way young British men talk about their bodies and the bodies of other men, Rosalind Gill, Karen Henwood, and Carl McLean found that 'being thought vain or narcissistic was clearly something profoundly feared by the vast majority' of the 140 men they interviewed. 'Our interviewees,' they wrote, 'were not prepared to admit that any of their bodily practices might have anything to do with the desire to look attractive. Clearly there is a powerful taboo in operation which makes this very difficult for many men.'[102]

On some level, the desire to look good is also the desire to be looked at, which is not a desire easily accommodated within mainstream notions of heterosexual masculinity. The look at another can be both a privilege and an instrument of power, potentially a tool of mastery and degradation. Television critic Margaret Morse has written that the strong cultural inhibition against 'the look' at the male body has been rooted in a reluctance to turn the male body into an object of desire, particularly into an object of homosexual desire.[103] Steve Neale makes a similar argument in a discussion of men in mainstream cinema: any 'erotic elements involved in the relations between the spectator and the male image have constantly to be repressed and disavowed.'[104] Garry Whannel claims that the 'cultures of hardness' that are pervasive in sport are a consequence of this disavowal. The 'muscular invulnerability'[105] that many male athletes aspire to is, at least in part, a way to 'preserve fragile [sexual] barriers and to police heterosexual masculinity.'[106] Morse says that broadcasters – who tend to design their programming for a predominantly male audience – try to counteract the potentially homoerotic look at the male athlete by focusing on statistical and technical details. Viewers are invited to engage with the male bodies on their screens not as objects of desire but as exemplars of human physical potential. So, for instance, during coverage of the 2003 world championships on Canada's CTV network, colour commentator Elvis Stojko simply failed to mention any of the aesthetic aspects of the men's skating. He drew no attention to what the skaters looked like nor to the purposefully aesthetic moves between their jumps. He focused mainly on the details that affected their jumping: dropped shoulders, over-rotated torsos, shaky take-offs. While it is not within broadcasters' power to determine the way viewers actually take up the images on their TV screens – where you might see a statistic in action, I might see a terrifically sexy body – such attempts to frame what we see are pervasive in televised sports. A focus on statistics and technique is a way of de-eroticizing the relationship between male viewers and players.

Although sport is one of the few contexts in which men's bodies are on display, figure skating presents unique problems for male skaters and viewers. In figure skating, competitors perform alone, sustaining the gaze of an audience for more than four minutes in the long free skating program – an eternity (and gold mine) in broadcast terms. With only one player on the ice at a time in singles competitions, few commentators can maintain their pattering hold on our attention for a skater's entire performance. In terms of both time and content, it would be impossible for an entire skating program to be incorporated within a typical athletic or technical discourse. At some point, viewers are inevitably left to their own interpretive frameworks and they just might end up looking at bodies and not technique. What might it mean for a man to subject himself to the gaze of women? What might it mean for a man to perform in front of male viewers and to *invite* their gaze? What might it mean for male viewers, including broadcasters and journalists, to watch other men perform in an activity popularly seen to be gay or effeminate (in part because of the performance)? The potential for homoeroticism in the relationship between the male skater and the male viewer is likely part of the reason that figure skating audiences are primarily made up of women – and perhaps also why many adult gay men recollect watching so much figure skating when they were younger.[107]

Figure skating is full of contradictions. For many fans its greatest appeal is its multi-faceted nature, a hybrid of sport, art, and entertainment spectacle. Competition and performance. Risky and lyrical. Skating does not fall easily within standard definitions of sport. This hybridity is part of what gives skating its reputation as an endeavour more suited to girls and women, which leads to assumptions that male skaters are effeminate and/or gay. In a culture where it is still difficult for many men and boys to be in situations where they might be compared to women and girls or where they might be thought to be gay, this reputation and these assumptions are a source of anxiety. Since the mid-twentieth century, there have been ongoing attempts to construct a new public image for skating, one that is more appealing to men. I find it interesting that these efforts were most pronounced throughout the 1990s, the era in which skating's popularity was at its all-time height. Figure skating has not always needed to pander to reluctant male spectators or to worry about the gender reputations of its male competitors. In an effort to understand how men's figure skating came to have an 'image problem,' the next three chapters trace the transformation of skating, over one hundred and fifty years, from gentlemanly art to sport for young girls.

4 Manliness and Grace: Skating as a Gentlemen's Art

A sombre man, middle-aged, dark-suited, glides across the ice. He folds his arms firmly before him, raises his free leg behind him, toe pointing downward, the silver buckle on his boot catching the tiniest bit of light. His posture is dead straight and his face, from beneath the brim of his hat, wears an expression of bemused confidence. Painted by American Gilbert Stuart in 1782, 'The Skater,' a portrait of William Grant, inspired one enthusiastic critic to write, 'The figure is splendid. Seldom were manliness and grace more winningly joined.'[1] Seldom now, and more is the pity, are they joined at all. Since Stuart created his work, grace has fallen from favour as a valued marker of masculinity. Stuart and Grant would both likely be shocked to learn that grace and beauty are rarely the primary aims of men who skate and that skating is now so thoroughly associated with girls and women that some male skaters feel intensely the need to protect their manly reputations.

Over the past two hundred years, figure skating has gone from a gentlemanly art to a sport that is seen to be particularly suited to young girls. Along the way grace has fallen almost completely from view as a celebrated quality in men's skating. In this chapter I look at the early development of figure skating, a pastime that was pursued almost exclusively by men of rank and privilege until well into the second half of the 1800s. I pay particular attention to the way skaters understood and expressed the gendered qualities of grace and beauty, two important signifiers of eighteenth- and nineteenth-century upper-class masculinities. Over the course of the nineteenth century, the meanings of these qualities shifted in accord with masculine ideals that were themselves being transformed by the coming to prominence of bourgeois moral values and the embourgeoisement of established upper-class physical and aesthetic cultures. While figure skating was certainly never a major 'art,' nor a major sport, episodes from its history provide useful evidence of the ways in which discourses of class and gender came together to influence the look and experience of men's physical activities and pastimes. By the latter decades of the 1800s, these were increasingly understood in terms of athleticism and of the sporting cultures by which athleticism was rapidly being subsumed.

Historian J.A. Mangan argues that ideas about manliness were at the centre of the games ethic that flourished in England's Victorian public schools and that gave rise to the 'cult of athleticism.'[2] Games were meant to develop in boys and young men physical vigour, courage, and tenacity. Games would demand self-control and discipline. They would help boys develop hard muscular bodies that would symbolize the moral virtues required by a society increasingly defined by middle-class values, a society in which these particular boys were expected to take up positions of influence. More than a century and a half since the enthusiasm for sport recast male physical culture, many people continue to understand athletic prowess as a key component of virility. While the Victorian manly ideal described by Mangan has certainly changed, significant remnants of it continue to influence many contemporary sporting cultures – the valorization of self-discipline and stoicism, the glorification of the muscular male body and aggressive action, the marginalization of sports that emphasize aesthetics or that simply do not promote aggression, brawn, and physical contact. It is a twenty-first-century version of this manly ideal that frames contemporary figure skating as effeminate.

Figure skating grew out of a different masculine tradition. Its roots lie with a 'refined' version of masculinity that produced 'the man of feeling,' a late-eighteenth-century ideal that privileged politeness, sensibility, expressiveness.[3] Early styles of aesthetically defined skating were a careful mix of feeling and control and would have fit well in this tradition. But as the 'man of feeling' was replaced by what Mangan and Walvin have called a 'neo-Spartan virility'[4] in the second half of the nineteenth century, English skating changed dramatically to maintain its status as an activity appropriate for men. Men's skating bodies represented the changing ideal.

This chapter presents a discussion of nineteenth-century men's figure skating that draws primarily on instructional texts from Britain, with additional sources from Austria, Germany, France, Canada, and the United States. While there were skaters in North America in the nineteenth century, the skating that evolved into figure skating has roots that are primarily European, and it is these roots that are the main focus of the narrative I piece together here. I am interested in how men skated, what their skating looked like, and what they hoped to accomplish on the ice. Men's skating reflected their privileged class backgrounds and the gender norms that were particular to them. Later in the chapter I look at the different shapes these gender norms took in different national contexts and at how skating evolved differently to meet them. I discuss the two main stylistic branches of skating that emerged in the 1860s, the English style and the so-called International or Continental style. By the end of the century the latter had eclipsed the former and had become the skating that was featured in international competitions. The formal organization and institutionalization of skating as a sport, a process referred to by some sociologists as sportification, will be addressed in the next chapter. My focus here is on the skating itself and the meanings it was seen to convey.

A note about the class of men who feature in this story: I refer to them variously as 'elite,' 'privileged,' or 'upper-class' gentlemen, and in so doing 'fudge over' complex historical and sociological debates about class formation and class power in nineteenth-century England and Europe. Who exactly do I mean by these terms? At the risk of oversimplification, I am referring to people of wealth and social status, white people who, unburdened by the need to work (which is not the same as saying they did not work), would have been able to engage in conspicuous consumption of leisure. They were members of the aristocracy and the gentry, certainly, but they might also have been members of the upper middle class, the bourgeoisie – industrialists, military officers, lawyers, or other professionals.[5] To varying extents they had access to and constructed class identities based on social, economic, and political power, cultural exclusiveness, and, most important to us here, leisure.[6]

My emphasis on men in this chapter and on the relationship of skating to masculinity is not meant to suggest that women were not participants in the 'gentlemanly art.' Evidence suggests that some women did skate in various locations and circumstances in the early decades of the 1800s, as I will show in the next chapter. But such women were definitely exceptions and were not a primary influence on the early development of the type of skating that would turn into figure skating. The stories in this chapter show that today's emblematically feminine sport was once a fine way for certain privileged men to express their masculinities. Indeed, the kind of skating that would turn into figure skating was designed by men to meet their interests and needs. In addressing early skating texts and advice written for skaters on how to manoeuvre their bodies over the ice, the chapter points to the historical specificity of today's limits on what constitutes appropriately masculine forms of movement. It is intended to provide historical context to figure skating's current gendered reputation and the notions of effeminacy that give it meaning.

Early Days

A sixteenth-century painting by Dutch artist Pieter de Hoogh shows two women skating with baskets on their heads, perhaps en route to market. Other Dutch paintings show men, women, and children from all classes, including the aristocracy, skating together on crowded canals. In Holland, skating evolved as both recreation and transportation. Long distances were covered, races were held, and a thriving ice-surface economy ensured that skaters were well shod, well watered, and well fed. The easy integration of skating into everyday life seems to have been unique to Holland. Throughout the rest of Europe and in North America, skating evolved primarily as a form of recreation, albeit one with class- and gender-specific histories.

Seventeenth- and eighteenth-century skaters were tied to the landscape in obvious ways. If there was no ice, there was no skating. If the river was long, and the ice was solid, skaters might run races or use their skates to travel quickly and pleasurably over distances, as in Holland. On small ponds, skaters challenged themselves by inventing new ways of using their blades. Different landscapes led to different kinds of skating and these became associated with the people who practised them. In the Fen District of England, for instance, where the still, flat water froze in great smooth stretches, it was mostly, but not exclusively, male farm labourers who invented courses and formats for racing on skates. In London and other European cities, skating was a pastime of young boys and of well-to-do men. While the boys played games on frozen ditches or canals – on any bit of ice they could find – the gentlemen practised a sedate and dignified style of gliding on the ponds and lakes in urban parks and estates. This 'gentle art' is the skating that would eventually turn into figure skating. A popular court entertainment, it was honed at ice balls and masquerades and at other aristocratic gatherings across the Continent.

As with so many games and physical pastimes, aristocrats had the time and resources to develop skating beyond the basics. The gliding that would eventually turn into figure skating was a product of elegant, noble, and exclusive manners. It developed in distinct, and in some cases deliberate, contrast to the less 'refined' forms of skating practised by the common people. The first member of British royalty to learn to ice skate was James, Duke of York, the future James II of England / James VII of Scotland. When his father, Charles I, lost the throne during the English Civil War, James fled to Holland, where he was taught to skate by the women of the Dutch court. With the restoration of the monarchy in 1660, James returned to England, bringing with him iron skates and an advanced skating move called the Dutch roll. Two years later, a winter of hard frosts gave him and his courtiers a chance to demonstrate their skills before astonished onlookers in London's St James Park. Before bicycles or downhill skiing, the only experience of speed available, even to aristocrats, required horses or sailing boats. Skating – gliding – allowed people to move quickly, with very little effort, under their own steam. Unlike running, skating appeared smooth and elegant and fit easily with the graceful image cultivated by the nobility.

Interest in the imported amusement spread and several decades of unusually cold weather provided rare excellent conditions for practice. By the mid-1700s (the exact date is unknown) a small group of enthusiasts in Edinburgh had founded the world's first skating club.[7] Not for them the egalitarianism of the Dutch, who came from all classes to skate together – women, men, and children – on the frozen canals. Membership in the Edinburgh club was restricted to upper-class men who could perform the manly feats of skating a circle on each foot and jumping over three hats stacked on the ice. As historian Dennis Bird points out, the club was more like an exclusive social club than a sports club; its membership was heavy with lawyers, landowners, Army officers, and the sons of peers. No women were admitted until 1910.[8]

Introduced by royalty, 'fancy' skating grew to be an acceptable pastime for men of elite classes in England and Scotland. Such was also the case in Austria and France, where skating was introduced as a popular amusement at court. The scant evidence that suggests how early skating was perceived or practised outside elite circles comes from Austria and Germany. According to German skating historian Matthias Hampe, acceptance by the nobility did not necessarily translate into the broader acceptance of skating as a pastime for the middle classes. In Austria, beyond court circles, early forms of skating were practised by boys and 'street urchins.'[9] In Germany, Hampe writes, a strict middle-class morality cast skating for adults as overly frivolous. He says it was the Romantic poets, in the late eighteenth and early nineteenth centuries, who eventually brought respectability to skating in Germany. Goethe himself was responsible for having a ban against skating lifted in the city of Weimar.[10]

Goethe exalted in the physical freedom of gliding over ice and in the closeness of the skater (before indoor rinks) to nature. For him and for a number of other German poets, skating was a metaphor for their protests against traditional social constraints. Skating signified the individual autonomy that was seen as central to the political emancipation of the middle classes. On skates an individual could find achievement through personal effort and could, it seemed, overcome physical limits, even those imposed by gravity. While to Goethe has gone much of the credit for liberating German skaters from moral pressures and from their fear of social judgment,[11] Friedrich Gottlieb Klopstock was the first ice skating propagandist, writing odes to skating as early as the 1760s.[12] Klopstock had both a political and an artistic vision of how skating might develop, proposing an academy of ice skaters that would be organized like the academies of artists that existed in Europe at the time. Austrian writer Helga Glantschnig notes that Klopstock did not see skating as just an amusement or a sport but as an art, an imaginative contrast to the stylized and 'forced' social dancing that took place in the enclosed halls of court society.[13] And, in an era when the German states were fragmented, Klopstock also saw skating as an important part of a broader national culture in which frozen rivers and canals and the skaters who plied them would help to constitute a united Germany.

In the more than two centuries since Klopstock was writing, few other skaters and few other skating writers have seen in skating such political potential! Klopstock's view of skating as a type of art, however, came to be widely shared by certain communities of skaters in both Europe and North America over the course of the nineteenth century. The notion that skating was not just an exercise or a form of locomotion but a means of expressing sensation, feelings, and aesthetic ideas came to define the type of skating that would, in the late 1800s, turn into figure skating.

Manly Amusement

Everywhere but Holland, early skating was an almost exclusively male pursuit. So what were men doing in the first decades of the nineteenth century when they had the ice almost completely to themselves? At first, they were gliding forwards on the inside and outside edges of their blades, making pleasing arrangements with their arms. Once transferred from the open spaces of Holland to the more constrained ponds and canals of London, Paris, or Vienna, skating began to grow technically and artistically. With no hope of distance to hold their imaginations, skaters began to explore the possibilities for movement presented by the curved metal blade on ice. They perfected the basic edges – forward inside, forward outside – and then the same backwards. They experimented with gliding poses to which they attached tremendous, evocative names – the Forward Mercury, the King of Rome, the Nymph, the Adonis. They began to work out all manner of turns. In all of this experimentation, nothing was of greater concern than grace and ease of manner.

Easy movement and grace are the sole object of skating, wrote Robert Jones in skating's first textbook, published in 1772. Jones said that skating on curved lines on the outside edge – rolling – when 'performed by a person of a genteel figure, is the most graceful and becoming movement of all others; and must appear to those who neither consider, nor understand, the reason of the body's being preserved so long in a falling state, as it were, somewhat amazing.'[14] The amazement of onlookers notwithstanding, rolling was one of the easiest elements of the skating repertoire, yet Jones, like other writers after him, considered it the height of skating art. In 1814, in *Frostiana or A History of the River Thames in a Frozen State* (a book actually published from a stall on the frozen river), George Davis wrote that 'nothing can be more beautiful than the attitude of drawing the bow and arrow while the skater is making a large circle on the outside.'[15] Writing half a century later, Viennese authors Demeter Diamantidi, Carl von Korper, and Max Wirth saw the forward outside edge as the most beautiful and gracious movement on the ice, one that brings out the poetic side of skating.[16] Parisian George Vail wrote that with the outside edge 'the delight of the skater is suddenly born. One feels lifted up by enchantment, one gets a taste of the bird's flight.'[17] For each of these writers, technique was less important than aesthetics. The goal of their skating was not to be higher, faster, stronger, but to be more beautiful, to feel more acutely the joy of their motion. In a revised edition of his book, published in 1823, Jones actually argued against adroitness. 'It wants,' he said, of 'that bold sweep which is an essential requisite of gracefulness in this agreeable recreation.'[18] Too much bravado would get in the way of the glide. Or as the author of a little book from 1832 put it, 'Let grace be aimed at always ... Such feats as leaping on the ice are awkward in the extreme and please no one.'[19]

Nineteenth-century North American books made the same point. *The Skater's Textbook*, written by Frank Swift and Marvin Clark in 1868, goes to some length to advise against an over-emphasis on technical prowess, especially speed: 'Rapidity is very pleasing, but it is a noted fact that our most artistic, and particularly our graceful skaters are light in their movements without rapidity. Brilliancy and dash are too often indulged by skaters, and should, to a reasonable extent, be avoided. Grace is antagonistic to rapidity.' Excessive rapidity, they wrote, creates in the spectator 'an undue and painful sympathy for the performer, and always leaves a bad impression.'[20]

Textbook authors counselled skaters to avoid ungainly positions or awkward movements. More than one text had a chapter devoted solely to the 'disposition of the arms,' and all writers mentioned them. For the earliest skaters, who were working with a limited technical range, arm movements allowed them to vary their look, their attitude. When both feet had to stay fairly close to the ice and the design of the blade did not allow for much beyond the four basic edges and simple turns, arm movements were the primary means of showing elegance, of practising skating as an art. Elegant arm movements were a way of keeping skating close to its aristocratic roots. By his arm movements a skater demonstrated grace or its lack.

> The habits of skaters in disposing of the arms in various unnatural and uncouth manners, to the utter destruction of the beauty of the figure, calls for a correction, the severity of which must be equal to the disease. We have seen skaters ruin all the grace which they naturally possessed by spasmodic clutching of the fingers, continual swinging of the arms, bending the arms to a right angle, holding the arms out from the body, or spreading the fingers, until the three Graces must have wept in anguish and hidden their faces in sheer vexation.[21]

This particular bit of text, written by Americans Swift and Clark, made such an impression on Canadian writer George Meagher that he plagiarized it almost word for word in his *Lessons in Skating*, published in 1900.[22]

In the late eighteenth and early nineteenth centuries, skating was one of a number of activities through which aristocratic and upper-class men might exhibit their grace and elegance. Among men of the upper classes in Europe and North America grace was considered an essential characteristic of masculinity. Men of privilege were expected to demonstrate their refinement by the grace of their demeanour and by their knowledge and mastery of graceful arts and skills, including dancing and fencing. Indeed, in 1793 German physical educator J.C.F. GutsMuths complained that grace had come to be valued too highly in comparison to other manly qualities such as strength and robustness. 'People of rank,' he wrote, 'regard nothing but gracefulness of demeanour and health.' In his famous treatise about the importance of gymnastic exercises for youth, GutsMuths argued that an overemphasis on grace was turning boys soft. Educated by bookish ecclesiastics, surrounded at home by women and girls, with few opportunities for vigorous exercise and access to too much luxury, upper-class boys were at risk of effeminacy. As a solution, he proposed a program of vigorous physical exercise that included skating:

> I am come to an exercise superior to everything that can be classed under the head of motion. Like the bird sailing through the air with wing unmoved, the skater now glides along as if impelled by the mere energy of volition; now gracefully wheeling in all the intricate curves fancy can conceive, he wantons securely on the slippery surface, that the unpractised foot dares not tread; anon the rapidity and ease with which he glides along astonish us. I know nothing in gymnastics, that displays equal elegance … I would recommend it as the most efficacious remedy to the misanthrope and hypochondriac.[23]

Far from being a cause or product of effeminacy (as many modern-day fathers seem to fear when their sons express an interest in figure skating), skating was its cure. Like dancing, skating promoted a useful combination of gracefulness, strength, and agility. GutsMuths endorsed a masculine bearing that included suppleness, an upright posture, a lack of stiffness, an easy natural movement of the arms, and a 'light yet firm and manly step.'[24] His goal was not to eliminate training in gracefulness – he expected boys to grow up into graceful men – but to encourage educators to promote other manly qualities as well.

While grace was important to most nineteenth-century writers on skating, none described it with such detail or exuberance as did Jean Garcin, who published the first French text on skating in 1813: *The True Skater or Principles of the Art of Skating with Grace*. Addressed to a masculine reader who valued art, beauty, and the public display of emotions, Garcin's text opens with a rapturous dedication to Mlle Gosselin Ainée, *Première Danseuse de L'Académie Impériale de Musique.* 'To whom else,' asked Garcin, 'could such a book be dedicated, but to one equally involved in an art of suppleness and vitality and grace?' Dance and skating, he wrote, are similarly possessed of charms that could 'seduce weak mortals.'[25] Garcin carefully qualified the type of skating to which he referred. He found speed skating vulgar, and had no time for artistic skating from other countries. It is not, he wrote, that

> the Germans, English, Danes and people from other cold places are incapable of skating otherwise, but look at them the first time they show their knowledge here: [T]he body is bent, the arms swinging, the derriere pitched, or straight as a picket, all stiff, inflexible, without grace, without attitude. It is surprising to us, but after a few winters here with our skaters, they change ... though they are always missing a little softness of their movements and abandon.[26]

While Garcin seems to have believed that French skaters had natural corporeal gifts, he must also have believed that they needed the benefit of his counsel to make those gifts evident. In the first instance, he advised skaters to pay attention to their arms. It is the attitude of the arms, Garcin wrote, that 'contributes most to the aplomb and grace of the skater.' Garcin counselled against carrying anything while skating, although a small cane would not have been out of order, were it to be held by the thumb and the first two fingers, fingernails facing up, fingers spread. By no means was the skater to grab the cane 'like a baguette': closed fists appear 'stiff and take away from the softness and grace of the arms.' When skating with empty hands, the skater was advised to hold them open, 'as if you are presenting them to a friend' or to raise the arms, as when 'one implores favours from heaven.' To be avoided at all costs were mannerisms that were too feminine. This age especially, he wrote, 'does not permit men to join the thumb and the index finger while holding the other fingers spread and rounded or stretched and turned in the air.' These gestures are too childish and 'fit poorly with our corpulence.'[27] From such minutiae are masculine reputations gained or lost.

Garcin's detailed descriptions convey a sense that skating is something to be enjoyed by both skater and audience. He offered suggestions to make moves prettier; he noted those moves that attract the most admiration (much more for a nice step backwards, he said, than the same step forwards). He also described facial expressions appropriate to certain positions, surely a consideration only when someone is watching. Writing, for example, about the inside backwards edge, he said that a skater could change the meaning of the move without changing the body position. He needed only to replace a timid mien with the expression of one who, fleeing reluctantly from an indiscretion, 'cannot hide the sweet smile that betrays the state of his heart.'[28] Garcin also understood that the visual effect of a move could be heightened by the physical pleasure of the skater. Nothing is as beautiful, he wrote, as a skater who simply abandons himself to the edge. And nothing feels better to the skater. The French poet Alfonse de Lamartine, writing in 1849, elaborates on Garcin's point:

> To be carried with the speed of the arrow, and with the gracious swoops of the bird in the air, on a surface that is smooth, brilliant, resonant and treacherous; to print with a simple lean of the body, and, in this manner to describe, guided only by the rudder of the will, all the curves, all the inflections of the boat on the sea, or of the eagle hovering in the blue sky, it was, for me, such a drunkenness of the senses, and a voluptuous exhilaration of the mind that I can no longer reflect on it without emotion. Even horses, which I love very much, do not give to the rider the delirious melancholy that the great frozen lakes give to skaters.[29]

Cited on the opening page of George Vail's 1886 book *L'art du Patinage*, Lamartine's rapturous prose captures the physical and expressive possibilities the French found in skating. English textbook writers would have found it somewhat distasteful. While English writers also mentioned the physical pleasures of skating, they certainly did not dwell on them, and they never talked explicitly about skating as a means of expressing ideas or emotions – although the body positions described by Robert Jones were clearly intended to express something beyond the run of the blade over the ice or the facility of the skater with his edges. In the English reluctance to make explicit the expressiveness of the movement lies the seed of what would eventually grow to be a substantial difference between English and Continental skating.

Two Styles: The English

For most of the nineteenth century, skaters experimented with patterns and turns on the ice, perfecting a small standard repertoire and working out innovative designs. Skaters in Canada and the United States were keen on tricky footwork combinations and spins. French skaters continued for some time to practise Garcin-esque poses. In England and elsewhere in Europe, stunts like jumps and spins were frowned upon and considered by many not to be true skating.

At some point in the mid-1800s, the pleasurable freedom that had been found in skating by early practitioners of the art stopped being a major concern for English skaters. Rejecting the expressive possibilities of skating, they turned instead towards technical innovation and 'combined skating,' a type of formal group skating that required an exacting and regimented uniformity. What would come to be called the English style of skating emphasized long edges and turns and required a large ice surface. It was practised with a stiff upright posture. Knees were not to bend. Arms were not to lift. Nothing fanciful was to interfere with precision.

Once mastered, basic turns and edges were skated in unison by groups. Although groups sometimes had up to ten skaters, the usual number was four. One skater would act as a caller, giving instructions to the others. The goal of the exercise was conformity. An orange was used to mark a central point on the ice and the skaters would perform their turns and edges moving towards and then away from the orange. The more perfectly they could match each other's movements, the more successful the exercise. Anything difficult to match, for instance, the degree of bend in a knee, was eliminated. All flourishes were eliminated. Anything that would set one skater apart from the others was eliminated. Skating, which had once offered the possibility of individual expression and freedom of movement, evolved mid-century into a kind of regimented team activity. As one writer said, it took a 'good fellow' to skate combination figures well.[30]

Victorian England was the birthplace of modern team sports. Good team players – good fellows – were expected to be strong, calm, and well disciplined. They worked hard. They rose to a challenge. They were stoic in defeat and modest in victory. They avoided emotional display. For such fellows, the earlier, freer style of English skating would have held little appeal; gender expectations were changing and with them notions of what kinds of movements were appropriate for male bodies. As early as 1830, one English writer was complaining that skating had grown too 'florid' and that the 'fine art [was] degenerating.'[31] The upper-class men who formed the majority among English figure skaters until the turn of the twentieth century needed to develop a style of skating that fit well with the character of the time.

PLATE III.—THE OUTSIDE EDGE FORWARDS.

Correct Attitude.   Incorrect Attitude.

Figure 4.1 'The Outside Edge Forwards – Correct and incorrect attitudes.'
An illustration showing proper skating technique from *A System of Figure
Skating* by Maxwell Witham, published in 1893 (Trustees of the
National Library of Scotland).

Reserve, discipline, and self-control were all prized moral virtues of
the era. As historian Linda Young writes, 'Self-possession in public was
a primary aim' of the culture of gentility that was key to the middle
class cultures that came to dominate English social life in the nineteenth
century. Emotional and bodily control were both encouraged. 'Calm

control of the limbs and facial expressions evidenced an untroubled soul in command of all faculties, one who could be trusted.'[32] While the new style of skating was nothing if not controlled, it was still, nevertheless, a form of elegant gliding through space. Thus, it met expectations for middle-class restraint without denying its aristocratic roots. It might be argued that in this sense, skating epitomized gentility, a system of middle-class values expressed largely through adaptations of aristocratic cultural forms. As Linda Young argues, the 'stickiest step in understanding middle-class construction is to disentangle its relations with aristocratic culture, at once yearned for and yet moralized as decadent and unproductive.'[33] In English skating one sees a creative negotiation as traditional aristocratic aesthetics were adapted to middle-class norms.

In the new Victorian style skating was no longer motivated by artistic or expressive concerns; it had become instead a kind of science. And yet, writers continued to stress the importance of grace and, not infrequently, to refer to skating as 'a fine art,' as in a fat little book by Douglas Adams, published in 1890.[34] George Anderson (under the pseudonym Cyclos) entitled his 1880 book *The Art of Skating, with illustrations, diagrams, and plain directions for the acquirement of the most difficult and graceful movements*. Even Montagu Monier-Williams, who prized the sober English style of skating above all others because of its strict rules of form and its uniformity of method, still wanted skaters to show grace:

> Should the would-be figure skater have an instinctive idea of what constitutes grace in movement, he is more likely to become a really finished performer than if he not be so gifted. How often do we see really fine powerful skaters fail to reach the first rank from lack of this gift, and from whom no amount of practice seems to be capable of eradicating a natural clumsiness of movement! It will often be noticed that good figure-skaters are also easy and graceful dancers.[35]

Of course, grace is a culturally and historically specific concept. The grace spoken of by Garcin in Paris in 1813 was not the grace spoken of by Robert Jones in London in the 1770s, and it was not the grace spoken of by Monier-Williams in London in the 1890s. But whatever form it took, they all expected it, could not imagine skating without it. And, for the most part, they discussed grace as an inherent quality. American authors Swift and Clark wrote:

> There are those who are naturally graceful, the bulk of which are women.

There are those, also, who are naturally *ungraceful*. There are few, however, especially among those who possess symmetry of form, incapable
of attaining a graceful bearing by close attention to every movement ... A
natural air, an unassumed easiness of motion, elasticity and lightness of
step, harmony of movement, softness, pliability, and elegance in the disposition of the limbs, an insensible melting of one movement into another
– this is grace.[36]

As English skating in the Victorian era became more closely governed by rules, as it became stiffer and more controlled, grace ceased to
be equated with beauty. Previously grace and beauty had been seen as
synonymous, as they remained throughout the century in French and
Viennese skating texts. By the end of the nineteenth century, however,
English writers begin to speak of grace simply as ease of movement.
They no longer emphasized beauty, which, like art, was increasingly
relegated to feminine spheres of life. The appearance of ease, however,
was a central marker of aristocratic and bourgeois identities.[37] Members
of the upper classes were to be seen to move easily through their lives.
According to historian Michael Curtin, 'ease and elegance' have 'been
at the center of the aristocratic ideal of manners at least since the Renais-
sance.' He writes, 'the easy style was an invention of an aristocratic age
and was meant to exalt its possessor above his fellows.'[38] In his book
Distinction, French sociologist Pierre Bourdieu argues that manners,
gestures, posture, and styles of moving through the world are forms
of class embodiment that become markers by which groups of people
are distinguished from each other. Bourdieu would say that easy styles
of movement are forms of physical capital, that is, vehicles by which
individuals gain status, access to resources, and power.[39] They are one
example of the 'substantial inequalities in the social values accorded
to particular bodily forms.'[40] The requirement of ease in figure skating
made sure that skaters did not contravene the norms of appearance or
movement – the requirements of taste – that helped to constitute the
privileges and rewards of the class from which they came. The marvel
of the English style was that the skaters managed to balance the aesthetic demands of one form of class embodiment while also meeting the
athletic and sports-related demands of another.

The English style accommodated the public reserve that was a key
feature of late-nineteenth-century gentility.[41] Writing in the 1930s,
Ernest Jones (the prominent psychoanalyst who was also a keen figure
skater) argues that Victorian skaters devised their stiff, upright style
as a reaction to 'the self-display and gasconnade of the eighteenth

Figure 4.2 'The Flying Mercury.' From *The Art of Skating* by Cyclos [a pseudonym for George Anderson, MP for Glasgow], published in 1852. At that time such expressive poses were no longer in vogue. Instead, skaters were adopting a less 'florid,' more upright style that fit more closely with their ideas of how men should look and move (Trustees of the National Library of Scotland).

and early nineteenth centuries.' Not only in Europe, but also in England, he writes, skating of the early 1800s had 'flowed into an excess of gesture and posing.' As evidence, Jones points to the 'well-known illustration' of a position called 'The Flying Mercury' that appeared in several books (see figure 4.2).[42] What counts here as an 'excess of gesture and posing'? A gentleman skates on his right foot. His left leg stretches behind him, slightly bent at the knee. His left arm holds a graceful curve, his hand suspended beside his left hip. He stretches his right arm before him and points to the sky, following the gesture with his gaze. Such 'excess' could have formed the basis of a uniquely English artistic skating. But shifts in the English cultural climate forestalled its development and artistic skating would eventually have to come to England as a Continental import.

Two Styles: The Continental

While English skaters were perfecting their stiff turns and combination figures, a different style of skating was taking hold across Europe. Its founder was American skater and dancing master Jackson Haines. Like Garcin, Haines saw in skating tremendous theatrical and artistic possibilities. While other American skaters paid little attention to style or rhythm as they drew designs on the ice or practised acrobatic movements, Haines experimented with a form of skating inspired by dance. He fit his skating to music, developed new moves (including the sit spin, which for many years was called the Jackson Haines spin), and invented a one-piece skate. Yet, even after winning championships in 1863 and 1864, Haines gained few converts among North American skaters. In 1864 he left the United States and travelled to Europe in search of a more receptive audience.

Haines stayed in Europe for eleven years, giving exhibitions and collecting disciples. American and Continental sources routinely say that he was given a frosty reception in England, although not a single English source gives any specific information about him skating there. Whether this means he was completely discounted in that country or that, in fact, he never went there, it is impossible to know. There is, however, evidence that he skated to warm receptions in Norway, Sweden, and Russia and that his exhibitions in those countries prompted the founding of figure skating clubs and the building of ice rinks. But it was in Vienna where Haines had his greatest success and where his performances changed the future development of skating.

In 1810 a Viennese bookseller named Franz Gräffer – a 'fanatical skater' who, decades before Haines, had wanted to combine skating with music – tried to open an ice rink.[43] He was refused permission by the police and for another fifty years Viennese skaters had to make do with the uncertain ice on the narrow River Wien and on ponds in city parks. Unreliable ice and the lack of comfortable facilities limited the popularity of skating, and by the 1860s Viennese skating culture needed a boost. In 1867 a group of aristocratic men founded the Wiener Eislaufverein (WEV), the Vienna Skating Club. In January 1868, Haines gave his first exhibition on the club's rink. The weather was a balmy sixteen degrees Celsius and the ice was terrible. Yet, three thousand spectators gathered to watch the American perform, including Kaiser Franz Joseph I, 'the cream of Viennese aristocracy,' and other members of the city's elite – that class of people who 'attended all important theatre events.'[44]

In 1868, Vienna was in the midst of waltz fever. Balls and dances featured prominently on the local social calendar. In what was surely a calculated move, Haines took to the ice to the strains of a waltz. An American spectator described his entrance:

> [H]e shot in on a long outside roll (spiral) which took in the whole circumference of the area, and gradually narrowed down until he came to the centre, where he performed a pirouette and took off his hat to a Grand Duke who was present, continuing with a series of evolutions on both feet, something in the style of a Philadelphia twist or grape-vine; and when the band turned from the overture to the waltz-tune, he broke into a double cross-roll backwards ... Haines's advent caused a great sensation, and I have no doubt that this was the beginning of the modern art of skating in Vienna.[45]

Haines wanted to turn skating into a spectacle, to present it as a form of dance or theatre. He exaggerated poses, teased his audience, wore special costumes – all to great effect. Apparently he received tumultuous applause and the reviews in the next day's papers were glowing. He was declared to be marvellous, gracious, skilful, beautiful, and powerful. One newspaper talked about the grace of his elegantly proportioned movements, the ease of his pirouettes, his dainty and delicate turns, the way he followed the music as he 'floated in wide curves or whirled and jumped on tiptoe.' It was, they said, a most pleasant performance and Haines had shown better than any stage performer how 'perfect the beauty of human movement can be when one trains one's physical strength.'[46]

There is no sense in the coverage of his performance that Haines's style was too florid, his movements unbefitting a gentleman. Indeed, his musicality and style, his showiness and posing, brought him accolades and disciples. If it is, in fact, true that he performed in England and received a chilly reception there, perhaps it was as much a reaction to his version of masculinity as to his version of skating. Self-control and physical and emotional restraint were not part of Haines's program. He was concerned with style and expression, with using the unfettered motion of the skate against the ice to interpret the feel of the music. He concentrated on the aesthetics of the movements. Thus, Haines is considered the father of artistic skating, what we now call free skating. It is his legacy that is reflected in the French term *patinage artistique* and in the German term *Eiskunstlauf*. It is surely no coincidence that while those terms highlight art, the English term, figure skating, emphasizes technique.

Haines's style gained many converts in Vienna. Members of the WEV were said to have left his performance promising to follow his example. The book *Spuren auf dem Eise* [Tracks on the Ice], written in 1881 by WEV members Diamantidi, von Korper, and Wirth, turned Haines's technical accomplishments into a system which served, eventually, as the basis for international competition rules. In Haines's wake, Vienna became the most important skating city in the world. Eduard Engelmann, one of the spectators at Haines's performance, was so impressed by the American's performance that he went home and ordered a rink to be created in his (obviously sizeable) garden. His descendants would go on to create a skating dynasty that included four Olympic champions, seventeen world champions, and eleven European champions in the years between 1892 and 1936.

At its roots, Viennese skating was about pleasure – the pleasure of moving to music, the pleasure of the easy and long-held edge, the pleasure of the spectator. But it was also about the pleasure to be gained from the social aspects of skating. After Haines's exhibition, skating became a fashionable bourgeois pastime in Vienna. Masquerades, ice balls, and cotillions were a regular part of the skating season. By 1912, the Eislaufverein had more than 8500 members, a huge number.[47] By comparison, the Toronto Skating Club had 1200 members in the 1920s.[48]

Dancing was in large measure responsible for the popularity of skating in Vienna, and for the impressive numbers of women who took it up. As German historian Hugo Winzer wrote in his 1925 history of figure skating, the Viennese realized that 'it is wonderful to flirt while skating' and that skates could be used to dance on the ice. Winzer complained that skating historians had neglected to give the Viennese credit for inventing ice dancing – perhaps, he said, because they are non-Germans and have not the 'sense or ability' to understand it. He went on to say that 'the art of gracious dance figures on the ice could only be invented in Austria in accord with the cheerful people's character.'[49] Having enough women skaters (whom I will talk about in the next chapter), enough musicians, a sizeable rink, and the ballroom experience of the bourgeois social calendar probably helped too.

Winzer argued that, left to the English or the Americans, skating would never have been subjected to a proper system. It was 'German carefulness,' he wrote, and the 'German sense of systematizing'[50] that gave the Austrians the wherewithal to develop a system from Haines's innovations. Carefulness, maybe, but also a critical mass of skaters to practise the system, good ice to facilitate their practising, and three well-to-do men with the desire and the time to 'systematize.' It surely also helped that orderliness and rational modes of thought were increasingly promoted in the growing capitalist economies of Europe and in the educational institutions that supported them.

So what was this system that allegedly grew from the Germanic character? It was the technical foundation upon which artistic skating could grow: edges and turns. For the first time the turns were skated as part of large figure eights (later known in English as school figures), a concept that revolutionized skating. Guidelines for how the figures were to be skated stressed the importance of beautiful figures, beautiful 'tracks on the ice,' and a beautiful posture. Diamantidi, von Korper, and Wirth spoke of grace, of the 'aesthetic moment,' the 'aesthetic spirit,' of feelings. They also talked about dance steps, pirouettes, and other free-skating moves. About jumps they wrote: 'Although jumps on the ice are not part of figure skating, they result from practical need: in increasing coldness there appear wide gaps on extensive ice-areas that can be surmounted by jumps.'[51] The idea behind the system was that once skaters had mastered the basic techniques and understood the theory of skating, they would be able to engage with it as an art.

The Demise of the English Style

While some English-language writers claimed that the English and Continental styles of skating were different but equally valid ways of using the same technology, skaters themselves were not always so free of judgments. Miss M. Bland Jameson, a skater in the English style, began practising in Davos in 1902. Seventy-five years later she wrote to skating historian Dennis Bird:

> To us sober English-style skaters – with our severely-controlled move-
> ments, these exuberant (International) skaters seemed to be showing off
> and performing circus stunts. We looked askance at their black tunics and
> tight-fitting breeches, trimmed with Astrakhan fur. Discourteously, and
> not to their faces, we called them 'lion tamers' ... I think it is possible, even
> probable, there really was deep feeling that amounted to animosity ... Our
> efforts at combined figures must have appeared joyless and solemn to the
> International skaters, just as their efforts at spins seemed to us grotesque.[52]

In British criticisms of the international style, ideas about gender were
never very far from the surface. Figure skating was developed by and
for male bodies and what was seen to be correct, appropriate, or even
possible was tied to beliefs about masculinity, despite the increasing
numbers of women skaters by the end of the nineteenth century. In the
above quote it is not women's costumes but men's that roused British indignation. The difference between the two styles of figure skating
reflected different understandings of the male body and how it should
look and move – two perspectives forged in distinct national contexts.
   Figure skating is just one of an endless number of cultural forms
where we can see the way gender and national identity give each other
shape. As English magazine writer H. Goodwin put it in 1930, the English style 'was our true national style ... As far as men are concerned [it]
is the style which is most in accord with our national characteristics.'
According to Goodwin, the characteristics of Englishness were specifically masculine traits:

> An Englishman has a natural aversion to making an exhibition of himself,
> even in the most literal sense, and there are several characteristics of the
> [international] style which to an Englishman were at that time somewhat
> objectionable, not least, perhaps, the orthodox costume which consists of
> black tights and a closely fitting jacket trimmed with braid. Apart from
> the costume there is a certain degree of rhythmic abandon, best compared
> perhaps with ballet dancing. I venture to suggest that it is because this
> particular feature is unnatural to us as a nation ... The International Style
> is a style better suited to the fairer sex than the more athletic but less spec-
> tacular sport of the English style.[53]

Apparently the women Goodwin skated with were not quite as English
as he was. His conflation of masculine and 'national' characteristics is

certainly not unique, nor is it yet an anachronism. One sees it today in the continuing gender exclusivity of most national sports.

Skating in groups while wearing tall hats, black frock coats, and trousers, English men held their arms by their sides, their legs stiff and straight. They took their pleasure in overcoming difficulties rather than in the freedom of moving. And in all this they were perfect, moving representations of middle-class Victorian norms. Their style of skating was shaped by and, in turn, helped to maintain Victorian ideas about masculinity. To skate as the other Europeans did was not simply an issue of bending one's knees; it was a question of what a soft knee might say about one's identity as an Englishman. At stake was not just a method of gliding on ice but the ideologies attached to the method, including, in this case, notions of British superiority in the realm of physical exercise.[54] In 1897, sounding like a defeated politician, Herbert Fowler reflected on the increasing influence the international style was having in England:

> Great Britain has been, if not the Mother, at least the Governess of Continental schools of skating ... Great Britain may well be proud of her pupils in other lands and other tongues, in this as in so many branches of sport; let us hope that they are not wholly ungrateful to her! Is it nothing to have opened the chests, hardened the muscles, and increased the gaiety of nations? Friends and fellow-skaters – Here's luck! A votre santé, Messieurs! Prosit! Skal![55]

What would have been the cost of admitting that while the English style of skating had had some technical success – with the invention of certain turns, for instance – it was basically a dead end in terms of the ongoing development of *figure* skating? The German writer Hugo Winzer responded to Fowler's patronizing suggestion with his own misogynous brand of national chauvinism. In his 1925 article on the history of figure skating (by which time the English style was dying out), Winzer blamed the 'ossification' of the English style on a lack of aesthetic sense and rhythm. The English, he wrote, skate with a stiff posture and their turns 'appear as ugly convulsions.' He scoffed at Fowler's suggestion that other skating nations owed England a debt of gratitude: 'It seems better to see England as a daughter who became an ugly old spinster and who stayed infertile.'[56] Obviously, there was more at stake here than skating technique.

By the turn of the twentieth century two prominent London figure skaters, Edgar Syers and Herbert Yglesias, had begun to lobby for the adoption of the international style in England. To that end, they invited the International Skating Union (ISU, founded in 1892) to hold the third official world championships in London in 1898. The event gave many English skaters their first opportunity to see the international style in action. Not all were impressed:

> It would be ungracious to criticize in any adverse tone the style of foreign skaters ... But probably no one will feel aggrieved if we go as far as to regret the concession made by Mr. Grenander [of Sweden] to what was once considered in England the degenerate practice of bending the knees.[57]

Other commentators were more open-minded:

> Indeed it must have been a revelation to the English skaters that with so much swinging of the arms and legs there could yet be an appearance of grace and beauty. [Huegel's] skating was quite free from the jerkiness or stiffness which is so common in Englishmen, who try to conceal every movement as much as possible. If movement is to be allowed ... as one thinks it must be, then let it be free and open. Properly developed it certainly gives a rhythm and vitality which are very charming to watch.[58]

And which, apparently, inspired audiences to cheering and great applause.

Eventually, Syers and Yglesias met with success. The style of skating developed by Haines's disciples eclipsed the Victorian poker style (although the English style remained popular among some skaters through the 1930s and, apparently, is still practised today at a rink on the outskirts of London). The international style held the promise of ice dancing, it allowed skaters more individual freedom, and, as Madge Syers (wife of Edgar and the first Olympic champion in the women's competition) wrote, agreeing with the magazine writer, Goodwin, above, it was less jerky and so seemed better suited to the requirements of femininity. While for some English skaters the artistic and social possibilities of the new style made it desirable, for others the switch may have been based on more practical concerns. The international style required less space and so was easier to practise in the indoor ice palaces that were built around the turn of the twentieth century. And, finally, the new style offered the chance for international competition. The spread of middle-class values meant that little was more manly in Britain than an athletic competition. What a lovely irony it is that to take part the 'good fellows' had to bend their knees, raise their arms, ever so slightly, and put themselves on display. To prove their mettle, English skaters had to temper their manly reserve, adopt a more expressive style, and skate like 'effete' Continentals.

Ideas about class and gender were key to the development of skating. The competing styles of skating that developed in England and in Vienna show us two different configurations of how these categories shaped a unique physical activity and the meanings that came to be associated with it. The story of figure skating reminds us that not all sports had a similar relationship to the notions of manliness that drove the mid-Victorian English games ethic. As John Lowerson has written, the majority of research on Victorian sport in England has investigated only a handful of athletic and team activities, with most attention being devoted to cricket and the various forms of football.[59] We need more research on a greater variety of sports to learn whether sporting masculinities are as coherent as they can seem to be in the literature, where they are often lumped together under the undifferentiated category of dominant or hegemonic masculinity. While these can be useful concepts, their boundaries need to be determined by empirical research. Figure skating provides a very good example of how participants in one sport managed to negotiate traditional and emerging masculinities to produce styles of movement that met the requirements of both gender schemes. Discourses of dominant masculinity were represented very differently on the skating rink than they were on the football pitch, but they were still central to the ways in which the sport would develop.

In the next chapter I look at the organizational structures and regulations that supported the transformation of skaters' 'art' into a competitive international sport. The institutionalization of figure skating, as a specific branch of skating and a formal body of knowledge developed, shared, and governed by its practitioners, was well under way on both sides of the Atlantic by the end of the 1860s. This was the era in which women began taking to the ice in significant numbers. Their participation in skating – as it became more formalized, more rational, more competitive – is an interesting variation on the usual story of 'sportification,' a process that has generally been considered in relation to the pastimes of men. Here too, skating offers another reminder that the field of sport history could benefit from study of a broader range of sports.

5 Women Start Skating, Skaters Form Clubs, Their Art Becomes Sport

In the 1860s, skating was touted as the ideal winter pastime for a democracy like the United States of America. According to the handbook of the Brooklyn Skating Rink Association, the 'millionaire and mechanic, the lady of fashion and those of humbler rank, all meet together to enjoy this fascinating and beautiful exercise. All can skate alone or associate with those most agreeable to themselves.'[1] And skate they did. Throughout the 1860s, on cold winter days, New Yorkers flocked to Central Park. When the weather was right and the ice was good, the lake at 110th Street could be crowded with tens of thousands of skaters.[2] Between the 1860s and the 1890s, skating was in vogue in cities and towns in the eastern United States, a sign of increasing interest in urban recreation and a general expansion of sport and other vigorous pastimes. Some US historians argue that ice skating was the first recreational activity promoted to men and women equally, by both commercial establishments and community organizations.[3] And, while claims about skating's accessibility to the 'humbler ranks' were undoubtedly exaggerated, it was certainly the case that recreational skating attracted a great deal of attention among the middle classes. So much so, Paul Renwick writes, that in New York City more privileged skaters felt the need to retire from the busy lakes of Central Park to private ponds and rinks, where admission was controlled.[4] As in England, there were skaters and there were *skaters*. The denizens of exclusive clubs and private rinks considered themselves not just a different class of people but a different class of skater. In 1867 Edward Gill wrote that the goal of the New York Skating Club (founded in 1863) was not simply pleasure but 'the advancement of the art of skating,' which, he notes, would have been impossible on the crowded ponds of Central Park, with all the 'crowds that gather round good skaters, and interfere with their evolutions.'[5]

In the nineteenth century, in both Europe and North America, it was in an elitist network of clubs that skating skills beyond the basics were developed and passed on. And skaters in such clubs clearly understood that what they did differed from what they saw on local ponds and rinks in public parks. In London, thousands of skaters took advantage of good winter days. But, as Vandervell and Witham noted in the late 1860s, 'the mass is made up of young and old *learners*, who having, with all respect to them, but hazy ideas how to acquire this art properly, arrive only at a certain low degree of skill, and never seem to progress as they ought to do ... The truth is that the deep mysteries of our art are known only to the select few.'[6] The select few to whom the authors referred were those same few with the time and resources to practise and the social capital that would permit them entry to the clubs where skating skills were shared. Vandervell and Witham claimed that there were

> very few figure-skaters of any pretensions at all, in this country at least, among the lower classes, notwithstanding that as a class they excel in most of the manly exercises, including rapid skating. Yet, when we come to figure-skating, we shall not fear contradiction when we assert that the most graceful and finished skaters come from the better educated, or the middle and upper classes, the clergy and military, and gentlemen belonging to any of the higher professions, being at the top of the scale; very few of the lower class, as we descend the social scale, knowing more than to 'go ahead.'[7]

Not quite the sport of kings, skating was at one time a diversion for dukes, barons, earls, and princes. The Cercle des Patineurs, for instance, was founded in 1865 in Paris by two marquis, a pair of princes, a count, a viscount, and three of their non-titled peers.[8] When and where titles were in short supply, skating clubs on both sides of the Atlantic maintained their exclusivity by other means. Membership fees or requirements to buy shares in a club, the vetting of prospective skaters, and the expectation of upper-class manners kept figure skating an elegant pastime done by the right kind of people. As late as the 1920s, the well-to-do members of the Toronto Skating Club were greeted by a uniformed butler as they entered the rink.[9]

Elegant skating, like skill at dancing or refined table manners, was a means through which the highest classes constructed their social identities. But while dancing skills and table manners were displayed primarily to other upper-class people – as a way to mark shared membership of that class – skating was on display to anyone who happened to pass by the skater's frozen pond. In this sense, skating made class differences visible. Huge homes, servants, and fines carriages did the same thing, of course. But while the ability to own a fine carriage could seem a simple question of wealth, the ability to skate in an elegant fashion could seem a question of inborn physical ability. Rich people and poor people, even now, learn to move their bodies in different ways. They walk differently, they sit differently, they have different sets of physical skills. These different styles of moving can make it seem that there are actual physical differences between upper- and lower-class people, that richness or poorness are inherent rather than the product of social and economic practices. The notion that people of different classes are fundamentally different kinds of people helps to naturalize class disparities and makes economic inequality seem inevitable and, therefore, easier to maintain. Bodies and the movements they make are tremendously powerful representations of ideology. The roughhousing of boys on a frozen ditch and the studied gliding of top-hatted men in London's finest parks sent different messages to the onlooker. And those messages were not just about skill on skates.

This chapter looks at the processes and structures through which certain kinds of skating were transformed by certain kinds of skaters into a highly stylized competitive sport. One wonders that skaters felt the need to shoehorn themselves and their 'art' into the narrow framework offered by competitive sport. But over the course of a few short decades, they homogenized diverse approaches to movement on ice and contained their efforts within a standardized repertoire and a formal set of rules. I look here at the organization of skaters into clubs, the formation of national associations, and the efforts to give a shape to the first competitions. Once again, this chapter moves somewhat freely among national contexts, with London and Vienna providing most of the evidence for the arguments I make below.

While early figure skating was largely a male pursuit, women were starting to skate in significant numbers by the end of the 1860s and they were integrated into clubs over the last few decades of the century. The presence of women did nothing to change the class boundaries that kept figure skating an exclusive pastime. Indeed, the exclusivity of this kind of skating and the venues in which it was pursued were part of what made it possible for privileged women to take it up. As compared to many other activities that were newly formed as sports in the late nineteenth century, figure skating stands out for the fact that women were not just token participants in the structures that provided the context for its transformation.

Women's Early Skating

In countries outside of the Netherlands, a female skater would have been an unusual sight in the late 1700s and early 1800s. Yet, textbook authors generally presented positive views on the possibilities of women's skating and complained about the social conventions that kept women from the ice. In 1772, Robert Jones, author of the first skating textbook, wrote:

> I see no reason why the ladies are to be excluded; to object to it as not being hitherto practised, is the effect of prejudice and confined ideas ... No motion can be more happily imagined for setting off an elegant figure to advantage; nor does the minuet itself afford half the opportunity of displaying a pretty foot: a lady may indulge herself here in a *tête à tête* with an acquaintance, without provoking the jealousy of her husband; and should she unfortunately make a slip, it would at least not be attended with any prejudice to her reputation.[10]

While Jones was the first, he would not be the last writer to recommend women's skating as much for the pleasure it would bring to men as for any benefit it might bring to women themselves. German physical educator Gerhard Vieth made the same argument in the 1790s:

> Consensus of opinion denies the feminine sex this pleasure as indecorous; but, to my mind, without reason. In my opinion, a girl on skates is a far pleasanter sight than an amazon on horseback. A girl can, in the motions of skating, display much grace, and it is surprising that our ladies, who otherwise understand so well what is to their advantage, do not make use of this. What could be more becoming to them – than to float along on a crystal mirror, like the divinities of the poets.[11]

Long before women's skating was commonplace, Vieth and Jones were presenting it as a matter of display, as something to be watched, as much for the pleasure it would bring to men as for the pleasure it would bring to women themselves. These writers were foreshadowing the heterosexual sociability that would prove to be an important reason for the substantial increase in skating's popularity among both women and men in the 1860s and after.

In the late eighteenth and early nineteenth centuries, skating was a popular entertainment in European court society. But while men attempted to master the new art, women were far more likely to take to the ice in ornamented wooden sleighs. Historian Matthias Hampe writes that in France, the symbolic figure of women's 'skating' in this early period was the Marquise de Pompadour, the mistress of Louis XV, being pushed about in a sleigh that was shaped like a swan.[12] Swan-shaped wooden sleighs also appear in accounts of the Congress of Vienna – a seven-month-long conference at which European rulers met to negotiate the borders of a post-Napoleonic Europe (1814–15).[13] Other women and other sleighs feature in descriptions and imagery of skating and ice spectacles from France, Germany, Austria, and North America. The first skating club in Russia, founded in 1865, even had a special 'chaise' skating department.[14]

It is not clear why so few women skated. Decorum? Moral prohibitions? A lack of experience with physical pursuits? The problem of inappropriate clothing? While one late-eighteenth-century German writer lays the blame on women themselves – 'in the Netherlands the feminine sex finds itself strong enough to defy the cold with nimble feet, while our simpering creatures embroider filet behind the stove'[15] – most authors blamed moral restrictions and limited views of women's physical potential. Americans Swift and Clark drew on orientalist rhetoric to scoff at physicians who claimed skating was too violent a pastime for women: 'In this country, where woman is regarded more particularly than in any other land, except perhaps Turkey, as a delicate organization, incapable of sustaining any amount of burden because she is the weaker vessel, it is not strange to us that such an opinion obtained.'[16] An article in the popular American magazine *Godey's Lady's Book* blamed overprotective fathers,[17] while an 1895 history of the Philadelphia Skating Club suggested that women were constrained by their fear of falling on frozen lakes and rivers, as well as of the 'rowdies' who would sometimes bother skaters.[18] A history of ice skating in Germany, published in 1925, blamed 'philistine-like modesty and hypocrisy' and claimed that early women skaters were looked at suspiciously and regarded, unfavourably, as emancipatory women.[19]

Regulatory moral discourses and the conventional limitations on women's freedom of movement did not prevent all women from skating. Nor did they prevent some men, like Gerhard Vieth and Robert Jones, from encouraging women to do so. The late-eighteenth-century German poet Friedrich Klopstock was also a great promoter of skating for women,[20] as was Goethe, who has been credited with getting women up and out of their ice-chairs in Weimar.[21] Evidence of women's skating comes from a range of textual and visual sources – letters, paintings, diaries, lithographs, magazine and newspaper articles. The images of women's skating that are perhaps most well known today are those that appear in Dutch paintings from the seventeenth and eighteenth centuries; they provide irrefutable evidence that women could skate and skate well. Writing in 1814, George Davis, an English printer, seems clearly to have been impressed by the culture he saw on the Dutch canals: 'These instruments [skates], indeed, are indispensable to the Dutch in the winter season; and are used by men, WOMEN, and *children*, constantly. The women skate to market with provisions, and *children of five or six years old* and upwards, accompany them, not lazily hanging at their backs or on their arms, but each little skater with *winged feet* flies after its mother, and carries a little basket of eggs, or other articles along with it. *Interesting scene!*'[22] In 1847 the duke of Wellington used the example of women skaters abroad to encourage his friend Angela Burdett Coutts onto the ice: 'Don't repine! My dear! that you are a woman. There is nothing to prevent you skaiting [*sic*], excepting the difficulty and the want of opportunity ... Women skait habitually in the countries in which the ice is certain annually, and in England I have seen ladies skait beautifully ... as well at least as most men.'[23]

Further examples of women skaters are scattered throughout the skating literature. In Vienna, opera singer Henrietta Sontag skated in public in the 1820s, as well as in Berlin in the 1840s. Married to an Italian count, Sontag's fame and title gave her the social weight to ignore popular opinion and to circumvent the moral retribution that would have befallen a woman of lesser privilege. German skating author Fritz Reuel claims, for instance, that in 1851 Maria Weigl, the daughter of a doctor, was stoned by farmers who disapproved of her skating in the German countryside.[24]

Despite Sontag's example, Viennese women did not start to skate in significant numbers until the mid-1860s, inspired by the example of Auguste Willibrandt-Baudius, a well-known actress who, protected by her popularity, not only skated with men in public but sometimes did so in trousers. A curious account of her skating appears on the opening page of Franz Biberhofer's history of the Wiener Eislaufverein (WEV, the Vienna Skating Club), published in 1906:

> Then something extraordinary, something unbelievable happened. It was true for it was reported in all the newspapers. But in order to make sure one had to go the next afternoon to the City Park in order to see for one's self.
>
> There were many curious people gathering around the pond, three-quarters of whom were women of all ages. On the ice there were gentlemen skating. There is a movement through the crowd ... So it is true! The unbelievable is true: A lady on the ice! The newspapers were right. Now, this must be the peak of female emancipation. The elder 'young ladies' found it especially insolent because the female skater was young and beautiful and her companions were very elegant and distinguished young gentlemen. One of them was the son of the famous court opera singer. The truly young ladies watched with envious admiration: 'It must be wonderful, one needs only courage.' Yes the woman on the ice had it easier, she was the unequaled ingenue of the theatre, a favourite of the public. She can do such a thing, but could we? And with a shock each thought of her mother.
>
> This public act made evident the secret tension between obsolete traditions and the demand for liberated exercise for women. Like all revolutions, this one too ended with the triumph of the modern idea.[25]

Once women started to skate in Vienna, their numbers increased rapidly. When the WEV was founded, in 1867, there was no question that women were an important part of Viennese skating culture. Descriptions of club activities include accounts of parties and ice festivals at which women were present. In 1875 the club took the unusual step of showcasing its female skaters by holding a competition only for women.[26]

In both Europe and North America, skating's general popularity increased in the 1860s and women were part of the trend. The increase was due in part to an overall expansion of leisure activities for middle- and upper-class people and to the increasing attention paid to the health benefits of physical exercise, especially when conducted out of doors in fresh air. Improved designs made skates more comfortable and more effective, and new skating venues reduced the danger of venturing onto ice. The removal of skating from lakes and ponds to flooded fields and rinks in urban areas made it much safer. Some rinks were made accessible at night by the installation of electric lights. In Canada the development of covered rinks in the late 1850s brought skating new converts, among whom were many women. The new rinks still relied on natural ice, but they had heating and lights and some even had band platforms. In these hospitable conditions skating became a popular hetero-social entertainment for the well-to-do. Masked balls and fancy dress carnivals could draw hundreds of skaters in elaborate costumes; such events required the presence of women for their success. It was this hetero-social aspect of skating that contributed the most to its attractiveness as amusement and/or exercise for both women and men.

Before the development of urban skating clubs and supervised rinks in the United States, skating had been, as in Europe, mostly 'confined to irrepressible school-boys and the rugged and reckless of our youth.'[27] Once it became possible to skate in good company, on good skates, under night-time lights in the city, women took to the ice in large numbers. Lithographs from the 1860s show crowded outdoor ice rinks with many women skaters. So many women took up skating in the 1860s, 1870s, and 1880s that it became profitable for skate manufacturers to produce special skates and to design skating clothing for women. Some American scholars have argued that skating was the first 'nonutilitarian physical recreation in which women actively participated in large numbers.'[28]

The hetero-sociability of skating seems to have been key to its growth among both women and men. Skating offered freedom of movement and exhilarating exercise out-of-doors. But it also permitted women and men the possibility of unchaperoned private conversations in public spaces and the chance that men and women might touch each other. It is perhaps not surprising then that upper-class skaters would want to limit their interactions to people of similar backgrounds. To do so, they contained their skating in private clubs.

A Rink for Their Sole Use: Maintaining Class and Organizing Skaters

The first formally organized skating club was established in Edinburgh some time in the mid-1700s.[29] Skating on the 'picturesque' Loch at Duddingston, club members found congenial company while they worked on the development of their art – no simple feat when the loch could go several years in a row without freezing. All members were men of excellent social standing and able skaters. New members were vetted for social compatibility and were required to demonstrate their competence on skates by skating a circle on each foot and jumping over three hats stacked on the ice. Women were not admitted until 1910, and then only through family ties.

'There can be few more animating sights than a meeting of the Skating-club there [on the lake] on a clear bright winter's day during a season of hard frost – enhanced as it is by the singular beauty of the locality, with the overhanging hill, the ancient church on the margin, and the fringing woods of the Marquis of Abercorn and Sir William Dick Cunningham,' wrote the author of an 1865 history of the club.[30] While the location may have been beautiful, aesthetics alone could not guarantee good conditions for skating. Annual suppers for members included toasts to John Frost,' the 'patron saint of the Club.' Just as important, but less recognized, was the small band of labourers who maintained the club's ice. According to a letter written by the club's treasurer, at least one good frost in 1814 was 'of little avail from want of funds to clear the ice.'[31] Far be it for gentlemen skaters to sweep the snow themselves.

Of course, once having paid for the clearing of the ice, members of the club had then to pay for the clean ice to be protected from boys or others who might damage it. The club employed labourers and watchmen who were both overseen by a paid officer. It was the task of the officer to report on the condition of the ice to the club's secretary or treasurer every evening. If the ice were indeed suitable for skating, the officer would post notices around the city the next morning or deliver a note to the home of each member. No need, therefore, for gentlemen skaters to venture out needlessly into the cold.

Similar practical concerns motivated the founding, in 1830, of what would become Britain's most prestigious nineteenth-century club, the Skating Club in London. An invitation sent to potential members made no mention of the shared pleasures of skating, but described an organization that would provide 'notice of when the ice will bear, in what place all probability the Members will meet to have the ice properly swept and watched, a convenient booth for putting on skates, keeping great coats, &c., &c., &c.'[32] The club, like others that followed it, provided a structure for gentlemen skaters to hire out the work that made skating possible. Depending on the weather, that work could be considerable. For instance, on the lake at Wimbledon, home of the Wimbledon Skating Club, an extravagant area of twenty acres was cleared for the exclusive use of figure skaters, curlers, and bandy players. After a heavy snowstorm, the club might employ up to 170 men to clear the ice with 'scows and snow boxes.' In the 1890s the average cost of a snowstorm to the club was one pound per minute.[33] During one series of heavy snowstorms, one hundred men worked constantly for ten to twelve days to keep the ice clear.[34]

As sport historians routinely point out, the play of the few depended on the work of many. The wealth and leisure of the privileged classes depended on the labour of employees or tenants as well as on an economic and political system shaped by and for the upper classes. On a far more practical level, the games and pastimes of the rich depended quite directly on the work of people less well off than themselves: people who would maintain the stable or riding course, wax the rowing shells, sweep the rink, and mind the coats. Henry Vandervell and T. Maxwell Witham write about the particularly cold winter of 1860–1: 'The well-known words, "'Ave a pair on, sir? Skates on, sir?" invited the promenaders in the London parks in every direction, and it was apparent that thousands of the humble classes were getting their daily bread in a most inclement season by ministering to the wants of the skater.'[35] And while some among the 'humble classes' may have found the means to skate, it is unlikely that they would have gained access to the 'deep mysteries' of skating art.

For almost forty years, members of the Skating Club had permission from the Ranger of Woods and Forests to skate on a section of the Serpentine, a small lake in London's Hyde Park. They were also permitted to erect a marquee on the bank. But when the weather was cold and the untutored skating masses descended, club members found it hard to protect their space. 'All attempts to carry out those beautiful figures which give such delight to the on-lookers were frustrated, and many of the strongest members of the Club, well-bruised all over, departed in disgust to other parts of the Serpentine, or more frequently to the outskirts and environs of the metropolis.'[36] Beyond the infringements on their private ice, the gentlemen skaters were horrified to think that unknowing spectators might confuse the awkward and unskilled hordes with bona fide club members. To stave off such mis-identifications, the club adopted a small silver skate as a badge, and any member who appeared on the ice without it could be fined. Complaints about the club's privileged access to a piece of London's best ice were much harder to stave off.

In the late 1860s, the gentlemen skaters finally constructed a rink for their sole use on the flooded archery pitch of the Royal Toxophilite Society in Regent's Park. After the opening of the new private rink, measuring 150 yards long by 50 yards wide, club memberships were much sought after. Worried about crowding on the new but limited ice surface, members voted in 1870 to restrict the total membership to 120 gentlemen and 20 ladies. They also instituted skating tests as a means – beyond the existing requirement for sponsorship and a formal balloting system – of screening applicants.[37] With their new ice and new procedures, members of the Skating Club transformed an exercise that had previously been synonymous with personal freedom and unencumbered space into a carefully circumscribed practice. Skating as they organized it became increasingly exclusive in terms of class background and level of skating skill – the two being closely related – even as it opened up a tiny bit for upper-class women.

Drawing on the work of French historian Philippe Ariès, sports theorist Henning Eichberg argues that the enclosure of outdoor activities was an exclusionary process that was as much about separating activities from each other as it was about dividing people of different social rank.[38] Eichberg is concerned mostly with enclosed indoor spaces like training halls or indoor riding arenas. In the case of the Skating Club, the members did not yet have the option of fully enclosing their pastime, although entrepreneurs in Canada had begun to build enclosed structures over natural ice in the late 1850s. It would be a few more decades before skating in Britain could be an indoor pursuit. Nevertheless, the wealthy skaters did what they could with the technology available to them, removing themselves, their distinctive style of skating, and the knowledge of how to perform it, to private grounds.

Historian Dennis Brailsford argues that nineteenth-century sports clubs were fundamentally about exclusivity.[39] In the 1870s, English figure skating was not yet considered a sport; however, it was in many ways organized like one, with clubs promoting a shared body of technique and emphasizing the achievement of physical skills. Yet knowledge and performance were not necessarily, as any number of historians could remind us, the main reason for joining a sports club – 'The company came first.'[40] In this regard, skating was definitely sport-like.

In sports like cricket and rowing, the social opportunities occurred before and after the game. In skating, as in golf, they were central to the main activity, which was all the more reason to guarantee that skaters shared the same class background. The screening of potential members was a common practice in nineteenth-century sports clubs; it was not unique to skating nor to England. Prospective members had to be sponsored or nominated for membership and then approved by existing members. Black-ball voting systems were typical. For instance, the 1875 by-laws of the Toronto Curling and Skating Club stated that applicants would be rejected on the basis of a vote of one black ball – a negative vote – for every five members.[41] At most clubs this voting system applied only to male applicants. Women's memberships, at those clubs where they were actually allowed to join, generally came through their ties to husbands, brothers, or fathers, a practice that would have made joining difficult for single women without family connections (who, in any case, would probably not have had the means to do so) or for women whose family members did not care for skating. At the Wimbledon Skating Club, a lady who ceased to reside with a member – for instance, a daughter who married or who for some other reason moved from the family home – had to forfeit her membership.[42]

Published in 1909, the history of the Skating Club makes no mention of when the first women members were admitted. However, the provision of twenty spaces 'for ladies' in 1870 suggests that at least some women were skating at the club before this time.[43] The privacy offered by clubs freed some 'ladies' to take their first precarious steps in skates. As a combination of art, exercise, and social event, skating fit somewhere between the categories of walking and dancing, both of which were, within limits, considered appropriate for upper-class women in the nineteenth century. But, unlike dancing, skating often took place before crowds of curious onlookers in public places. And, unlike walking, competence in skating was hard won. Few skaters would have had the resources to practise their art in private. What gentlewoman could suffer the humiliation of falling before men and women of lower classes? What father would permit his daughter to do so? Those forms of exercise that were considered appropriate for privileged women in the 1800s tended to take place in the confines of the home. Jennifer Hargreaves argues that, in England, games like croquet and lawn tennis fell into the same category as piano-playing, drawing, and needlework. They were fashionable accomplishments that allowed women to lay claim to the status of 'cultured ladies.' They gave fathers and husbands an opportunity to be proud of feminine talents, as long as they could be displayed in the respectable context of home and family.[44]

Clubs were public, but in only the most limited sense of being outside the home. On club ice women could experience the precariousness of their first attempts at skating surrounded by others of their own class. Indeed, it is almost certain that a woman would take her first steps on the ice accompanied by someone from her own family, as women's access to skating clubs was mediated through male relatives. A woman could not join the Skating Club in London of her own accord, no matter how high her social standing or how proficient her skating. What's worse, the gentlemen members of the club restricted the number of women using their rink and permitted it to grow only slowly. It took almost twenty-five years to raise the number of women members from twenty to fifty, an increase so great that it necessitated the enlargement of the women's club room.[45]

Unlike men, ladies who sought membership in the Skating Club were not subjected to public testing of their skating skills. The sponsor of a woman's application had only to attest, in writing, to her skill at skating a forward edge on either foot. Gentlemen, by contrast, were required to skate before a committee to demonstrate their proficiency. They had to skate forward and backward cross rolls, and a large three on each foot. (A three or a 3-turn is a turn on one foot, either forwards to backwards or backwards to forwards, in which the blade 'draws' a number 3 on the ice.) Clearly, the club was not looking to its women to uphold the highest standards of the art. It is a sweet irony, then, that the member of the club who made the most significant contribution to the history of skating was a woman named Madge Syers, about whom more later.

In Canada, where skaters were most concerned with staging elaborate balls and ice carnivals, there was no question of women not skating – men needed them for partners. This does not, however, mean that women were equal members of skating clubs. The Montreal Skating Club, as one example, had no female members in 1860, although they certainly held balls with women present. A rule requiring gentlemen to restrict their smoking to the gentlemen's dressing room suggests that there might well have been ladies, if not a ladies' dressing room, on the premises.[46] In 1870, at the Victoria Skating Club in Saint John, New Brunswick, only 10 of 348 members were women. To maintain decorum, club by-laws stated that anyone guilty of rudeness to a lady would be struck from the subscribers' list.[47]

In Vienna, the skating club adopted a far less exclusive approach to membership. In 1874, the membership rules changed so that 'every friend of ice-skating – without distinction of sex and age – may become a member of the WEV.'[48] It might have been more correct to say every friend of ice-skating who could afford the fees. Nevertheless, the club's less-exclusive policy is evident in a membership list that after just four years included more than one thousand names.[49] Photographs of skating sessions on the WEV's huge outdoor rink show crowds of women and men, skating alone and in pairs and groups. Despite the club's location in the centre of the city, there was no call – as there had been in London – to protect upper-class skaters from the prying eyes of the masses, and thus elegant skating became part of the urban scene. Accounts by Biberhofer and other Viennese writers suggest that in Vienna skating emerged as a fashionable – desirable – entertainment, akin to dancing. The skating rink of the WEV was just one of many cultural venues in the city centre that catered to the leisure pursuits of the bourgeoisie. It was not just a place for learning new skills, but one for socializing in elegant and tasteful company, as were ballrooms and theatres. Given their background in developing skating as a cultural activity, it is ironic that Viennese skaters would play a dominant role in its transformation into a highly structured, competitive sport.

Women as Skaters

By the last decades of the 1800s one begins to see regular references made to women in the skating literature. American writers Swift and Clark use female skaters as inspiring examples. Monier-Williams, an English writer, actually addresses women as readers.[50] Austrians Diamantidi, von Korper, and Wirth write for readers without specifying gender, and praise the talents of female skaters in Vienna, where, they say, the women were as powerful as the men. After almost two centuries as a gentlemen's pastime, 'the graceful art' went co-ed.

While it was expected and desired that women skate, it was not, at first, expected that they would skate like men. It was often assumed that women would prove to be timid skaters – and this may indeed have been the case, given that dancing, walking, riding, and perhaps lawn tennis, were the physical exercises most likely to be available to the bourgeois and upper-class women at whom the textbooks were aimed. As Miss L. Cheetham wrote, 'Ladies as a rule mistrust their own physical powers.'[51]

The Viennese authors of *Tracks on the Ice* reassured women that it was okay for 'the beautiful sex' (but not for the 'strong sex') to ask for help when learning to skate.[52] In England, George Anderson invented the safety frame so they wouldn't need to. This wooden device, shaped like the railing on a small balcony and affixed to runners, supported the skater as she pushed it in front of her. (It was the Victorian version of the overturned plastic garbage can or the chair that sometimes supports beginning skaters today.) The frame was meant to free women from the fear of falling and the possibility that they might expose their underclothes. Practising in a location separate from men was one option – though not a very practical one – for anxious women. Anderson gave such advice: 'I like to see ladies skate; though, no doubt, the early steps must be rather trying to female nerves and female draperies; but more in idea than in reality, for with careful instructions, a lady may acquire sufficient skill to move about freely without any extensive ordeal of falls. At the same time, where the opportunity can be had of a private pond, these little difficulties may be more easily surmounted.'[53]

Anderson made a point of giving the same technical instructions to male and female readers, and he chastised previous authors for not having done so: 'In the latest work on skating, the instructions for ladies learning are different from those for the other sex, but as it seems to me that whatever is easiest and best for the one sex is equally so for the other, I mean the same instructions for both. Fair readers have therefore only to substitute the feminine for the masculine pronoun as they read,[54] – a bit of semantic gymnastics that would have made it clear to women they were not his primary audience. Similarly, Anderson's decision to include a chapter directed to ladies with 'a few hints' on how to proceed in the course of their practice told female skaters they were a special case. Did men not need similar advice?

In Vienna, ice dancing was the motivation for many bourgeois women and men to take up skating. In Britain, skating with a partner (without music, of course) was called hand-in-hand skating. It was promoted as a method by which women – never men – could learn to skate more quickly. Hand-in-hand skating was generally performed by a woman and a man together. One of its touted advantages was that a strong gentleman could keep a novice lady from falling; gentlemen were encouraged to learn hand-in-hand figures specifically to have the pleasure of teaching them to ladies. One never reads of a more experienced woman, or man for that matter, offering the same assistance to a novice gentleman. Men were simply expected to buck up and learn the basics on their own.

Beyond the basics, hand-in-hand skating was said to present the opportunity of 'teaching ladies how to skate all sorts of figures that they would probably never otherwise learn.' For instance, 'When a gentleman asks a lady who has never attempted a rocker [a type of turn] to skate one with him, the suggestion is generally looked upon as a joke,' wrote T. Maxwell Witham, 'as the very term rocker implies a degree of perfection that very few ladies hope to attain; but, although they might not be able to execute this awe-inspiring movement as an individual figure, they will find that it is by no means difficult when attempted with a partner.'[55] In a special chapter for ladies in Douglas Adams's 1890 book *Skating*, Miss L. Cheetham wrote that hand-in-hand skating was 'pre-eminently suited to ladies ... The figures are ... *the* prettiest things on the ice ... More than all, hand-in-hand figures are easy.'[56] She too found them a great encouragement to the beginner.

The advice regarding rockers notwithstanding, there is little sense in any of these texts that women, once past the treacherous and embarrassing beginning stages, were not as capable as men. Indeed, Madge Syers – the first female world and Olympic champion – foreshadowed attitudes to come when she wrote in 1908 that men are often too slow and heavy to be good skaters.[57] Other writers suggested that women should excel on skates because they were naturally more graceful than men. Diamantidi, von Korper, and Wirth found women more graceful and their skating more delicate than men's. Swift and Clark thought likewise. Some writers noted the appropriateness of certain moves, steps, or techniques for women. Parisian George Vail wanted women to show off their feminine grace with long, undulating steps. Miss Cheetham wanted women to focus on moves that look pretty. While she found women capable of performing the same things as men, 'there are some figures which, though they do not look bad for them, are not really elegant or graceful for us.' For example, Cheetham argued, a continuous figure – a complicated series of movements performed on one foot, a North American speciality – was not pretty enough for a woman. It wasn't a question of not being able to do the one-foot figures, as she herself sometimes practised them, but to achieve the required speed 'necessitate[d] so much kick [of the free leg] as to make them ugly ... I know that this was the case as regards some foreign champions whom I have several times seen. Their speed and agility were marvellous, but, in my opinion, too acrobatic to be quite gentlemanly, to say nothing of ladylike.'[58] And English skaters were meant to be, above all, ladies and gentlemen.

The social aspects of skating helped to get women on the ice. And it was to women's benefit that skating in the last decades of the 1800s had yet to be fully recast as a sport – for sport in that period was still no place for ladies. The longer it took for figure skating to be seen primarily as an athletic rather than a social or artistic pursuit, the easier it would be for women to choose to do it.

Making Competitive Sport of the Pretty Art

In many ways it is surprising that figure skating ever became a competitive sport. At the time of the first competitions in the 1860s, the equipment was still awkward and ice conditions were unreliable or dangerous – practising was not always possible. Moreover, figure skating bore scant resemblance to other competitive sports: it was not suited to head-to-head competition; it was not about speed or strength or endurance or goal scoring. In Vienna, where some of the best-documented early competitions took place, figure skating was about performance and aesthetics. Comparisons between skaters were likely inevitable: Who looked better while cutting their figures? Who left the best tracings on the ice? Who invented the most interesting moves? That skaters attempted to answer such questions in the context of competitive sport suggests the rising prominence of sport in late-nineteenth-century culture. It also points to the narrowing of the realm of men's physical culture in an increasingly bourgeois environment, particularly in Great Britain and North America: sport provided one of the few social contexts in which middle- and upper-class men could receive social approval for using their bodies. Did the framing of figure skating as a sport make it seem more in line with changing conceptions of masculinity that were emerging as the middle class achieved greater social and cultural power at the end of the nineteenth century?

The unusual mix of aesthetic and competitive concerns that shaped skating over the last decades of the nineteenth century was a product of its development among well-to-do men and, increasingly towards the end of the century, women. Whether in Vienna, London, Montreal, or Boston, figure skating was just one of the many activities that set the privileged apart. Style had been central to definitions of skating skill since the first texts of Jones and Garcin in the late 1700s and early 1800s. And while notions of style were different in different national contexts, as we saw in the previous chapter, its importance to skaters did not diminish even as they bent their art to fit a competitive framework. And thus, figure skating was, according to at least one commentator, the first judged aesthetic sport: 'Skating is absolutely the only sport in which competitors are marked both for the doing of a thing and for the way it is done, it is the only one in which grace is a factor to which such a special recognition is awarded.'[59]

Figure skaters were on new ground as they attempted to develop a manner of comparing performances. The persistent definition of skating as an art seems not to have gotten in the way of attempts to make it a contest. Nor, apparently, did the presence of a significant, if not yet equal, number of women skaters. Somehow skaters managed to reconcile an understanding of competitions as demonstrations of manly competence with the fact that many women skaters had technical abilities equal to those of men. In some cases, this contradiction was resolved, so that women figure skaters had competitive opportunities far in advance of women in other sports. In other cases, women were simply left off the schedule, as we will see below. One wonders how skating would have evolved had women rather than men been predominant in its early years, as they are now. Would it have become a sport? Would figure skating have progressed as a branch of the performing arts, as Jackson Haines had wanted it to, or would it simply have remained a pleasurable social skill?

We don't know much about early figure skating competitions. Who competed? For what rewards? How? Early competitions in Canada were often held as profit-making ventures for promoters or for the owners of private rinks. Some of these events tested the better performers at fancy-dress ice balls, providing prestige for the rink and entertainment for the other skaters and spectators.[60] A competition in Troy, New York, in 1863 was called the Championship of America and was won by skating artist Jackson Haines. With no overseeing body, any contest could be dubbed a national championship, and more than one skater may have made claim to the title at any given time. Because rules varied from town to town, competitors were often asked to sign an 'article of agreement' that outlined the figures to be skated and the points they were worth.[61] It was a situation that made a home-ice advantage quite real.

Early Viennese competitions are better documented than those in North America or elsewhere in Europe; in them we can see the roots of modern championships. At an event in 1872 called the International Ice Sport Day the best male skaters from Vienna competed against the best from northern Germany. They had to perform compulsory figures, special figures (newly invented by the competitor himself), and a free skating program which likely would have been a series of turns or figures joined together and perhaps embellished with spins or spirals. Three years later, in 1875, the WEV held the first documented women's competition. The twelve local competitors did forward and backward threes, forward and backward figure eights, double and triple threes on one foot (two or three 3-turns, in a row), waltz steps, loops (a figure in which the blade draws a large loop on the ice), spirals, and the Flying Mercury pose (see figure 4.2; described by the English writer Robert Jones in 1772 and later denounced by some English skaters as overly florid, although they probably would have approved of women doing it). One newspaper took pleasure in the fact that Viennese women could perform feats that 'in some cities no man is able to do,'[62] suggesting that in the context of regional rivalries, the prowess of women skaters was cause for pride rather than alarm. Was this because skating itself did not seem, despite its competitive framework, like other sports and so was not considered inappropriate for women? Or because women were able to compete in their usual feminine garb without challenging feminine standards of deportment?

At a competition at the WEV in 1879, the novelty of electric lights was as big a draw as the skaters. The night-time competition for male skaters from the club was meant to showcase the developments in skating since the Ice Sport Day seven years earlier.[63] The men performed threes and double-threes, eights, loops in all directions, and combined special figures. Mr Schönbach skated twenty figure-eights on one foot, Mr Biberhofer did an artful three and loop combination, Mr Bellazi skated most elegantly, and Mr Röhringer did a huge spiral backwards.[64] Local critics were well pleased with the progress of the sport. In 1882, the Viennese club invited male skaters from Austria, Germany, England, the United States, and Norway (though not all attended) to compete for prizes worth 8500 francs in gold. In anticipation of the event, which was promoted as an ice party, the WEV constructed stands for eight hundred spectators. As the first important international competition, organizers had hoped that it would 'lead to fraternization of all skating nations on neutral terrain of a sport that strengthens and refreshes the spirit.'[65] They also wanted to 'try out' and, no doubt, promote the Viennese system of figures that had been developed by Carl von Korper, illustrated by Demeter Diamantidi, and given a historical context by Max Wirth in the 1881 book *Tracks on the Ice*. It is interesting that the events in 1879 and 1882, both intended as technical exhibitions, were organized not simply as demonstrations but as competitions.

On the first day of the International Figure Skating Competition in 1882, the skaters were required to do either eighteen or twenty-three figures (depending on which source one consults), in all four directions (backwards and forwards, left and right), including 'daring threes and snake-threes'[66] (a change of edge from outside to inside or inside to outside that was followed by a 3-turn on the same foot, so that the drawing

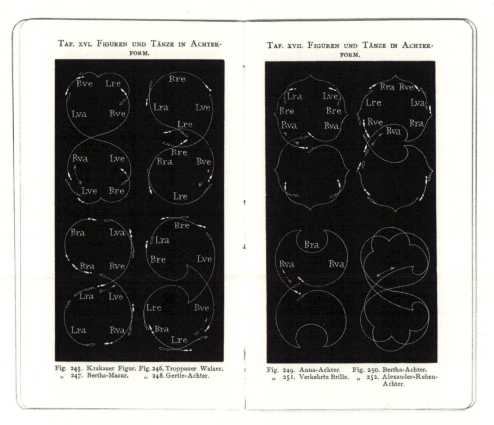

Figure 5.1 Figures and dance steps in eight-form. The notations identify forward and backward outside and inside edges. The image is taken from a pocket-sized supplement to the second edition of *Spuren auf dem Eise* [Tracks on the Ice] by Demeter Diamantidi, Carl von Korper, and Max Wirth, published in Vienna in 1892. Skaters could have referred to the booklet while practising.

on the ice would be a large 'S' joined to a 3). In either case, this was a staggering number of figures and would have tried the stamina of judges, participants, and spectators, thousands of whom gathered outside the rink, had the unusually warm weather not limited the field to only two skaters.[67] Conditions were more favourable the second day when the special figures were held. These were figures that combined turns and free skating moves or fancy designs of a skater's own invention. The judges were looking to award the prize to the skater 'who does his figure in the most correct and most certain way.' Audience members had different criteria, and gave the most 'vivid applause' to skaters 'with an admirable competence who skated daring and hair-raising figures.'[68] It was at this competition that Norwegian Axel Paulsen performed the jump that still carries his name, one and a half revolutions that begin on a front outside edge and end on a back outside edge on the opposite foot. In an era when most skaters kept their feet firmly planted on the ground and when many skaters felt that jumps contravened the elegance of their art, Paulsen must have given spectators a thrill. But despite his now famous jump and his ability to spin as 'fast as a storm,' he placed third. Dash and athleticism were obviously not all that mattered to the judges. With an emphasis on both technical and aesthetic dimensions, figure skating was clearly not evolving along the lines of other competitive sports.

Over a period of slightly more than a decade, Viennese skaters developed the framework of what would become a long-standing format for competition. The skating that was performed at competitions was based on a particular repertoire of figures (theirs, of course) that highlighted technique and style. To compete, a skater needed to master a shared body of knowledge that was assumed to represent the apex of skill and accomplishment at the time: various kinds of figure eights, turns, and changes of edges, all carefully illustrated in *Tracks on the Ice*. This formal skating repertoire was *figure skating*, a very different kind of skating than the sociable waltzing or pleasant, unencumbered gliding that had prompted the increases in skating's popularity. The institutionalizing of this version of skating helped to ensure that only those skaters with considerable leisure time and, therefore, the money that made it possible, could participate. While the special figures, which might include step sequences, new figure designs, or completely new techniques like Paulsen's jump, allowed skaters to express some creativity, they were, in these early days, of secondary importance, at least to the Viennese who were trying to institutionalize their time-consuming system of compulsory figure exercises.

Skating competitions could have been organized to measure a whole different set of skills or qualities, ones that might have seemed more akin to the skills measured in other sports. Judges could have chosen to measure the height of jumps, the number of revolutions of spins, the length of time a skater could perform combinations or figures on one foot, the number of turns a skater could perform in a given time or over a given distance. Or judges could have dispensed altogether with figures to focus solely on imaginative sequences of moves or on innovation and daring skills like Paulsen's jump (as contemporary competitions do). That figures became paramount says much about the distance of late-nineteenth-century, upper-class sport from spectacle. Two- and sometimes three-day-long figure competitions in cold outdoor rinks could not have been any less spectacular.

For all their geometrical precision, the exacting technique required to perform them correctly, and the tracks they left on the ice, figures must have seemed like the most objective part of skating to evaluate. The process of assessing them was not quite as clear-cut as measuring the speed of a running race or the distance of a javelin throw, but it would have seemed far easier than comparing a new jump, for instance, to a new spin, although judges did compare these as well. Of course, it was not too long before the sport was hit with the first judging controversies and the difficulty of marking figures consistently and objectively became apparent. Nevertheless, the heavy emphasis on figures would have left an impression of skating as something other than a frivolous social pastime or a fanciful art. Figures were the masculine, rational side of skating. Figures were science. At a time when the athleticism of free skating was not yet fully developed, figures definitely made sense within the discourses around technical innovation that were key to the development of many late-nineteenth-century sports. Figures also permitted well-to-do men to perform and compete in public without contravening upper-class standards of dignified bodily comportment. It would be a century before the changing exigencies of the mediated sports world would render figures obsolete and they would be eliminated from competition altogether.

National Associations

Attempts by skaters and officials to promote their own versions of the new sport led to disagreement and frustration, and it is often argued that this was the ground from which national skating associations grew. It is somewhat ironic, then, that the first association, the National Skating Association of Great Britain (NSA), had little to do with the desire of competitors for consistency. Indeed, the figure skating department of the NSA had nothing whatsoever to do with competition – many of the gentlemen figure skaters felt competition to be incompatible with their sporting ideals. The NSA was conceived by James Drake Digby, a Cambridge journalist who was concerned about the cheating that stemmed from betting on speed skating races. He thought the sport of speed skating needed to be standardized and that the speed skaters themselves needed greater recognition. So in 1879 a committee of fifteen men founded the NSA. As Dennis Bird writes, 'All of course were gentlemen; it was not intended that the Fen speed skaters from the agricultural labouring classes should control their own sport.'[69] One of the early decisions made by the organization was to stop awarding prize money as lump-sum payments to speed skaters. Instead, the NSA officials decided to bestow a 'moderate amount' of money at the time of the race, with the rest to follow in the form of an annual income. Their goal was to 'make the champion keep himself temperate.'[70] This kind of patronizing behaviour was an inevitable product of the heavily stratified class system that dominated English Victorian society. Members of the upper classes felt that they had the right to control working-class behaviours and that such control was for working-class people's 'own good.' Underneath such attitudes was a firm belief that members of the upper and working classes were different types of people, with not just different resources but different innate capacities. Their two very different kinds of skating confirmed the point.

Figure skaters were not included in the NSA at the outset; Digby and members of his committee did not want to be seen to be stepping on the toes of their social equals. Figure skating was already organized by the clubs, and it was not clear that these clubs would want to affiliate with a national body. But in 1880 a meeting was held in London to discuss such an affiliation. The main object of a governing body would be to organize for figure skaters a series of graded tests that had been proposed and designed by Henry Vandervell as a means of encouraging beginners and improving the general level of skating. The proposal was not looked upon favourably by all skaters. Some feared that tests and any awards that might follow from them would lead skating down the dreaded path of professionalism. Others thought the tests would help skaters and the sport itself to advance. The testing advocates won out. In 1880 the figure skaters elected to join the NSA, and a three-part series of tests was introduced that same year. By the end of the first season there were fifty bronze medalists. By 1883 there were ninety-two bronze medalists, sixteen silver medalists, and seven gold medalists, 'including a lady,' Miss Lily Cheetham of Southport, whom we met earlier.[71] Other women, including her sister, followed in due course. Women's proficiency on the ice did not, however, translate into power in the organization; they were not permitted on NSA committees until 1939, presumably because male skaters were unavailable during wartime.

Although some British skaters and officials participated at international meets during the last decades of the 1800s, British skaters resisted competition. As late as 1900 a proposal to hold British championships for individual skaters was met with derision by some members of the NSA. In the previous year, the organization had sanctioned the first competition among combined-skating teams (which was won by a mixed team, composed of three men and one woman). While no harm was seen in competitions between teams, a quest for individual glory at the expense of another skater was thought to be unseemly and not befitting a gentleman: 'The idea of a British figure-skating championship is undoubtedly repugnant to most members of the leading figure-skating clubs.'[72] Dissenters argued that individual competition would lead to the crowning of champions, and from there it was a slippery slope towards professionalism and its attendant problems of unsportsmanlike behaviour, cheating, or gambling.[73] Nevertheless, the promoters of individual championships eventually won out with their argument that competitions were the best way of propelling the technical advancement of the art. The first championship in the English style was held in 1902. The first British championship in the international or continental style of skating was held in 1903 and was won by Madge Syers.

Three more national skating organizations formed in the 1880s, in the Netherlands (1882), in Canada (1887), and in Germany and Austria (1888). These new organizations helped to channel some of the frustrations of early international competitors and set the ground for the emergence of an international governing body for speed and figure skating. While much of the impetus for the International Skating Union came from speed skaters looking to promote their competing views on what a race should look like, figure skaters also contributed to the process. In an era long before state sponsorship of athletes, the prospect of international competitions must have seemed more within the grasp of upper-class figure skaters than working-class racers.

In 1890, what is now called an 'unofficial world championship' (that is a pre–International Skating Union championship) was held in St Petersburg. The participants probably felt official enough at the time, even as they argued over the format of the competition and the advantages it gave to certain skaters. Canadian skater Louis Rubenstein was the only North American competitor at the event. As a Jew, Rubenstein faced the anti-Semitism of the tsarist regime. He was repeatedly pressured by the police to leave the country, and was only permitted to stay and compete after intervention by the British ambassador. By all accounts, Rubenstein hated the set-up of the Russian competition, and he worried about the absence of restrictions on conflict of interest. As he told the *Montreal Gazette*, 'There were nine judges, but with the exception of two, they appeared to know very little about fine skating ... Of the nine judges, seven of them were local men ... [and they] acted as coaches to the home men, instructing them what to do. Three of them made a regular practice to watch me at work.'[74] No doubt Rubenstein would have been supportive of the Europeans who met in 1892 to set up an international body to codify and regulate the sport.

Founded in 1892, the International Skating Union (ISU) adopted rules for speed skating immediately. Rules for figure skating were not adopted until 1897. The delay signalled differences of opinion, tense relations between some of the early members of the ISU (the result of judging controversies at European championships held in Hamburg in 1891 and Berlin in 1893),[75] and, one might reasonably assume, the difficulty of squeezing the slow, graphic exercise of compulsory figures into a competitive sporting framework. There is a sense in much historical writing about figure skating that its transformation into a sport was inevitable. It's almost as if the activity itself had some germ of 'sportness' inside it just waiting to be set free by the men of the ISU. It is an assumption that is not unique to figure skating; it appears in a lot of historical writing about sport. But it is important to remember that the development of modern competitive sports was in no way inevitable. Competition is no more naturally a part of physical activity than it is a part of painting or gardening. Certain physical activities became competitive because people made them competitive. Competition emerges and is promoted as a way of organizing physical exercises because there are – especially in capitalist societies – valuable social, political, and economic benefits to be gained from 'naturalizing' it.

Ironically, the first official ISU world championship was held in 1896, one year before the rules of figure skating were approved; all 'official' meant in this case was that the governing body gave its stamp of approval. At this championship and at the five that followed, all the competitors were men, although the competitor lists were so small that this may have been as much a question of logistics as gender. In 1896, for instance, there were only four entrants; in 1900 there were only two. So when Madge Syers of England entered the world championship in

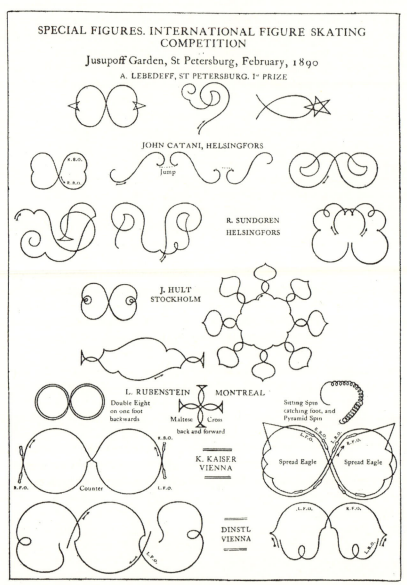

Figure 5.2 Special figures performed by the competitors at an international competition in St Petersburg in 1890. The illustration is taken from *The Art of Skating* by Irving Brokaw, published in London by Letchworth at the Arden Press in 1910.

London in 1902, she joined a select group of skaters, perhaps character-ized more by their ability to train and to travel internationally, that is, characterized more by their class than their sex. With no specific provi-sions to prevent women from skating, ISU officials had to allow Syers to compete. She placed second behind the Swedish skater Ulrich Salchow (after whom the jump is named). ISU officials were not impressed. At their next meeting in 1903 they voted six to three to bar women from future ISU championships. In 1905 they relented, agreeing to set up a separate women's event the following year.

The British association was among the minority advocating for women competitors. British ISU delegate G.H. Fowler said that several issues were raised to justify what he believed to be an unfair ban:

(1) that the dress prevents the Judges from seeing the feet; to this we answer that it is impossible to skate figures properly in a long dress, the dress *must* be short;

(2) that a Judge might judge a girl to whom he was attached; we reply that if a man were so little of an honourable sportsman as to be willing to judge in this case, his Association would certainly not permit it;

(3) that it is difficult to compare women with men; we respond that the woman must be judged in every respect exactly as a man is judged.[76]

Fowler's responses were well in keeping with British practice. Wom-en not only competed as part of four-member teams in English-style events (Madge Syers was, again, the first to do this), but British women and men also competed against each other for the Swedish Cup, the prize for the British figure skating championship in the International Style, from 1903 until 1926. Separate women's and men's champion-ships were not held in Britain until 1927. Madge Syers was the first winner of the Swedish Cup in 1903. She won again in 1904, beating her husband Edgar, who placed second. In North America women and men were also competing against each other in some events in the 1910s. Boston skater Teresa Weld, as one example, beat men on more than one occasion. A report of her win at a 1917 competition at New York's Hippodrome claimed that even the 'veriest tyro among the spec-tators knew that she would. And her sumptuous ... crimson costume and her attractive girlish vivacity had nothing to do with the decision, either.'[77] As the professional skating star Charlotte wrote in 1916, 'Up to within a few years ago, the figure skating championships of Europe were open to both men and women on equal terms. Perhaps the fact

that women excelled in grace was partially responsible for the separation of the sexes in these championships.'[78]

That women and men once competed against each other is a remarkable piece of sporting history, although figure skating is not unique
in this sense, as we will see in the next chapter. Long before skating
became a jump fest in which technical achievement was prized above
artistic development, it was assumed that men and women were capable of similar levels of performance. Today some people laud figure
skating because it is one of the few sports where male/female teams
compete against other male/female teams. While this is true, figure
skating's pair and dance events are structured by strict notions of heterosexuality and by the idea that the differences between men and
women need not just be accommodated but be advertised. Early competitions made evident no such assumptions. Not only did men and
women compete against each other, but pairs could be composed of
two men or two women or a man and a woman. To an extent that is
unimaginable today, skaters were skaters, despite clothing and commentary that may have suggested otherwise. Indeed, the present-day
viewer of filmed skating competitions from the 1920s cannot help but
remark at the similarity in the styles of male and female singles skaters.
The steps are mostly similar, the embellishments are similar, the technical abilities are similar. Were the skaters dressed alike, there would be
little difference. In today's skating, one of the main differences between
men's and women's performances lies in the use of the arms and the
upper body. But in the 1920s, skaters only rarely raised their arms above
waist-level, so this avenue through which they might have constructed
gendered impressions was not open to them. Overall, skating in the
1920s was less embellished; it had not yet become the kind of theatrical performance that we are used to today. And so skaters had fewer
mechanisms through which to present themselves differently from
each other, whether in terms of gender or other aesthetic qualities.[79]

When ISU delegates finally instituted a championship for women,
they did not completely let go of their prejudices. From 1906 until
1924 the women's event was held separately from the men's and was
known simply as the Women's Championship of the ISU – the title of
world champion was available only to men. The International Olympic
Committee was not so stingy. Figure skating was the fourth sport to be
opened to women, after golf and tennis in 1900 and archery in 1904. A
woman's event was included on the schedule of the first Olympic skating competition, which was part of the 1908 London summer games,

held at one of London's glamorous indoor rinks. Madge Syers won the gold medal. The presence of the figure skaters brought the total number of female athletes at the Games up to 43, or 2.1 per cent of all the athletes competing.[80] Figure skating appeared once more at the summer Olympics in 1920 in Antwerp. When the winter games began in 1924, figure skating was the only sport for women until skiing was added in 1936.

By the end of the nineteenth century figure skating had been 'sportified.'[81] But it was a sport unlike any other at the time: with its emphasis on aesthetics it confounded definitions of sports as rational, easily measurable activities; with its large number of female participants it defied the notion that sports were the makers of men. Yet the fact that the male skaters who controlled the organization of figure skating felt the need to force their 'art' into a competitive framework suggests the social value which accrued to sports and the power of sporting discourses as a way of making sense of men's physical cultures in the late 1800s. But while other sportsmen invoked competition to see who was the strongest or the fastest, skaters competed among themselves and with and against women to see who looked the most beautiful, who performed the most gracefully, who drew the best tracings on the ice. These were not the gendered values that prevailed among the increasingly powerful white bourgeois classes in Europe and North America. Nor were they the values of the men who looked to field sports or team games to prove their masculinity. They were not the characteristics required by empire. The values promoted in skating were remnants of an elegant upper-class physicality; the actual movements performed by skaters continued to show clear links to figure skating's aristocratic past. But, its new context as competitive sport suggests the ascendency of middle-class values and middle-class discourses about gender. As we see in the next chapter, figure skating's increasingly middle-class character was eventually an important aspect of its feminization.

6 'They Left the Men Nowhere': The Feminization of Skating

By the early 1900s, figure skating was a distinct branch of skating, established as a competitive sport in Britain, much of Europe, and North America. It was no longer the exclusive preserve of men, as it had been just half a century before. In many contexts it was no longer even male dominated. In North American and European cities, gendered membership practices were being abandoned, with women and men both having access to ice, clubs, and competitions. While the skating bureaucracy would not approach gender equality for decades (and still has not in some jurisdictions), the culture of most rinks was, for the time and the sporting context, *relatively* gender balanced, a fact about which some skaters boasted. This is not to say that gender was irrelevant in figure skating, but it does seem to have been less central to the explicit organization of skating than it was to the organization of other sports at that time (or this time!). While women in many other sports were struggling to establish their credibility and to gain access to athletic venues and tournaments, women in skating were not only training with men but were often beating them in competition. How was it that figure skaters had the opportunity to develop and demonstrate their physical skills while many other sportswomen did not?

Female skaters, of course, wore skirts and moved gracefully, they didn't sweat too much or come into physical contact with their opponents. As more than one writer claimed, skating seemed well suited to the 'natural' characteristics of ladies:

It may be said without fear of serious contradiction that ladies not only skate as well as men, but that as a body, they are the better skaters. They seem to pass more readily, more smoothly and with less conscious effort, from one edge to another, from one position to another. Their lack of physical muscularity, so far from being a disability, is a positive advantage, and serves to enhance the quality of their skating, making it more feathery and less compact than that of the male skater.[1]

Skating's emphasis on aesthetics and its requirements for ease and fluidity contrasted markedly with the intentional 'roughness' of sports like field hockey or basketball. There is no question that the advancement of women in figure skating depended heavily on their ability to achieve high levels of technical skill while respecting the exigencies of narrow feminine norms, norms that defined vigorous sport as not just unbecoming but debilitating to ladies. It also probably helped that – in spite of its competitive structure, its trophies and champions – figure skating did not look much like other sports. Although some middle-class sporting women in Western industrialized societies had begun to gain ground in the late nineteenth and early twentieth centuries, competitive feeling and athletic ability were still widely considered to be masculine traits. The fact that skating did not fit easily into the prevailing model of (manlier) sports must have made it easier for women's husbands or their parents to condone their skating, and must, therefore, have made it easier for women to succeed. As one critic noted of the 1908 Olympic Games, 'Figure skating on artificial ice ... seemed a very long way from manly athletics, whatever its beauty.'[2]

While this view of skating as not quite like other sports may have facilitated women's participation, what did it mean to men? Did it not bother them that their sport of choice was perceived to be of a different character than manly athletics? Skating texts from the early twentieth century present little evidence of the kind of defensive response that this view has elicited from male skaters, especially in North America, since the Second World War. A rare example appears in a First World War–era interview with Edgar Syers (husband of the more famous Madge):

And if any of your muscular, brawny, and deep-lunged B.O.P.-ites [readers of the English magazine *Boys' Own Paper*] chance to make the mistake of imagining figure skating to be just a 'soft thing,' they should sample the five minutes' 'free skating' to music such as is involved in any bid for figure skating championship honours. It is real hard work, as I can readily testify, and when the five minutes are up, I doubt if any contestant regrets their passing.[3]

Syers goes on to point out that many 'champion skaters are men of fine physique.' He claimed to know one 'genial Continental champion who had six poached eggs in his soup every day just as a start before dinner!'[4]

Syers's claims notwithstanding, figure skating did not explicitly offer the muscularity or homosocial male-bonding opportunities that advocates of boys' and men's sports found so important. Yet male skaters do not appear to have minded. Had they been heavily invested in a different kind of manly contest or in man-to-man bonding they certainly had the power to design a competitive version of skating to fit that model and to make it less accommodating to women. But they did not. There is very little suggestion in the skating literature – almost all of which was written by men – that the manliness of skating (or lack thereof) was cause for concern or that women's presence on the ice was in any way questioned. In general, men who wrote publicly about skating seemed very much to want women to skate and to skate well, and not only because they wanted female waltzing partners or because they appreciated the heterosexual social opportunities that skating provided. Indeed, some skating writers seemed quite chuffed to be involved in a form of physical exercise that was open to both sexes. Some even hoped their sport would inspire women's involvement in other athletic pursuits. The following, from a chapter on skating, appeared in the final report on the 1908 London Olympic Games, the first at which figure skaters competed:

> More [Olympic] events, in fact, might be open to women, whether they are permitted to compete with men or not. They have already so competed, successfully, in the case of Mrs. Syers in international skating meetings. They have competed in skating, archery, and lawn tennis in the Olympic Games. Perhaps it may be worth considering whether in future Olympiads they may not also enter for swimming, diving, and gymnastics, three branches of physical exercise in which they gave most attractive [noncompetitive] displays during the Games in London. In rifle-shooting, and possibly in other sports, they may also have a fair chance of success in open [mixed-sex] competitions. But it is not probable that in any physical exercise they will ever both demonstrate their superiority and also preserve their characteristic charm so convincingly as in such skating as was seen at Prince's [Skating Club] during the Autumn Games of 1908.[5]

The plea here is definitely to increase women's involvement in high-level competitive sport, though only in sports of a certain kind, of which skating stands as the finest example. The argument rests on an understanding of skating as a sport particularly suited to women.

Advocates for female athletes have been justifiably critical of attempts, historical and contemporary, to divide sports into those suited to men and those suited to women; they are well aware that 'sport' and 'women's sport' are not equal categories and that in the present day the labels 'women's sport,' or worse, 'girls' sport,' tends to mark a sport as inferior and inappropriate for men. We need to be careful, however, not to impose today's gender categories on sports in earlier time periods. In looking back at calls for women to participate in gender-appropriate sports, we are right to see the constrained gender ideology and limited understanding of women's physical capabilities from which they grew. Women were not, after all, being encouraged to take up football. But we also need to see these calls as efforts to gain for women access to sports that still belonged to men. To say that they were appropriate for women was not to mark the sports as inferior, which would have been to insult male participants, but to suggest that women deserved to and were capable of playing them as well. It was not until women began to surpass men in terms of skill and to outnumber them on rinks that figure skating came to be seen as feminine and therefore inferior to those sports in which men continued to predominate.

Gendered sport categories are not natural or inevitable. One of the main tasks of this book is to demonstrate how historically contingent our notions of men's and women's sport categories are – figure skating, as an excellent example of this, managed to cover all points on the continuum in less than a century. There is nothing inherent in forms of movement that makes them masculine or feminine. Gendered adjectives are applied to sports, and other forms of human behaviour, in accordance with the culturally specific definitions of masculinity and femininity that circulate at particular times and that are given shape by discourses of race, nation, and class. These definitions change.

In this chapter I look at how the gendered adjectives applied to figure skating shifted over the first half of the twentieth century. From a relatively gender-balanced (if not completely equitable) sport at the turn of the century, figure skating was widely identifiable as a girls' sport by the end of the Second World War. By that time, clubs were struggling to attract boys and men. Girls and women were dancing without male partners. Skating officials were having to work hard to promote the value of their sport as a masculine pursuit. What conditions brought about this shift in skating's image? From where did the notion of skating as a 'girls' sport' come?

Unremarkable Similarities

With their physical accomplishments buffered by their 'characteristic charm,' women figure skaters made significant headway after the turn of the century, and not just in segregated corners of their sport. Indeed, the segregated corners that did exist were relatively few in number, the single-sex events at some competitions being the main example. Men and women practised almost all the same moves, on the same ice, at the same time, as they do today, with some technical exceptions and gendered stylistic differences. They were evaluated on the same skills on their proficiency tests. Surprisingly, the sameness of women's and men's skating does not seem to have put feminine or masculine gender identities at risk – as it would come to do only a few decades later. In accounts of skating competitions in Europe and North America, men and women were both described with adjectives like 'graceful,' 'beautiful,' and 'powerful' that might in other contexts have been strong signifiers of normative gender attributes. An Austrian sport newspaper, for instance, complimented Swedish skater Henning Grenander on his 'delicate graceful legs and his flexibility.'[6] By contrast, the *New York Times* praised a Mrs Beresford for a 'bold and athletic' style and 'strong sweeping strokes.'[7]

In Britain it was considered appropriate for men and women to compete against each other for the national title until 1927. There had certainly been no consternation on the occasion of Madge Syers's second-place finish when she competed with men in the 1902 world championships, as evidenced by the fact that even the king and queen sent a message expressing their pleasure 'that an English lady had created a unique and permanent record by her beautiful skating and remarkable success.'[8] By the 1920s, in both England and the United States, skating observers were commenting favourably on the fact that women and men were equally competent skaters.[9] Some male writers argued explicitly against those International Skating Union (ISU) regulations, like the shorter required times for women's free programs (which persists today) or the fewer required figures in women's events, that suggested women were not as capable as men.[10] Two things are important here. First, women were not considered to have been 'masculinized' by their sport by performing the same skills as men, by competing against men, or by beating men. Second, men do not appear to have felt threatened by women's ability to match them.

From the perspective of the present day, this indifference surprises. The traditional plot of the history of women's sport tends to emphasize exclusion, gender segregation, and the role sport played in helping to constitute and support cultural understandings of men's and women's different – unequal – physical capabilities. As historian Kathleen McCrone has put it (while also acknowledging that sport did have some liberatory potential for Victorian women), sport 'was a repressive and constraining mechanism that deliberately idealised maleness and kept women separate and inferior to men.'[11] There is certainly plenty of justification for such an emphasis.[12] With a few exceptions, like lawn tennis and riding, the basic story line of the gender history of sport goes something like this: In the nineteenth century, middle-class English men made of earlier games and physical activities highly structured, competitive sports. Sport became associated with socially valued masculine characteristics. Men's ability to play these sports was thought to contribute to and validate their virility. Sport made obvious the differences between masculinity and femininity that were important elements of Victorian upper- and middle-class cultures; it helped to justify and uphold the binary organization of gender in the culture at large. Women's participation and success in sport would have helped to minimize those differences and to undermine the whole ideological framework through which gender was constituted. For this reason, 'men's and women's sport, with a few exceptions, remained strictly segregated, and women's sport was severely circumscribed by the patriarchal nature of social relations.'[13] When women did get to participate in sport, they played apart from men, following different rules and styles of play. The typical story of women in sport, therefore, is a story of the efforts made to break through gender barriers that kept women from soccer pitches, golf links, and hockey arenas, and that constituted women's physicality as different from and lesser than men's.

In far too many instances, this story rings true. Nevertheless, segregation and exclusion are not the only themes in the history of women's sport. There were also sports, in the late nineteenth and early twentieth centuries, figure skating among them, in which gender segregation seems, during certain periods, not to have been central to the organization of the activity. The history of women in these sports is not a simple story of attempts to wrench the sports open to female participants; rather, it is a more complicated tale of women achieving, losing, and then trying to regain ground, a tale of women's achievements being redefined (read: de-valued) in light of shifting gender norms. The emergence and growth of male-controlled sporting bureaucracies often features prominently in this narrative. In their drive to codify certain competitive physical activities as sports and to impose upon them international standards, sporting officials – in some instances, on the advice of medical experts – enacted policies that made gender segregation seem normal and natural in sports.[14] In the worst cases, like ski jumping, skeleton tobogganing, and bobsledding, the institutionalization of the sports led not just to separating the sexes, but to prohibitions against women competing. For example, while the first official rules of bobsledding, written in the 1890s, *required* mixed-sex teams, women were completely excluded from the sport by the end of the 1930s.[15] Founded in 1923, the Fédération Internationale de Bobsleigh et de Tobogganing (FIBT) banned women from international competition in time to keep them out of the first Olympic bobsled competition in Chamonix in 1924. As Mike Cronin writes, once bobsledding came to be an elite sport, it was, all of a sudden, too dangerous for women.[16] National governing bodies followed the lead of the FIBT. In the United States women were barred from competition at the end of the 1930s, right after Katherine Dewey won the United States championship in 1938. It was not until the 1990s that women were able to compete in the sport at the Olympics, although they are still not permitted to compete in the same number of events as men. Had women simply been excluded from bobsledding from the beginning, the story would be far less troubling in terms of the way sport has not just reflected but contributed to the discourses and practices through which gender difference and, therefore, gender inequality, is constituted.

Synchronized swimming and skeleton tobogganing also had periods in which women and men competed against each other. In Olympic skeet shooting, total gender segregation was not established until 1996 – after a woman won the gold medal in 1992. What can we learn about gender from the non-segregated episodes in these sports? In figure skating, mixed gender competitions occurred in an era when men were clearly considered to be superior to women. What made it possible for women skaters to demonstrate equality with or superiority over men in competitive sport, a realm that was, according to most accounts, considered to be not just an important masculine domain but an important way of maintaining gender difference?

The pessimistic answer to these questions is that the gender discourses through which men's superiority over women was constituted may simply have been flexible enough to assimilate and dilute evidence of physical equality between the sexes, thus keeping men from feeling humiliated. However proficient women skaters had become, their talents and achievements were likely no match for overarching discourses of gender and sexual difference that framed women and men as inherently different and unequal in society generally. In the report on the Olympics that I cited above, the call for women's increased participation in the Games was justified by claims of its benefit to women's traditional maternal role and their potential contribution to the eugenic project. The report notes the 'successful appearance of ladies in these competitions,' and then suggests that 'since one of the chief objects of the revived Olympic Games is the physical development and amelioration of the race, it appears illogical to adhere so far to classical tradition as to provide so few opportunities for the participation of a predominant partner in the process of race-production.'[17] Giving women a chance to compete in Olympic sport would make them better mothers. American author Edward Gill used the same argument to promote recreational skating:

> If young ladies would become good skaters, they would be much better fitted to become mothers of American children. Let the ladies betake themselves to skating, and we shall doubtless see a more robust generation of children growing up betimes. This is an important consideration. Weak and sickly women are not good mothers. If the children are born of puny mothers, the race degenerates, mentally and physically ... Let the girls prepare their skates and spread themselves, when the skating carnival begins, for they will not only do themselves good, but will enhance the glory of the American eagle, the star-spangled banner, and all that sort of thing.[18]

The assumption that skaters would be healthy white middle- or upper-class women was key to the racial betterment argument. So was the notion that the white race should be 'better' than the racial groups against which white people constituted their identities.

Some historians have suggested that sportswomen were 'permitted' to excel or to compete with men only in those situations where the outcomes were not important.[19] The elite classes in North America and Europe had a history of mixed-gender recreation and play. Tennis, archery, and various winter sports, including recreational skating and figure skating, all provided opportunities for upper-class men and women to socialize with each other in an environment of respectability and exclusivity. In the proper company, these activities were as much about flirting, courtship, and meeting the right kind of people as they were about physical achievement and competition. A woman beating a man at Sunday afternoon tennis was nothing more than a bit of fun, a conversation piece to present at the evening's supper. As Ellen Guber wrote in an early feminist article on the history of women's sport, the level of play was so low, no one cared who won.[20] But this was definitely not the case when Madge Syers won the silver medal at the ISU-sanctioned world figure skating championship in 1902. Nor was it likely the case over the almost three decades of mixed-sex national championship meets in England, nor during the many mixed-sex competitions that took place in the eastern parts of North America in the 1910s. While some skaters pursued figure skating as a simple recreational pastime, the men and women who competed nationally and internationally made considerable investments in their sport. At the very least, we know this because of the enormous repertoire of school figures they needed to be able to perform – more than eighty variations, a number far too great to be mastered by casual skaters.

In the case of figure skating, the indifference to women's competence was not related to low levels of competition. These events were taken seriously by their competitors: they were attended by royalty and other dignitaries; they were reported upon in respected newspapers; they were dissected and reviewed in widely circulated sports magazines. It is therefore difficult not to conclude that the men who participated in them did not consider it humiliating to be defeated by a woman or to have that defeat broadcast in the press. In England, where the practice of holding mixed-sex events was most widespread, it is reasonable to assume that had male participants felt badly enough, the men in charge of the National Skating Association would have eliminated the opportunity for open competitions long before they actually did. The examples of figure skating and other sports where men and women achieved the same levels of competence, and where they tested their skills against each other, suggest that sport scholars need to develop more layered narratives of women's and men's experiences of sport and our understandings of sport's relationship to gender in earlier time periods.

Of course, what makes figure skating unique among sports is that its many dimensions are not completely contained by standard definitions of sport that privilege the fastest, highest, and strongest performances. And it is perhaps this fact that accounts best for the acceptance of women's skating abilities. For instance, the ISU took very different approaches to women's participation in speed skating and figure skating. Speed skating, more easily recognizable as a typical sport, was not granted a women's world championship until 1936 and women speed skaters were not allowed to compete in the Olympics until 1960 – more than half a century after women figure skaters. In contrast to speed skating, figure skating was something of a hybrid, considered by some proponents to be a singular example of a manly sport and by others to be a fine art. The possibility of understanding figure skating through more than one discourse meant that male and female skaters, should they have desired to, could have judged themselves and their behaviour by standards unrelated to sport. Here, the relationship between upper-class identities and cultural ambitions was likely key to the meaning skaters took from what they did. The arts, skating included, offered the privileged classes an opportunity to demonstrate the refined tastes and elegance that were expected of men and women of high social and economic standing. No doubt the ability of upper-class male figure skaters to endure unfavourable comparisons with women skaters in their mutual sport had something to do with it not being just a sport.

The argument here is not that the success of women skaters, as compared to men, eliminated gender inequities or gender difference from the sport. While women had many opportunities in figure skating, they still experienced the effects of broadly inequitable gender ideologies that prevailed in the culture at large. Any number of small injustices let women know that they were still not the norm as athletes, especially at the level of international competition. Women's supposedly weaker constitutions were accommodated by the ISU requirement that, while men skated for five minutes in their free programs, women skated for four. At the 1908 Olympic Games, men competed in two events, women in one. From 1906 until 1924 women competed not for the title of world champion, as men had been doing since 1896, but for the generic title of ISU champion. To make sure that no one got confused about the difference, the ISU women's championships were held in a different location and at a different time than the men's world championships. European championships for ladies (and pairs) were not held until 1929, although Madge Syers competed against men in at least one of the earlier events. Most national skating organizations did not permit women to judge skating events until the mid-1900s. At the first Winter Olympic Games

in 1924, the women competing in figure skating were put in the immodest position of having to share a dressing room with Canadian male
speed skaters.[21] In 1932, women on the US Olympic figure skating team
received the following instructions for ordering their uniforms: 'WOM-
EN will have measurements for warm-up suits taken according to the
chart for men, and will furnish their hat size in accordance with men's
sizes … Where "Socks" appears on the Blank, WOMEN will substitute
the word "Stockings" and furnish the size required … All necessary
measurements for WOMEN'S CLOTHING not covered by the Men's
Chart are to be noted in a separate letter.'[22]

These and many other examples reflected prevailing discourses
about women's anomalous position in competitive sport. While wom-
en's participation in figure skating was certainly more extensive than
their participation in many other sports, it was influenced by the same
discourses that limited women's opportunities to engage in competitive athletic endeavours generally.

Figure skaters were privileged men and women who practised their
sport in exclusive private clubs. They performed and competed in a
style of skating that threatened the gendered identities of neither ladies
nor gentlemen. In the overall picture of late-nineteenth- and early-
twentieth-century sport, figure skating provided some upper- and
middle-class women with opportunities to develop skills at the highest
level, to pit themselves against men, to share resources and facilities. It
stands as a compelling, if small and short-lived example of how sport,
in general, might have developed differently in terms of gender. It is
also a strong reminder of the importance of class background in facili-
tating athletic experiences and, also, in shaping what those experiences
look and feel like.

Sonja Henie and Skating's Transition to Girls' Sport

In a few short decades, what had once been a relatively gender-neutral
sport came to be seen as a feminine activity not quite suitable for men.
Two key factors account for this change. First, and without a doubt
most important, was the tremendous influence of Norwegian skater
Sonja Henie, who became the dominant force in competitive figure
skating in the late 1920s and early 1930s. The second key factor was
the dramatic improvement in women's skating generally. Henie was
just one of a cohort of women skaters who were responsible for major
technical and stylistic advances in the sport. Henie's huge popularity,
alongside the increased prowess of women skaters, meant that men

began to be overshadowed; women's events became figure skating's main public attraction. And then, in 1936, Henie retired from competition, moved to Hollywood, and transformed herself into a film star. Her films introduced figure skating to a broad public not as a serious competitive activity but as a sparkly entertainment. At the same time as she was becoming the face of figure skating, the Second World War was drawing men away from their peacetime leisure pursuits. For the first time in figure skating's history, the majority of skaters were female.

International skating came to a halt during the First World War. Olympic competition resumed in Antwerp (as part of the 'summer' Games) in 1920, without skaters from Germany or Austria. ISU European, world, and women's championships resumed in 1922. At that time, international events were still predominantly contested by Europeans. Men's championships tended to attract more competitors than did the 'ladies" events, which were held separately, and figure skaters were quintessential amateurs – wealthy adults with the money and time to pursue their sport and travel to championships.

Austrian Herma Planck Szabo, women's world champion from 1922 to 1926, launched one of the trends that would lead to huge demographic changes in the sport. Szabo, who began to skate at the age of two, was raised and trained from childhood to be a champion. German skating historian Matthias Hampe writes that she was the first girl to be systematically trained at such a young age.[23] In 1927 Szabo lost her title to Norwegian Sonja Henie, one of the most successful child stars in the history of sport. Within two decades, *adult* women would become the minority and young girls the majority in high-level competition.

Sonja Henie won Olympic figure skating championships in 1928, 1932, and 1936. She also won ten consecutive world championships from 1927 to 1936. Only one other skater, Soviet pairs skater Irina Rodnina, who competed first with Alexei Ulanov and later with Alexander Zaitsev in the 1970s, has matched Henie's total number of world and Olympic gold medals. Immediately following the 1936 Olympics, Henie retired from amateur competition and went to the United States with the singular goal of becoming a movie star. She signed a five-year contract with Twentieth Century Fox that led to ten films and a huge new audience for figure skating. Her popularity was key to figure skating becoming a 'girls' sport.' As skating historian Nigel Brown writes, before Sonja Henie, figure skating drew a 'limited circle' of 'elegant elite adults' and attracted only small crowds of spectators. 'Artistic skating remained a pleasant winter pastime with appeal principally for those who indulged in it.'[24] Henie's fame and popularity brought figure skating to a large public for the first time, turning it into a commercial entertainment with mass appeal.

Henie made her first international appearance at the age of eleven at the 1924 Olympics in Chamonix. She won her first Olympic gold medal four years later. Wilhelm Henie had groomed his daughter to be a champion from the time she was a child. By the age of eight she was already following a strict diet. She practised for three hours every morning and two hours every afternoon. She received lessons from the best coaches in Europe. She studied ballet. To have the time to become a champion, she stopped going to school and completed her education with private tutors.[25] According to her American contemporary Maribel Vinson, Henie became figure skating's first 'full-time champion.'[26]

In the brief historical overviews that introduce glossy coffee-table books on figure skating, Sonja Henie is usually noted for three things: winning more singles championships than any other skater; introducing short skirts, white boots, and a fashionable image to women's skating; and making a name for herself and for figure skating in Hollywood. While Henie may not have been the fashion innovator she is made out to be – Canadian Cecil Smith claimed that Henie got the idea for white boots from her[27] – she was truly a force in her sport. Other skaters of the time were impressed by her unique combination of athletic and artistic abilities, her musicality, her attention to choreography. Her performances inspired no end of superlatives, such as in this review, published in 1931 in the American magazine *Skating*:

> She is more than a skater, she is an artist. Her figures were executed almost flawlessly … With each new figure she seemed to justify herself as the champion. Her free skating was the ecstasy of all beholders. I sat there in amazement trying to absorb all that I saw. Her opening spiral was done at terrific speed, with marvelous control, in fact so was her entire performance. Her Axel Paulsen was simply a dream and its landing extraordinary; I have never seen a better one. Her spins are astounding, for they are longer and faster than ever, and are finished on a inner back edge in beautiful positions …
>
> Miss Henie is unique in one thing, and that is an appealing attraction which is hard to describe in words. It is, perhaps, a combination of personality, charm, and perfection; but whatever it is, it blossoms forth to captivate her many followers.[28]

In her 1940 autobiography, *Wings on My Feet*, Henie claims for herself the distinction of being the first to base a free skating program on ballet. She writes that prior to the 1928 Olympics in St Moritz, free programs 'had been little more than [a] series of school figures and minor stunt figures strung together on an abtrusive thread of navigation from one spot on the ice to another.' Her 1928 program, by contrast, had 'introduced dance pattern into free skating ... It gave form and flow to the sequence of orthodox spins and jumps. As a matter of history, good skaters in all countries since then have come to build their free skating programs to a large extent on dance choreography.'[29] Henie's claim to be the first to tie ballet and free skating is an exaggeration. English champion Arthur Cumming performed balletic programs in the 1910s after consulting with no less an authority than Serge Diaghilev of the famed Ballets Russes. The professional skater Charlotte (about whom more later) also put ballet on ice in the 1910s. During some of her performances, the famous ballerina Anna Pavlova danced on a wooden stage right beside the ice. But whether Henie's innovations were original or not, they came at the right time and in the right context to have a huge influence on the development of free skating.[30]

Turn-of-the-century skaters had considered balletic moves and attitudes to be inappropriate and a sign of 'false grace.' Such moves, which included any that raised the arms higher than hip level, were considered superfluous to a style of skating that emphasized flow and glide rather than ornament. But Henie pulled attention up from the blade to the performer herself. She wanted her skating to express more than her technical mastery of the medium, although her artistic impact would have been far less significant without her outstanding technical skills. Nigel Brown argues that Henie brought 'vigour' to figure skating – a quality generally associated with men. He suggests that her youth allowed her an athleticism and abandon that mature, lyrical skaters of either sex lacked and that she was the first to blend the 'highly athletic element with pure artistic skating.'[31] In so doing she changed free skating from a somewhat arcane exercise that was difficult for non-skaters to appreciate into an exciting and moving, almost theatrical performance that could appeal to spectators with no prior knowledge of the sport. In some circles skating achieved a new social status and became a fashionable form of entertainment.[32] While competitions provided opportunities for people to watch skating, it was skating's proximity to dance that prompted an increase in its popularity. And, in the late 1920s and 1930s, the skaters who grounded their programs in dance were most likely to be women.

American and British reports on the 1928 Olympics suggest that the women's competition at those Games took figure skating to a new level. They also make it clear that Henie, while important, was not the only skater pushing the boundaries of her sport. The reports are unanimous in lauding the overall standard of the women and in expressing surprise at their youth. 'It is astounding,' writes one critic, 'when one thinks how much there is to learn in skating, that such a tremendously high standard of proficiency can be attained by youngsters still in their teens. One can almost imagine these infant prodigies being wheeled out in their perambulators with skates attached to their wooly boots just to accustom them to the feel of the things.'[33] Another writer claims the young women's free-skating, 'with a few exceptions, was magnificent. An American observer, well qualified to judge, was heard to say that it "left the men nowhere," and as he was one of the men concerned he can hardly be accused of bias in the ladies' favour.'[34] Long-time English skating writer T.D. Richardson speculates, 'One cannot help thinking what a fine contest could be arranged between a team of the above-mentioned five girls [1928 Olympic competitors], and five stalwarts picked from the rank of the male skaters … Total marks count. I should back the ladies every time, and it would undoubtedly take a brave bookmaker to lay a shade of odds on the men!'[35]

The overall standard of men's competitions had changed little since before the First World War. While a skater like Gillis Grafstrom of Sweden, three-time Olympic champion and three-time world champion, was routinely referred to as a genius and a poet on ice, his unique skill lay in pushing the skating of his time to the highest possible level – not in transforming its fundamentals. According to T.D. Richardson, Grafstrom's 'personality combine[d] the greatest knowledge of the art of skating possessed by any living soul, with a rare intelligence, intense artistic feeling, perfection of technique and supreme athletic achievement.'[36] His edges were sublime. His technical innovations, like the change-foot-spin, complex. Other skaters found his performances spell-binding; they were clean, subtle, and erudite. Grafstrom was the skater's skater. There was nothing of the spectacle or the showman about him. And there was nothing about his performances that would bring skating to a wider audience.

Apart from Grafstrom, the men who competed in the 1920s seem to have inspired more concern than awe among skating critics. In 1929 one English critic wrote that the 'standard of ladies skating has risen enormously,' while 'it is doubtful if the standard of men's skating has risen at all. In fact it may be lower now than in 1914.' He goes on to say: 'Few men today can excel these young girls at compulsory figures and the situation is the same with regard to free skating ... It is really amazing how these young girls from the Continent, America and Canada can have achieved such a pitch of perfection in such a short time.'[37] As the calibre of women's skating improved, the men seemed to be left behind. Some writers speculated that boys' education left them less time to practise[38] or that changing economic conditions meant that more young men than previously had to work and that fewer of them, therefore, had the leisure time that high-level skating required.[39]

In England, the instigation of separate women's and men's championships in 1927 highlighted the differences between male and female skaters. What sparked the decision to separate them? Any conclusions I might draw from the available sources can only be speculative: Was the move internally or externally motivated? Was it an effort to bring figure skating more in line with other sports? Did the women get their own championship when they started to surpass the men in overall ability? One thing is certain: once established, the women's championship 'quite eclipsed the other events in public interest ... Every contest attracted large crowds to see the girls compete. On the other hand, the men's events received comparatively little attention from the general public until the N.S.A. put all the British amateur championships – men's, women's and pairs – together in one combined programme at Wembley Sports Arena in December 1937.'[40] Did the men object to riding on the women's coattails? Certainly men's interest in participating seemed to drop off. In 1936 only two men competed for the national championship of Great Britain, although their numbers started to increase again in 1938, just before the war put an end to competitions.[41] By the time skating competitions resumed in the post-war period, the gender reputation of the sport had already changed.

Some writers attributed the growing popularity of women's skating to Sonja Henie, some to the novelty of the women's youth, others to their appearance and to the appeal of their twirling skirts (!), an advantage not available to men.[42] This is as close as the commentary comes to suggesting that skating was developing along feminine lines that might not have been suited to the demands of a competitive sporting masculinity – even in a relatively upper-class context where that version of masculinity was far 'softer' than it is today. The new emphasis on dance-like free skating programs certainly would have made skating appear less than manly to some observers.

The Henie Factor: Skating Finds a Public

Sonja Henie's youth, her blonde cuteness, and her amazing string of victories made the women's event the lead figure skating story in English-language reports on the European, world, and Olympic championships, no matter how outstanding the competitors in other disciplines. The interest of the press was only increased by the controversies that regularly attended her. For example, Henie won her first world championship on home ice in Oslo in a split decision from a five-judge panel, three of whom were Norwegian – the resulting scandal would lead to a rule that allowed each country only one judge per event. Throughout her career, Henie remained the lead story in skating as much for her entourage as for her skating. As the American skater Maribel Vinson wrote from the 1933 European championships, Henie's 'popularity at the competition was peculiar. The public had evidently got fed-up with six weeks of Pop Henie's ballyhoo for Sonja and were praying for anyone to beat her.'[43] Vinson continued: 'The Henie organization is unbelievable and has had as bad an effect on the internals of the sport as Sonja's real virtuosity has had a good effect in spreading the popularity of skating through the world.'[44] According to historian Nigel Brown, in 1936 the possibility of Henie losing her Olympic title to fifteen-year-old Cecilia Colledge of England drew a crowd of 200,000 to the women's free skating at the Games in Garmisch-Partenkirchen, Germany.[45] When Brown was writing, in the late 1950s, the results of the competition were still under dispute.[46] The suggestion was, and remains, that Henie's father and professional promoters who hoped to benefit from her victories exerted influence on the judges and the results. Maribel Vinson describes how 'a minor drama developed over the right back bracket-change-bracket,' one of the school figures skated by the women competitors. Vinson – who of course had a vested interest in Henie's mistakes – wrote:

> She had almost no speed for the second half of the figure, she came up to the second bracket right on the flat of her skate instead of on an edge, a major fault, and after the turn she had to wiggle and hitch her skating foot to keep going, and then she pushed off for the next circle a good four feet before she reached her center, another very major fault ... and when she had turned her twelfth and last bracket, she was at a dead standstill. So making no pretense of trying to finish out her circle, she just put both feet down, smiled a gay camouflage smile, and walked off the ice. We gasped

to see the world champion do such a thing. The figure as it stood, deserved no more than Vivi's [Vivi-Anne Hulten of Sweden] 3.8 average, if as high as that, AND YET when the judges put up their cards, not one, not even Mr. Rotch, who does indeed know correct figures, had given her less than 5! We competitors and those on the sidelines who knew laughed in derision and with a 'what can you expect' tone – I looked at Mr. Rotch with the question, 'How could you honestly do such a thing?' in my eyes, and he just shrugged.[47]

The assumption made by the other skaters was that Sonja Henie's transgressions, on ice and off, were overlooked because of her ability to fill the stands, thus benefiting rink owners and the amateur associations that sponsored competitions.[48]

Throughout Henie's competitive career it was alleged that she failed to conform to the amateur rules of the times. In their book *Queen of Ice, Queen of Shadows*, Raymond Strait and Leif Henie, Sonja's older brother, write: 'Rumors were rampant that she was "the richest amateur in sports," and that her father was demanding and receiving astronomical fees (for the era) to assure Sonja's appearances [at amateur exhibitions]. Wilhelm Henie was a clever man, and there were never any checks or bank drafts. Cash was the policy, and the money that changed hands never appeared on official ledgers or tax reports.'[49] Strait and Henie say that no formal complaints were ever lodged against his sister or his father. Maribel Vinson, however, claims that the National Skating Association in Great Britain did lodge complaints, but they were never acted upon by the ISU.[50]

Henie's popularity grew not just from her championship titles but also from the demanding circuit of exhibitions she skated throughout the season. Her father understood very early in her career the importance of keeping the young star in the public eye: exhibitions gave her a chance to get used to performing before crowds; they generated (undeclared) income for the family; and the buzz that followed them could not help but influence any skating judges who happened to hear it. In 1930 Henie travelled to New York to compete at the world championships, which were being held outside Europe for the first time. It was the first opportunity that North Americans had to see the type of figure skating that had taken hold overseas. And it was a huge opportunity for the United States Figure Skating Association to generate wider interest in their sport. To this end they took full advantage of Sonja Henie's visit. On arrival, her family was greeted at the pier, amid great fuss, by the mayor of New York and a gaggle of journalists who would be key in constructing her North American fame.

Prior to the competition, Henie was invited to take part in a carnival at the New York Skating Club's third-floor rink at Madison Square Garden. Her father agreed on the condition that the show be moved to the main arena. The club agreed to the upgrade only after Wilhelm Henie offered to rent the arena himself and to keep for his family any profits from the show. Club officials declined his offer but, inspired by his confidence, moved the show downstairs. Father Henie then went to work drumming up an audience among the large Norwegian community in New York. Twelve thousand tickets were bought the first day they went on sale. The show easily sold out the Gardens – the second largest indoor rink in the world – and garnered a lot of favourable press for Henie. When the world championships were held a few weeks later, 13,000 spectators attended the competition – an unprecedented number in a country that had previously been quite indifferent to the sport: 'This huge turnout of spectators … was the first dramatic proof that skating, without embellishments of props, scenery or special effects, could be a major arena attraction. It was an eye-opener to promoters and officials as well.'[51] Henie's financial success inspired amateur carnivals and commercial ice shows all over North America and Europe, and promoters began to troll the halls of amateur competitions. In an era when the demand for light, popular entertainments was huge, the novelty of figure skating held the potential for huge profits.

The 1930s was not the first era of professional figure skating. In the early years of the twentieth century, small ice shows were staged in theatres and hotels in North America and Europe. The most famous of these was the show at New York's Hippodrome in the 1910s. As in the 1930s, the headline attraction was Charlotte Oelschlägel, who, as a teenager, had starred in the Ice Revue at Berlin's Admiral Palast until it was closed down because of the First World War. Hippodrome producer Charles Dillingham initially signed Charlotte (who didn't use her surname) and her sixty-five-member skating troupe for a run of six weeks. They stayed for almost three years, performing two shows a day in the six-thousand-seat theatre. Charlotte became a Broadway star. Her ice show spawned numerous small imitations in cities across the north-eastern United States. It inspired the construction of rinks and launched a small boom in first-time skaters. Charlotte endorsed skates, dolls were made in her likeness, she appeared in magazine advertisements. She was, from all accounts, an amazing talent, well ahead of her time. To her goes much of the credit for first transferring ballet vocabulary to the ice. She was also the first woman to execute an axel jump and the first figure skater to perform at Madison Square Gardens. In 1916 she appeared in 'The Frozen Warning,' the first film to feature ice skating. She was young and beautiful and she became the public, commodified face of skating. Her success made youth and femininity the framework within which figure skating would be commercialized and turn a profit. Charlotte was the first ice princess.

This initial foray of theatre and entertainment promoters into ice skating only lasted a few years. Writing with the advantage of hindsight, one commentator suggests that the sport's popularity waned in the United States after the imposition of prohibition in the 1920s: 'The theory was circulated that only the patronage of a drinking public could support skating shows and the cost of the necessary ice.'[52] It may have simply been that the novelty of ice shows diminished or that no new stars emerged to take the place of Charlotte or that the consumer's desire to pay for such a European style of entertainment diminished after the war. In any case, investors stopped investing and ice shows became yesterday's fad until the arrival of Sonja Henie.

With Henie's competitive and popular success, promoters again saw the potential for profits. Fifteen thousand people watched the free skating competitions of the world championships in Montreal in 1932. Clearly, skating had a market. Maribel Vinson writes, 'Every rink manager in Europe [is] interested in champion figure skaters to fill their pockets with exhibitions.'[53] These 'sports impresarios,' as Vinson called them, hoped to make money from the combination of youth, beauty, and skill that was attracting ever larger crowds to competitions on both sides of the Atlantic. Yet sport had very little to do with the new product they were developing. The skating they wanted to sell was pure spectacle. With the right music, enough rhinestones, and theatrical lighting, figure skaters could turn their athletic routines into glamorous entertainment that would have mass appeal – and the skaters who appealed to audiences the most were women. No one knew this better than Sonja Henie, whose entrepreneurship would put the sports impresarios to shame.

In 1936, immediately after winning her third Olympic and tenth world titles, Sonja Henie embarked for New York. She did screen tests for Metro-Goldwyn-Mayer, skated before a crowd of ten thousand at Madison Square Gardens, and gathered a lot of positive publicity. The next stop was Los Angeles, where father Henie rented an ice rink and

Sonja performed for the cream of Hollywood society. According to New York's *World-Telegram*, the morning after her first performance, 'Hollywood had elbow bruises on its ribs, and Sonja Henie was the talk of the town. Studios were cooing at her. Universal, Paramount, MGM wanted her. It has been a long time since Hollywood's producer contingent has devised as many attractive contracts for one person.'[54] A few days later Henie had a lucrative five-year contract with Twentieth Century Fox. From Fox's initial offer of $75,000 for a supporting role in one film, Henie managed to negotiate $125,000 per film, with star billing in five films over five years. Not bad for an athlete who had never acted before.

Sonja Henie's first film, *One in a Million*, was released in January 1937. An immediate success, it grossed $2 million and gained Henie eighth place in polls measuring box-office popularity. Two movies later she was ranked second. While her popularity was never again so high, she stayed in the public eye for more than a decade; between 1937 and 1952 she appeared on at least twenty magazine covers. As Jack Cuddy wrote in the *Toronto Globe and Mail*, she was the 'greatest sensation ever to graduate from athletics to entertainment.'[55] Two things appear without fail in news accounts of Henie's professional adventures: first, admiring descriptions of her 'pert,' 'blonde,' 'curvesome' appearance; second, breathless accounts of her spectacular knack for making money.

Films were just the beginning. They created an audience and a consumer demand for a new, glitzy skating that Henie was only happy to meet. In 1938 she teamed with Chicago promoter Arthur Wirtz to found the Hollywood Ice Revue, a touring show that would present figure skating as a 'big extravaganza.' While the Ice Revue was not the first touring show (the Ice Follies began in 1936), it was the biggest, the most lavish, and the only show fronted by a bone fide Hollywood star. Sports writers in Canada and the United States marvelled at Henie's ability to sell seats and turn profits. One columnist called her 'the sell-out queen' after an alleged twenty-two thousand people were turned away from sold-out performances in New York City.[56] In her 1940 autobiography Henie claimed that they had not yet had a vacant seat in the house.[57] In addition to her tours, she also capitalized on her fame by opening a chain of franchised skating rinks, endorsing products, and selling Sonja Henie souvenir merchandise. According to her brother, who managed this aspect of Henie's business, one particular line of brooches, shaped like silver skates, brought in $300,000.[58]

In an era when foreign actors did not always fare well with the North

American film-going public, writes film theorist Diane Negra, the exaggerated whiteness of Henie's public persona was central to her popularity.[59] Henie's connection to winter sports (in which, even now, the vast majority of athletes are white), her 'safe' ethnic status, her frequently mentioned fondness for white things – bedrooms, cars, and clothes – all helped to position her in terms of a racialized femininity that contributed to her appeal and made possible the reception she received from American audiences. Henie's carefully constructed and emphatically white cuteness provided a means through which her foreignness (evident in her films because of her accent) could be negotiated in a relatively unproblematic way. Citing Lori Merish, Negra argues that cuteness is a means through which 'the Other' can be 'domesticated and (re)contextualized.'[60] Cuteness allowed the foreign-born Henie to transcend her status as outsider and to avoid the negative reaction that greeted some other ethnic stars in Hollywood, especially amid the xenophobic forms of nationalism that arose during the Second World War. Cuteness, expressed through the most appropriately feminine version of athleticism, permitted Henie to be assimilated and to find a place in American popular culture.

It would be hard to overstate the effect Henie's visibility had on figure skating and public perceptions of it. In a pre-television era, her touring shows and films brought figure skating to a huge public for the first time. In earlier periods, figure skating had been a pastime of the elite, practised behind the walls of private clubs – most people had actually never seen it until Henie appeared on screen at their local cinemas. In this context, she and figure skating became synonymous. Her sequined and bejewelled costumes, her use of toe-steps, her wide-eyed, doll-like appearance led to popular understandings of figure skating as a feminine form of dancing on ice, rather than a competitive sport. While male skaters appeared in Henie's films, their roles were secondary. The effervescent Henie, 'a sort of grown up Shirley Temple,'[61] always took centre ice. And thus the public image of skating was one of youthful, white femininity.

As precocious girls had once sought to emulate Shirley Temple (who Henie surpassed in box office popularity in 1938), they now begged their mothers for skating lessons. Between 1935 and 1937, the number of skates produced in the United States doubled and the value of the skate market increased by $900,000, even as the cost per pair decreased.[62] Demand for skating clothes and apparel was so high that Saks Fifth Avenue opened its own Figure Skating Center in the store.[63]

According to a 1941 issue of the North American magazine *Skating*, 'The Sonja Henie boom spread [figure skating] to the thousands beyond the USFSA's [United States Figure Skating Association's] immediate reach, made it big enough to command the manufacture of good skates and boots at reasonable prices, and popular enough to justify the construction of scores of artificial ice rinks.'[64] In the same year, the Works Progress Administration in the United States funded construction of more than one thousand ice rinks. The number of figure skating clubs also increased, while the number of proficiency tests taken during the 1940–1 figure skating season was 63 per cent higher than in any previous year.[65]

While the *Skating* article does not say so explicitly, it becomes apparent in later issues of the magazine that this huge growth was a feminine phenomenon: the majority of new skaters were girls. As facilities became more accessible, skating clubs opened in public arenas, the population of figure skaters grew, and the sport became less exclusive in terms of class. By the early 1940s, what had once been a relatively gender-balanced sport practised by privileged white adults was well on its way to becoming a sport of young middle-class white girls.

The Boy Problem

The influx of young girls was not the only thing that changed during the Second World War. As girls were coming into the sport, older boys and men were leaving for military service. One observer wrote: 'A trend common to all war-torn countries is becoming increasingly evident. Skating is carrying on, but it is becoming more and more of a woman's sport. Most of the men skaters are in military service, many overseas.'[66] Clubs did what they could both to support the war effort and to keep men on their rinks. The Toronto Skating Club organized practice times around the militia duties of male skaters. Other clubs offered free memberships or skating passes to men stationed nearby. The editor of *Skating* encouraged clubs to open their doors to service men, to encourage them to skate, and to invite them home for supper.[67] While these efforts may have been appreciated by those who took advantage of them, they did little to address skating's growing gender imbalance.

In 1945 *Skating* published the first of many articles that considered the 'boy problem': 'Round Table Talks on Boy Skaters' (1945) was followed by 'Where Are the Boys?' (1946), 'Where Are the Boys?' (1954), 'Bring in the Boys' (1955), 'My Advice to Other Dads' (1957), and 'For Boys Only' (1966), among others. The reasons offered by the writers of such articles for the 'shortage' of boys continue to circulate in skating venues today: boys like things rough; boys hate being compared to girls; boys don't like sports where girls excel; boys like team sports. The general assumption at work in the articles was that figure skating was misunderstood. As one writer said, 'There is in the minds of many boys the idea that we offer a "sissy" sport. Many football heroes are frightened from our doors, because they believe it is a graceful endeavour solely for girls.'[68] Swedish skater Maj Britt wrote in a British skating magazine, 'It is regrettable that boy skaters seem to have almost disappeared from the British rinks. I do not know if it is for the same reason as in Sweden, where they seem to think figure skating is something for girls only and are ashamed even to put on a pair of figure skates. For them exists only ice hockey.'[69] Britt sounds both surprised and frustrated that male figure skaters were becoming scarce. In most of the articles, the decline in the number of male skaters is presented, erroneously, as if it were a long-standing historical fact and not a fairly recent development, exacerbated by the war. There is no discussion of the sport's changing demographics, no serious consideration of why things might have changed. None of the writers consider anything beyond boys' own attitudes as an explanation for their diminishing numbers. Even in the skating press, figure skating's history as a gender-mixed sport was being lost. It was beginning to appear as if skating's greater appeal to girls was natural and, therefore, inevitable and as things always had been. The taken-for-grantedness of skating's gender imbalance was key to establishing figure skating's new identity as a girls' sport; it was made possible by the fact that skating's new feminine image fit easily into mid-century, middle-class gender norms. Notions of how girls and boys, women and men should appear and behave were so powerful that skaters themselves found it hard to see past them, even as these norms radically altered their sport.

Once figure skating came to be seen as a feminine sport, boys and men who skated risked being seen as effeminate. Tightening gender norms during the Second World War and the post-war period limited the socially acceptable options for behaving as a 'proper' man and contributed to perceptions of skating as fey. A boy's interest in feminine concerns such as skating could be seen as a dangerous sign of abnormal gender development or sexual deviance. In an era when military drill was the standard curriculum for physical education, figure skating, like ballet, became an inappropriate way – an unpatriotic way – for a male to use his body.

In response to the shifting reputation of their sport, male skaters changed how they skated, adopting a less lyrical, more athletic style. The two men who had who dominated skating during the 1920s and 1930s, Gillis Grafstrom of Sweden and Karl Schäfer of Austria, had been lauded for creating poetry on ice. American Dick Button, Olympic gold medallist in 1948 and 1952, was lauded instead for his athletic prowess, especially for being the first skater to land a double axel and a triple jump in competition. A Viennese newspaper claimed that Button marked a significant shift in skating: 'The figurative and soft-dancing style retreats before the artistic-athletic combination. The skater of today must be hard, a daring jumper, an athlete, thoroughly trained on the athletic field, so that he masters the technical side to such an extent that that comes naturally, and allows him ever to increase the refinement and musical adaptation of the performance. That is the lesson of Button's skating.'[70] Button's new style was feted for being distinctly 'masculine.' Historian Nigel Brown says he ushered in a 'new athleticism' that was less likely to attract artists than skaters with courage. Brown called Button 'a gymnast possessing all the virile qualities of our century.'[71]

In his autobiography Button writes that when he was a boy, his participation in figure skating made his masculinity an issue among his classmates. As he put it, public perceptions of skating during his era were based on the image of Sonja Henie 'in a ballet costume.' Button's father invited Dick's classmates to dinner and then took them to watch Dick skate an exhibition. Button writes, 'I tried to do the most difficult program of jumps and spins I knew. The Englewood delegation was surprised. They didn't see a ballet toe-run, but a strenuous athletic performance.'[72] This was the impression Button hoped to leave on spectators throughout his career. His jumps were higher and longer, his spins faster than those of his competitors. He termed his approach to skating aggressive, exuberant, and American. While Button combined his athleticism with a strong sense of musicality and style, many of the men who followed him seemed to focus only on jumps, forgetting that in figure skating 'the manner of performance' is also important.[73] Post-Button, an over-emphasis on athleticism became the hallmark of men's skating.

Button was a student of Gustav Lussi, a Swiss expatriate who coached in the United States. Lussi developed new techniques for both jumping and spinning that allowed his skaters to push the technical bounds of the sport. While women also trained with Lussi, their athleticism did not generate the same response in Europe as Button's did. The female champion in the first post-war Olympics was Canada's Barbara Ann

Scott, who was known not for the difficult elements she performed but for her precision, delicacy, and grace. The word routinely applied to her skating was 'feminine.' If Button represented daring and risk, Scott represented reliability and beauty. While Button kept spectators on the edge of their seats, Scott's smooth perfection kept them calm and mesmerized. Both skaters fulfilled the gendered expectations of their time, and they were rewarded handsomely for it.

The lesson to be found in the history of figure skating – along with the history of bobsledding and other sports that have gone through periods without a heavy emphasis on gender segregation – is not new: the social organization of gender is historically and culturally contingent; the 'games and pastimes of the other sex' in one era might at another time be the games and pastimes of my own. The categories of feminine-appropriate and male-appropriate sports are socially constructed. They represent and help to constitute particular understandings of gender difference that make it seem inevitable and relatively inflexible, whether due to social convention or biology. These categories can make it seem like women and men are more different than they are the same. And, in contributing to the separation between genders, these categories can make life difficult for people, like present-day male figure skaters, who transgress the boundaries between them. But what the story of figure skating also makes clear is that the relationship between gender and sport has not always been and does not need to be structured or understood as it is now. Women and men have not always needed to compete separately; men have not always needed to eschew activities that emphasize the aesthetic; women have not always been required to compete in versions of sport that are less valued than men's. Figure skating has not always been so heavily invested as it is now in producing male and female skaters as different.

If the legacy of Sonja Henie put North American skating at the feminine end of a gender continuum, then Dick Button increased the measure of gender difference in the sport with a type of skating that was decidedly not like hers. As skaters' movements became more gendered, skating seemed to confirm popular notions about fundamental differences between men's and women's physical capabilities. Men's and 'ladies'' skating began to develop along distinctly different stylistic and technical lines. Men became the technicians and athletes, while women were expected to be the artists. It was a division of labour and talents that Henie, Grafstrom, and skaters of earlier times would have rejected.

The combination of art and athletics is, for many skaters and fans, the special appeal of the sport. But this is also, in large part, the root of skating's effeminate image. In the next chapter I look at debates over these two aspects of skating for what they can tell us about the changing understandings of class and gender that have shaped figure skating over the past century. They are debates that are ongoing and that are fundamentally concerned with the public image of male skaters, that is, with the effects of their 'artistic impressions.'

7 Artistic Sport or Athletic Art? Class and Gender and Shifting Definitions of Skating

During his past four years of monopolizing championships, [Dick] Button has created a new era in world skating. He has literally taken skating away from the ballroom and put it on the athletic field where it belongs.[1]

Debates over where on the cultural landscape figure skating belongs have occupied skaters and those who write about them for more than a century. By the end of the 1800s, figure skating had already acquired the official trappings of a competitive sport: championships, governing bodies, and a complicated, evolving set of rules. Yet skaters were by no means unanimous in their acceptance of the sporting framework that had come to govern what they could do on the ice. They continue to be divided on the same topic today. Should skaters concern themselves more with aesthetics or athleticism, artistic expression or competitive drive, style or stunts? Simply put: Is skating an art or a sport? In the present moment, one might as easily ask, Is skating for girls or boys, so gender-coded are these two categories in popular culture. At the beginning of the twentieth century, however, the relationship between art and sport in figure skating seemed to raise more questions about class than it did about gender. Some skaters hoped a heavier emphasis on art would help to keep skating an elegant, upper-class concern. As we saw in chapter 5, they feared that too much emphasis on sport would push skating towards prize-winning, professionalism, and, heaven forbid, mass appeal. Debates over which direction figure skating should take were, in essence, debates over who should skate and how skating and skaters should appear to outsiders. In this chapter I look at these debates for what they might tell us about the historical context of skating's current North American reputation as a sport for sissies and girls, a reputation that has a lot to do with the artistic demands of the sport.

The requirement that skaters demonstrate both aesthetic and technical skills has remained consistent throughout the institutional history of the sport despite lobbying from officials, some of whom place more value on art and some of whom place more value on sport. Early judges marked skaters for 'contents of program' and 'manner of performance,' categories that were changed to 'sporting merit' and 'general impression' in 1959 and then to the more familiar 'technical merit' and 'artistic impression' in 1961. The former addressed the level of difficulty and the cleanness and sureness with which the program was skated, the latter addressed the composition of the program and the quality of its performance and relationship to the music.[2] In 1994 the 'artistic impression' mark was replaced by a mark for 'presentation.'[3] While the terms have changed, a scoring system that accounts for both technique/athleticism and performance/aesthetics is a large part of what makes figure skating figure skating and not something else. In the current 'code of points' marking scheme, judges no longer give a distinct mark for each of the two categories; instead, they award points to the various aspects of a program according to lists of criteria grouped under the two headings, 'technical elements' and 'program components.' Although the method of calculating scores and ranking has changed significantly in the new system, the requirement that skaters develop two sets of skills – athletic and aesthetic – remains.

Skating's requirement for 'artistic impression' positions skating as akin to dance and is, therefore, a large part of what puts figure skating outside the bounds of normative masculine behaviour. In North America and western Europe dance is generally considered an odd and inappropriate pastime for boys and men, as the English film *Billy Elliot* made clear. For well over a century men's dance, particularly in North America, has been seen as effeminate.[4] Social critics routinely point out that the arts, generally, are seen as feminine: 'Do *real* men "go for" ballet, poetry, pictures or do they go for sports? Isn't the culture sector the province of the ladies' committees? Aren't the arts seen as girlish frills in the education system? What papa is pleased that his son wants to be an artist?'[5] The disapproving papa is a recurring figure in such arguments, standing in for masculine norms and dominant social conventions. Carolyn Parks invoked him in a piece written for *Dance Magazine* in 1953: 'The American public has always looked at art in any form as suitable for its girls, but sissy for its boys ... Most shocking of all seems to be the idea that any boy should put on a pair of tights, and thus brand himself a fop. The American father howls his indignation at the thought ... He declares he'd rather see his son dead than up on the stage cavorting with those fools.'[6] Dance critics have euphemistically referred to this attitude and its consequences as 'the problem of the male dancer.'

Rarely mentioning the homophobia or misogyny at the root of this 'problem,' critics have decried the fact that presumptions about the effeminacy of male dancers have resulted in a tremendous gender imbalance among both dancers and spectators. They have tended to respond to these presumptions, not by defending, validating, or praising so-called effeminate characteristics in men's dance, but by challenging the attribution of these to male dancers. In so doing, dance writers have borrowed heavily from discourses about sport and male athleticism:[7] dancers aren't fey, look how strong they are! Look how high they can jump! Unlike art, sport is an important cultural site for the constitution of mainstream masculinities, as sport scholars routinely point out.[8] What better tool, then, for reframing understandings of men's dance?

Those concerned with the reputation of men's figure skating have taken the same rhetorical route, playing up the athleticism of skaters, trying to present skating itself as dangerous and difficult. In early 2009, marketers for Skate Canada talked in the press about the need to 'rebrand' the sport by playing up its risk and athleticism.[9] It's a strategy skating officials have been pursuing for fifty years in their attempts to make the sport more acceptable to boys and men. If people could just see how hard they work, how difficult it is to do what they do, male skaters, the argument goes, would get more respect and boys might want to emulate them. But the 'problem of the male skater,' like the 'problem of the male dancer,' isn't that he isn't strong, or doesn't work hard, or that his sport isn't risky enough. The problem is more about the tights and the music and the many, many girls with whom he trains. It's about the fact that his athleticism is not simply directed towards mastery of time, space, or an opponent, but that it is meant to be expressive and compelling to watch. His athleticism is developed with its aesthetic qualities in mind. It is supposed to produce art. In a heavily gendered culture, where art is a dubious sphere of interest for boys and men, figure skating – *patinage artistique*, *eiskunstlaufen* – by definition will have a hard time solving its 'boy problem.'

As we saw in the previous chapter, it wasn't until the 1940s and 1950s that figure skating, newly available to the burgeoning post-war middle class, came to be seen as a feminine sport, not altogether appropriate for men and boys. In the century before the Second World War, figure skating had been positioned much differently in terms of gender and class. In the late nineteenth and early twentieth centuries figure skaters were privileged people whose notions of gentlemanly masculinity were validated by the sport's aesthetic requirements for ease and elegance. Indeed, in that period, many male skaters, as we will see below, hoped to keep the explicit sporting aspects of skating to a minimum. At a time when sport was rapidly becoming the primary form of cultural and physical expression for men of the middle classes, the emphasis on skating's aesthetic aspects was a means of setting figure skating apart from other types of athletic exercise, of ensuring that it remained a refined activity with echoes of its aristocratic beginnings. Far from being a threat to their virility, as it could be today, an interest in art and aesthetics helped to secure for elite men their status and prestige and their group identity as men who were not like most men and who were, therefore, justified in their privileges and access to power.

But as female skaters began to outnumber male skaters in the post–Second World War period, and as new clubs began to cater to the 'plain old middle class,' and to children rather than adults, gentlemanly elegance lost its value in skating, as it had in the culture at large. Some skaters, officials, and coaches set out to reframe the sport to fit within the tightening gender climate of the 1940s and 1950s.[10] To do so, they tried to fashion for *men's* skating a new identity as an athletically demanding, clearly defined sport. This effort has continued until the present day with varying degrees of intensity, but only mixed success. Some skaters have resisted the impulse entirely, refusing to tone down their artistic inclinations; among these, 1976 Olympic bronze medallist Toller Cranston of Canada and 1976 Olympic gold medallist John Curry of England are the most well known.

The division of skaters into artists and athletes, as if these were mutually exclusive categories, is now a common feature of skating commentary. This polarization, beneath which lies a host of normative ideas about gender and sexuality, peaked in the 1990s with the emergence of a group of self-consciously manly skaters, among whom Canadian Elvis Stojko, intentionally or not, was the emblematic example. While journalists and broadcasters continue to sort skaters into categories, the recent trend among skaters has been towards more well-roundedness, a better balance between the aesthetic and athletic aspects of performance. The best examples of this trend, in my view, have been the programs of Daisuke Takahashi of Japan, who won the world championship in 2010 and who is one of the few skaters capable of combining dense choreography, original expression, and quadruple jumps.

The struggle over figure skating's identity as artistic sport or athletic art has been a struggle over status and privilege. It is a struggle that has rarely been about women who, even today, are represented as if they quite naturally hold up the artistic side of the binary, against men's athleticism. The primary positions in the art versus sport debate have always been represented by men – Gillis Grafstrom in the 1920s, Dick Button in the early 1950s, Toller Cranston in the 1970s, Elvis Stojko in the 1990s. Proponents on either side, whether motivated primarily by concerns of class or gender, have had little to say about women, even during the long period that women have dominated the sport in terms of numbers and popular interest; their goal has been to protect the reputations of men and to define skating to meet their ideas of how and in what types of public contexts male bodies should move.

Worrying about Status and Privilege: Promoting Skating as Art

In his instructional book *A Skating Primer*, American George Browne wrote: 'In the skating we have in mind, there is an element of beauty … The Germans have a more expressive name for this art than we, *Kunstlaufen* – artistic skating, or skating as a fine art – skating that appeals to the esthetic sense as well as to the desire to excel, to win … The skating we have in mind, then, is not so much a competitive sport as a graceful accomplishment.'[11] While it would have been impossible for Browne to ignore completely the athletic aspects of figure skating, he pays them little attention. The frontispiece of the book's first edition (1910), for instance, displays two photographs. One shows a male skater on the left outside edge, free foot raised, arms outstretched. The other shows a classical Greek statue, in a somewhat similar position: a nude, muscled male figure, standing firmly on the right foot, the left foot stretched behind with heel raised, one arm held in front, parallel to the ground, the other reaching behind, following the line of the outstretched foot. The caption reads: 'Note the resemblance of the Modern Champion, Gustav Hugel of Vienna, in Good International Form, to the Ancient Greek Athlete, [from] the Borghese [Gallery] in the Louvre.'

Browne's reference to a piece of classical Greek art and to its home in the Louvre, one of the emblematic temples of European high culture, tells us a lot about the frame through which he wanted his readers to see skating. In the late nineteenth and early twentieth centuries, neoclassi-cism influenced home design, fashion, visual arts, dance, and forms of physical education. Familiarity with classical Greek art allowed 'cultured' Europeans and North Americans to signal their refinement and their taste. In her history of the Anglo middle classes in Britain, the United States, and Australia, Linda Young writes that taste is 'most obviously described as the sum of correct knowledge or cultural capital with which the genteel person distinguished himself or herself from people who did not have it.'[12] Produced at 'the intersection of learning and money,'[13] taste was part of how the middle class constructed itself as a class.

Some scholars suggest that the investment the middle classes made in their knowledge of Greek art allows us to see that this process of class formation was also fundamentally concerned with the produc-tion of whiteness as a privileged category. Nude male sculptures, like the one shown in Browne's book, were seen as examples of masculine physical perfection in which the middle class saw represented their defining virtues – strength, rationality, democracy, independence. Art historian Daniel Purdy argues that the colour of these statues, which were made of brilliant white marble, was central to interpretations of their beauty and inspired those who looked upon them in nineteenth-century museums to see their own values reflected in the stone. Would the sculptures have generated so much interest in northern Europe and North America if they had been made of brown, black, or red stone? Would they have been called upon to perform the same ideological work? Purdy writes that 'enthusiasm for ancient white statues' justified the claim that white Europeans were more 'beautiful' than were peo-ple of other races, including, most importantly, the 'primitive peoples' Europeans had colonized in the age of imperialism.[14] This was a judg-ment that was not simply about appearances. Beauty was a moral term that carried connotations of right character and health; it also served as a symbol of the sacred. What was not beautiful was seen as degener-ate, as lacking purity.[15] The male standard of beauty, represented by sculptures like the athlete that appears in Browne's book, was linked to notions of cultural superiority that grounded the imperialists' defini-tions of themselves as civilized and their definitions of those they colo-nized as inferior and needing intervention. The 'need for intervention' was one of the fundamental justifications of imperial conquest. It grew out of notions of racial difference that received support from practices and ideas that circulated in Western cultures – religion, science, government, art, and leisure activities, including sport. In presenting the statue of the Greek athlete as a model for skaters Browne was locating skaters and his readers as part of this heritage.

In his comparison of the two photographs, Browne highlighted aesthetics – line, posture, and form – rather than instrumental strength or physical ability. The images helped to support his view of skating as primarily an artistic rather than athletic endeavour, presumably best represented by men, and fundamentally concerned with beauty and grace. Historian Doug Brown reminds us that not all of George Browne's contemporaries saw the distinction between sport and art as a sharp one. Pierre de Coubertin, founder of the modern Olympic movement, had hoped, for instance, that the revived Olympic Games would be 'a union of art and sport.'[16] Writing about a 1906 conference initiated by de Coubertin and focused on the arts, literature, and sports, Brown argues that Coubertin and his colleagues worked with theories of sport that were 'greatly influenced by theories of art and beauty.'[17] While they were not talking about self-consciously aesthetic sports like figure skating, their investment in beauty and grace as one of the effects of athleticism drew on the same kinds of Hellenist discourses that motivated Browne. But conference delegates were focused on the beauty of the athletic body as a source of inspiration for artists. Browne saw the athletic body itself as a producer of art that was beautiful.

He was not the only writer to see skating in this way. In 1927, German skating historian Hugo Winzer wrote that 'the true and highest goal of figure skating is the enjoyment of that movement which can only have an aesthetically pleasing appearance.'[18] In 1929, American Roy W. McDaniel wrote in the North American magazine *Skating* that 'the ultimate object of figure skating ... is to enable the skater to render a performance, pleasing in effect to the spectator.'[19] These authors had very little to say about winning or breaking records or pushing the technical limits of jumps or spins. They worried instead about composing harmonious programs, developing good body lines, and avoiding ugliness.

In his later writings, which were directed at experienced rather than novice skaters, Browne argued quite explicitly against the framing of skating as a sport. He worried that competitions and exhibitions of skill impeded the aesthetic development of skaters and their art. 'The tragedy of sacrificing considerations of art to considerations of prize-winning,' Browne wrote in *Skating* in 1925, 'has serious consequences.'[20] He claimed that skating had the potential to rival the Russian ballet, if only skaters would give up on competition, and release themselves from the 'over-legislation' of competitive rules. 'Hampering fetters and narrowness,' Browne wrote, 'should be sedulously avoided. The devotees of the art of Skating should not put shackles upon it.'[21]

Although not as emphatic as Browne, English writer and former Olympic skater T.D. Richardson spent decades making the same point in both specialist figure skating magazines and general skating textbooks. In a tribute to three-time world and three-time Olympic champion Gillis Grafstrom, Richardson lauded the Swedish skater as a 'great artist ... [The Russian ballet dancer] Nijinsky at his greatest was no finer exponent of the dance than is Grafstrom of *his* art, unrivalled in delicacy or poise on skates that flash like sword blades. The time has come,' Richardson wrote, 'to raise skating out of the realm of *mere athletic prowess*, to remove for all time the horrible commercial scramble in championships for honours, to place it in [the realm] of the arts; and to give the world a new art as Grafstrom and his followers conceive it' [emphasis added].[22]

Richardson's disparaging of athleticism and his disdain for the 'the horrible commercial scramble' of competition evoke the nineteenth-century gentleman's view of competition as the bane of true amateurism. In chapter 5 we saw that many nineteenth-century English skaters initially rejected the idea of competitions because they thought it unseemly for gentlemen to compete against their peers. They also worried that competitions would precipitate a slide to professionalism in figure skating and attract those who skated for prizes (as had been the case with speed skating) rather than those who skated for more intrinsic, refined motivations. While Richardson could see how prize money might be important for athletes from 'the masses,' he remained committed to a definition of amateurism that would not accommodate their circumstances. Thus, he wrote, 'it is to those who can afford time and money to study skating at home and abroad and pay for lessons with the recognized masters, that we must look for our national champions.'[23] And so begins a circular process: national championships are institutionalized by upper-class sportsmen as amateur contests; members of the upper classes are the only ones able to expend the time and resources needed for training, and thus it is they who win the honours; once won, these honours come to signify the superiority of the upper classes and to justify the privileges, like freedom from work, that made it possible for them to compete in the first place.

Historians have made a strong case that notions of amateurism in sport evolved as a way to foster and maintain class differences and exclusivity and that concerns about professionalism were in large part a response of middle- and upper-class sportsmen (and they were men) to working-class involvement in sport.[24] The introduction of amateur rules was a means of making sure that competitors of different class backgrounds – for instance, those who required prize money in order to live and to train and those who did not – did not mix. In actual practice there was little chance of professionalism 'contaminating' the exclusive upper-class world of figure skating in the late nineteenth or early twentieth centuries, when access to ice, clubs, and competitions was very well regulated by both economic and cultural means.

Concerns about the relationship between competitions and professionalism were not unique to figure skating. But some figure skaters took a position on the issue that participants in other sports might have found surprising. Writers like Richardson and Browne, for example, worried not just about competitive rewards or about who was permitted to compete but about the fact of competition itself. They claimed that competitions were pushing the emphasis in figure skating away from artistry to 'stunts,' that skaters were giving precedence to difficulty rather than aesthetics. In the 'scramble for honours' skaters were behaving like typical athletes, focusing on the technical aspects of their sport to gain advantage over others in their field. In most sports, critics would have been thrilled to see technical boundaries expanding. But critics in *Skating* magazine complained regularly that competitors were focusing too much on the obviously difficult elements of their programs in an effort to please the judges.[25] In a review of the 1931 world championships, Roger Turner wrote:

> One of my first impressions of the World Championships which were recently held in Berlin, Germany, was the exhaustive enthusiasm of the press for acrobatic skating. It would be unfortunate if the exponents of the Art should acquire an indelible image on their minds of acrobatics – stunts performed by [*sic*] a disharmonic nature – rather than a free and harmonious expression – the true continental school … There is danger … if perverted opinions predominate, of losing much of the glory and fineness of the present style; and figure skating like the Russian ballet, which has given way for a coarser school, would decline.[26]

As skaters attempted increasingly difficult jumps and spins, they were more likely to stumble or fall. While the resulting uncertainty made skating more exciting to many spectators, it also made it less elegant and less graceful, pulling it away from its aristocratic roots and the genteel demeanour prized by many of its participants.

What also rankled some critics was the way that the obviousness of difficult jumps and spins opened up the appreciation of figure skating to a larger audience. Refusing to be impressed by technical achievements, by skaters who 'showed off' with 'acrobatic stunts,' critics of this trend signalled their own refinement. They were marking themselves as members of the class of people who did not need to be dazzled by big leaps to appreciate a fine performance. Even as late as 1949 – the era of Dick Button's groundbreaking and huge double axels – the International Skating Union (ISU) vice-president responsible for figure skating could write: 'We do not want to promote showmanship combined with a lot of technical stunts; we want to see figure skating developing more and more into an *art* again, tastefully executed without skaters playing to the gallery.'[27] By rejecting the 'cult of obvious feats and visible virtuosity'[28] – by rejecting the gallery – those who disapproved of stunts were setting themselves up as 'connoisseurs,' distinguishing themselves from the uninformed masses. As Richardson put it, figure skating was just too hard for 'the man on the street to understand.'[29] Here again, we see the distinction between high and low culture and the positioning of skaters and skating as part of the former.

In his book *Distinction*, French sociologist Pierre Bourdieu argues that aesthetic tastes and the taste for certain cultural products, including sports, is not 'natural' or inborn, but is produced through social practices and follows a logic derived from class inequalities. He writes:

> The denial of lower, coarse, vulgar, venal, servile – in a word, natural – enjoyment, which constitutes the sacred sphere of culture, implies an affirmation of the superiority of those who can be satisfied with the sublimated, refined, disinterested, gratuitous, distinguished pleasures forever closed to the profane. That is why art and cultural consumption are predisposed, consciously and deliberately or not, to fulfil a social function of legitimating social differences.[30]

Bourdieu argues that an educated 'aesthetic sense' lends status to members of the privileged classes. Its exercise serves as a means of maintaining or proclaiming one's rank, 'asserting one's position in social space.'[31] As Linda Young explains it, 'distinctions of taste' transpose into 'distinctions of class.'[32] Produced in specific class conditions – a combination of upbringing and education – aesthetic sense unites those who share those conditions while dividing them from those who do not. Such divisions, of course, are not innocent or benign. They help to constitute and maintain social and economic class hierarchies rooted in domination and exclusion; they help people to know their place; they make class and race differences seem natural and like they are linked to inherent personal characteristics and abilities rather than differential access to economic and cultural capital.

Until the mid-1930s, figure skating was still very much an upper-class sport in Europe and North America, especially at the highest levels, and skaters were a relatively homogeneous group. Authors of an early history (1902) of the National Skating Association of Great Britain (NSA) claimed that the NSA figure proficiency tests – known as the bronze, silver, and gold medals – had been designed to 'take in the masses as well as the classes.' The masses, however, 'never appear to have caught on to any extent, but it might be well to remember that we had their interests at heart, if they knew what was good for them.'[33] While this type of patronizing, elitist attitude diminished somewhat over the first few decades of the twentieth century, the financial costs associated with competitive skating did not. Skaters needed plenty of money to ply their craft in private clubs, to pay the not inconsiderable costs of travel to competitions, to hire private coaches. They also needed cultural and social capital to gain a place in the skating world. In London and in many other European cities, clubs were exclusive social environments with fabulous facilities – 'warm dressing rooms, lounges, reading rooms, writing desks, glassed-in restaurants'[34] – staff members who actually took care of members' skates,[35] and noble, if not always royal, patrons. Competitions often involved social events, like cocktail parties and formal post-skating banquets, that demanded both proper attire and proper etiquette. Even while training, skaters were expected to fulfil the requirements of 'good taste' in terms of dress and behaviour, an expectation reflected, for instance, in rules that prohibited men from skating in their shirtsleeves.[36]

Wealth alone was not always enough to ensure entry or acceptance into clubs. Well into the twentieth century, some figure skating clubs continued to employ the type of exclusionary vetting policies that were once common in country clubs and other elite sporting clubs. Such policies kept the population of skaters firmly located in dominant racial, ethnic, and religious categories. In a letter to her family written in 1933, American skater Maribel Vinson reported on a club in Edinburgh: 'Mr

S is the Mussolini of it – he turned down six applications on Sunday because he didn't consider them desirable – and he gets away with it.'[37] Vinson doesn't say what Mr S was screening for. It could have been skating skills, sociability, or financial position. He also could have been looking for markers of religion, race, or ethnicity that would have threatened the homogeneity of his club.

In an expansive article on Jewish history and modern sport, George Eisen writes that, after the Second World War, European sports clubs gave up what had once been the common practice of barring Jews from membership. In North America, such anti-Jewish policies continued at some clubs into the 1970s. In January 1962, the Anti-Defamation League of the B'nai B'rith in the United States issued a report on discrimination in country clubs. The researchers found that of the 803 clubs surveyed in the United States, 576 engaged in discriminatory practices. Four hundred and sixteen clubs, almost 52 per cent, prevented Jews from joining, while 89 clubs had quotas that restricted the number of Jews who could be members.[38] When we think of the kind of social and athletic clubs that discriminated against potential members we tend to think of golf clubs and maybe tennis clubs. But some figure skating clubs also engaged in anti-Semitic and racist membership policies. Legendary Canadian skating coach Ellen Burka emigrated to Canada from Holland at the start of the Cold War. A Jewish survivor of concentration camps, Burka kept her religion to herself when she came to Toronto looking for coaching jobs: 'When I entered Toronto not only was it very WASP-y but it also was very anti-Semitic. There were many, many clubs which didn't allow any Jews in there. I am quite sure if I would have told anyone I was Jewish I wasn't able to teach in some clubs. So this way it was much safer. My children were brought up as Anglicans and myself, I didn't have any religion.'[39] Toronto's Granite Club, an exclusive social and athletic club where Burka now coaches, is one of the clubs that would have prohibited Jews from joining. Its anti-Semitic membership practices were not discontinued until 1970, when members of the Anti-Defamation League of B'nai B'rith Canada launched an opposition campaign against discrimination at the club.[40]

Like other elite sports clubs, the more prestigious figure skating clubs were as much an excuse for socializing as they were for skating. It was not until the widespread construction of public and commercial rinks in the late 1930s and 1940s that new clubs were founded to cater to a less-exclusive middle-class clientele. But even some of these less prestigious clubs maintained exclusionary policies. Mabel Fairbanks was a

'Never were manliness and grace more winningly combined,' wrote one reviewer of 'The Skater,' a portrait of William Grant by Gilbert Stuart. 1782. Oil on canvas. Andrew W. Mellon Collection, National Gallery of Art, Washington.

THE COMBINED-FIGURE.

"Twice back centre-change entire."

In the mid-1800s, English gentlemen rejected the expressive possibilities of skating, turning instead towards technical innovation and 'combined skating,' a type of formal group exercise that required a regimented uniformity. It emphasized long edges and turns and required a large ice surface. It was practised with a stiff upright posture. Knees were not to bend. Arms were not to lift. Nothing fanciful was to interfere with precision.

JACKSON HAINES.

JACKSON HAINES.

JACKSON HAINES.

JACKSON HAINES.

American Jackson Haines saw in skating tremendous theatrical and artistic possibilities. When his innovative ideas failed to take hold at home, he travelled to Europe looking for receptive audiences. Haines's 1868 performance in Vienna caused a 'great sensation' and is said to have launched the 'art of modern skating,' the skating known today as figure skating.

At its roots Viennese skating was about pleasure – the pleasure of moving to music, the pleasure of the easy and long-held edge, the pleasure of the spectator. But it was also about the pleasure to be gained from socializing on ice. In the late 1860s skating was becoming a fashionable bourgeois pastime in Vienna, and masquerades, ice balls, and cotillions were regular events at the Vienna Skating Club. Eislaufplatz vor dem Stubentor [Skating rink before the Stubentor] by Franz Kollarz. 1869.

In 1902, Madge Syers of England was the first woman to compete for the world championship. She placed second behind the famous Swedish skater Ulrich Salchow. In response the ISU quickly enacted a rule prohibiting women from competing against men in international meets. A separate ladies' championship was established in 1906. Syers was the first champion. She won again in 1907. She also won the gold medal when skating first appeared at the Olympics, in London in 1908.

PANIN, ST PETERSBURG. AT CHANGE FROM OUTSIDE TO INSIDE.

Above: Nikolai Panin won the gold medal for special figures at the first Olympic skating competition in 1908, the first and only gold medal ever awarded for special figures at the Olympics. Panin's medal was also the first and only Olympic medal to be won on behalf of Tsarist Russia. Here he is practising school figures on a beautifully cleared and sizeable rink.

Below: Henning Grenander of Sweden was the 1898 world champion and helped to introduce the more artistic continental style of skating to England. Here he demonstrates the kind of free skating moves that were not yet part of the English repertoire. Once again, notice the expanse of well-cleared outdoor ice.

THE SPREAD EAGLE, GRENANDER.

GRENANDER. DOUBLE TOE PIROUETTE.

Gillis Grafstrom was Olympic champion in 1920, 1924, and 1928. He was lauded by English writer T.D. Richardson as a 'great artist ... [The Russian ballet dancer] Nijinsky at his greatest was no finer exponent of the dance than is Grafstrom of *his* art, unrivalled in delicacy or poise on skates that flash like sword blades.'

Karl Schäfer of Austria won seven world championships, from 1930 to 1936. He was the Olympic champion in 1932 and 1936. In Schäfer's era figure skating competitions and shows were becoming increasingly popular spectator events. In this 1932 press photograph Schäfer is skating in front of a huge crowd at the Engelmann ice rink in Vienna.

Sonja Henie of Norway won ten world championships and three Olympic gold medals. After she retired from competitive skating in 1936 she became a Hollywood film star. Her movies brought skating to a mass audience for the first time and played a large role in the development of skating's reputation as a 'feminine' sport.

For Cecile Grafstrom, with my kindly wishes and English regards — Dick Button

Two-time Olympic gold medalist (1948, 1952) Dick Button of the United States introduced a new level of athleticism to men's figure skating. While many men tried to copy his powerful style, few paid attention to his equally strong aesthetic sensibilities. Men's programs became so packed with jumps that there was little opportunity to demonstrate or develop their artistic skills. As Button himself commented in 1966, 'The majority of male skaters have awkward positions and very little flair in presenting their programs. Are they ashamed of making a beautiful line?'

John Curry of Britain was the 1976 Olympic and world champion. Known for his 'ravishingly beautiful' body line, Curry was heavily influenced by ballet. After retiring from competition he established the John Curry Skating Company in New York and set out to turn skating into a performing art. 'What I try to achieve,' said Curry, 'is something that cannot be done in any other medium.'

1976 Olympic bronze medalist Toller Cranston of Canada is considered by many to have been one of the most innovative skaters in the history of the sport. Described as operatic and baroque, Cranston's skating was full of angles, passion, and embellishments, and it pushed men's skating in new expressive directions.

Canadian Kurt Browning was part of a 1990s cohort of male skaters who were lauded by the press as much for their masculinity as for their skating. Canada's *Saturday Night* magazine claimed that 'Kurt Browning's macho ice image … startled the skating world.' The *Globe and Mail* credited him with 'wiping away the stereotype of effeminate male skaters.' Browning was a four-time world champion and was the first skater to land a quadruple jump in competition.

Nicknamed 'The Terminator,' Elvis Stojko of Canada won the world championship in 1994, 1995, and 1997. He is shown here skating at the 1994 Canadian national championships. During his competitive career Stojko attracted a lot of media attention for his explicitly macho style. More recently, Stojko has been in the news as a vocal critic of figure skating's new scoring system, which, he suggests, is making men's skating too soft.

2008 world champion Jeffrey Buttle of Canada was among the first generation of skaters to compete under the ISU's new scoring system. Noted for his
musicality, his complex choreography, and his superior technique in all the
elements of his performances, Buttle was exactly the kind of well-rounded
skater the system was designed to celebrate.

Patrick Chan is the current Canadian national champion and a two-time world silver medalist. He has grown up with the new scoring system and the expectation that even male skaters should be more than jumpers on skates. He is fortunate to be skating in an era when men's skating seems to be less constrained by gender stereotypes than it was in the 1990s. Here Chan performs at the 2009 Skate Canada International competition.

pioneering African American figure skater and coach. As a young girl, in the mid-1930s, she was refused entry to public rinks in New York City. But she was persistent in her attempts and one rink manager eventually relented and allowed her to skate. Once on the ice, Fairbanks was noticed by coaches Maribel Vinson and Howard Nicholson, who gave her free lessons and advice. But, despite completing all the United States Figure Skating Association (USFSA) proficiency tests, Fairbanks was never permitted to join a figure skating club, and thus she was unable to compete.

With no chance for a competitive career, Fairbanks turned professional. In an era when racism kept the big ice shows like Ice Capades and Ice Follies from considering a black performer, Fairbanks skated in benefits for black community organizations and charities and in nightclubs. According to the *Los Angeles Times*, the nightclubs always billed Fairbanks as an 'extra added attraction.' They never let her 'dazzle the audience with her skill and amazing jumps and spins because "none of the white skaters wanted to be outshone by someone black."'[41] In 1947 Fairbanks took a job performing with Rhythm on Ice, a previously all-white ice review that toured in the southern United States and Mexico. She was hired because the show's management wanted 'someone to skate in the dark countries.'[42]

One of Fairbanks's early coaching jobs was at the Pasadena Figure Skating Club, where a sign posted at the rink entrance read: 'Colored Trade Not Solicited.' Fairbanks called in the media before taking up a position at a rival club. In the 1960s, two of her students, Atoy Wilson and Richard Ewell III, became the first black skaters to be admitted to figure skating clubs in the United States. They both went on to win gold medals at national championships. Wilson won in novice men's and Ewell in junior men's and in junior pairs with Michelle McCladdie.[43]

Discriminatory practices like those confronted by Burka and Fairbanks were not just about prohibiting access to ice or lessons or the experience of skating. They were also about protecting what Pierre Bourdieu called the 'social profits' of skating; they were the means by which such profits were hoarded by dominant social groups. In this regard, figure skating shares a background with golf, equestrianism, and other sports pursued in private clubs. Like these other elite sports, figure skating brought 'gains in distinction' to those with the cultural, social, and economic capital required to participate. Before, during, and after their skating, members of private skating clubs were able to mingle with the 'right kind of people' – people who looked like them and shared their privileges. Skating offered club members the opportunity to display their privilege through forms of movement and carriage produced by training and practice in environments that were not open to all. Spectating offered them the opportunity to exercise and demonstrate their educated aesthetic tastes. Shared skating knowledge helped skating insiders to confirm their identities as members of a select group who knew how to 'read' the sport; it set them up as connoisseurs, as distinct from those who watched only for sensational moves and from those who did not watch at all.

Institutionalizing Aesthetics in an Institutionalized Sport

Debates over the value and place of athleticism and aesthetics in figure skating did not just take place in the pages of skating magazines, they also figured on the agendas of the biannual congresses of the International Skating Union – as they still do, although perhaps less explicitly, today. From the very earliest championships, as we saw in chapter 5, skaters have been judged on style. It is not enough in figure skating to get from point A to point B, to spin quickly or to jump a great distance. Skaters have always been required to meet aesthetic criteria as they perform; even the first set of international rules was very specific regarding style.

Late-nineteenth-century competitions included both figure and free skating events. The latter were fairly tame, involving turns, connecting steps, simple spins, small jumps, and gliding movements like spirals. The regulations adopted by the ISU for both parts of the competition detailed basic principles regarding carriage (easy, graceful, and upright) and general movement (swinging, supple, purposeful, and controlled). Skaters were admonished not to perform stiff or angular movements, or to adopt an affected bearing, or to demonstrate 'cramped, spasmodic, exaggerated, or aimless action.'[44] Judges were required to look at both performance and difficulty. In the freestyle portion of the competition, judges based their scores on (a) the contents of the program, including the difficulty and diversity of the various elements, and (b) the manner of its performance, including harmonious composition, confidence, posture, and quality of movement.

The first ISU freestyle regulations had no requirements about specific moves, music, or clothing, as they do today. German skating historian Matthias Hampe claims, rightly, that this left skaters a lot of freedom to expand their repertoires and to exercise their creativity and artistry.

In his opinion, technical requirements are too weighed down by 'moral conventions,' which present a great obstacle to artistic development.[45] Of course, aesthetic and artistic standards can be equally heavy with moral conventions. Skaters' freedom to perform to their own aesthetic criteria has been limited since the first rules were published. Even the basic prohibition against stiff, angular movement – which until recently was an unquestioned norm of skating style – suggested a very particular take on what skaters' bodies should look like, what ideas or feelings they should communicate by their performances. In this way figure skating codified general, often unspoken, norms concerning bodies and forms of movement that were rooted in bourgeois and white European traditions that contrasted clearly with movement norms from other cultures like, for instance, those evident in South Asian or African styles of dance that employ angular or bent limbs.[46]

The regulation of the body is a particularly powerful means by which we come to internalize – to live – various forms of power. Limitations on the kinds of gestures we might make in certain situations, on the types of clothing we wear, on the speed with which we move, on the public, physical expression of emotions or ideas are all examples of embodied forms of power. Ideologies around gender, class, race, and nationalism are articulated through forms of physical comportment like walking, sitting, and standing. The admonishment to stand up straight is not given to children simply out of concern for their spines; it is a way of building into the very structure and feeling of their bodies discourses about what an upright person represents.

The graceful movement and upright posture demanded of competitive figure skaters was not in any great way different from the same qualities expected in the everyday movements of well-to-do people. Erect postures have long been an important means of representing and reproducing the fundamental moral values of the genteel classes, symbolizing self-discipline, moral fortitude, and dignity. Upright bodies are assumed to be controlled, to resist impulses and the public expression of too much emotion. They are a fine mark of what Peter Gay has called the 'regulated will,' a central defining characteristic of the Victorian bourgeoisie and their cultural heirs.[47] A potent and easily visible sign of class difference, 'good' posture is one of the less tangible effects of a privileged upbringing. It provides daily rewards that can be easily taken for granted: ease of interaction with officials like teachers, police officers, bank employees; respectful treatment in public environments like stores and restaurants; opportunities for casual social interactions with other similarly embodied people. In this sense, Bourdieu would say that 'good' posture provides evidence of the way bodies serve as physical capital, that is, as vehicles by which individuals gain status, access to resources, and power. In common-sense knowledge about different postures, we can see the 'substantial inequalities in the social values accorded to particular bodily forms.'[48] The requirement of an erect posture in figure skating made sure that skaters did not contravene the norms of appearance or movement – the requirements of taste – that helped to constitute the privileges and rewards of the class from which they came.

While rules about posture and style of movement guaranteed that skaters paid attention to their appearance as well as their technique, some commentators felt that the ISU should have gone further to promote artistry in skating. In such discussions the term 'artistry' rarely functioned as anything more than a simple synonym for beauty. What counted as beautiful, however, remained largely unstated, its definition assumed to be self-evident. In this sense, the beauty promoted by skating critics was not in the eye of the beholder but was seen as timeless and universal, an obvious cultural value. But beauty is no different than any other cultural value, as dance historian Evan Alderson reminds us: 'Our sense of the beautiful ... is ideologically conditioned ... When we are moved by the beauty of something, it is difficult to see it also as expressing a specific social interest.'[49] Indeed, we learn a lot about social values and social hierarchies through definitions of what is *not* beautiful. In figure skating, both the demand for beauty, like the demand for good posture, and its definition (or lack thereof) expressed the specific interests of the 'cultured classes' of the industrial metropole. Shared notions of beauty that derived from knowledge of ballet and from other elite performing and visual arts, especially the art of classical Greece, were part of the language of good taste that gave figure skating its refined and elegant image. A skater who failed to demonstrate such taste risked being labelled 'ugly and uncouth,' as the always frank T.D. Richardson put it.[50] The notion that beauty might be open to various definitions or that its definition might be a vector of power had no place in Richardson's many commentaries, nor indeed in the rules themselves, which applied equally to all skaters, male and female.

From our contemporary vantage point, it is surprising to find that, for at least several decades at the beginning of the twentieth century, discussions of beauty in skating were relatively silent on the subject of gender. While some skating textbooks suggested that beauty and grace came more naturally to women, their authors still expected men to develop these qualities in their skating, and it was assumed that men and women needed to move their bodies in similar ways to look good on the ice. It was not until the mid-1940s that *Skating* magazine published its first challenge to prevailing notions of artistry in the sport. William Grimditch, men's silver medallist at the 1942 US national championships, argued for wider notions of art and a more complex understanding of aesthetic effectiveness in figure skating rules. He quoted the rulebook disparagingly: 'Speed should be gained as inconspicuously as possible ... Everything violent, angular, or stiff is to be avoided. There should be no visible strong effort and the impression should be given that the entire program is executed with ease.' His own definition of what worked was clearly influenced by wartime masculine norms and by a particularly American set of values. Using other male skaters as evidence, Grimditch made a case for the thrill of speed and effort and the appropriateness of a 'stiff' form in certain contexts, like a 'military spread-eagle.' He criticized skaters (presumably male) who looked like 'graceful "weak fishes."' He found the overemphasis on grace and erect carriage in free skating dull:

> In the ideal academic skating, the skater's arms are always 'extended, and hands are at waist height'; he shows no sign of effort, no sign of gaining speed, his carriage is always erect, in fact, if you only saw the upper half of him you would think he was riding a bicycle or at home sitting on the sofa, except that he sways very gracefully and easily to the music – like a lullaby. Give me energy, vigor, and occasional violence!
>
> We need more than the type of skating which belongs with eighteenth or nineteenth century art – art which embodied only the beautiful, the graceful, the sweet and frilly, the effeminate.[51]

Grimditch claimed to have nothing against beauty and grace, he was simply against the notion that 'these two rather effeminate qualities' should be the only thing that counts as 'good art' in skating. Art in the twentieth century, he wrote, is 'manly, forceful, shrill, vigorous, energetic, dynamic and intense.' It obviously did not hold much place for women.

It's hard to argue with Grimditch's criticism that figure skating was governed by a narrow and historically particular set of aesthetic criteria. Yet his concerns were clearly about masculinity as much as they were about art. What is interesting about Grimditch's argument is that he makes the case for virility from the *art* side of the art/sport binary. Later advocates of a greater athleticism in skating, who espoused an understanding of masculinity very similar to his, would see the concept of art itself as not just limited or badly interpreted, as Grimditch did, but as fundamentally problematic for male skaters.

Worrying about Masculinity: Promoting Skating as Sport

By the 1940s and 1950s, calls to protect and augment skating's artistic side were growing fewer in number and tamer in rhetoric. Increasingly, skaters were drawn from the middle class and thus they did not have the same investment as had their more wealthy predecessors in main-taining their sport as a symbol of elite good taste and refinement. Dick Button had made it clear that the technical bounds of the sport could be pushed further than once believed. Most important, what had once been a mixed-gender sport for adults from culturally and economically privileged backgrounds had turned into a sport primarily pursued by young girls from the growing post-war middle class. In the immediate post-war period, skating clubs were faced for the first time with a short-age of boys and men, and officials and coaches began to speak publicly about the problem of attracting male skaters to their rinks.

While upper-class men of earlier decades seem to have had little dif-ficulty reconciling their gender identities with the artistic demands of skating, such demands conflicted with prevailing post-war masculine norms and the heavily gendered definitions of sport that supported them. Hence, debates about the relative weight of aesthetic and ath-letic aspects of skating that had once been proxies for discussions of class, came to centre instead on gender. Concerned about the possibil-ity that male skaters might be perceived to be effeminate or gay, some skating insiders began to push for skating to present a more sporting image, that is, an image that could be read easily as masculine, given the fact that sport was (and continues to be) seen primarily as a field of masculine endeavour. The irony of this strategy was that by the late 1940s, the level of athleticism in skating had skyrocketed. Both men and women were paying more attention to the fine technical points that made it easier to perform multiple revolution jumps or to spin more quickly and efficiently or to maintain their stamina throughout their programs. Pairs skaters were starting to experiment with overhead lifts and throw jumps that demanded strength from the men and strength, control, and fearlessness from the women. Despite these innovations, popular discourses about the relationship between sport and gender framed skating as a girls' sport and, therefore, not much of a sport at all. The ill fit between skating and definitions of sport as a straightforwardly manly endeavour put the gender reputations of male skaters at risk. In an attempt to salvage the masculine image of men who skated, some skaters and officials drew on discourses of athleticism, as dance critics had done before them, to try to constitute for skating and skaters a more virile image. If skating were seen to be less of an art and more of a sport, perhaps boys and men would see it as compatible with mainstream masculine norms and, thus, not be afraid to try it.

The 'American style of high-powered athletics' introduced after the Second World War by Dick Button 'and his merry henchmen,' as one enthusiastic critic called them, set the scene for the recasting of men's skating as a solidly masculine and not terribly artistic pursuit.[52] Throughout the 1950s and 1960s, many men tried to copy Button's powerful style, but few of them paid attention to his equally strong aesthetic sensibilities. Men's programs became so packed with jumps that there was little opportunity to demonstrate or develop their artistic skills. As Button himself commented in a review of the 1966 world championships,

> The men's free skating performances were marked by unpointed toes, unstretched legs, bent backs, a notable lack of spinning ability and very little interest in relating choreography to music ... [T]he majority of male skaters have awkward positions and very little flair in presenting their programs. Are they ashamed of making a beautiful line? Do they realize that a masculine performance doesn't necessarily mean an awkward one?[53]

This is as close as skating critics came to identifying the 'problem' of men's skating. Button was one of only a few writers able to acknowledge that gender had something to do with it. He was also unique in presenting his concerns without a call to cleave the art from skating's athleticism. Other writers tended to keep their underlying gender concerns implicit as they argued for less art and a lot more sport. USFSA official Alan Zell, for instance, wrote a piece in 1970 in which he asked, 'Are we going to sit back and be known as an "athletic art form" rather than a sport?' Vice-chairman [sic] of the USFSA Public Relations Committee, Zell wanted figure skating to adopt a more 'sports-oriented image' and to show a more 'athletic front to the public.'[54] At issue was not skating per se, but the context within which it took place. Zell wanted the printed programs at competitions to provide statistical details on each skater and to include scoring charts. He wanted to see large scoreboards in arenas so spectators could more easily follow the standings. He wanted skaters to 'dress more like athletes, not like people in show business.' And while he criticized the chiffon, the rhinestones, and the 'high hairdoes' worn by the women, his main concern was for the men: 'Some of the [men's] costumes are just too trim, neat and show-biz. The stretch suits that most male skaters are wearing might give us a better sports image if they'd allow for a shirt tail to stick out near the end of a program.' He claimed that spectators found it surprising that a man could 'look trim and neat after three or five minutes of rigorous participation in any sport.' To look like real athletes – to look manly – skaters apparently needed to show their effort and sweat, exactly the sort of thing that would have appalled the elegant men who had competed in earlier times.

Zell also worried about language. He wanted commentators to use 'masculine and powerful terms, especially,' he wrote without irony, 'when [they] talk about men skaters.' He offered a few examples: 'He *spikes* the ice, not toe-picks. He *jumps*, not leaps. He uses his *strength*, not extends to get height. He has *muscle, power, control* and he *attacks*. Use any word you can think of which connotes a virile image' (emphasis in original).[55] And, finally, he wanted skating to be portrayed as a rugged physical exercise – in other words, something befitting a man.

Clearly Zell was not that troubled about the image presented by female skaters. For commentators like Zell, the question of skating's definition as either art or sport was (and continues to be) a decidedly masculine concern. Rather less ink has been spilled in the contemplation of whether female skaters should be, or should be perceived to be, athletes or artists. Certainly no one has proposed that women wear less tidy costumes, that their skating be discussed in more powerful and virile terms, or that they be described as rugged.

Zell never explained why skating needs a more sporting image. He wrote only that 'sports editors, teachers, coaches and the general public have come to regard figure skaters as participants in a semi-art form rather than in a sport. Most of us in skating think they are wrong, but we have done little to dispel their misconceptions.' Does it matter whether skaters are seen to be participating in a sport or in an art? For male skaters in North America it matters a lot. The desire to present skating as sport rather than art is a bid for respect in a culture that sees sport as masculine and art as feminine, a culture that gives priority to endeavours defined as male rather than female, hetero- rather than homosexual. Despite the impressive headway made by women into the broader realm of sport, the default category for athlete remains male. Art, by contrast, is assumed to be a feminine pursuit in North American culture. It is rare (think rock musician or film actor) that a man's virility is confirmed by his artistic talents or inclinations.

Sport and art are generally seen as separate domains that share little in terms of the values they promote or the practices they generate. Some commentators have found it difficult to accept that figure skating draws on both traditions. Journalists, officials, and even skaters have questioned the sport's reliance on costumes, makeup, and music, claiming these are incompatible with the athleticism of skating.[56] Their concerns have nothing to do with the quality of skating performances nor with the competence of skaters; they are, simply, criticisms of their image – it is not sporting enough. Does a skating program become less difficult or less athletic when the skater wears sequins? Would a record-breaking sprint be any less impressive were the runner to wear makeup or jewellery, à la Florence Griffith Joyner? Is this issue only a problem when the competitors are men? Concerns about the presentation and image of skaters belie the fact that sport is defined not just by the movements athletes make but also by the context within which they make them, a point not lost on public-relations man Zell. We understand certain activities to be sport because they take place in a sporting context. It is not physical activity per se that makes sport but the meanings we give to it, and those meanings are heavily shaped by discourses about gender and sexuality. Beneath worries about the image of male skaters lies an understanding that physical demands alone cannot guarantee skating's right to be called a sport, and thus they cannot be relied upon to validate the masculinities of male skaters.

Resistance from the Artists: Cranston and Curry

Throughout the 1970s and 1980s the art versus sport debate continued in the pages of skating magazines: 'Which Is It – Art or Sport?' 'Athlete or Artist,' 'Are Skaters Athletes?' 'Sport vs. Art,' 'Athletes and Artists.'[57] But it also played out dramatically on the ice. Forceful interventions were made by Canada's Toller Cranston, 1976 Olympic bronze medallist, and by England's John Curry, 1976 Olympic gold medallist, both

of whom voted with their feet, their arms, and their torsos for the proponents of art, emphatically defying the version of figure skating promoted by writers like Zell. Cranston was all angles and passion and
baroque embellishment, Curry was the cool danseur, perfecter of the
elegant edge and an impeccable, 'ravishingly beautiful' line. While they
worked from different aesthetic sensibilities, both hoped to push the
artistic development of figure skating to where it could hold its own
against other performing arts. Technically accomplished skaters, they
valued skating as a medium for self-expression. They understood their
music, they attended to the fine details of body line, and they certainly
did not allow prevailing notions of masculinity to curtail their creativity. As a consequence, they both struggled throughout their careers to
gain acceptance in a sport that had grown aesthetically timid in the
face of narrow but popular ideas of how male bodies should move and
perform in public.

Curry and Cranston both weathered criticism of the way they performed gender. Both were told explicitly that their skating was too
effeminate. In the days before computerized marking, Curry faced
judges who, in protest against his style, refused to lift their scorecards
higher than their shoulders.[58] Even as these two men were winning
their Olympic medals, that is, when they were the best free skaters in
the world, some commentators could still not accept that they did not
perform from the point at which sport and gender norms usually con-
verge. A German reporter described Cranston as a 'clown on ice.' An
Austrian television announcer introduced Cranston's Canadian team-
mate Ron Shaver by saying, 'Now we will see more of a male performance.'[59] One London newspaper announced Curry's Olympic victory
– the first figure skating gold medal for an English man – in a story
with the following opening line: 'They played God Save the Queen last
night. It was for John Curry.'[60] And here is a German writer in a book
commemorating the 1976 Games:

> Nobody will deny that the lovely Dianne de Leeuw of the Netherlands
> has real curves above her blades; but with the male skaters some doubts
> threaten to overshadow the future. If either the handsome Toller or the
> graceful John had worn a small skirt they could have become the best
> female figure skater of this year's winter games. Prof. Dr. Ivan Maur of
> Bratislava has found that to be successful, a female figure skater must
> have long legs. Those of John Curry are the longest. But he is a man. Never
> before have men skated so femininely.[61]

Of course, the derision was not universal, as Curry's and Cranston's Olympic medals suggest. Skaters and spectators who valued the artistic side of skating hailed Curry and Cranston as revolutionaries. The two skaters sent appreciative writers stumbling after adjectives. They were declared geniuses for their innovative contributions. Both were at various times compared to Vaslav Nijinsky and Rudolf Nureyev. In Germany – the 'clown' comment notwithstanding – Toller Cranston was feted as the 'skater of the century.' Curry was publicly lauded by the widows of the great Swedish skaters Ulrich Salchow and Gillis Grafstrom. The widow of Salchow presented Curry with her husband's 1908 commemorative Olympic medal. The widow of Grafstrom presented Curry with a small gold skate that she had engraved with a congratulatory message. According to the *London Times*, Mrs Grafstrom 'was only too anxious to sing the praises of a man whom she regards as having turned back the clock to the unhurried, graceful, elegant days of the 20s.' She apparently told Curry that he reminded her of her husband, Gillis, because of his 'musical interpretation and lack of acrobatics' which, she said, 'belong to the circus.'[62]

In the 1970s, men's skating was often underdeveloped except for the jumps. As Curry himself put it, 'People can now do three turns in the air but cannot skate round the corner.'[63] Many male skaters seemed wooden. Their backs were stiff, their arms were rigid. They ignored their music. This was the crowd out of which Cranston and Curry emerged. Watching them on YouTube today, it takes no special knowledge of skating to note their different approaches. Here were skaters who did not feel the need to conform to a typical sporting persona, who saw technique as a means to an end, and who understood the potential of the gliding, skating body to open up unique aesthetic and expressive opportunities. Thirty years later, Curry's ability to compose a gorgeous body line has yet to be matched. He was the skater for whom pre–Second World War critics like T.D. Richardson had been waiting. Cranston was something else. His bent elbows and knees, his curving torso and electric hands all challenged skating's conventional notions of line and grace. Where Curry was supple and stretched, Cranston appeared taut and brimming with unspent energy. Sports writers, straining for vocabulary outside their normal range, frequently described Cranston as 'balletic.' Yet there was no ballet in his background; indeed, his ability to skate with exuberant abandon was the antithesis of the dignified control trained into ballet dancers. Cranston was the answer to William Grimditch's call, in the 1940s, for new ways to conceptualize beauty on ice. Although, in a classic case of 'Be careful what you ask for,' Cranston's skating came nowhere close to fitting the manly post-war American aesthetic Grimditch seemed to have had in mind.

After retiring from their amateur careers, Cranston and Curry both launched professional skating companies through which they hoped to escape the limitations of sport and to realize their visions for a truly artistic form of skating. John Curry produced and choreographed shows in England and the United States, collaborating with a number of well-known dance choreographers – Twyla Tharp, Sir Kenneth Macmillan, Peter Martins, Laura Dean. From 1977 until 1985 he directed the John Curry Skating Company, setting out to assemble a repertoire of skating pieces that could be performed, as dance pieces are performed, by different skaters at different times in different places. Like dancers, Curry's skaters attended daily class, where they worked on perfecting a shared movement vocabulary and a company style. The approach was novel in the world of skating. And while it met with great critical success, Curry never found the financial security that would have permitted his company to continue without him. In 1991, Curry announced publicly that he was living with AIDS. He moved back to England, where he died in 1994.

Whereas Curry's professional efforts were about skating as a 'high art,' Cranston's were spectacular and designed to showcase his own charisma. 'Toller Cranston's The Ice Show' opened on Broadway in May 1977. Like the big touring ice shows, Cranston's was full of glitz and glamour; unlike Ice Capades or Ice Follies, it was built around a small troupe of champion skaters. There was no mistaking, however, that he was the star. Here's a writer from the *New York Times* describing one of Cranston's entrances: 'Mr. Cranston, wearing a black beaded jumpsuit cut nearly to his navel, his head thrown back à la Nureyev, slowly descends to the stage in a huge illuminated star. The entrance regularly causes Mr. Cranston's admirers, many of them male, to break into laughter and enthusiastic cheers.'[64] Critics loved the show, but more for Cranston's personal style and aesthetic than for the troupe or any long-term impact it could have had on the development of skating itself. Despite the accolades, Cranston, like Curry, was unable to secure solid financing.

In their own ways, Cranston and Curry were both trying to explore what figure skating might become outside the realm of sporting competition and the big mass-market commercial shows like Ice Capades. 'What I try to achieve,' said Curry, 'is something that cannot be done in any other medium.'[65] As Cranston put it, skating was a 'virgin area' in the world of the performing arts, its vast potential yet to be met. But, while Cranston and Curry both wanted to push skating in new artistic directions, their legacies have been greatest within the sport itself. In the years after their amateur retirements, television announcers talked frequently of Tollerisms and Curryesque movements. As skaters had once tried to emulate the board-clearing jumps of Dick Button, they now tried to paint themselves as artistic in the manner of Curry or Cranston. In 1975 Frank Loeser, Canadian correspondent for *Skating* magazine, and probably one of the best writers ever to comment on skating, wrote that the work of Cranston and his teachers Ellen Burka and Brian Foley had already influenced skaters across Canada: 'The result is a more flamboyant style. Unfortunately, when the Tollerisms are copied directly, they are irritating and almost always second rate. Skaters do not seem to take from Toller a more valuable awareness; and that is, that even in figure skating (where the social demands for conformity often seem Victorian), one can still be original and individual – and succeed.'[66]

It's not altogether surprising that Cranston and Curry would show up at the same time, in the mid-1970s, to challenge, in different ways, the narrow masculinity that had taken hold of skating in the late 1950s and 1960s. In western Europe and North America in the 1970s and early 1980s, space was opening for men to represent a broader range of masculinities in public. Alternative arts and styles that had emerged in the counter-cultural movements of the late 1960s were moving into the mainstream. Singers like David Bowie and Freddie Mercury were flamboyant, androgynous, visible, and popular. Feminism and gay liberation movements, while still marginal, had had some success in forcing issues of gender and sexuality onto the public agenda. Outside the world of sport, traditional images of masculinity were clearly being contested. For skaters who did not define themselves solely as athletes, the culture at large provided a lot of material for inspiration. With Curry and Cranston having broken the ground with great competitive success, some male skaters became more willing to experiment with new ways of skating. While stiff arms and rigid backs were not (and still have yet to be) wiped out, they were no longer the only option for men. A little bit of space had been created within figure skating for men, once again, to pay more attention to artistry. But not all skaters wanted to claim it.

In discussions about figure skating, debates over the relative weight of art and athleticism conceal worries about what people outside the sport think of it, especially people who are men. Will they respect it? Will they sign up their sons? Will they validate skaters' skills and talents? Will they let skaters into the privileged society of athletes? Or will they write off male skaters as effeminate sissies? In a 1983 article, world champion Scott Hamilton of the United States (who became the 1984 Olympic gold medallist) said it was a shame that men's skating had 'been marketed as mostly artistic' (a statement which would have shocked many skaters). Hamilton wanted to help make skating more athletic. 'Artistry,' he said, 'comes down to taste and people that are interested in the arts ... But everyone enjoys athletics.' Everyone? Would Hamilton have been more precise to say 'all men enjoy athletics'? Hamilton said he had always wanted to bring figure skating 'out into the public eye to let people enjoy it more – I wanted to involve the whole sports community. I kind of wanted to gain the public's respect as an athlete ... Skating is for everybody, not just for people that have a taste for artistry. It's something that everyone can enjoy.'[67] In this formulation, people with a 'taste for artistry' are likely women and gay men. Hamilton seemed to understand that the only audience that could validate his athleticism was made up of straight males, but they were unlikely to flock to anything that seemed too arty and, thus, too fey.

The Stojko Effect

The art/sport opposition is one of the primary structuring devices of figure skating commentary. While this binary is used to categorize skaters within women's and men's competitions, it is also assumed to be the primary difference between male and female skaters. Artistic ability is supposed to come more naturally to women, while technical virtuosity is seen as the domain of men. Hence, the suspicion and uneasiness caused by men who excel in the former and women who excel in the latter. More damaging, the opposition between technique and artistry makes it seem like artistry is not in itself technical. It suggests that the ability to look a particular way, to interpret music, to be expressive comes naturally to some skaters, mostly women but also certain men. The opposition discounts, for instance, the effort and technique required to hold a strong line.

For much of the 1990s, Canadian discussions about the boundary between sport and art in skating centred on Elvis Stojko, in skating circles and in the press. From the time he first came to public attention in the early 1990s, Stojko was heralded for his tremendous jumping ability. But he was also widely criticized within the skating world for his limited choreography and the quality of the skating between his jumps. Stojko's programs often received higher marks for technique than for presentation. His critics claimed that he relied on the same movement vocabulary for different kinds of music, that he telegraphed his big tricks, that he inserted too many rest breaks into his programs. In response to the criticism and to his lower presentation marks, supportive sports journalists tried to construct Stojko as a misunderstood underdog, unappreciated by an effete 'skating establishment' because of the overt masculinity he showed on the ice.

With his three world championship titles and two Olympic silver medals Stojko was an unlikely underdog. Nevertheless, here is Steve Keating writing during the 1998 Nagano Olympics: 'Don't expect to see Canada's Elvis Stojko crying if he doesn't win an Olympic figure skating gold medal. In a sport full of sensitive performers, Stojko, a karate black belt and dirt bike rider, stands out as one of the tough guys. But once again, Stojko believes he felt the backlash from the judges for being too macho when he was marked down for artistic impression during Thursday's short programme.'[68] And here is Dave Perkins of the *Toronto Star* writing about the same event, as Stojko sat in second place after the short program, behind Russian skater Ilia Kulik, the eventual winner: 'For Stojko who ... possesses a quadruple jump that can be a direct ticket to a gold medal, the uneasy feeling needs to be defeated that nailing everything [in the long program] might not be enough. There is this perception problem. You can say again or still, but it is here at the Olympics and it is this: Artistically, Stojko is always skating uphill when a willowy wonder like Kulik, or [American Todd] Eldredge on a good day, is in the competition.'[69] In an adjoining article Perkins referred to Kulik and Eldredge (many skating fans would have found the link between these two very different skaters surprising) as 'two lean and reedy skaters of the more classical type usually favoured by the more conservative judges,' most of whom, Perkins claimed later in the article, 'own their own fur coats.'[70] One suspects that the author is not pointing here to his views on animal rights.

Writer David Staples also wove the underdog theme into his 1997 profile of Stojko for *Saturday Night*, 'Skating Is No Wussy Sport,' which I discussed in chapter 3.[71] Staples used verbs like 'sniff' and 'natter' to evoke effeminacy when he cited skating officials. He claimed that less-skilled jumpers were 'invariably boosted' by the judges so their artistic marks would be higher than Stojko's – as if the more than four minutes of skating before and after their seven or eight jumps was nothing of consequence. Staples found it shocking that ties between competitors in the long program were broken by the artistic and not the technical mark. He never mentioned that the procedure was reversed in the short program.

To paint Stojko as the underdog, Staples had to adopt a position where the artistic aspects of skating held no value. He had to reject an understanding of 'artistic impression' as something requiring effort and the development of skills, as something that adds a level of difficulty to a performance. Staples, like Perkins, saw the so-called classical look of other skaters – stretched limbs and pointed toes – as little more than flourish, as the inevitable product of 'lean and reedy' bodies. Like other journalists, Staples seems to have assumed that the men who skate with such flourish (and to be honest, in Stojko's era there were not that many of them) do it 'naturally.' It's just the way they are. The irony here is that these two writers, both of whom wanted skating to be tougher and more sport-like, end up discounting the skaters who performed the most difficult programs: 'Kulik ... certainly seems able to get his performance widely accepted with far less sales pitch than Stojko,' wrote Perkins.[72] Indeed, he did and for good reason. Kulik performed the same jumps as Stojko did, but he did them in the midst of more complicated choreography, with more stretch, and he never seemed to forget that he was possessed of arms, as Stojko sometimes did. Aesthetic tastes aside, skating with a good stretch and a commitment to some kind of obvious body line (whether inspired by ballet or not – Kulik's was not) is harder than skating without them. Kulik had the more difficult program and he won. Of course, once Kulik and company were painted as naturally 'classic,' then the corollary was that Stojko was 'naturally' not classic. Stojko's thinner choreography and neglected arms were, therefore, not about limited technique, they were about his nature as a man.

As part of the construction of Stojko's masculinity, stories about him, in print and on television, inevitably mentioned his refusal to take dance classes. Staples wrote that Stojko 'refused to be a ballet dancer, polishing the air with sweeping arm movements.'[73] Stojko himself often addressed the same theme, as if this is what most set him apart from his competitors. In a televised profile from early in his international career, Stojko said, 'I was never into taking ballet. That's not me ... That's not where I'm at – how can I say ... Of course you can be powerful in ballet, but I more try to be the macho kind of guy, that's the way I am.'[74] In *Toronto Life* James Chatto wrote: 'Stojko has never felt comfortable with ballet. Perhaps he finds it effeminate, perhaps his body is not suited to it, but his skating is free of the classical balletic influences upon which so many skaters rely.'[75] The fact that, among male competitors, Stojko would not have been alone in his lack of ballet training is less important here than the way these comments counterpose macho-ness to ballet and the way they suggest that the difference between a man who might draw on ballet and a man who would not is somehow inherent within the men themselves – 'that's the way I am' – as if something like ballet, which requires years of daily training, is in any way natural for anyone.

Dance is, almost without exception, the reference point for the art side of the art/sport binary that is so prevalent in present-day figure skating commentary. The fear that skating is too easily conflated with ballet motivates much of the effort to make sure that the athletic abilities of male skaters are more highly valued than the artistic ones, to make sure that male skaters are understood to be athletes rather than artists. In the context of North American ideas about gender, ballet signifies effeminacy as almost nothing else can, despite the technical wizardry, bulging leg muscles, and huge performance fees of well-known male stars. Efforts to portray male skaters as jocks are intended to interrupt an equation that leads from skating to dance to ballet to effeminacy, and from there, of course, to homosexuality.

And the Problem with Ballet Is What, Exactly?

The biographies of male dancers, including Rudolf Nureyev's,[76] are littered with stories of fathers troubled by their sons' interest in dance. Young Billy Elliots, prepared to defy family and friends for their love of dance, remain the exception and not the rule. 'For the public at large that sees a performer in leotard and tights,' says American choreographer Bill T. Jones, 'dance is about display and seduction. And most believe men should be watching it, not doing it.'[77] Yet even watching is an issue for some men. Dance historian Ramsay Burt has argued that in a cultural situation 'in which it [has] seemed "natural" not to look at the male body,' it has also been 'problematic and conflictual for men to enjoy looking at dancing.'[78] By corollary, it has seemed somewhat transgressive and odd for men to dance on stage. It wasn't always so. Expectations for appropriate forms of gendered behaviour change historically. From the history of ballet, as with the history of skating, we learn that the meanings ascribed to men's public deportment and to male movement have changed profoundly since the 1700s, when, for instance, in Italy, ballets were performed by all-male dance groups. In France, during the same era, the king himself initiated and performed dances before the court. According to Burt, prejudices against European male dancing did not arise until the nineteenth century.[79] With the invention of the strengthened pointe shoe (used only by women), female dancers appeared weightless and otherworldly. Cast as ethereal creatures in narratives shaped by nineteenth-century Romanticism, women came to define the feel and potential of the balletic imagination; they became the ballet's main stars. Female dancers became objects of desire for male spectators and, thus, male dancers 'seemed hardly necessary, and even unnatural'[80] – they got in the way of the male spectators' enjoyment. Men on stage were seen as 'mere attendants, sturdy but dull, perambulating pedestals for the display of the ballerinas' charms ... The new fashion resulted in the eclipse of male dancing for a hundred years.'[81] By the late 1800s, men had become so marginalized that some theatres were casting women *en travesti* to perform male roles.

As dance came to be seen as a feminine art, prejudices grew up around male dancers. Burt argues that these prejudices initially had nothing to do with homosexuality or effeminacy, as they do now; rather, they were rooted in class difference during a period when bourgeois norms were gaining prominence, the same norms that led to more rigid, less expressive forms of figure skating in Victorian England. What was at stake with male dance performances was 'the development of modern, middle-class attitudes towards the male body and the expressive aspects of male social behaviour.'[82] Criticism addressed towards male dancers focused on the inappropriateness of bourgeois men allowing their bodies to be put on display, of allowing their bodies to give visible meaning to feelings. Moreover, while their physical strength made male dancers seem akin to working-class men, their costumes and their lack of regard for middle-class norms aligned them with 'the degenerate style of the old aristocracy.'[83] In either case, Burt writes, it was 'the inability of the male ballet dancer to represent the power and status of men in bourgeois society which was proposed by one nineteenth century writer as being the trouble with the male dancer.'[84]

So how was it that dance – and by association, figure skating – came to be linked with the version of effeminacy with which we are more familiar today, that is, with effeminacy as a marker of homosexuality? Joseph Bristow and Alan Sinfield have each written about the evolution of effeminacy as a concept. Sinfield argues that before the trials of Oscar Wilde in the 1890s, effeminacy was more likely to be seen as a sign of excessive leisure and luxury or as a sign of a man being overly fond of women (including in the sexual sense) than a sign of homophilic attraction.[85] But in the extensive coverage of Wilde's trials, his effeminate aesthetic and behaviour and his homosexuality were conflated. Once Wilde became *the* public homosexual in Britain and in many parts of Europe and North America, effeminacy came to be 'the main stigma attached to male homosexuality.'[86] This is the version of effeminacy that keeps present-day fathers from registering their sons in ballet and figure skating classes and that determines the overwhelming femaleness of ballet and skating audiences.

With effeminacy increasingly linked to homosexuality, the problem with the male dancer was no longer simply a matter of whether his gender behaviour matched the expectations of his class; rather, the issue was the fit between his gender and what we would now call his sexual identity and sexual orientation, all of which were assumed to be essential physical attributes. Effeminacy and homosexuality were no longer seen as things one did, they were things one was. Thus, it could be claimed that it was an inborn effeminacy that led dancers to the unmanly acts of displaying their bodies and emotions on stage, and of mingling too closely with women. A truly manly constitution would have precluded such actions. This is a bald, early version of the argument sports journalists used to diminish the accomplishments of Elvis Stojko's competitors and to excuse the limitations of his free skating programs.

It was not until the early years of the twentieth century, with the arrival of Serge Diaghilev's Ballets Russes in the West, that the problem of the male dancer became an effeminacy that led to presumptions about his homosexuality. Diaghilev reintroduced men to the Western ballet audience. But while the traditional Russian repertoire featured princely roles and emphasized masculine strength, this was not the repertoire performed by the Ballets Russes. The men of Diaghilev's company represented a much broader range of masculine identities. According to dance historian Lynn Garafola, they 'traced a spectrum of male roles that transcended conventions of gender while presenting the male body in a way that was frankly erotic. Ballet after ballet celebrated its physique, dramatized its athletic prowess, and paraded its sexual availability.'[87] Diaghilev reversed the trend of the feminized ballet, promoting the men in his company at the expense of the women.

In his productions men were the stars. Some of them, including Vaslav Nijinsky, were also his lovers.

Garafola writes that before Diaghilev there may well have been individual dancers who were homosexual, and there may have been homosexuals in the ballet audience, but ideologically and socially ballet itself remained heterosexual. Diaghilev's work changed that and 'ballet in Western Europe, no less than in America, became a privileged arena for homosexuals as performers, choreographers, and spectators. It was a feat unparalleled in the other arts, and for gay men (to use a modern term) it was a revolution.'[88] Maybe so, but, as with the successful creation of gay cultural spaces later in the twentieth century, the visibility that would have been a draw and an invitation to some men would likely have been for others, perhaps in greater numbers, a source of fear. Although dance has provided a home for many gay men, there have certainly been others who have shunned it, not wanting the exposure that might come with association.

While the visibility of Diaghilev and his lovers did much to make possible the equating of dance with effeminacy and homosexuality, the equation depended on more than this. Before the first decades of the twentieth century, such an equation would have made little cultural sense – it could not until (a) homosexuality existed as a popular concept and (b) it was linked conceptually to effeminacy. As historians of sexuality have repeatedly pointed out, the notion that humans have essential sexual identities that shape our individual capacities is a modern one, only put into circulation towards the end of the 1800s.[89] The notion did not work its way into popular discourses until well into the twentieth century. In earlier times, same-sex acts were seen as sinful activities that anyone might engage in, much the same as adultery. Once again, it was the trials of Oscar Wilde that helped to spread the idea, at least in Britain, that the homosexual (and, conversely, the heterosexual) is a particular type of person and that homosexuality is more than a simple case of who one might choose as a bedfellow. Wilde's mannerisms, his dandyish style of dress, his aesthetic interests, his effete demeanour came to be read as marks of homosexual inclination. His effeminate version of masculinity was no longer understood to be a cultural, political, or aesthetic choice, but was seen instead as a physical mark of his homosexuality. Effeminate behaviour came to be seen as the male body's way of displaying the homosexuality lodged within it, of displaying an abnormal constitution.

Ironically, the performer who did the most to elevate the status of the male dancer also contributed the most to the link between effeminacy and male dancing in popular commentary. Vaslav Nijinsky was a huge star despite being described by critics as both androgynous and feminine. His dancing was said to be erotic and feline. In their book *Men Dancing*, Alexander Bland and John Percival refer to him, with obvious regret, as 'notably unmasculine.' His body was not suited to the traditional aristocratic male roles and he was unconcerned with the bravura performances and technical proficiency audiences would eventually come to expect from men. Instead, Nijinsky was obsessed with developing his body as an 'expressive instrument.'[90] A spellbinding performer, Nijinsky drew tremendous crowds, including many people who were new to ballet. Some critics were able to accept Nijinsky's unorthodox performances and unmanly eroticism by labelling him a genius. For others, however, particularly in the United States, his emotional, seductive style of dancing was altogether too feminine and his 'effeminate quality' came to be seen as 'almost inseparable from the male Ballet dancer.'[91]

In the post-Nijinsky era, many male dancers have spent their careers trying to construct for themselves an image more manly than his. As numerous writers have pointed out, this task has often resulted in a 'macho overcompensation,' as men have tried to prove just how tough ballet is or how similar dance is to sport.[92] In their efforts to cast a new image for themselves, many dancers have turned to mainstream discourses linking sport and manliness – the very discourses by which they were marginalized in the first place. In attempts to validate men's dancing, the dancer-as-athlete argument has drawn on popular assumptions that athletic men are, naturally, not effeminate. The hope is that dancers' often extraordinary physical prowess will win the respect of, and perhaps even some converts from, regular guys and their sons. If dads could only see how physically hard dance is, the argument goes, they might allow their sons to take lessons.

As in figure skating, dancers' attempts to represent themselves through sport discourses have had little effect on either the number of boys who register for lessons or the number of men who attend live dance performances. The world of dance, ballet especially, is still primarily populated by women and girls. As we saw in chapter 3, the context within which men's athleticism is on display in skating and dance – as performance and art, conducted in female company – continues to present a challenge to mainstream notions of how and where men should move their bodies. Despite their bulging calves and well-developed torsos, male dancers remain well outside everyday norms of masculinity.

Appeals to athleticism in men's figure skating and dance reflect the assumption that gender is rooted in our bodies. Sport has been valorized at least in part because it allows men to produce hard muscular bodies that seem to set them apart from women, bodies that are both representations of and literal repositories of male power. 'True masculinity,' writes R.W. Connell, 'is almost always thought to proceed from men's bodies – to be inherent in a male body or to express something about a male body.'[93] Attempts to use discourses of sport, rather than discourses of art, to make sense of men who skate and dance are attempts to restrict the meanings that can be made of their bodies. They are intended to preclude understandings of those bodies as effeminate and, therefore, probably homosexual. They certainly do nothing to help increase the range of ways boys and men might choose to express themselves physically without fear of ridicule or other more serious forms of censure.

'The male skating's gotta be stronger'

With recent changes to the judging system in figure skating, the impulse to overemphasize the athletic aspect of men's competitions seems to be on the wane. Introduced in 2004, the new system forces skaters – as formal skating regulations have always tried to do, despite the concerted efforts of some coaches, judges, and skaters to thwart or ignore them – to pay attention to both aesthetic and athletic skills and to make sure that they do not reduce their athleticism to jumping. The new rules are intended to augment rather than diminish the uniqueness of figure skating as a complex, competitive activity that demands more of its participants than a simple commitment to bigger jumps. The scoring system's refusal to allow jumps to outweigh other skills or performance quality and its recognition that aesthetic factors add to the physical difficulty of a program, mean that to excel in the competitive context, male figure skaters won't be able to hide behind a narrowly defined athleticism. They will have to embrace fully the aesthetic aspects of their skating and concentrate on every element of their programs.

Unfortunately, the new system does not seem to be encouraging creativity or originality, as many observers had hoped it would; in their efforts to maximize their scores, skaters have all ended up doing the same difficult, high-scoring moves. The new system has, however, been widely heralded for having rejuvenated the non-jumping elements of the sport, in particular, spins and footwork. But not everyone in the skating world is in favour of this change. For some skating insiders the reduced importance of jumps has been harmful to the sport – to the men's events in particular. Such criticisms have been widely publicized during the last two Olympic competitions, both of which were won by men who did not perform a quadruple jump.

After the men's event at the 2010 Vancouver Games, silver medallist Evgeny Plushenko of Russia got a lot of press for his complaints about the state of figure skating and the fact that he was beaten by American Evan Lysacek, who executed a clean, complex program without attempting a quad jump. 'If the Olympic champion doesn't know how to jump a quad, I don't know,' Plushenko said. 'Now it's not men's figure skating, now it's dancing.'[94] As has been the case for the past sixty years, debates around the shifting relationship of art and sport in figure skating are debates about men, and they tend to draw on simplistic discourses of athleticism and masculinity. One of the most vocal participants in recent versions of this debate has been Elvis Stojko. After the men's event in Vancouver, Stojko scoffed at the suggestion that the new system broadens the requirements of the sport, suggesting that programs without quads turn the competition into more of 'a recital.'[95] Stojko claimed the new system was taking the sport backwards, that it was 'eliminating the risk' from men's skating.[96]

Stojko had made similar arguments during coverage of the 2006 Olympic Winter Games in Turin when he was called upon by the Canadian Broadcasting Corporation (CBC) to give post-competition comments. Stojko clearly disapproved of the fact that some male skaters – bronze medallist Canadian Jeffrey Buttle among them – competed and placed well without landing quadruple jumps. (According to Skate Canada's director of High Performance, Michael Slipchuk, Stojko also won his own two Olympic medals without attempting a quad).[97] Under the new system, a skater is awarded points for every part of the program: jumps, spins, footwork, 'moves-in-the-field' like spirals and spread-eagles, edgework, turns, and basic forward and backward skating. While a quadruple jump will garner a skater a lot of points, a program has to have more than a quad to score well – as we saw in Vancouver when Plushenko, who landed quads in both the short and long programs, placed second. Judges are looking for a range of qualities, including speed, surety, strength, and flexibility, not all of which can be demonstrated by jumping. As a consequence, freestyle programs in both Turin and Vancouver looked very different than the programs of Stojko's era. They were fuller and more complex, if perhaps less spectacular in the realm of big tricks. For this reason, especially, they failed to make Stojko, who is not moved by demonstrations of flexibility or complex footwork, happy. He wants to see more risk, more and bigger jumps. 'The betweens [the moves between the jumps and spins] are fine,' he said. 'But it's not a stretching event.' He thinks men's skating should be about 'athleticism, power, speed and strength ... You gotta do the hard stuff. We come to see the hard stuff.'[98] In his lexicon, holding your foot directly above your head while spinning doesn't qualify as hard, nor does complicated footwork, edge control, or the ability to use every beat of a piece of music.

The desire to claim jumps as the only 'hard stuff' comes out of a need to play to those who don't understand and, more important, don't want to understand how difficult it actually is to skate with stretch, to spin in positions that require flexibility, to hold a position in a spiral, to maintain strong postures and awareness of the whole body. While these skills look easy, that is a mark of skaters' technical competence. If they were actually easy everyone would do them. To suggest that skating should revolve around jumping, the most easily identifiable and spectacular athletic skill, is a plain bid to make figure skating more appealing to men, a bid to find male validation.

Stojko told CBC, 'The male skating's gotta be stronger.' And that's the key to his argument – it's all about men. It's not simply about what is hard or risky or exciting – any move can be made to be so. It's about precluding the appearance of too much similarity between male and female skaters and strength is always, in skating and elsewhere, the fall-back position for emphasizing sexual difference, that is, the difference between women and men. Stronger-appearing skating would confirm notions about the difference between men's and women's bodies. Male/female. Sport/art. The overemphasis on sport in men's figure skating, at the expense of art, has been the primary strategy used to make distinctions between men and women on the ice. But it certainly hasn't been the only one. In the next chapter I look at some of the techniques that have been used to keep men and women from appearing too much the same, and at how anxiety over the reputation of male skaters has led to figure skating being one of the most gender-differentiated sports.

8 Sequins, Soundtracks, and Spirals: Producing Gender Difference on the Ice

After the imperative of competition, institutionalized gender difference is probably the most fundamental aspect of contemporary elite sport. For many people, high-level sport would be unthinkable without it. While women and men often play on the same teams and compete against each other in recreational leagues, almost all contemporary elite-level sports maintain separate events for women and men, and some sports subject women and men to different rules. In gymnastics, women and men perform on different apparatuses. In golf, men's tees are further from the green. In tennis, men play more sets in the major tournaments. In hockey women are not allowed to body-check. Physiological explanations are almost always given as justifications for such gender-specific rules. But physiology cannot explain why some physical differences are emphasized and not others, or why these differences are assumed to be worth promoting in the first place. Sociologists and historians argue that the practice of treating male and female athletes differently and drawing strict boundaries between them helps to prop up ideologies that constitute women and men as not just different but as unequal. As an institution, sport makes it hard for us to see similarities between women and men and, in this sense, helps to support ideologies of male supremacy.

Sport, of course, is not the only sphere of life through which gender difference is constructed. Institutions like commerce, religion, and the family also contribute to understandings of masculinity and femininity that emphasize the differences rather than the similarities between the categories. This binary view of gender is both a product and a requirement of the normalizing versions of heterosexuality that pervade everyday life in contemporary North America. In a culture in which heterosexuality is a primary organizing principle, masculinity and femininity must not grow too similar. Refracted through heteronormative discourses that present gender as a function of biology, men and women are constructed as 'opposite sexes,' as the 'two halves of a whole,' as Mars and Venus. The segregation of men and women in sport confirms and also helps to reproduce gender polarization in the culture at large.

Almost all elite sports are organized around gender, with equestrian events being a notable exception. What sets figure skating apart from other sports is the degree to which the production and maintenance of gender difference is integral to the activity. If not the most gender-differentiated sport – that distinction should probably go to those sports, like rhythmic gymnastics or North American football, pursued primarily by one sex – figure skating certainly ranks among the top few. It has gender-specific equipment and costumes, gender-specific music, gender-specific rules, gender-specific moves. Its system of evaluation explicitly regulates and rewards the performance of gender as much as the performance of athletic or aesthetic skills. In few other sports are gender concerns so central to the spirit of the game.

In previous chapters I have been primarily interested in issues of masculinity in figure skating, especially how these have been shaped by the tenacious popular notions that figure skating is a 'girls' sport' and that men who skate, therefore, must be effeminate sissies and/or gay. For at least half a century, this notion, rooted in both misogyny and homophobia, has been a heavy influence on North American men's skating, affecting male participation rates and provoking a whole series of efforts to secure for men in the sport a more manly heterosexual image. These efforts, which peaked in the 1990s, have had an impact on the rules, on the way men actually skate, and on the ways they are judged by officials and covered by journalists. What is perhaps less obvious is that these efforts have also had a detrimental impact on women's skating. In this chapter I look at the way anxieties around the reputation of men's skating have influenced the performances of male *and* female skaters.

It may seem odd to be concerned about women in figure skating, a sport in which many of the gender conventions that shape other sports are reversed: women far outnumber men; women, especially in the United States, have been the biggest stars and, historically, they have had the most lucrative professional careers; women make up the majority of coaches; women constitute the greater part of the audience; and, in some jurisdictions, women fill high-level administrative roles (the ISU is one organization that is still heavily dominated by men). Given its unique position, one could easily assume that figure skating must have made significant contributions to improving the broader realm of women's sport. Unfortunately, this has not been the case. Despite having been, until the 1970s, one of the few outlets through which women and girls could express their athleticism without recrimination, figure skating has done little to make general sport discourses and practices more accommodating to women. Figure skating has certainly done nothing to shift mainstream representations of athletic female bodies or women's experiences of athleticism – as sports like speed skating, triathlon, and, even, boxing have done. As it has for decades, figure skating continues to support and reward only a limited range of intransigently traditional femininities, none of which foreground women's strength and power, none of which pull skating any significant distance from its white, upper-class European roots. Female figure skaters are almost always positioned as elegant princesses, bubbly pixies, or alluring vixens; women and girls who cannot or who choose not to fit these stereotypical roles face an uphill battle achieving success in this sport. The image presented by figure skating's world champions has remained relatively constant since the heyday of Sonja Henie.

This image is deeply rooted in the sport's privileged heritage. While figure skating is an increasingly global sport and the population of skaters has been growing more diverse, the femininity represented through women's performances remains homogeneous. Women who succeed in figure skating are never not graceful (even when they are being bubbly pixies), their skating is 'light' and they are often praised for seeming to float across the ice. Such qualities are the traditional marks of femininity that we see in ballet and in some forms of North American and European contemporary dance. Brenda Dixon Gottschild writes that European theatre dance traditions privilege 'pointed, lifted feet, tentative contact with the ground, so there is a light airy feeling ... The characteristic quality is airborne.'[1] She contrasts this with African, South Asian, and other dance forms where women bend their knees, flex their feet, and maintain strong contact with the ground. The point Dixon Gottschild makes is not just about difference but about the value ascribed to difference. In her book *The Black Dancing Body* Dixon Gottschild notes that in some quarters of the North American and European dance worlds there is an unspoken assumption that white European forms of dance are not just different but superior and that ballet is the pinnacle of dancing achievement. European forms of dance serve as the norm, while other forms are seen as 'inferior/auxiliary.'[2]

In skating, the assumption of superiority is made clear by the fact that the same version of femininity is rewarded year after year, decade after decade, while alternatives to it are disparaged or simply ignored. As Ellyn Kestnbaum has written in her book *Culture on Ice*, female skaters who have tried to define 'an artistry appropriate to their own styles of movement' have gone largely 'unappreciated.'[3] Kestnbaum notes that the most well-known of these skaters have been women of colour (Debi Thomas, Midori Ito, Surya Bonaly) or women from working-class backgrounds (Elaine Zayak and Tonya Harding). In her ethnographic project on Canadian figure skating, anthropologist Karen McGarry shows the kind of racialized and classed discourses of femininity that have marginalized skaters who have tried to present a different image. In the course of her research, McGarry asked a Canadian coach about the technical superiority of female skaters from other countries. In his answer he referred to former world champion and Olympic silver medallist Midori Ito of Japan and to three-time world silver medallist Surya Bonaly of France. Ito was the first woman to land a triple axel in competition. Bonaly, also known for her jumping, remains one of only two black skaters to have won a medal in the women's event at the world championships (1986 champion Debi Thomas of the United States is the other). Both Ito and Bonaly were regularly presented in the press as not having the style or elegance of skaters who matched more closely the standard that has dominated women's figure skating since before the Second World War, a standard defined by a particular genre of movement, a particular physical type – small, slender, not obviously muscular – and a certain 'way of being' on the ice. It is a standard constituted through stereotyped ideals of white femininity, as we see in a quote from McGarry's interview with the Canadian coach:

> If we want to be at the top, then our girls have to have all that, you know, classic sort of a grace like Barbara Ann [Scott]. You know, competitors like Surya and Midori Ito, they had the really masculine, exotic sort of style and yeah, it got them some great technical marks. I mean not many women are out there attempting triple axels. But skating is really all about beauty and sophistication and all the really powerful women skaters have modeled themselves after Grace Kelly or Audrey Hepburn, or that sort of a thing. That's what our women have to offer and it just comes natural to them. And I'm not saying they're not up there technically. I mean, they're obviously not as aggressive as someone like Surya, but she's never really

had the respect, you see. She's a great skater, in an exotic kind of a way I suppose, but she's missing the classic basics our girls have.[4]

A distinct contrast is being constructed here between 'our women' and skaters like Bonaly and Ito. 'They' are masculine, technical, exotic, strong, clearly not as feminine as 'our women,' who have classic grace and thus fit a definition of skating – 'beauty and sophistication' – that evokes the sport's elitist roots. Our women 'naturally' model themselves on glamorous, iconic white Hollywood stars. The fact that glamorous iconic movie stars are, almost without exception, white says as much about the racism of Hollywood as it does about the narrowness of what counts as a 'classic sort of grace' in figure skating.

The idealized femininity against which skaters are judged harkens back to the era of Sonja Henie, when figure skating clubs were enclaves of white upper-class exclusivity. Usually represented by a small, slender body, this ideal femininity is synonymous with the performance of whiteness – by way of an 'elegant' and 'graceful' movement vocabulary – even if the skating body itself is not white. Between 1989 and 2010, fifteen of the twenty-two women's world champions have been Asian skaters or North American skaters from Asian backgrounds. Except for Midori Ito (1989), all of these skaters have had bodies that were slight and not obviously muscular,[5] and they have demonstrated the kind of elegant graceful style that has come to be expected of women who win in the sport. Even Miki Ando of Japan (2007), who was the first woman to land a quadruple jump in competition, and Mao Asada of Japan (2008), who has successfully landed triple axels, leave an impression of gracefulness rather than assertive athleticism when they skate. They achieve this through the kind of movement vocabulary they employ, but also through their choice of hairstyle and makeup, costuming, and music. A similar impression is left by 2010 Olympic champion Kim Yu-na, widely heralded as one of the best skaters, male or female, ever to have competed in the sport. While technically Kim is an extraordinary skater, her athletic brilliance is not the 'take home' message when she skates. Here is the *New York Times* describing her gold medal–winning long program in Vancouver: 'Dressed in azure, accompanied by Gershwin, Kim Yu-na of South Korea seemingly floated to the clouds with her soaring jumps and airy elegance Thursday night, winning an Olympic gold medal and her rightful place as one of the greatest women's figure skaters of any era.'[6]

Like other winter sports, skating is predominantly white in terms of who has access to rinks, coaching, travel, and equipment – although in urban centres in North America the demographics are shifting.[7] But figure skating's whiteness is not just a question of who actually makes it onto the ice. The racialization of skating is also about who has access – literally and symbolically – to the history of the sport and to the traditions of performance that that history has spawned. And these traditions are maintained by expectations, expressed through judging and coaching practices, that produce conformity to a narrow range of femininities that have their roots in white cultural environments. The skating world seems not to have noticed that the overall sporting landscape has changed tremendously for women since the 1970s. When women softball players no longer wear skirts, when women ice hockey players receive mainstream endorsements, when girls' high school rugby is one of the fastest growing sports in Canada, why is it that representations of femininity continue to be so narrow in figure skating? Why are skaters still so girlie?

If figure skating were a minor sport, its gender politics would be less troubling. But from a Canadian perspective this is no minor sport. While the popularity of televised figure skating in North America has fallen off in recent years (due to saturation coverage in the decade following the Kerrigan-Harding incident), it remains an important sport for Canadian broadcasters. According to research conducted by CTV, a major private network, figure skating was the 'number one television sport for women in Canada' in 2002/3.[8] Elsewhere in the world, figure skating coverage tends to wax and wane with the success of individual skaters. In South Korea, for instance, the success of Kim Yu-na has made figure skating the most popular televised sport. Even before her Olympic win, Kim was the biggest celebrity in the country. The broadcast of the 2008 ISU Grand Prix Final, which was held in Seoul and which Kim won, was the most highly rated South Korean television program that year.[9] Her Olympic performances brought the nation to a standstill.[10]

In the United States, figure skating is a minor television sport except during the Olympics, when women's skating is one of the highlights of network broadcasts. Andrew Billings's important empirical work on US television coverage of the Olympic Games shows the privileged position of figure skating in relationship to other women's sports at the winter games. In studying the time allotted to each of the twelve sports in which women are able to compete, Billings found that women's figure skating accounted for almost 40 per cent of all coverage of women's events during the 1998 Olympics. It accounted for 26 per cent of the coverage of women's sports during the 2002 Olympics and slightly more than 35 per cent in 2006. When Billings added up the amount of coverage received by all sports for men and women over the three years, women's figure skating had the second highest total number of minutes, behind men's skiing.[11]

Outside of Olympic years, no matter how limited the coverage, figure skating is still one of the only opportunities for female athletes to perform on television, in prime time, on major networks. As Duncan and Messner have shown in their ongoing research on the coverage of women's sports on television news and sports highlights shows, major networks provide women athletes a 'backdrop of near-silence.'[12] Figure skaters, therefore, are still among the most visible female athletes – visible as they actually compete, not just in magazine photo spreads or in ads for milk or Nike. So, despite vastly improved access for girls to sports that have not traditionally been seen as feminine, skating continues to play an important role in representations of women's competitive sport and, therefore, in the construction of mainstream ideas about women's athleticism and women's physicality.

How might one explain figure skating's seeming imperviousness to expanding gender boundaries in sports (for women, at least) and in the culture at large? How might one explain the anachronistic femininities that prevail in skating? In her excellent article 'A Radiant Smile from the Lovely Lady,' Abigail Feder says the hyper-femininity of women's figure skating is a consequence of the fact that there is almost no difference between the athletic repertoires of male and female skaters.[13] In skating, 'athleticism' is usually understood to mean jumps. At the elite international level, the triple axel is now a standard part of the men's repertoire. Some men also land quadruple toe loops and/or salchows and a smaller number land quad jumps in combination. In women's events, the triple axel and quadruple jumps are still rare, but they have been done. Mao Asada of Japan, the 2010 Olympic silver medallist, landed two triple axels in her long program and a triple axel–double toe loop combination in her short program. 2007 World Champion Miki Ando, also of Japan, has landed a quad salchow. Other women have successfully landed quad toe loops in practice. The only thing a woman has yet to do that men have done is land a quadruple jump in combination in a competition. Unlike gymnastics, where men and women develop different skills and use different apparatuses, men and women in skating generally perform the same 'tricks,' although, as we will see below, they often do them in very different ways. And this, Feder argues, is at the root of figure skating's pronounced girliness: 'When physical capabilities no longer distinguish men and women, femininity is overdetermined to keep female athletes from being labelled as masculine or lesbian.'[14] This would certainly be the case were we talking about sports that are largely understood through discourses of masculinity, like ice hockey, rugby, or wrestling. Women who participate in these traditionally masculine sports still suffer scrutiny of their femininity and sexual orientation as Dayna Daniels shows in her book *Polygendered and Ponytailed: The Dilemma of Femininity and the Female Athlete*. But the gender dynamics of figure skating are different. In this sport even the men struggle to be seen as masculine. While some female skaters with exceptional jumping skills and more muscular bodies, like Midori Ito, Tonya Harding, and Surya Bonaly, have been compared to men, they have clearly been seen as exceptions. It is also likely that they were only compared to men *within* their sport and not, for instance, at school or within their families. Figure skating does not submit women to the kind of gender surveillance faced by women who are good at softball or weightlifting. It would be the rare female figure skater who would be asked pointed questions about her sexual or gender identity because of her choice of sport. Indeed, interest in figure skating fits easily with a socially acceptable heterosexual femininity. Male skaters have no such security. They leave their gender and sexual identities open to question simply by participating in the sport.

I agree with Feder that the overdetermined femininity we see in 'ladies' skating, as the ISU persists in calling it, is related to the lack of significant difference between men's and women's athletic abilities in the sport. Still, I would argue that it rises less from a need to protect the gender identity of the women than from a need to protect the gender identity of the men. To understand the pervasive 'girliness' of women's figure skating, we need to look at skating's reputation as a girls' sport and at what that reputation has meant for men. In a sport where the men are popularly considered to be effeminate and, therefore, presumed to be gay, the presence of hyper-feminine women helps to constitute for the men a more manly image, it helps to construct what feminist theorists call gender difference by allowing the maintenance of a distinct masculine/feminine binary in the sport. In other words, hyper-femininity ensures that the women and men do not seem too much alike. In the context of a so-called feminine sport, anything that diminished the contrast between male and female skaters – for instance, an influx of 'tomboys' to the ranks of the 'ladies' – would reinforce the perception that the men are sissies and/or gay. Rigid gender boundaries, as reflected in the different appearance (clothing, styles of grooming) and behaviours (styles of basic skating, gestures, choreography, choice of music) exhibited by male and female skaters, help to keep that perception at bay. As long as the figure skating community, within which I include broadcasters and journalists, continues to care whether members of the general public think male skaters are gay, gender difference will be promoted in figure skating and the sport will produce and reward mainstream heterosexual versions of masculinity and femininity that seem very obviously to differ from each other.

In the discussion that follows I unpack some of the ways that gender difference is constituted in skating through rules and aesthetic choices around costuming, music, and styles of movement. My focus is on practices within the sport rather than on commentary or the way such practices are given meaning through media discourses.[15] The purpose of the exercise is not simply to catalogue examples, but to suggest how skating's obsession with gender helps to perpetuate pernicious and harmful discourses of misogyny and homophobia in the culture at large. This obsession also hampers the creative and technical development of the sport by limiting the ways skaters might express themselves on the ice. The assumption behind the discussion here is that skating could be better than this. As an expressive, creative medium, figure skating could, like some other forms of physical activity, add to the store of images and experiences that expand how people understand their bodies, their capabilities, and the options they have for how they might choose to be in the world.

At the risk of confirming popular critiques of sociology or cultural studies, some of the examples I use here will seem very obvious. Certainly, you do not need any special critical skills or academic training to be able to see the profound opposition between masculine and feminine performances in this sport. The importance of the examples I give lies precisely in their obviousness – they remind us of how pervasive and powerful gender remains in everyday life and of how small, often simple, practices help keep it that way. Figure skating, like sports in general, could be organized differently. There is nothing inherent in the movements that can be made on skates that demands they be performed in gender-specific ways. The narrow representations of gender in skating, as opposed to, say, the more complicated explorations of gender one sees in some contemporary dance, suggest the limitations of sport discourses for expanding the terms of what it means to be feminine or masculine in mainstream North American culture. As long as people are not at liberty to express themselves as they would like to, as long as people continue to be marginalized for trying, those terms need to be expanded.

Once again, I need to make clear that I am only speaking of singles skaters in this discussion. While pairs and dance events are also extremely interesting to anyone concerned with representations of gender and sexuality, they have their own vocabulary and conventions that demand their own specific analysis.

Skating Apparel: Sequins, Skirts, and Exposed Skin

In no other sport, except synchronized swimming, are athletes required to pay so much attention to aesthetic factors that are not embedded in the actual physical movements that make up the competition – not even in 'artistic gymnastics.' The simple fact that skating requires music and costumes is key to its effeminate reputation. Costumes provoke concern from critics on two sides: those who want to see women's skating become less feminine and those who want men's skating to become more manly. Costumes provide quick visual evidence of how thoroughly skating is coloured by ideas about gender.

Most figure skaters confront the sport's binary gender norms as soon as they put on their skates. As any toddler who has ever been to a rink can tell you, boys wear black skates and girls wear white skates. Hand-me-down skates of the wrong colour are one of the potential traumas of childhood skating. More than one parent – like the father of 1962 world champion Donald Jackson of Canada – has spent time trying to bring the colour of second-hand skates into line with gender norms. After bugging his parents for skating lessons in the late 1940s, the young Jackson took one look at the 'sissy' white skates that had been bought for him and 'declared that he would never skate in anything like them.'[16] After his father's painting efforts, he didn't have to.

Women and men have been wearing differently coloured skates since the 1920s. White boots presented a more formal image and made women's feet appear lighter, less clunky. Men, presumably, did not feel the need to go for the same effect, and contrasting boot colours for male and female skaters have remained one of the most simple and enduring means of visually establishing gender difference in the sport.

While contemporary male and female skaters sometimes train in similar clothing – lycra tights and close fitting T-shirts – their competitive costumes are always gender-specific. Men compete in trousers topped by various kinds of shirts, T-shirts, or jackets, baring their skin only when they wear short sleeves or open V-neck collars. The majority of women, by contrast, compete in very short dresses. Exposed skin – or the illusion of exposed skin made possible by fabric that matches a skater's skin tone – is common. Some dresses have low-cut fronts and/or backs, some are backless and, these days, most are sleeveless. Skating costumes ensure that women and men look very different from each other even before they start to skate. Only someone completely unfamiliar with contemporary gender norms would be unable to identify male and female skaters by virtue of what they wear, a task that would prove difficult in most other winter sports.

What is important here is not so much the clothes themselves but the way they lead to different expectations of how women and men might skate. For instance, the contemporary woman's skating dress is unlikely to provoke thoughts of power or athletic prowess. Costumes that speak of elegance, cuteness, or sexiness can make it hard for us to see women's strength. In a non-sport context like dance, masked power is sometimes an important goal of a performance, and if successfully achieved it can enhance the enjoyment of the spectator. But in the context of sport, strength and power reign and masked power can simply appear as weakness, a possibility compounded by the surprisingly tenacious notion (given much evidence to the contrary) that women are the weaker sex.

Up until the late 1980s, there were no specific rules regarding skating costumes. In 1988, after American skater Debi Thomas wore a unitard (a one-piece leotard and tights also known as a catsuit) for her Olympic short program, the International Skating Union instituted a costume rule which held until 2004: 'The clothing of competitors must be modest, dignified and appropriate for athletic competition – not garish or theatrical in design. Clothing may however, reflect the character of the music chosen ... Ladies must wear a skirt. *The ladies dress* [sic] *must not give the effect of excessive nudity inappropriate for an athletic sport.* Men must wear full length trousers; no tights are permitted and the clothing must not be sleeveless'[17] [emphasis in original]. In one short paragraph, the ISU reminded skaters of both the importance of bourgeois standards of taste and the necessity of reflecting them in gender-specific ways. One wonders at the ISU's definition of 'excessive nudity inappropriate for an athletic sport,' a term which some skaters seem to have stretched past the breaking point without suffering any consequences. The directive to wear skirts, by contrast, was assiduously followed.

In men's competitions, the trousers rule, which remains in effect, also seems to have been fairly well enforced. The prohibition against tights maintains widespread Western cultural norms that keep the shape of a man's body, especially his genitals, concealed by his clothing. But this was not the only purpose of the no-tights rule. In addition to concerns about the tightness of tights, the rule responds to the greater fear that tights might lead spectators to associate figure skating with ballet. For all the reasons I've discussed in earlier chapters, skating officials want to make sure their male competitors are seen as athletes not dancers. They exhibit no similar concern about the women.

In requiring skirts of the women and trousers of the men, the ISU eliminated the possibility that women and men would have a similar 'look' on the ice. The fact that the sport's governing body enforces any restrictions on appearance in a so-called artistic sport is bad enough. What's worse, the requirement for skirts guaranteed that female skaters would be positioned in the first instance as women rather than athletes. The lenience shown by the ISU in terms of the 'modesty' of women's costumes suggests an institutional investment in women displaying as much 'sex appeal' as possible. The admonition against men baring their arms while women routinely expose (or pretend to expose) most of their bodies, is a stunning double standard. In the case of costume requirements, the ISU legislated not just gender difference but gender inequality.

It was not until the 1970s and 1980s that skaters began to wear clothes that could actually be described as 'costumes' rather than skating suits/ dresses or outfits. In the nineteenth century, women and men wore apparel on the ice that they could have easily worn on the street. While most skating textbooks devoted at least some space to the discussion of appropriate skating wear, questions of style were of secondary importance to more practical concerns like warmth, protection from the wind, safety, and ease of movement. In the early days of the sport, female skaters wore long skirts and corsets, jackets with fitted bodices, and, sometimes, small hats. As everyday skirts gradually grew shorter so too did the skirts worn for skating, with skaters being careful to maintain standards of decorum. American Theresa Weld Blanchard fretted about a dress that she had had made for the 1920 Olympic Games: 'I insisted the result was far too immodest as it was only six inches below my knees and I knew the audience would see my bloomers when I jumped.'[18]

It would not have been easy to jump or spin in heavy wool or velvet skirts. It is likely no coincidence that critics began to remark on the superior technical ability of women towards the end of the 1920s, by which time skirt hems had climbed considerably. The shorter skirts were a product of (1) increasingly liberal attitudes towards women's dress in general and (2) the decreasing age of the 'ladies' in international competitions. Younger skaters had more freedom to display their legs than did women like Weld Blanchard, who was twenty-four when she skated in the Olympics. By the early 1930s, knee-length dresses with full skirts, designed specifically for skating, were standard. They allowed women freedom of movement and lent an elegant effect to spins and turns. They also gave skaters the opportunity to express – within the bounds of the bourgeois manners that shaped their sport – their own sense of style.

Women's skirts continued to rise over the next few decades. They became more colourful and more form-fitting with the invention of new types of stretch fabric. After television networks began broadcasting figure skating in colour, dresses became brighter and incorporated more beading and other forms of ornamentation, but the basic form of a competition dress was no different than a dress a woman might have worn for practice: they had full backs, long sleeves and simple skirts, all of which were generally made of the same fabric. During the 1980s, dresses started to become more like costumes. They became more elaborate and more risqué. Skirts rose, necklines and backs fell, and sleeves disappeared. Today, a woman competing in a dress with a 'regular' neckline and long sleeves would seem overdressed.

Flashier, theatrical costumes emerged as part of a general shift that saw figure skating becoming more spectator-friendly. Free skating competitors played more to the crowd, behaving not just as competitive athletes but as entertainers. According to historian Matthias Hampe, 'sensation,' rather than beauty or other aesthetic motivations, had become a primary value or emphasis in free skating by the 1990s, a transformation Hampe attributes to new forms of commercialization in the sport.[19] Showier costumes were perhaps intended to make figure skating appeal to a wider – non-skating – audience, to give it a bigger profile on television, particularly in the United States where interest in the sport routinely wanes between Olympic years. The ISU launched the restrictive costume rule at the same time as the sport was building

on the popularity it had achieved with television audiences and marketers during the 1988 Olympics. In this regard, it is not surprising that
officials gave only the most heteronormative portions of the rule any
teeth, that is, that they made sure to enforce the rule in ways that would
most effectively give skating a heterosexual image.

In 2004 the ISU liberalized the skirts-only rule by permitting women
singles and pairs skaters (not ice dancers) to wear trousers or tights
in competitions. Interestingly, coaches and skaters heralded the move
not as a sign that women skaters were being taken more seriously as
athletes or as adults able to decide for themselves what to wear, but as
a chance to increase the 'artistic possibilities' of women's choreogra-
phies.[20] That is, a woman wearing pants or tights would be able to skate
to different kinds of music than a woman in a dress. A few seasons into
the new rule, it seems only a handful of women have chosen to give up
the skirt. Spectators and fans who were hoping that tights or unitards
would bring a less 'girlie' image to the ice have been disappointed.
Broadcasts of the 2006 Olympics on Canadian television showed only
two skaters wearing unitards. In both cases the one-piece outfits stayed
firmly within current conventions of female costuming. For instance,
without a skirt to contend with, Swiss skater Sarah Meier was able to
drop the back of her costume well below her waist, exposing quite a
bit more skin than she could have done had she been wearing a dress
with a skirt. For those of us who welcomed the rule change, this was an
outcome we had not expected.

Over the years, men's costumes have not changed as drastically as
women's have. In the nineteenth century, men wore trousers and jackets
that were quite similar to those they would have worn for other forms
of recreation and leisure. By the 1890s some European men had started
to wear tights rather than trousers. Tights allowed a skater to show
a good body line while giving him more freedom of movement than
woollen trousers did. Many writers advised against regular trousers,
fearing that they might catch upon a skate blade. In Europe and, eventually, in North America too, tights were standard apparel for men's
competitions until the Second World War. In 1944 the American magazine *Skating* reported that tights seemed to be 'fast disappearing from
our rinks to be replaced by tapered slacks.'[21] Within a decade tights
were completely gone, despite the fact that they were far more suitable to free skating than were the trousers that replaced them. In 1954
a skater from Philadelphia wrote: 'Thank goodness the era of tights

for men has passed, never, I hope, to return!'[22] In the 1950s and 1960s, men competed in suits and ties and 'monkey suits,' short-waisted, buttoned jackets with matching trousers. Not the most comfortable or the most practical outfit, the suit brought skating clothes closer into line with men's street clothes while simultaneously making the difference between men and women on the ice more apparent.

Serious and conservative, the monkey suit was reminiscent of both business and military attire; however, it did little to signify the athletic context in which it was worn. And as we saw in the last chapter, critics who worried about the reputation of men's skating were coming to understand that a sporting image was as important as sporting ability in the quest to make skating seem more manly. In the 1970s, some skaters adopted the one-piece stretch jumpsuit in an attempt to wear something appropriate to the actual physical demands of skating. The jumpsuit was more practical and more comfortable than the short jacket and pants that it replaced, but it was criticized for the message it might convey about skaters. While traditionalists found jumpsuits too casual for competition, those worried about representations of masculinity on the ice thought they looked too much like dance-wear. Jumpsuits did not look like the uniforms worn by men who participated in other sports. Neither did they look like men's street clothes. Even the plainest jumpsuit could make a skater stand apart visually from other men. And to the horror of some critics, not all male skaters wanted to keep their jumpsuits plain.

Until the 1970s, all male skaters wore pretty much the same thing, with the only variations being in terms of colour or trim. But, as women had done, men began to cultivate an individual approach to costuming in the late 1970s and 1980s. They started to wear outfits that would help draw out the themes of their programs and bring coherence to their music and choreography. Coaches and choreographers began to speak of a skater having the 'entire package' – technical skills, well-chosen music, effective choreography, and a costume and 'look' that would pull it all together. It was in this era that skating outfits became costumes. Men took to the ice dressed as matadors, princes, generals, and characters from film, opera, and theatre. Satin, sequins, and brocade became common embellishments. Uniformity of dress – one of the defining characteristics of masculine appearance norms over the past two hundred years[23] – ceased to be a feature of men's figure skating competitions. In refusing to follow a standard prescription for competitive apparel, men were adopting what fashion historians would call a feminine approach to dressing.[24] They were also rejecting the conformity that tends to be a salient feature of contemporary sport.

Beyond issues of fit and comfort, costumes have nothing to do with the actual physical skills involved in skating. They are packaging, adornment, extra to the athleticism. There is no way to assimilate the use of costumes within any sort of traditional athletic framework. One cannot, for instance, make an argument that they facilitate the skating itself, as one may say of swimsuits designed to reduce drag in the water. Costumes push skating beyond the comfortable limits of sport discourses. They draw attention to the fact that skating is not just about objective skills but about performance and display, and thus it exceeds not just the usual boundaries of sport but those of normative masculine behaviour as well. Despite the increasing commodification of men's appearance, mainstream heterosexual masculine norms still have little room for men who are openly invested in what they look like.[25] The simple fact that they wear costumes seems to suggest that male skaters are concerned with matters related to appearance. And thus, costumes are a good part of what makes figure skating seem fey. It's no surprise then that critics find them troublesome. As international figure skating judge Jon Jackson writes in his memoir *On Edge*, his own father found the idea of costumes a bit hard to take. Putting words into his father's mouth, Jackson writes: 'This was no sport for a boy. A costume? Not my son. It was bad enough he was going off every day to the ice rink to dance around with girls.'[26]

In criticism of men's costumes the sparkly little sequin functions as the primary target of concern. In such discussions the inappropriateness of sequins for heterosexual men is taken as a given; to meet the norms of mainstream masculinity, a man should not sparkle. In the early 1980s, American skater Scott Hamilton drew praise for wearing a plain blue jumpsuit with a simple stripe on the sleeve, in 'an effort to give skating a more masculine image.'[27] In 1992 the world championships were held in Oakland, California. Reporting on the competition, the *San Francisco Chronicle* printed a story under the headline 'Men Dump Sequins, Try More Macho Style.' *Chronicle* writer C.W. Nevius opened the article with a reference to a sign he saw in the stands of the men's event:

'Kick some butt,' it said.
Maybe that's not your impression of what happens during a men's com-

petition. Maybe you think in a case of a tie, the winner is the man with the most sequins on his costume. Maybe you should have taken a look at the victory platform last night ...

On the top step was Viktor Petrenko, who is ending his well-documented career as a ladies [sic] man with his impending marriage. Petrenko banged out five triple jumps and clinched the world title with a strong, athletic performance.

Next there is macho Kurt Browning, a Canadian heartthrob who became so annoyed with his costume during the short program that he ripped part of it off and tossed it onto the ice ...

And finally, in third, was a karate-kicking, motorcycle racing Elvis Stojko, another Canadian.

Are you sensing a trend here? Some of skating's insiders are, and it's not toward more sparkly costumes and cute dance steps. At the end of the competition, the gaudiest item any of them was wearing were their championship medals. There was barely a sequin in the bunch.[28]

A quick look at the medal ceremony on YouTube confirms Nevius's observation; there were, indeed, no sequins.[29] However, each of the three skaters was wearing a shiny satin shirt with puffed sleeves. Petrenko's was plain but for the white cummerbund that remained hidden until he raised his arms; Browning's had quite beautiful coloured beadwork across the yoke and down the sleeves; Stojko's was made of a glittery fabric that precluded the need for sequins. Two of three shirts were definitely sparkly; none would have passed muster with the average guy on the street. So why bother making the remark about sequins?

The reference to sequins was a bit of shorthand. It allowed Nevius to call attention to the popular assumption that skaters are effeminate and/or gay without having to state that assumption outright. The representation of Petrenko, Browning, and Stojko as sequin-less helps readers to infer that these men are straight. Nevius has set us up for that reading with the short descriptions of the men in the opening paragraphs of the story – Petrenko is a ladies' man, Browning is a heartthrob, Stojko rides dirt bikes. There is very little discussion of skating in the article; the new 'macho style' is clearly about something else. Elaborating on the sequin theme Nevius quotes from Linda Leaver, coach of 1988 Olympic champion, Brian Boitano of the United States: 'I think getting away from the sequins is good for the sport. I think both men and women like to watch men be masculine on the ice and women be beautiful.'[30] Leaver did not say exactly what the problem with sequins is, but one assumes it has something to do with keeping masculine and beautiful as separate categories. We learn more of Leaver's view of masculinity when she says that male skaters 'should compete full out, full risk ... That's the way it should be, aggressive, athletic men, fighting it out on the ice.'[31] It sounds like she's talking about hockey instead of a sport where competitors never actually face their opponents, perform to music, and receive marks for style.

In a 1994 interview, Elvis Stojko was more explicit about the root of sequin-anxiety: 'I like a simple, effective, masculine outfit. As my Mum would say, You don't want to go out there looking like a fruitcake, lit up like a Christmas tree.'[32] Who else but a fruitcake would actually choose to wear sequins in public? Real men wear clothes that do not catch the light. Of course, not all little boys know this when they first begin to skate, and for some of them, the chance to wear sequins is one of figure skating's primary allures. Jon Jackson writes about his own first costume:

> I was steered toward the plain black fabrics. Not the satins and sheers, just the plain black polyester gabardines. What about Mr. Carmen Miranda in the Ice Follies [whom he had just seen]? Why couldn't I be him? ... I would have settled for a nice blue. Maybe even a robin's-egg blue. But black? Blah. Who would ever notice me in that?
>
> My mom could tell I was disappointed, but tried to explain, 'Your dad will never go for anything other then black. Maybe we could sew some sequins on it to make it sparkle?' Ah, now she's making sense; a glimmer of hope. A language I understood.[33]

Anxieties over men's costumes are based on some kind of Liberace-stereotype of gay men. They ignore the fact that almost any masculine image can be assimilated by or associated with gay cultures. The popular link between skating and gay men depends on a lot more than sequins. The feminine context of their sport means that even the most macho skaters can be read as gay. In the 1990s, when some skaters tried to mark their masculinity in an aggressive fashion by sporting tight black T-shirts, studded wrist cuffs, and (fake or real) leather trousers, they were simply trading one set of gay signifiers for another. Indeed, when I have presented video clips of men's skating to gay audiences, some viewers have argued that skating's leather-clad, tough guys fit more easily into a contemporary gay image than do skaters wearing satin shirts or beaded boleros.

Admonishments to tone down men's costumes fail the boys who come to skating looking for something they can't get from Little League. They also ignore the simple fact that it is costumes, period, rather than any particular element about them, that put skating outside mainstream masculine norms, especially as these are constituted in sport. No amount of fiddling with costume design will save the masculine reputation of male athletes who compete in individualized outfits designed to meet the aesthetic and not the technical requirements of their sport. Critics inside and outside skating sometimes suggest that male skaters – no mention of women – should adopt plainer outfits that look more like uniforms in other sports, simple tights and T-shirts, perhaps. The danger is, of course, that tights could veer too close to dance-wear. Costumes are one of the things that make skating unique. They are part of the sport's appeal on television and part of what delivers an atypical sports audience to advertisers. Costumes also give many skaters – male and female – a lot of pleasure, as do the other more theatrical aspects of their sport, like the music.

If It Has a Soundtrack, Is It Really a Sport?

In the sport of artistic gymnastics only women perform to music and only in the floor exercises. In figure skating all events – women's, men's, pairs, ice dance – require music. For those parents who look at figure skating and say, 'No way! That's not for my son!' the sport's music is likely as much of a problem as its costumes. Nevertheless, so integral is music to the sport that, unlike costumes or some of the other aesthetic aspects of figure skating, there have never been any serious debates from inside or outside the skating community about getting rid of it.

Coaches and choreographers spend enormous amounts of time searching for music that will bring out the personalities of their skaters, help them demonstrate their strongest skills and appeal to audiences and judges. In the conservative environment of figure skating, part of that appeal depends on hitting just the right gendered note. Is there such a thing as feminine or masculine music? Critical musicologists argue that there is nothing inherent in a piece of music that gives it a gendered sound. What sounds masculine or feminine shifts over time and varies across cultures; our interpretation of it as such depends on the particular gender ideologies of our own time and place. In the constrained gender climate of the 1940s, for instance, American dance choreographer Ted Shawn made a strict separation between music he thought appropriate for women and music he thought appropriate for men. Shawn was the founder of the first all-male dance company in the United States, and he was very concerned about the public image of men who danced. One of the goals of the company was to change American perceptions of men's dancing. As with some present-day figure skaters, Shawn thought the way to go about doing this was to minimize the similarities between male and female dancers and to construct for the men a more virile image. Shawn thought that music for men should have a rhythmic rather than a melodic stress and it should be written with a time signature of 4/4 or 2/4 to emphasize men's big steps and big movements. Men's music should be slow and heavy, marked 'forte,' and written in a major key, with 'abrupt and rough' phrasing. By contrast, women's music should stress the melodic line. It should have a 3/4, 3/8, or 6/8 time signature to highlight women's less weighty movements. It should be light and fast, marked 'piano,' and written in a minor key, with legato phrasing.[34] Today Shawn's guidelines seem narrow and outdated. Yet the principle upon which they are based – that gender norms can be represented by music – has had a heavy influence on free skating.

In early international competitions, skaters performed to music played by a rink-side orchestra. The skater would simply request a march or a waltz and then skate a loosely connected series of moves to whatever music the orchestra provided. It was not until the 1920s that skaters began to choreograph specific programs to specific pieces of music. At that time figure skating remained firmly ensconced in a world of upper-class privilege and taste, and skaters' musical choices reflected this context. Classical Western orchestral music became the norm on the ice.

For women, the fact that their sport demands music is completely congruent with normative versions of femininity. Female athletes perform to music in rhythmic and artistic gymnastics and in synchronized swimming, the other sports most likely to be seen as primarily appropriate for girls. Indeed, music is part of what defines the category of 'feminine sport.' Still, not all styles of music are considered appropriate for female figure skaters. Music, supported by costumes, helps to constitute the conventional and narrow sphere of identities that bring women success on the ice. As Ted Shawn might have predicted, we do not see women skating to 'big' orchestral sounds, to a lot of brass, to jagged or startling rhythms, or to music that evokes masculine characters or narratives. As few women have been ready to give up their skirts, few have attempted to push the boundaries of acceptable music. These two phenomena are not unconnected. In the design of a program, the choice of music comes first, and from this follow decisions about movement and costumes. When choreographers choose music that falls into traditional feminine ruts, as they frequently do, we see traditional feminine costumes and traditional feminine programs.

Male skaters have had more leeway to explore a range of identities on the ice, hence their musical choices have been somewhat less constrained than women's. While the broad category of classical music was once the main source of skating music, Hollywood film soundtracks now seem to fill that role. Soundtracks are considered less abstract than classical music and so more accessible to mainstream audiences and to skaters themselves, who are now less likely than they once were to come from the kinds of elite backgrounds where knowledge of classical music would have been expected and nurtured. Soundtracks often provide choreographers with a ready-made theme or 'hook' for a program. They can also give a program an instant racial, ethnic, or gender identity. While Elvis Stojko was certainly not the only male skater to adopt this strategy, he became expert at it over the 1990s, skating to music from *Dragon: The Bruce Lee Story* (1991), *Total Recall* (1992), *The Killing Fields* (1993), *1492: Conquest of Paradise* (1994), *Speedway* (1995), *Dragonheart* (1996), *The Rockateer* (1997), *Ghost and the Darkness* (1998), *Merlin* (1999), and *The Mummy* (2000).[35] Some of his musical selections could evoke masculinity with their sound, but equally important was the way they could evoke masculinity with their titles. Television broadcasters now routinely post the title of a skater's music on the screen at the start of a program: 'The Godfather.' 'The Matrix.' 'James Bond: Live and Let Die.' The words on the screen can associate the skater with particular types of masculinity even before he takes his first step.

While soundtracks are popular, they are not the only type of music used by male skaters. To a much greater extent than women, men have been experimenting with styles of music that earlier skaters would have found too risky or that earlier judges would have rejected out of hand. Over the past two decades we have begun to hear rock and techno music in men's events. The best example is Kurt Browning's 1993 short program that he skated to a drum solo called 'Bonzo's Montreux' by Led Zeppelin. In 1998 Elvis Stojko skated a well-received short program to a recording of Japanese Taiko drums. At the height of skating's macho period, men flagged their virility with fast, hard pieces of music that contrasted significantly with the classical music most people associate with the sport. What, after all, is more effete than classical music, with its easy links to aristocratic drawing rooms, ballet dancers, and bookish intellectuals? But, as with costumes, no amount of tinkering with men's music to make it faster, harder, or in any other way more macho can cancel the fact that it's the very presence of the music – rather than its style – which puts skaters' reputations as athletes and as men into question.

Do Men Do Spirals?

> I have a sinking feeling that I'm probably setting myself up for public humiliation here, but how come the men never put spirals in their routines? Okay, I shouldn't say 'never' in case someone has actually done one, but I haven't seen it. Anyway is it just considered too femme?[36]

It's not surprising someone felt the need to ask this question on a popular figure skating website. In men's singles competitions, spirals are few and far between. When men do perform them they tend to look very different than women's. In the physical vocabulary through which skaters communicate, spirals say a lot about gender.

A spiral is skating's version of what ballet dancers call an arabesque. The skater glides on one foot while bending forward at the waist to hold the torso parallel with the ice. The back is arched, the arms are, usually, spread out like wings, and the free leg (the leg that is not on the ice) is stretched behind and lifted above the hips, in some cases until it is almost perpendicular to the ice. Like almost no other move in the skating repertoire, a spiral expresses the freedom and joy found in the long running edge. For the child who is just learning to skate, it is an exciting marker of the transition from pleasure skater to figure skater. For the experienced competitor, it is an opportunity to compose a beautiful or striking shape in space and to feel the pull of the music. While some skaters execute spirals that require tremendous strength and flexibility, the basic move is neither difficult nor spectacular, part of the reason perhaps that many coaches and skaters feel the spiral is not an appropriate move for men, a view confirmed by the rules of the sport.

Anyone who has watched skating on television will be familiar with 'the spiral sequence,' a required element in the women's, but not the men's, short and long programs. Introduced to the short program in 1983, the spiral sequence has to include one change of foot and at least two changes of body position. The full sequence must cover the length of the ice in a large S-shape or follow a large circle or oval that stretches across the width of the rink. As a required element, the spiral sequence is intended to demonstrate edge control, creativity, and flexibility, characteristics that could certainly be developed by men as well as by women were the rules to demand it, which they do not.

During the Canadian Broadcasting Corporation's coverage of the 1992 Winter Olympic Games in Albertville, France, Canadian skating judge Jean Senft explained the gender-specific rule about spirals:

> Only the women perform this sequence and you might wonder why that is. As women's skating moved from the traditional graceful approach to concentration on sheer athleticism, we began to lose something in the transition. A few years ago, women began trying many triple jumps without much success, falling too often and destroying the beauty of their programs. The spiral sequence was brought in to help restore the grace and beauty of women's skating. Here the emphasis is on artistry and not on jumping … While women are very capable of performing difficult triple jumps, the spiral sequence is there to remind us all of a little bit of our past and to preserve an element of beauty and dignity in our sport.[37]

As Senft says, the spiral sequence was introduced at a time when many women were struggling with the increasing technical demands of the sport. What she does not say is that, a decade earlier, men experienced their own technical growing pains. German skating historian Matthias Hampe writes that men's efforts to manage more difficult and more frequent jumps led to a lot of 'technical messiness.' While they were struggling with new techniques, the quality of men's programs degenerated, with too much empty choreography and too much similarity among the skaters. The push for bigger tricks made competitions far less interesting to watch.[38] As evidence, Hampe says only 557 spectators – instead of several thousand – showed up to watch the men's event at the 1971 European championships in Zurich.[39] But even in the face of dwindling audiences, the ISU obviously did not feel the need to impose compensatory regulations on the men as they later did on the women. In pushing themselves to try elements beyond their immediate capabilities, men would have been fulfilling masculine stereotypes. They would have been admired as courageous risk-takers who were expanding the boundary of possibility in their sport. Such risk taking is not, generally, read as compatible with femininity. Thus, in similar circumstances, women were just seen as messing up. Almost all contemporary books on skating make sure to note that women's first attempts at multiple triple jumps were not always pretty. To my knowledge, only Hampe acknowledges that men struggled with them too.

Like the spiral sequence, the layback spin has also been institutionalized as one of skating's principal 'feminine' moves; it too is a short-program element for women but not for men. To execute a layback, the skater spins with the free leg bent softly at the knee and raised slightly to the side or behind. She holds her arms in a graceful position, perhaps over her head or dropped behind her, while arching her back as far as possible. The ideal is to turn the spin with the back parallel to the ice. The position requires tremendous flexibility and a precise body control that allows strict attention to detail – the placement of the knee, the shape of the arms and hands, the stretch of the neck. The skater uses her body to compose a beautiful shape that is, at once, moving and still. But, as more than one feminist writer has pointed out, despite the skill and strength required to perform it well, the layback presents an image of vulnerability. Abigail Feder suggests that the extremely arched back and exposed neck make it 'like nothing so much as popular conceptions of female sexual climax.'[40]

Dance theorist Jane Desmond reminds us that the body itself is a form of representation, a vehicle through which social ideologies are constituted and made available to us.[41] While bodies are certainly more than texts, we do read them like texts; we take meanings from what they look like and the way they move. These meanings are shaped by our social and historical locations. So, when we look at a skater performing a layback spin or a spiral, or any other movement, we do not make sense of what we are seeing in a vacuum. We make associations between it and other things we have heard, seen, or experienced. Hence, Feder's association of the layback with the sexualized images of women that appear regularly in contemporary advertising and soft-core porn. Skaters – particularly women who perform laybacks – might find her analysis hard to swallow, steeped as they are in the conventions of their sport. But for the average non-skating spectator, the links between a woman doing a layback on TV and a model swooning with sexual desire in a perfume ad would not be that hard to see. Where else in public might a woman arch her back to drape her head and hair behind her?

Desmond writes: 'By looking at dance we can see enacted on a broad scale, and in codified fashion, socially constituted and historically specific attitudes toward the body in general, toward specific social groups' usage of the body in particular, and about the relationships among variously marked bodies.'[42] We can make a similar point about skating. The layback provides a perfect embodied example of attitudes about gender. The spin represents dominant gender ideologies that make it not at all unusual for women to convey vulnerability with their bodies. By contrast, it is not usual to see men in the head-thrown-back position – not in skating, not anywhere. It is a position of surrender; it fits poorly with notions of masculinity that emphasize control, independence, or dominance.

Explanations of why men do not perform laybacks or spirals are far more likely to be made in biological terms than in ideological ones. One of the main arguments against requiring men to perform such moves is that these skills require flexibility and this is seen as a characteristic strength of female and not male bodies. It is often suggested – in popular writing on sport, in research on sociobiology, in the letters pages of the daily newspaper – that the differing capabilities of men's and women's bodies are simple biological facts. Men are naturally stronger and taller and women are naturally more flexible. There are a number of problems with this perspective. First, it assumes that the category of humans divides neatly into the subclasses of male and female. But this is much easier said than done. Upon which criteria will we determine who belongs in which category? Genitalia? These are indeterminate in one out of every 1500 or 2000 births.[43] Hormones? All of us produce so-called male and female hormones and there is no absolute level or ratio that separates one sex from the other. Chromosomes? Even the IOC eventually admitted that these are unreliable when, after three decades, it abandoned the practice of trying to verify the sex of all female athletes. The IOC and other major sports organizations gave up the practice of across-the-board 'gender verification' (as they call it) on the grounds that it is simply too difficult.[44] These organizations do, however, cling to the notion that it might be possible, continuing to test individual athletes, as we saw in 2008 at the Beijing Olympics and in 2009 with the horrific treatment of the South African world champion 800-metre runner Caster Semenya by the International Association of Athletic Federations (IAAF).

The desire to see physical characteristics like flexibility and strength as simple biological facts ignores the way such characteristics are produced through an interplay of biology and culture. Biologist Anne Fausto-Sterling talks about the powerful impact of cultural factors on the materiality of the body. Looking at bones, Fausto-Sterling talks about how factors linked to gendered experiences, like women's and men's different histories of exercise and diet, have contributed to bone density levels that are highly variable between the sexes and across cultures. As Fausto-Sterling puts it, 'Culture shapes bones.'[45] What she wants to make evident is that cultural factors are not just the context for biology, they actually change it. They also, of course, shape how we understand biology, and those understandings, in turn, can have physical effects. As Susan Bordo writes, 'When we look at bodies (including our own in the mirror), we don't just see biological nature at work, but values and ideals, differences and similarities that *culture* has "written," so to speak, on those bodies.'[46]

Ideas about bodies and what they should and should not do, can and cannot do, give shape, quite literally, to the bodies in which we live. Our bodies then become promotional devices that reinforce those same ideas. For instance, the notion that physical flexibility is a feminine characteristic has contributed to many men not seeing value in working on their own flexibility and, therefore, living with muscles that are tighter than they would be if flexibility were considered a desirable measure of manliness. These discursively produced tight muscles then confirm the commonsense 'fact' that it is not normal for men to be limber, and thus they make the limber male skater or ballet dancer seem unmanly and strange. Even within the dance world, 'the facts' about flexibility have shifted over time, influenced by changing notions of masculinity. Bruce Marks is a dancer who performed with both the Metropolitan Opera Ballet and with the American Ballet Theatre in the 1950s. He wrote:

> For a man to lift his leg higher than hip level in extension [at that time] just wasn't done. A man's leg was to be kept at a forty-five degree angle. And men were not to stretch … Men's legs now go up very easily in a stretch. There was no one who could do a split on the wall like Misha [Baryshnikov] does, when I started studying ballet – no men. None of them wanted to. The first year I danced, I remember Pierre Lacotte came from the Paris Opera and stretched constantly. I had never *seen* a man so stretched; it was considered taboo. We made fun of French male dancers for that. They were considered effete because they were looking for a kind of line that was forbidden to us as men.[47]

Gender is about limits, about not having free range to act or look or behave in any manner whatsoever. Men who are not only flexible but willing to show it seem to push against those limits. Many in the skating world, including coaches and choreographers, are committed to staying within the bounds of appropriate gender norms. They have tried to minimize the difference between skaters and other male athletes by emphasizing the development of stereotypically masculine capabilities like strength and speed rather than so-called feminine capabilities like limberness. Male skaters are taught certain ways of moving – and not moving – that minimize their difference from other men and maximize their difference from women.

Early skating textbooks were relatively silent on the difference their authors expected to see in male and female skaters. Indeed, gender difference seems to have been of relatively minimal concern until the 1930s. At that point, as we saw in chapter 6, some commentators considered the quality of skating in women's competitions to be overtaking that in men's. Women's technical skills were not only on a par with men's, but it was women who were pushing the sport in new directions. Was it anxiety about women's increasing competence that inspired some writers to try to separate gestures, styles of movement, and so-called innate abilities into masculine and feminine categories?: 'The Haines [sit spin] is properly a man's figure ... Now, with modern ideas and clothes, Mrs Jarosz and other lady skaters use the Haines in their program and do it quite well. Whether the esthetic and feminine appeal of their programs is aided by the use of this figure is indeed still very doubtful.'[48] The differences between men's and women's skating were attributed to physical and cultural factors. One English writer claimed: 'In the man one is impressed by strong curves of muscle and magnificent lines running from head to feet, whereas in the woman, the eye is caught by the flying draperies, and the lines of movement are more broken and unsettled.'[49] Willy Boeckl, an Austrian skater who moved to the United States to coach, took the same perspective in his 1937 textbook: 'There is a subtle difference between the programs of men and women. A good man skater jumps higher and with more abandon, skates his filling steps faster; the element of risk or danger should always be present in the mind of the audience when a man skates, while the woman should always represent grace and beauty.'[50] The suggestion that men should cultivate the element of risk or danger would have horrified turn-of-the-century gentlemen skaters, whose goal – in skating as in social life – was to communicate ease and grace. The element of risk or danger would have been at odds with the sense of calm and confidence they hoped to display as gentlemen. But figure skating, like other aspects of interwar culture in North America and Europe, was witnessing the declining influence of upper-class values. As the risk-taker gained currency in popular representations of masculinity, so he gained currency on the ice.

Skating writers have long recognized that even the tiniest movement carries social meaning. And, thus, they gave advice regarding not just hands, but also fingers and wrists. In terms of a skater's gender identity, a lot seems to ride on the hands. Even the 'genius' Gillis Grafstrom (Olympic champion in 1920, 1924, and 1928) was subject to criticism on this account. 'Graceful hand movements are surely aesthetically attractive,' wrote fellow Swede and ten-time world champion (1901–5 and 1907–11) Ulrich Salchow, 'but they leave too much room for femininity.'[51] An article published in England in 1930 claimed: 'Men may fold their arms, but not women. Women may make more use of the hands above the head. For a man to do so is to risk looking effeminate or ridiculous.'[52] By 1961 the advice had grown even more particular (note too the asymmetry between 'girls' and 'men'): 'Girls may slightly cock their wrists, but men never, otherwise instead of being male and virile they become effeminate which is most objectionable.'[53] In 1969 *Skating* magazine was giving counsel not just about hands and wrists but even about fingers: while girls could hold their fingers loosely and slightly spread, boys needed to keep their fingers closed for a 'more masculine expression.'[54]

No logical case can be made here to ground these gender-differentiated instructions about hands in the 'natural' physical differences between women and men. The sanction on certain hand positions or hand movements is nothing more than a reflection of and contribution to systems of meaning that rely upon bodily codes to render ideas about gender and sexuality visible. What is interesting in the recurring discussion about hands is how truly minor those codes can be. The actual content of the different prescriptions is less important than the simple fact that they were proposed at all, especially given the fact that, by the mid-twentieth century, skaters were awash in gender signifiers. One might imagine that someone already sporting a gender-specific hairstyle, gender-specific clothes, and gender-specific skates while performing gender-specific skills would not have to worry too about the angle of a wrist.

How was it that certain moves came to be identified with one sex or the other? In the 1920s and 1930s, the spiral, for instance, was a signature move for both Gillis Grafstrom and Karl Schäfer (who beat Grafstrom to become Olympic champion in 1932 and won again in 1936). Iconic photographs of both men show them doing spirals that differed in no significant way from those done by their female contemporaries. Yet, in his 1937 book, Boeckl wrote the following: 'Advanced men skaters are often of the opinion that spirals are only for the beginner or that they are too feminine. They are quite mistaken. A fast spiral on a strong slant in a good position requires courage and speed.'[55] Grafstrom and Schäfer, and the women who skated alongside them, would have found Boeckl's attempt to describe a masculine rather than a generic spiral both odd and unnecessary. They would have been even more surprised by the fact that many male singles skaters eventually stopped doing spirals altogether. By the time 1976 Olympic gold medallist John Curry began to skate in the 1960s, spirals were seen as questionable for boys. When Curry practised spirals on his own, 'the teachers would sort of watch me out of the corners of their eyes, obviously thinking: What *is* this child doing?'[56] The move would later come to symbolize the incomparable lyrical quality of Curry's skating. One British dance writer called it 'a miracle of poise and elegance.' Of course, these are exactly the type of adjectives that many male skaters and their coaches would have found problematic in the 1970s. Some skaters would have found it easier to avoid the spiral altogether than to risk being seen as elegant, a word that in a sporting context could be taken as synonymous with 'effete.'

According to American coach Jeff Nolt, there is still a stigma attached to men and boys who do spirals. 'Men and boys can do spirals,' he told figure skating journalist Lorrie Kim. 'I think it's misguided that they're not asked to … in the SP [short program] and FS [free skate]. They CAN do them.' Nolt rightly argues that 'avoiding certain kinds of movement' actually 'constitutes the stigma' that men are trying to avoid. 'It is important not to let fear of harassment keep a male skater from pointing his toe, or doing extension moves [like spirals], or showing good athletic form.' Yet despite his obvious desire to release male skaters from the constraints of normative ideas about gender and sexuality, Nolt still seems to believe that there are masculine and feminine ways of doing particular moves. Holding one arm out in front of him, he demonstrates a spiral position for Lorrie Kim: '"A woman might come *up* more," Nolt demonstrated, lifting his hand and wrist slightly before settling into the exit pose. "But men: just the way the arm is shaped – it's a thicker line, not as waiflike as a woman. Just the way they leave the floor out of plié, they can go higher. Just the flexing into the floor. The lines of the chin. The line of the front arm."'[57] Nolt says that men should not fear moves like spirals because they will project 'virility' as they do them. He seems to be suggesting that a male body will inevitably perform virile movements. But what of men who do not see virility as important and who do not see the need to inflect their skating with it? And what of not-so-waiflike women? Could there ever be room in skating for them to portray virility? Might we imagine a day when the gender of skating moves ceases to be tied to the presumed sex of the body that performs them? Could we imagine a day when skating moves cease to have gender connotations at all?

The notion that movements or styles of movement are or should be masculine or feminine continues to be widespread among skaters, coaches, and critics. It is unclear whether they consider gender-specific ways of moving to be a product of nature or of training.[58] Are they inevitable or a goal to be achieved? While such questions are, to my knowledge, not discussed at all in the skating literature, they have been under consideration for decades in the world of dance. One of the most prolific and passionate defenders of the notion of gender-specific movements was Ted Shawn, whose ideas about gender-appropriate music I introduced in the previous section. Shawn strongly believed that there are natural, fundamental differences in male and female movement. He wrote: 'If we can get these specific qualities of masculine and feminine movement separated, it will be like breaking up white light into the colours of the spectrum ... We shall then be able to split up our orchestra of dancers – the percussion and brass for the men and the woodwind and strings for the women, each sex contributing a different but complementary quality of movement to the enrichment of the art of the dance as a whole.'[59] He thought that a healthy respect for sex differences would make the virility of men's dance more obvious to the American public and thus make it easier for men to watch and do.

Men, Shawn wrote, make big movements; women make small movements. Men use their whole bodies. Their arm movements 'are a continuation of the body movement, as for example, the movement of a man using a scythe.' Women's movements are smaller, they use 'a great deal of arm and wrist movements of a small range ... the little, fluttery movements of the wrist and hands are legitimately a woman's movement.' Shawn described men's movements as 'positive, aggressive, forceful, definite, explicit.' Women's movements, by contrast, were described as 'tender, protective, conservative, conciliatory, delicate and tentative.'[60] On posture, he wrote: 'The man's stance is the forward thrust, the woman's the concave receptivity.'[61] He believed that different-shaped bodies are supposed to make – have the capacity to make – different kinds of movement. Shawn's was a perfectly binary view of gender that corresponded with the prevailing attitudes of his time and reflected his anxiety over the already feminized reputation of dance.

While more recent critics might not be so firm in their opinions nor rely on such rigid gender stereotypes, the notion that there are essential masculine or feminine styles of movement is not yet a relic of the past, as we see in ballet and some forms of contemporary dance and also in competitive figure skating. On the one hand, the assumption is that gender difference is natural – men are not capable of being flexible or graceful so they don't need to do spirals – but on the other hand, there is a fear that gender identity is not as fixed as it could be – be careful you don't cock your wrist or you might turn into a pansy.

In his 1985 book on masculine dance technique, Nikolai Tarasov, a noted teacher from the Moscow Choreographic School, cautioned that boys must be taught so that they don't develop 'that gracefulness so welcome in girls, and so unwelcome in males,' implying that gendered styles are a result of training (hence, the need for his book). Yet, Tarasov also believed that the differences between male and female styles of movement were inherent. But if that were the case, surely there could be no fear of boys developing feminine characteristics. Tarasov wrote: 'With boys, the movement has more resolve, physical force, simplicity, terseness and vigor in performance. If a boy and a girl execute an identical turn of the head, the boy will do it with more definite resoluteness than will the girl.'[62] Is this resoluteness a natural tendency or something that boys must be taught? Tarasov seems to suggest that it is both and, therefore, he recommended that boys not be taught by women. Ted Shawn made similar arguments, claiming, on the one hand, that gender differences in styles of movement are natural and, on the other, that men and women should follow separate training regimes to make sure that men do not develop an effeminate style, full of soft, pretty movements instead of vital and dynamic ones.[63] *New York Times* dance critic Tobi Tobias put it more bluntly, suggesting simply that men should focus on jumps – those all-important signifiers of masculinity – while women and girls should focus on 'fluidity and finesse of line.'[64] Is the point to create gender difference or to work with it?

Choreography reinforces the notion that there are specifically male and female styles of movement. If a choreographer believes that male and female styles of movement are inherently different, then she or he will choose music and design programs that reinforce that belief.

Shawn, for instance, claimed that one had to respect the limitations imposed by male and female bodies: 'Never under any circumstances should I require either sex to project through themselves the movement quality of the other sex.'[65] How does one project 'sex' qualities through movement? The usual convention in the Western styles of dance that echo ballet is for men to emphasize weight, muscle, hardness, and to sink into the ground, while women are to be seen to float over it. Men tend to use diagonals and forceful lines (as with skating's straight-line footwork sequences) to cover space, while women more frequently perform from a single position or follow smooth curves (as with the spiral sequence). Men's movements are full of straight lines and right angles, they move their bodies on square planes, for instance, with hips, back, shoulders moving as a unit. Women have more permission to twist and curve their torsos, to move shoulders and hips in opposition, to lean off the plane. Men's movements are expected to be more explosive, more powerful, more aggressive. And if the choreographer is concerned with such things, they will be. The corollary is that women will appear softer and less powerful, which is a problem only to the extent that 'softer' is less valued in our culture than 'powerful' and that women do not also have the option of appearing otherwise. In this sense, stylistic differences and gendered movement classifications are not equal. Indeed, they support broader cultural ideologies of male dominance.

In dance there are broad traditions – both mainstream and alternative styles of Western dance, and various styles of non-Western dance – in which dancers are not subject to, or in which they reject, the gendered styles of movement I have just described. In skating, however, we see few alternatives to the heavily gendered technical and aesthetic styles that prevail in ISU competitions. Gender norms continue to exert a huge influence on skaters and how they can present themselves, on women especially. And this I would argue is a result of the conservatism that comes from figure skating's structure as a sport, from the desire to win and the concomitant need to please judges. In singles skating, there are very few instances of women attempting to contravene expectations for how they should perform. Even those skaters, like Midori Ito and Tonya Harding, who were seen to fall shy of meeting the norms set out for 'ladies,' were still skating in a way that suggested they were trying to. Beyond the fact that they 'jumped like men,' these women were not explicitly challenging what it is that women do on the ice. Their choreography did not, for instance, project a sense of weightiness or include angular or purposely ungraceful positions or demand short choppy strides in transitional moves or footwork. They did not choose music that conveyed anger or aggression. Such innovations do appear in men's programs. But they would be too risky for any female skater attempting to do well with judges.

Figure skating no doubt attracts young girls who are inclined to enjoy the type of femininity they see in the figure skating that appears on television. And, once again, I need to make clear that I think it is a good thing that figure skating offers a venue in which girls and women can express their athleticism in a recognizably girly way. We need more such spaces in the culture and they deserve more respect. The problem with skating is that there is no room for boys and men to adopt this same style and no room for girls and women who want to express their athleticism in other ways. Young female athletes who choose skating are coached to perform girliness and they are rewarded for doing so. The narrow range of femininities that we see represented by elite skaters is, in part, the result of high-performance sport systems focused on reproducing success. Female skaters are the sport's most lucrative commodities. It seems no one is prepared to tinker with the formula that continues to churn out one media-darling ice princess after another. But even taking this into consideration, the homogeneity among female skaters at all levels is still remarkable.

The female skaters who win competitions perform a femininity that is the product of long-standing practices around costumes, music, and choreography. These practices have deep roots in skating's privileged white European history. But their remarkable consistency is also a product of post–Second World War efforts to ensure that female and male skaters look different, that there is no danger of overlap between the femininities and masculinities on display in the sport. Hence, figure skating is less open than it could be to varied styles of female movement, appearance, and body type. The creativity of female skaters who might like to stretch the definitions of gender that operate in their sport is constrained by the (perceived) need to protect the public image of skating's men.

Ironically, the concern about men who skate and the way they come across to the public ends up putting greater restrictions on women than men. While men are certainly limited by rules and by the expectation that they will avoid being too fey, they do exhibit more diversity than women do in their costumes, the styles of music they choose, and the kinds of choreography they use. As a group, they show greater variation in the way they perform gender than do women. In the 1990s, at the height of skating's macho trend, international men's events included skaters as different as Alexei Urmanov and Elvis Stojko, as Swan Lake and the Terminator. At the 2010 Olympics in Vancouver the final flight of skaters in the men's event included Johnny Weir and Evgeny Plushenko skating back to back. We never see such contrast among women. The greater number of female skaters at lower levels makes the sport more competitive for girls than boys, and this may promote a kind of conformity among girls as they try to emulate styles that get rewarded. Or perhaps boys develop the fortitude to weather disapproval by persisting in a so-called effeminate sport, and so they simply find it easier to skate as they would like to. The point, of course, is that all skaters should get to skate as they would like to without having to bend to gender-based rules or to conform to gendered norms around appearance and styles of movement. The point of this sport should be for athletes to push themselves technically *and* aesthetically, not simply to reproduce what has come before or to use their athleticism to reinforce unequal gender relations and the marginalization of people who do not conform to prevailing norms.

In the 1960s, 1970s, and 1980s, feminists pushed to expand the sporting opportunities available to girls and women. They wanted to promote female athleticism, to change sport from a 'male preserve' to a cultural site in which anyone who wanted to might discover and nurture their physical potential. In many ways this project has been tremendously successful. Girls and women now participate in a vast range of sports that were previously off limits to them. Athleticism is now an expected part of many girlhoods. But feminists had also hoped that the visibility of women's athletic achievements would help to shift ideologies about gender difference in the culture at large. Despite huge increases in the number of female athletes, many sporting institutions continue to needlessly exaggerate the differences between women and men. These differences are not neutral; they end up privileging men and devaluing women. They contribute to the whole package of ideas that support sexism and homophobia in our culture. In this regard, figure skating makes its own special contribution.

While I was working on this book I had the opportunity to talk with Patricia Chafe, a Canadian mathematician who acted as a consultant for the ISU when the new scoring system was being developed. Chafe is a critic of the way that gender has been structured into the new system. She mentioned a number of examples of how this works, but one in particular stands out. The new system is based on the familiar and annoying requirements that men and women execute different elements in both long and short programs and that men's long programs are thirty seconds longer than women's at both junior and senior levels of international competition. Chafe says that this extra thirty seconds is the justification the ISU has used for permitting men to perform eight jumps, while women can only perform seven. Because men have time to complete more elements they end up with more points. In other words, the greater number of elements means that, given a man and a woman of equal calibre, the man will inevitably receive a higher score. To make matters worse, the component score of a man's short program is multiplied by a factor of 1.0, while the component score for a woman's short program is multiplied by a factor of 0.8. Thus, her component score can only ever be worth 80 per cent of the value of his. In the long program, a man's component scores are multiplied by a factor of 2.0, a woman's by a factor of 1.6. Once again, her score is only worth 80 per cent of the value of his. This means, Chafe says, that a woman will likely never hold the record for the highest total score in the sport. The best skater, as determined by a comparison of scores, will likely always be a man.[66] And in an era when announcers and journalists have fetishized the total score, constantly hoping to announce the 'highest score ever awarded' or a 'new world record,' such records become a way of promoting men at women's expense.

The inequity of this practice was made evident at the 2010 Olympics, where Kim Yu-na won the women's competition by a huge margin. Many journalists noted approvingly that Kim's score was good enough to have placed her in ninth position in the men's competition. What the journalists did not say was that Kim had not had the same chance as the men had to generate points. She did not get to do the same number of elements as the men did and so missed out on possible points in her technical element score. And then her component scores were calculated at only 80 per cent of the value of the men's. If Kim had been allowed to skate for the same length of time as the men do, and thus do one extra jump, and if her score had been adjusted to remove the gender inequities that are embedded in the system – that is, if her score had been adjusted so that we could compare apples to apples – Kim would have placed even higher. I asked Patricia Chafe how much higher. A recalculation of Kim's component scores, using the same factor applied to the men's, would have put her in third place. Add to that the one extra jump that the men get to do – let us say a simple, well done *double* jump, which would be worth 1.9 + 1.0 points – and Kim would have had a total score of 257.85, as compared to first-place Evan Lysacek's score of 257.67.[67] Many people consider Kim the best skater in the world today. It's a view that will never be confirmed by her scores.

ISU officials could have done things differently. They could have used the development of a new scoring system to change long-standing inequities. They could have given male and female skaters equal time and required them to perform the same moves, the same number of jumps. So heavy is the influence of gender norms on the sport of figure skating that it is hard to imagine what skating could look like otherwise. Skating's large number of female athletes and its unique aesthetic demands could surely support and inspire new ways of thinking about sport and new ways of thinking about male and female athleticism. The emphasis the new scoring system puts on the full range of skating skills and on the development of complexity in choreography and performance does hold some promise. When we get to get to the point where male and female skaters execute the same required elements and where they may choose how they go about performing them, without penalty, skating will be helping to dismantle rather than shoring up ideologies that promote gender inequality. It will also get a lot more interesting.

Epilogue

In the fall of 2009, the CBC launched a *Dancing with the Stars* knock-off called *Battle of the Blades*. Television critic John Doyle called it gimmicky, 'totally dumb-as-a-plank TV,'[1] and he was right. Nevertheless a lot of us watched it. *Battle of the Blades* was such a huge hit that the network is airing a second season in the fall of 2010. The show paired former NHL hockey players – they would all be men, of course – with professional female figure skaters to compete as pairs teams in a weekly elimination series. It's hard to know where to start with an analysis of this show. The heterosexist commentary of the judges? The representation of hockey by men and figure skating by women? The heavily gendered, heteronormative choreography? The fact that the men were fully clothed and the women were not? Or, the fact that these men, like men pushing baby strollers, were praised over and over on the show and in the press for having the courage to try something that might put their masculinities at stake – all those sequins, the satin shirts, the arm movements.

A story about *Battle of the Blades* that appeared in the *Globe and Mail* quoted the mother of a young male figure skater. She thought the show would make life easier for her son.[2] My sense is that, on the contrary, it reinforces the very same notions that make skating a hard choice for young boys. Frequent comments by the show's judges framed the hockey players as unique and surprising in the figure skating context and emphasized their difference from regular male figure skaters. In general, *Battle of the Blades* produced a constant stream of talk that marginalized the men and boys who skate every day. The show certainly constituted a version of figure skating that was an impossible site for effeminacy or for gay men. In this way the show evoked the 1990s discourses of machoness that inspired this book. Thankfully, these days, such discourses seem to flourish more on reality TV shows than in the world of figure skating proper. In elite men's skating competitions they are becoming far less prevalent than they were a decade ago.

Figure skating's macho trend seems to have had its day. Symbolic of its passing, Kurt Browning, who may well have been the first figure skater in history to be labelled macho in the press, went on to become, in my view, the leading artistic skater of his time. The man once pegged as the Cowboy and known primarily for his jumps developed exquisite posture and control and a remarkable interpretive versatility. His professional career has demonstrated the artistic possibilities that lie in superlative skating technique.

The recent generation of male skaters puts Browning in good company. Most promising is the fact that the finest artistic skating does not scrimp on technique nor is it the sole property of professionals, as it would have been in the past. Johnny Weir of the United States, Daisuke Takahashi of Japan, Jeffrey Buttle and Patrick Chan of Canada stand out. Weir is, quite simply, gorgeous. Takahashi has everything – quads, spins, incredible choreography, and a compelling individuality. Buttle is so tightly meshed with his music that it seems the music is coming right from his skates. Chan's edges are so deep they defy gravity and rival those of any ice dancer. What makes possible the impressive aesthetic quality of their performances is their superior technique in all the elements of their free skating, including their basic stroking and their spins, elements that in the past have been neglected by many male skaters.

With the advent of the new scoring system, men's choreography has become thicker, more complex. It is less driven by a need to validate itself through conspicuous athleticism than it was a decade ago, and thus it shows more balance between aesthetics and technique. The best skaters today seem more fully developed as *figure skaters*, as opposed to jumpers on skates. While jumps remain important, they are more likely to flow seamlessly in and out of footwork, to be part of the whole rather than its reason for being. But despite this improvement in the overall quality of men's skating, there remain problems with the new scoring system. The emphasis on achieving the maximum number of points for each element means that skaters are focused only on difficulty at the expense of creativity or originality, at the expense of artistry. So we now have skaters who are highly skilled in the full range of skating elements, yet they are denied the opportunity to exploit their skills artistically. Were the scoring system to be reworked to allow more leeway for not just technical or aesthetic qualities but for 'artistic impression,' the current generation of technically well-rounded skaters would be able to push their sport in new directions. The best choreographers, like Canadian David Wilson, would have a greater ability to design men's programs in which the movement and stylistic qualities responded to the diverse inclinations, physical abilities, and talents of the skaters.

There are still male skaters who grumble about the aesthetic demands of their sport and who want the focus to be more clearly on jumps. A few years ago, 2010 Olympic champion Evan Lysacek of the United States talked to American skating officials 'about spinning off an ice-skating competition more like skateboarding's halfpipe where skaters focus only on jumps, flips and still undiscovered tricks – with no music in the background, except maybe hard rock.'[3] In 2009, a minor skating-world scandal erupted when French skater Brian Joubert and Patrick Chan scuffled in the press over the relative importance of quad jumps in men's skating. Joubert told the *Chicago Tribune* that he was 'very disappointed that other men do not try them … With the new system, you have to be clean, so people make it clean but simple.'[4] The notion that tightly choreographed programs full of complex spins and challenging footwork (along with all the usual jumps) are simple is a bit of spin meant to convince us that nothing counts but the one big trick. If Joubert were talking about boxing, he'd be discounting everything but the knockout. His comment to the *Tribune* was a criticism of skaters like Chan who spend time developing all their skills. Chan gains a scoring advantage by executing difficult footwork and spins and by attending to the presentation of these along with the jumps. Joubert, by contrast, puts all his eggs in one basket. He hopes to gather points by successfully completing the big jumps. As a consequence, his programs have been criticized for not fulfilling the requirements of well-roundedness demanded by the new scoring system.

The heavy emphasis on masculinity that influenced men's skating in the 1990s has been a casualty of the new judging system, of changes in the political economy of the sport, and in the culture at large. Skating is far less popular than it was in the wake of the Tonya Harding and Nancy Kerrigan story. There are fewer sponsorship opportunities, professional competitions, and television specials, and so less incentive for some male skaters to try to conform to mainstream gender norms. Figure skating is no longer as tightly associated with HIV as it was in the early 1990s after a number of prominent skaters had died of AIDS-related illnesses. There is, overall, less fear of HIV among the general public and so less fear of gay men. So skaters may feel less pressure than they once did to distance themselves from the disease by making themselves look straight. It is also the case that tough macho guys are not as dominant in North American popular culture, generally, as they were in the 1990s. In an era of ongoing war and global economic uncertainty, Rambo-style masculinities and the militarism they represent are, these days, heavily contested. In this sense skating is following larger cultural trends. Discourses on homosexuality have also shifted a lot over the past two decades. In Canada and elsewhere – most recently Argentina – lesbian and gay political movements have scored legislative victories and have had some success in changing understandings of sexuality and sexual identities. They've achieved human rights victories and successfully promoted greater public visibility of lesbian and gay people, issues, and cultures. More public space for gay people means more public space for things associated with gayness. All these factors contribute to a climate that, one hopes, makes it harder for coaches, officials, parents, media, and friends to push skaters to conform to mainstream gender norms or narrowly defined notions of what it means to be a male athlete. With any luck, fewer of them will want to.

When I wrote the first draft of this epilogue, it was the end of December 2009, during the quiet week between Christmas and New Year's. I had just been for a holiday skate with my friends Petra and Patrick and their daughter. At that time Julia was in grade 2, and was taking group lessons at the figure skating club where I also skate. She was very keen on skating, and she was good at it. Her skating teacher had suggested to Petra and Patrick that Julia would do well in private lessons. And from what I saw, that's true. She's coordinated. She has excellent body control for someone her size and age. She's strong and fast and, what's better in this sport, she seems to be fearless on the ice.

There are few things I love doing more than skating, and by skating I mean the endlessly interesting, perpetually challenging type of skating that is figure skating. I love the feel of it. I love the sound of it. Without exaggeration, it has been one of the greatest and most consistent pleasures of my life. Yet I have mixed feelings about encouraging Julia and her parents to keep on with it. I talked to her mother about moving from 'learn-to-skate' to figure skating and what an investment in the sport might mean for a little girl. Skating is expensive and, as sports administrators and sport psychologists would say, it's an early-specialization sport for girls, a sport like gymnastics in which female athletes reach their prime at a young age. Such sports force parents to make decisions about commitment earlier than they do in sports like skiing or soccer. In figure skating, talented children as young as Julia get streamed. Children and their parents can end up being pulled quite far into the culture and the commitments of the sport without really having planned to, especially if the child pursues tests or competitions as a means to progress athletically.

If figure skating were just about developing physical skills or helping children to learn how to interpret music with their bodies, the only questions that a parent would face would be fairly straightforward – time, cost, safety, enjoyment. But figure skating is not simply about the development of physical or aesthetic skills. It is about producing the kinds of people who win figure skating competitions. And this exercise influences the sport in competitive and non-competitive streams, at all levels. Little girls who skate, no matter the gender politics of their parents and coaches, are immersed in a culture that promotes certain narrow versions of femininity that are affirming and fun for some girls and a misery to others. Until there is room for all sorts of girls to be able to be who they are on the ice, and to have success in the sport for having done so, I hesitate to promote skating, especially to a girl like Julia, a wee tomboy, whose pleasure in skating is not about its prettiness but about its physicalness. My guess is that she would willingly try anything, and so she would be a wonderful skater to train. She is clearly not afraid of falling and she has a streak of intensity that would help her to master new skills. She is exactly the kind of girl that skating associations should be looking for. And yet, she is exactly the kind of girl who would be turned off by expectations on the part of test or competition judges that she wear a skirt or have her hair done in a certain way or skate more like 'a girl.' Julia seems to want to skate like a daredevil. In figure skating, there is too much of a risk that she would have that impulse trained out of her, or worse, be made to feel bad for feeling it.

The argument that I have been making in this book is that figure skating and figure skaters would be much better off if heteronormative expectations around gender stopped having such an important role in shaping our sport. When I began this project I was interested in the popular North American notions that skating is a 'girls' sport' and that male skaters must, therefore, be effeminate or gay. I wanted to try to make sense of the logic that linked skating to sissies and homosexuality; I wanted to get a better understanding of mainstream understandings of masculinity and the discourses that leave little space in this culture for effeminate boys and men. Over the long course of this research, it became obvious that the link between effeminacy and skating is historically specific and that the history of how this link developed presents us with a useful way of putting contemporary ideas about men, masculinity, and sexuality into context. But what has also become clear to me – although I have to admit it took a while – is that responses to the effeminate label have had important consequences for girls and women too. These responses are part of the reason that skating produces the limited, narrow versions of femininity that could make it a difficult sport choice for a little girl like Julia. They are part of the reason why skating has yet to embrace and put into circulation images of female athletes as strong, powerful, and substantial.

Making the sport better for Julia would also make it better for the little Johnny Weirs and John Currys, children who really do need some place where they can safely and confidently be themselves. Why not be the sport that lets children grow up into whatever version of themselves makes sense to them? Why not be the sport that lets boys and girls be the kinds of athletes or artists they want to be without worrying about how their image might be taken up outside of the sport? It only took a few decades for skating to go from manly to girlie. There is no reason it could not undergo another big change. The skating establishment, including journalists, could stop imposing gender norms on skaters. To the extent that it would be possible in a heavily gendered world, skaters could be left to determine for themselves the best way to negotiate gender on the ice.

After more than half a century of trying to make figure skating more appealing to boys and men, skating organizations have had little success. Efforts to push skating higher up in the hierarchy of men's sports have not worked. Maybe it's time for a new tack. Maybe it's time to embrace what is different about skating, to promote the qualities that separate it from traditionally male sports. There is no question that, like male ballet dancers, male skaters are strong and display incredible physical skills, but this does not mean they are just like other male athletes or that their sport is just like other sports. It diminishes both skaters and skating to try to make it seem like they are. Mastery of skating's physical and aesthetic skills can produce something that cannot be reduced to heights or speeds or distances. In this sport, statistics and records tell only part of the story.

For years the primary political strategy of lesbian and gay liberation movements has been to come out. Gay people have been encouraged to stop passing as straight, to claim their own identities, and stop catering to norms, structures, and values that were designed for and imposed by others. Once out, the assumption goes, all the energy that went into hiding could be turned to more important and more fabulous things. It's time for figure skating to come out, to stop trying to pass as just another sport. In 2009 Skate Canada marketing officials talked about wanting to rebrand the sport by playing up its athleticism. That would be like trying to rebrand Sprite by playing up its bubbles – they are not what makes it stand out, they will never be the thing that defines its market. It's time to claim skating's difference, to stop worrying about the sport's manly reputation, and to give up trying to make the sport appeal more to some generic category of boys and men. It's time to celebrate the men and boys who are drawn to the sport just as it is, whether they are attracted to the sequins or the triple jumps. The figure skating community needs to make banal and public the fact that a good number of male skaters are gay. And it needs to stop trying to enforce gendered versions of skating, a feminine one for women and a masculine one for men. There are many skaters who will want to follow this tradition, but some won't. We need to see what they can do. Figure skating has more potential than many sports do to help us think differently about the relationships between sports, gender, bodies, and styles of movement. It's a waste not to use it.

Notes

Chapter 1: Introduction

1 Internet Movie Database, 'Plot Summary for Blades of Glory,' http://www.imdb.com/title/tt0445934/plotsummary.

2 'Blades of Glory (2007),' http://www.rottentomatoes.com/m/blades_of_glory/numbers.php.

3 See, for instance, Eichelberger, 'Voices on Black Feminism,' 21.

4 See ibid. and also Silvera and Gupta, 'Women of Colour'; and Grewal, *Charting the Journey*.

5 Hill Collins, *Black Feminist Thought*; Siltanen and Doucet, *Gender Relations in Canada*; and Birrell and McDonald, 'Reading Sport/Articulating Power Lines.'

6 M.L. Adams, *The Trouble with Normal*, 13.

7 Foucault, *The History of Sexuality, Volume 1*.

8 Foucault, *Power/Knowledge*, 39.

9 See, for instance, Foucault, *The History of Sexuality*; Jonathan Ned Katz, *The Invention of Heterosexuality*; and M.L. Adams, *The Trouble with Normal*.

10 For discussions of these ideas, see Chauncey, *Gay New York*; and Kennedy and Davis, *Boots of Leather and Slippers of Gold*.

11 Kessler and McKenna, *Gender*; Butler, *Gender Trouble* and *Bodies That Matter*; Fausto-Sterling, *Sexing the Body*; and Stryker, '(De)Subjugated Knowledges.'

12 For excellent reviews of the field, see Sykes, 'Queering Theories of Sexuality in Sport Studies'; and King, 'What's Queer about (Queer) Sport Sociology Now?'

13 See, for instance, Wilkes and Cable, *Ice Time*; Smith, *Figure Skating*; and Ryan, *Little Girls in Pretty Boxes*.

14 The best of the institutional histories is Bird, *Our Skating Heritage*. See also Stephenson and Stephenson, *A History and Annotated Bibliography of Skating Costume*; Copley-Graves, *Figure Skating History*; and Thomson and Gladstone-Millar, *The Skating Minister*.

15 See, for examples, M.L. Adams, 'Freezing Social Relations'; Morrow, 'Sweetheart Sport'; Wenn, 'Give Me the Keys Please'; and Windhausen, 'Russia's First Olympic Victor.'

16 Monsma and Malina, 'Correlates of Eating Disorders Risk'; and Taylor and Ste-Marie, 'Eating Disorders Symptoms.'

17 Albert and Miller, 'Takeoff Characteristics'; Dufek and Bates, 'The Evaluation and Prediction of Impact Forces.'

18 Ferrara and Hollingsworth, 'Physical Characteristics and Incidence of Injuries'; Lipetz and Kruse, 'Injuries and Special Concerns of Female Figure Skaters'; and Porter et al., 'Sport-specific Injuries and Medical Problems.'

19 Deakin and Allard, 'Skilled Memory in Expert Figure Skaters'; and Haguenauer et al., 'Short-term Effects of Using Verbal Instructions and Demonstration.'

20 Delistraty, Reisman, and Snipes, 'A Physiological and Nutritional Profile'; and Ziegler et al., 'Eating Attitudes and Energy Intakes.'

21 Wu and Yang, 'Evaluation of the Current Decision Rule'; and Bassett and Persky, 'Rating Skating.'

22 Dufur, 'Gender and Sport,' 589; and Lenskyj, *Out of Bounds*, 143.

23 See, for instance, Feder, 'Big Girls Do Cry'; Feder, 'A Radiant Smile from the Lovely Lady'; Fabos, 'Forcing the Fairytale'; McGarry, 'Passing as a Lady' and 'Mass Media and Gender Identity'; Krause, 'The Bead of Raw Sweat'; and Foote, 'Making Sport of Tonya.'

24 Windhausen, 'Russia's First Olympic Victor.'

25 M.L. Adams, 'The Manly History of a Girls' Sport.'

26 Dufresne and Genosko, 'Jones on Ice.'

27 Wenn, 'Give Me the Keys Please.'

28 Morrow, 'Sweetheart Sport.'

29 M.L. Adams, 'To Be an Ordinary Hero.'

30 King, 'Consuming Compassion.'

31 Grenfell and Rinehart, 'Skating on Thin Ice.'

32 Rand, 'I Wanted Black Skates.'

33 McGarry, 'Performing Nationalisms.'

34 Kestnbaum, *Culture on Ice*.

35 A survey of tables of contents of the two major English-language sport history journals confirms this point. Between 2007 and 2009, the *Journal of Sport History* published work by 14 female and 43 male authors and by 3 three

authors who had non-gender-specific names or names with which we are not familiar. Assuming that there is a close fit between the gender identities of contributors and their names and supposing that each of the unclassifiable names belonged to a woman, that would still mean that only 28% of contributors were women. Over the same period, the *International Journal of the History of Sport* published work by a total of 269 contributors. We identified 163 names as male (61% of the total) and 51 as female (19%). There were 55 names (20%) that we could not classify. Even in the unlikely event that all the unclassified names belonged to women, that would still leave a significant gender imbalance. Thanks to Marty Clark for gathering these figures.

36 Between 2007 and 2009 the *Journal of Sport History* published 21 articles and 36 'forum' contributions. None of these was focused specifically on 'women's sport' or 'feminine sport.' All the articles and forums investigated either traditional 'masculine' sports or sport in general terms. Between 2007 and 2009 the *International Journal of the History of Sport* published a total of 215 articles. Twenty-one looked at 'women's sport' and three of these investigated 'feminine' sport or physical activity. The remaining 18 looked at women's participation in 'male sports' or at women's participation in sports generally.

37 A survey of the tables of contents of the *Sociology of Sport Journal*, 2007–9, shows that the journal published work by 62 male authors (50% of the total) and 53 female authors (42%). We were unable to classify 10 names (8%) because they were either not gender-specific or we were unfamiliar with them. Over the same period the *International Review for the Sociology of Sport* published work by 62 male (55%) and 37 female (33%) authors. We were unable to classify 14 names (12%).

38 Cited in Milton, *Skate*, 10. For the CBS television network in the United States, skating was targeted to help fill in the broadcast schedule after the network lost NFL football to Fox. Craig, 'CBS Is on Thin Ice.'

39 Connell, *Masculinities*, 54.

40 Burstyn, *The Rites of Men*; and Messner and Sabo, *Sex, Violence and Power in Sports*.

41 Alan Sinfield, *The Wilde Century*, 5.

42 Poovey, *Uneven Developments*, 12.

43 Daniels, *Polygendered and Ponytailed*; Hall, *The Girl and the Game*; Cahn, *Coming on Strong*; and Hargreaves, *Sporting Females*.

44 Tagg, '"Imagine a man playing netball!"'; Davis, 'Male Cheerleaders'; Anderson, 'Orthodox and Inclusive Masculinity'; and M.L. Adams, 'To Be an Ordinary Hero.'

45 Pawson Bean, 'Swimming, Synchronized.'

46 Cahn, *Coming on Strong*, 219.
47 Gruneau, 'Modernization or Hegemony?'
48 Laurendeau and Adams, '"Jumping like a girl."'
49 Ibid.
50 See, for instance, Connell, *Masculinities*; Kimmel, *Manhood in America*; and Daniels, 'You Throw Like a Girl,' 36.
51 Thanks to Mary McDonald for discussions on this matter.
52 Lee, 'The Joy of the Castrated Boy,' 37.
53 Daniels, 'You Throw Like a Girl,' 36.
54 Renold, 'Learning the "Hard" Way,' 377.
55 See Rottnek, *Sissies and Tomboys*; and Grossman et al., 'Comparing Gender Expression.'
56 See, for examples, Rofes, 'Making Our Schools Safe for Sissies'; Transgender Law Center, 'Transgender and Gender Non-conforming Youth.'
57 Hill and Menvielle, '"You have to give them a place."'
58 Cited by Burke, *Gender Shock*, 100.
59 American Psychiatric Association, *Diagnostic and Statistical Manual IV*.
60 Ibid.
61 Harris, 'Effeminacy,' 73.
62 Pronger, 'Outta My Endzone.'

Chapter 2: Tough Guys?

1 White, 'Figure Skating Gets Tough.'
2 Lawton, 'Sequins? What Sequins?'
3 Cyd Ziegler, Jr, 'Can Canada Make Figure Skating Tough?' http://outsports.com/jocktalkblog/2009/02/03/can-canada-make-figure-skating-tough/.
4 Skate Canada, 'A Message from CEO William Thompson.'
5 Donaldson, 'What Is Hegemonic Masculinity?'; and Connell, *Masculinities*.
6 West and Zimmerman, 'Doing Gender.'
7 Lorber, *The Paradoxes of Gender*.
8 Butler, *Gender Trouble*.
9 See Vertinsky, *Eternally Wounded Woman*.
10 Bordo, 'Reading the Slender Body.'
11 West and Zimmerman, 'Doing Gender.'
12 Hopkins, 'Switch Blades,' 7.
13 Leger, 'Here's Looking at You Kurt,' 7.
14 Smith, 'He's Soaring over Ice.'
15 Leger, 'Here's Looking at You Kurt,' 7.

16 D. Taylor, 'Looking Back, Moving Forward.'
17 'Rob McCall Dies after Lengthy Illness.'
18 Bondy, 'AIDS-related Deaths.'
19 Smith, 'Helping Buddies through Bad Times.'
20 Clarkson, 'Skating's Spectre.'
21 King, 'Consuming Compassion,' 157.
22 Springs, 'Skating's Shadow.'
23 Reed, 'Fear on the Ice.'
24 Ibid., 41.
25 CBC Radio, Toronto, Sports report on *Metro Morning*, 17 December 1992.
26 A. Stevenson, 'International Chit-chat,' 1.
27 Bondy, 'Skater Impatient with Reaction to AIDS.'
28 Simmons, 'The Last Word.'
29 Jeffords, *Hard Bodies*.
30 Ibid., 25.
31 Kimmel, *Manhood in America*, 192.
32 Ibid.
33 Connor, 'New Lad Emerges.'
34 Daniels, *Polygendered and Ponytailed*.
35 Bordo, *The Male Body*, 55.
36 McClintock, *Imperial Leather*, 55.
37 Rohanram, *Imperial White*, xxiii.
38 *Tough Guise: Violence, Media and the Crisis in Masculinity*.
39 Pope et al., 'Evolving Ideals of Male Body Image.'
40 Frias and Hartnett, 'Heavy Pressure.'
41 Kimmel, *Manhood in America*, 218.
42 Levine and Kimmel, *Gay Macho*.

Chapter 3: Girls' Sport

1 R. Wright, 'Blade Spinner,' 43.
2 Ibid., 44.
3 See, for example, Willis, 'Women in Sport'; Bryson, 'Sport and the Maintenance of Masculine Hegemony'; and Theberge, 'Toward a Feminist
   Alternative.'
4 M.L. Adams, 'The Game of Whose Lives?'
5 Allain, 'Real Fast and Real Tough.'
6 Wright, 'Blade Spinner,' 44.
7 Richards, 'Schmockey Night in Canada,' 28.
8 Wright, 'Blade Spinner,' 46.

9 Messner, Duncan, and Jensen, 'Separating the Men from the Girls.'
10 Hopkins, 'Switch Blades,' 73.
11 Ibid., 76.
12 Ibid.
13 Ibid.
14 Cox, 'Some Jump, Some Smile,' 105.
15 Proudfoot, 'Browning Is a Scrapper.'
16 Cited in Hopkins, 'Switch Blades,' 76.
17 Gary Salewicz and others, 'City of Athletes,' *Toronto Life*, November 2002, 92. This is basically a photo essay; the quote is taken from the caption.
18 For two examples, see Perkins, 'Elvis Dazzles'; and E.M. Swift, 'Spin City,' 53.
19 Staples, 'Skating Is No Wussy Sport,' 40.
20 Ibid., 37.
21 DiManno, 'Half-naked Candeloro fine ending.'
22 Kaufman, 'So They're All Gay, Right?' *Salon.com*, 22 February 2002.
23 CTV Television, Broadcast of men's long program at Skate Canada, 5 November 1994.
24 CTV, Broadcast of men's short program at Canadian championships, 5 February 1993.
25 CTV, Broadcast of men's short program at world championships, 28 March 2000.
26 CTV, Broadcast of men's long program at world championships, 30 March 2000.
27 Henderson, 'Changing Perceptions of Skaters.'
28 Figure Skaters Online, 'Evan Lysacek,' http://www.figureskatersonline .com/evanlysacek/index2.html.
29 Jennifer Kirk, 'More Masculinity in Figure Skating: The Way to Go?' *Skating the Issue* (blog), 25 June 2009, http://trueslant.com/jennifer-kirk/2009/06/25/more-masculinity-in-figure-skating-the-way-to-go/.
30 Andrea Chempinski, 'Biography,' *Simply Steven* (website), http://www .simplysteven.com/biography.html.
31 Hunter and Drummie, 'Orser in "Shock."'
32 Doran, 'Orser Wanted Palimony Suit Details Hushed.'
33 Ohler and Whyte, 'Orser Unmasked by Lawsuit.'
34 Barmak, 'No Giant Leap for Gays at the Games.'
35 Schwartz, 'Billie Jean Won For All Women.'
36 Deacon, 'Sex Sells – To a Point,' 79.
37 Gluckman and Reed, 'The Gay Marketing Moment.'
38 See http://www.katarina.de/76-1-endorsment-partners.html.
39 CBC Radio, *The Inside Track*, 'The Last Closet,' 16 October 1993.
40 Benet, 'Tanith Belbin and Evan Lysacek.'

41 Galindo, *Ice Breaker*, 25.

42 Ibid., 117.

43 Ibid., 141–2.

44 Cited in Kim, '"Gayest Sport in America."'

45 Jackson, *On Edge*, 121.

46 Kim, '"Gayest Sport in America."'

47 Jackson, *On Edge*, 136.

48 Jackson, 'Frozen in the Closet.'

49 Interview with Debbi Wilkes on *Ice Time*, Women's Television Network, 26 December 1998.

50 Kaufman, 'So They're All Gay, Right?'

51 Kim, '"Gayest Sport in America."'

52 Jackson, *On Edge*, 72.

53 See, for example, Thomas, 'College Team Teaches a Lesson in Tolerance.'

54 Clark, 'Gay Blade,' 154.

55 Lawton, 'Sequins? What Sequins?'

56 Christie and Longford, 'Pulling the Strings.'

57 Skate Canada, 'Associate Membership Profile Statistics.'

58 Orser, *Orser*, 12.

59 Brasseur and Eisler, *Brasseur and Eisler*, 18–19.

60 Lid, 'Elvis Lives,' 58.

61 'Emanuel Sandhu Speaks to MyBindi,' *MyBindi.com*, 2006, http://www.mybindi.com/lifestyle/perspectives/sandhu.html.

62 Brasseur and Eisler, *Brasseur and Eisler*,19.

63 Whitson, 'Sport in the Social Construction of Masculinity,' 21.

64 Walvin, 'Symbols of Moral Superiority,' 258.

65 Mangan and Walvin, introduction to *Manliness and Morality*, 1.

66 Mangan, *Athleticism*.

67 Sussman, *Victorian Masculinities*, 10.

68 See, for instance, Mangan, *Athleticism*.

69 H.S. Brown, 'Manliness.'

70 For discussions of effeminacy that might have influenced Stowell, see Gutsmuths, *Gymnastics for Youth*.

71 Kimmel, 'Consuming Manhood.'

72 Ibid., 21.

73 Ibid., 24.

74 Ibid., 21.

75 R.J. Parks, 'Biological Thought.'

76 Laberge and Albert, 'Conceptions of Masculinity,' 200.

77 Proudfoot, 'Dream Team Qualifies.'

78 Kane and Snyder, 'Sport Typing.'

79 For examples of such work see L.R. Davis, 'Male Cheerleaders'; and M.L. Adams, 'To Be an Ordinary Hero.'
80 Laberge and Albert, 'Conceptions of Masculinity,' 210.
81 Matteo, 'The Effect of Sex,' 424.
82 Riemer and Visio, 'Gender Typing of Sports.'
83 Schmalz and Kerstetter, 'Girlie Girls and Manly Men.'
84 Laberge and Albert, 'Conceptions of Masculinity,' 208.
85 Ibid., 214.
86 Metheny, 'Some Differences in Bodily Proportions.' For discussions of Metheny and other researchers involved in racial science, see Wiggins, '"Great speed but little stamina."'
87 Metheny, 'Symbolic Forms of Movement,' 49.
88 See Cahn, *Coming on Strong*; and Lenskyj, *Out of Bounds*.
89 Melody, 'At Home with the Jenkinses,' 25.
90 Metheny, Symbolic Forms of Movement,' 51–2.
91 Ibid., 53.
92 See, for instance, Jamieson, 'Reading Nancy Lopez'; and Douglas, 'To Be Young, Gifted, Black and Female.'
93 Hopkins, 'Switch Blades,' 74.
94 Brett, 'Musicality, Essentialism and the Closet,' 18.
95 Cited in Messner and Sabo, *Sex, Violence and Power in Sports*, 114.
96 Brett, 'Musicality, Essentialism and the Closet,' 12.
97 Bordo, *The Male Body*, 173.
98 Alexander, 'Stylish Hard Bodies.'
99 Trujillo, 'Hegemonic Masculinity on the Mound.'
100 Nixon, *Hard Looks*.
101 Ibid., 206.
102 Gill, Henwood, and McLean, 'Body Projects,' 51.
103 Morse, 'Sport on Television.'
104 Neale, 'Masculinity as Spectacle,' 15.
105 Whannel, *Media Sport Stars*, 69.
106 Ibid., 58.
107 See, for instance, Mitchell, 'How Queer Is Figure Skating?' 23.

Chapter 4: Manliness and Grace

1 Anonymous, quoted in Whedon, *The Fine Art of Ice Skating*, 42.
2 See Mangan, *Athleticism*.
3 Carter, 'An "Effeminate" or "Efficient" Nation?' 439.
4 Mangan and Walvin, introduction to *Manliness and Morality*, 1.

5 For a useful discussion of definitions of the British upper class, see Huggins, 'Sport and the Upper Classes.'

6 Volland Waters, *The Perfect Gentleman*, 16.

7 Elliot, 'The Edinburgh Skating Club.'

8 Bird, *Our Skating Heritage*, 2. For a discussion of the country club as a particular social phenomenon, see Daniels, 'Country Club.'

9 Hampe, *Stilwandel im Eiskunstlauf*, 26.

10 Glantschnig, *Meine Dreier*, 85.

11 Hampe, *Stilwandel im Eiskunstlauf*, 29.

12 Glantschnig, *Meine Dreier*, 79.

13 Ibid., 78.

14 Jones, *A Treatise on Skating*, 40.

15 Davis, *Frostiana*, 122. For a recent literary work on the frozen River Thames, see Humphreys, *The Frozen Thames*.

16 Diamantidi, von Korper, and Wirth, *Spuren auf dem Eise*, 161.

17 Vail, *L'art du patinage*, 5.

18 Jones, *A Treatise on Skating*, rev. ed., v.

19 A Skater, *The Art of Skating* (London, Basil Stuart, 1832), 16.

20 Swift and Clark, *The Skater's Textbook*, 40.

21 Ibid., 42.

22 Meagher, *Lessons in Skating*, 17.

23 GutsMuths, *Gymnastics for Youth*, 308.

24 Ibid., 331.

25 Garcin, *Le vrai patineur*, no page number.

26 Ibid., xiv.

27 Ibid., 8, 10–12.

28 Ibid., 12, 29.

29 Cited in Vail, *L'art du patinage*, opening page [no number].

30 Monier-Williams, *Figure-Skating*, 54.

31 North, 'Winter Rhapsody,' 303.

32 L. Young, *Middle-class Culture*, 112.

33 Ibid., 14–15.

34 D. Adams, *Skating*, 1.

35 Monier-Williams, *Figure Skating*, 3.

36 Swift and Clark, *The Skater's Textbook*, 81.

37 Curtin, *Propriety and Position*, 109.

38 Ibid., 110.

39 Bourdieu, *Distinction*.

40 Schilling, *The Body and Social Theory*, 116.

41 L. Young, *Middle-class Culture*, 16.

42 E. Jones, *The Elements of Figure Skating*, 280.

43 Wendl, *Eis mit Stil* [Ice with Style], 14.

44 *Die Presse*, 17 January 1868.

45 Cited by Browne, 'Figure Skating.'

46 *Wiener Zeitung*, 17 January 1868.

47 Heinlein, *100 Jahre Wiener Eislauf-Verein*, 34.

48 Toronto Skating Club, *Skating*, February 1924, 18.

49 Winzer, 'Geschichte des Eiskunstlaufs,' 39, 46, 47.

50 Ibid., 45.

51 Diamantidi, von Korper, and Wirth, *Spuren auf dem Eise*, 318.

52 Miss M. Bland Jameson, quoted in Bird, *Our Skating Heritage*, 40.

53 Goodwin, 'An Introduction to Figure Skating,' 21.

54 See Walvin, 'Symbols of Moral Superiority.'

55 Fowler, *On the Outside Edge*, 67, 70.

56 Winzer, 'Geschichte des Eiskunstlaufs,' 42.

57 A member of the Skating Club, 'The Skating Championships,' *Globe* (London), 17 February 1898.

58 'International Figure Skating,' *Manchester Guardian*, 16 February 1898.

59 Lowerson, *Sport and the English Middle Classes*, 64.

Chapter 5: Women Start Skating

1 'Rules and Regulations of the Brooklyn Skating Rink Association (1868–69),' cited in Lambert, *The American Skating Mania*, 1.

2 Rosenzweig and Blackmar, *The Park and the People*, 229. I learned of this reference in a wonderful unpublished manuscript by Paul Renwick, '"Ball Up!": Ice Skating in New York's Central Park, 1860–1870.'

3 Lambert, *The American Skating Mania*, 1.

4 Renwick, '"Ball Up!"' [unpaginated electronic file].

5 Gill, *The Skater's Manual*, 46–7.

6 Vandervell and Witham, *A System of Figure-Skating*, 17.

7 Ibid., 38–9.

8 Deney, *Traité du patinage*.

9 D. Young, *The Golden Age of Canadian Figure Skating*, 37.

10 Jones, *A Treatise on Skating*, xi.

11 Cited by Helfrich, 'Henriette Sontag,' 39–40.

12 Hampe, *Stilwandel im Eiskunstlauf*, 23.

13 Wendle, *Eis mit Stil*, 16.

14 Hampe, *Stilwandel im Eiskunstlauf*, 25.

15 Johann Peter Frank cited in Helfrich, 'Henriette Sontag,' 39.

16 Swift and Clark, *The Skater's Textbook*, 18.

17 J.M.L., 'Skating for Ladies. Why Ladies Ought to Skate, and Why They Do Not,' *Godey's Lady's Book*, December 1863 [viewed at http://www.accessible.com].

18 Lewis, *Skating and the Philadelphia Skating Club*, 25.

19 Winzer, 'Geschichte des Eiskunstlaufs,' 36.

20 Glantschnig, *Meine Dreier*, 80.

21 Hampe, *Stilwandel im Eiskunstlauf*, 29.

22 G. Davis, *Frostiana*, 124.

23 Cited in Bird, *Our Skating Heritage*, 5.

24 Reuel, *Das Eissportbuch*, 30.

25 Biberhofer, *Chronik des Wiener Eislaufvereines*, 3–4. Thanks to Ruba Turjman for the translation.

26 Ibid., 41.

27 *Champion Skate Book and Complete Amateur's Guide* (New York, 1879), cited in Lambert, *The American Skating Mania*, 3.

28 Melvin Adelman, cited in Renwick, '"Ball Up!"'

29 For discussions about the lack of an exact date, see Elliot, 'The Edinburgh Skating Club.'

30 Cited ibid., 96.

31 Ibid., 101.

32 The Skating Club, *Historical Sketch of the Club*, 3.

33 Monier-Williams, *Figure-Skating*, 30.

34 Ibid., 31.

35 Vandervell and Witham, *A System of Figure Skating*, 16.

36 Ibid., 19.

37 The Skating Club, *Historical Sketch of the Club*, 12.

38 Eichberg, 'The Enclosure of the Body,' 50.

39 Brailsford, *British Sport*.

40 Hutchinson, *Empire Games*, 144. For discussion of North American 'country clubs,' see Daniels, 'Country Club.'

41 Toronto Curling and Skating Club, *By-laws* (1875), 11.

42 Copley-Graves, *Figure Skating History*, 12.

43 The Skating Club, *Historical Sketch of the Club*, 12.

44 Hargreaves, 'The Victorian Cult of the Family,' 74.

45 The Skating Club, *Historical Sketch of the Club*, 19.

46 Montreal Skating Club, *Constitution of the Montreal Skating Club*, 5.

47 Victoria Skating Club, *Act of Incorporation*, 10.

48 Biberhofer, *Chronik des Wiener Eislaufvereines*, 38.

49 Ibid., 32.

50 Monier-Williams, *Figure-Skating*.

51 Cheetham, 'Ladies' Chapter,' 70.

52 Diamantidi, von Korper, and Wirth, *Spuren auf dem Eise*, 149.

53 G. Anderson, *The Art of Skating*, 12.

54 Ibid., 28.

55 Witham, 'Figure Skating,' 183.

56 Cheetham, 'Ladies' Chapter,' 77.

57 Madge Syers, 'Skating for Ladies,' in Syers and Syers, *The Book of Winter Sports*, 117.

58 Cheetham, 'Ladies' Chapter,' 84.

59 Edgar Syers, 'Skating,' in Syers and Syers, *The Book of Winter Sports*, 62.

60 Moore, *Reflections on the CFSA*, 25.

61 Ibid., 26.

62 *Neue Freie Presse*, 25 February 1875.

63 Ibid., 19 January 1879.

64 Ibid., 30 January 1879.

65 *Allgemeinesport Zeitung*, 30 June 1881, 360.

66 Matthias Hampe, who suggested the lower figure, is probably the most reliable source, *Stilwandel im Eiskunstlauf*, 45. The greater number of figures is suggested in an article in *Neue Freie Presse*, 22 January 1882.

67 *Neue Freie Press*, 22 January 1882.

68 *Die Presse*, 21 January 1882.

69 Bird, *Our Skating Heritage*, 13.

70 James Drake Digby, cited by Bird, *Our Skating Heritage*, 16.

71 Bird, *Our Skating Heritage*, 22.

72 Heathcote, Ellington, Syers, and Monier-Williams, *A History of the National Skating Association*, 46.

73 Ibid.

74 *Montreal Gazette*, 14 March 1890, cited by Moore, *Reflections on the CFSA*, 28–9.

75 Wright, *Skating around the World*, 18.

76 Cited in Bird, *Our Skating Heritage*, 36.

77 Perry, 'Boston Woman Skater Wins Championship.'

78 Charlotte, *Hippodrome Skating Book*, 7.

79 Films of the 1928 Winter Olympic Games are available for viewing (on video) at the World Figure Skating Museum in Colorado Springs, Colorado. For commentary on the relative merits of male and female skaters, see Richardson, 'Retrospection,' 5.

80 Guttmann, 'Olympics,' 823.

81 Lippe, 'Sportification Processes.'

Chapter 6: 'They Left the Men Nowhere'

1 'Sportswomen of the Day,' source unknown, 1907, exact publication date unknown, World Figure Skating Museum and Archives, file: Syers; see also Madge Syers, 'Skating for Ladies,' in Syers and Syers, *The Book of Winter Sports*, 117.
2 Cited by Lowerson, *Sport and the English Middle Classes*, 267.
3 Edgar Syers cited in 'The Art of Skating,' a published interview by Raife Raymond, source unknown, circa 1913 or 1914. Filed at the World Figure Skating Museum and Archives, file: Syers.
4 Ibid.
5 British Olympic Committee, *The Fourth Olympiad*, 295. The report refers to the Autumn Games because the figure skating events at the London Summer Games were held in October, several weeks after the rest of the competitions. The first Winter Games were not held until 1924.
6 Carl Fillunger, 'Zur Europa-meisterschaft [European Championship],' *Allgemeine Sportzeitung*, 26 February 1893, 193–4.
7 'Miss Weld Wins Laurels,' *New York Times*, 7 February 1918.
8 'The National Skating Association's Commemoration Week,' *The Field*, 22 February 1902, 256.
9 Beaumont, 'Some Aspects of Modern International Skating,' 5. For comments on the British championships in 1927 and 1928, see Wade, *The Skater's Cavalcade*, 59.
10 Browne, 'The International Skating Union (Again),' 28; 'Editorial,' *Monthly Freeze*, December 1931, 1.
11 McCrone, *Sport and the Physical Emancipation of English Women*, 2.
12 The history of the institutionalization of women's sport in Canada provides compelling examples of this point. See Hall, *The Girl and the Game* or Kidd, *The Struggle for Canadian Sport*.
13 McCrone, *Sport and the Physical Emancipation of English Women*, 13.
14 Williams, *A Game for Rough Girls?* 35.
15 Cronin, 'Bobsledding,' 144.
16 Ibid.
17 British Olympic Committee, *The Fourth Olympiad*, 295.
18 Edward Gill, *The Skater's Manual*, 13–14.
19 McCrone, *Sport and the Physical Emancipation of English Women*, 162.
20 Gerber, 'Chronicle of Participation,' 4.
21 Taped interview with 'Wag' Richardson at the Onslow Court Hotel, Lon-

don. Conducted by Ben Wright, 1979. World Figure Skating Museum and Archives.

22 George W. Graves, letter to Mrs Charles B. Blanchard, 4 January 1932. World Figure Skating Museum and Archives, box: Brunet, Blanchard, College; file: Graves to Blanchard.

23 Hampe, *Stilwandel im Eiskunstlauf*, 75.

24 N. Brown, *Ice Skating*, 161.

25 Strait and Henie, *Queen of Ice*, 22.

26 Vinson, *Advanced Figure S*, 287.

27 Cited by D. Young, *The Golden Age of Canadian Figure Skating*, 55.

28 G.E.B. Hill, 'Ladies' Championship,' 8–9.

29 Henie, *Wings on My Feet*, 8–9.

30 Earlier attempts to meld skating and ballet, specifically, were made in the 1910s by British champion Arthur Cumming, who was apparently so taken with the Ballets Russes that he sought advice from Serge Diaghilev on how to apply their approach to skating. I'll talk about Diaghilev more in the next chapter. Also in the 1910s, the professional skater Charlotte performed on-ice versions of Anna Pavlova's famous ballet solo 'The Dying Swan.' Henie too would be inspired by Pavlova and would do her own version of 'The Dying Swan' later in her career.

31 N. Brown, *Ice Skating*, 164–5.

32 Hampe, *Stilwandel im Eiskunstlauf*, 79.

33 Unsigned editorial, *Monthly Freeze*, April 1928, 1.

34 X, 'Olympic Skating: An Appreciation and Some Comments,' *Monthly Freeze*, March 1928, 7.

35 Richardson, 'Retrospection,' 5.

36 Richardson, 'The Master Skater,' 4.

37 Beaumont, 'Some Aspects of Modern International Skating,' 5–6.

38 Ibid., 7.

39 Richardson, 'Retrospection,' 5.

40 Wade, *The Skater's Cavalcade*, 59.

41 Ibid.

42 'Comparisons,' 12.

43 Vinson, 'Gay Blades,' 41.

44 Ibid., 58.

45 N. Brown, *Ice Skating*, 165.

46 Ibid.

47 Vinson, 'Gay Blades: Part II,' 47.

48 Ibid., 48.

49 Strait and Henie, *Queen of Ice*, 37.

50 Vinson, 'Gay Blades: Part II,' 48.
51 Goodfellow, 'When the Worlds First Came to America,' 22.
52 Claus, 'Skating as Dance and Theatre,' 20.
53 Vinson, 'Gay Blades: Part II,' 50.
54 Cited in Strait and Henie, *Queen of Ice*, 93.
55 Cuddy, 'Sonja Henie a Sensation,' 18.
56 Munns, 'Scanning the Field.'
57 Henie, *Wings on My Feet*, 92.
58 Strait and Henie, *Queen of Ice*, 166.
59 Negra, *Off-White Hollywood*, 89.
60 Ibid.
61 Hoffman, 'Sonja Henie – Queen of the Ice.'
62 'Ice Skating Goes into Big Figures,' 17.
63 Advertisement for Saks Fifth Avenue in *Skating*.
64 'Twenty Years of the USFSA.'
65 Ibid., 15.
66 'What Has Happened to Skating,' 7.
67 Theresa Weld Blanchard, 'Skating's Part in the War,' *Skating*, January 1942, 5.
68 Katherine V. Kasser, contributor to 'Round Table Talks on Boy Skaters,' *Skating*, December 1945, 18.
69 Britt, 'A Swede in Britain,' 17.
70 From the *Weltpresse*, cited in Button, *Dick Button on Skates*, 79.
71 N. Brown, 'Whither Skating,' 14.
72 Button, *Dick Button on Skates*, 18.
73 Ibid., 84.

Chapter 7: Artistic Sport or Athletic Art?

1 Chamberlain, 'The United States Championships,' 7.
2 International Skating Union, Regulations 1961, 58.
3 International Skating Union, Regulations 1994–1996, 126.
4 Burt, *The Male Dancer*.
5 Wayne, 'The Male Artist as Stereotypical Female,' 110.
6 Parks, 'Sex: Male, Profession: Dancer?' 42.
7 M.L. Adams, '"Death to the prancing prince."'
8 Whitson, 'Sport in the Social Construction of Masculinity,' 28.
9 White, 'Figure Skating Gets Tough.'
10 Dummitt, *The Manly Modern*.
11 Browne, *A Skating Primer*, 4–5.
12 L. Young, *Middle-class culture*, 88.

13 Ibid., 89.

14 Purdy, 'The Whiteness of Beauty,' 86.

15 Mosse, *The Image of Man*, 59.

16 D.A. Brown, 'Revisiting the Discourses of Art, Beauty and Sport,' 2.

17 Ibid., 15.

18 Winzer, 'An Outline of Figure Skating,' 36.

19 McDaniel, 'As to Figure Skating,' 31.

20 Browne, 'International Skating Union (Again),' 30.

21 Ibid., 25.

22 Richardson, 'The Master Skater,' 4.

23 Richardson, 'Retrospection,' 6.

24 See, for instance, Holt, *Sport and the British*.

25 Jakabsson, 'Criticism on the Modern Tendencies of Free Skating,' 47–8. For other examples of such commentary, see Theresa Weld Blanchard, 'The Fourth Olympic Winter Games,' *Skating*, April 1936, 9; and Howe, 'Report of Special Committee on Judging,' 43.

26 Turner, 'Sidelights of the 1931 World's Championships,' 19.

27 Witt, 'Letter to the Editor,' 34.

28 Bourdieu, 'Sport and Social Class,' 364.

29 Richardson, 'Retrospection,' 6.

30 Bourdieu, *Distinction*, 7.

31 Ibid., 57.

32 L. Young, *Middle-class Culture*, 20.

33 Heathcote et al., *A History of the National Skating Association*, 37.

34 Vinson, 'Gay Blades,' 13.

35 Baillie, *Figure Skating Simplified*, 24.

36 Hedges, *Ice-rink Skating*, 33.

37 Vinson, 'Gay Blades,' 15.

38 Eisen, 'Jewish History and the Ideology of Modern Sport,' 500.

39 Ellen Burka, quoted in the documentary film *Skating to Survive*, 2008.

40 Gasner, 'Life Experiences Forge Human Rights Champion.'

41 Quintanilla, 'Mabel Fairbanks.'

42 'Mabel Fairbanks, artist and icebreaker for black skaters,' African American Registry.

43 Scheurer, 'Breaking the Ice.'

44 Cited in E. and M. Syers, *The Book of Winter Sports*, 79.

45 Hampe, *Stilwandel im Eiskunstlauf*, 49.

46 Dixon Gottschild, 'Whoa! Whiteness in Dance?' 47.

47 Gay, *Pleasure Wars*, 19.

48 Schilling, *The Body and Social Theory*, 116.

49 Alderson, 'Ballet as Ideology,' 122.
50 Richardson, *Modern Figure Skating*, 144.
51 Grimditch, 'Dynamism,' 33.
52 N. Brown, '1968 World Championships,' 7.
53 Button, 'Worldscope/1966 World Championships,' 15.
54 Zell, 'A Sporting Image,' 16.
55 Ibid., 17.
56 For an example see comments by Geoff Gowan in J. Taylor, 'Athlete or artist ...?' 11.
57 See, for examples: Zell, 'A Sporting Image'; Colledge, 'Which Is It – Art or Sport?' 12; J. Taylor, 'Athlete or artist ...?'; McGillivray, 'Are Skaters Athletes?' 36–7. Also see Loeser, 'Sport vs. Art,' 18–19; and Frank Loeser Nowosad, 'Athletes & Artists,' *Tracings*, June/July 1992, 95–7, World Figure Skating Museum, file: Frank Loeser Nowosad.
58 'John Curry' *The Times* (London), 16 April 1994.
59 Cited in Posner, 'Just as Things Looked Hopeless,' 42.
60 Cited in Christie, 'Helped to Turn Skating into a Performing Art.'
61 Bizer, 'The Feminine Gentlemen,' 111.
62 Hennessy, 'A Monthly March to Immortality.'
63 Cited in Bird, 'Curry in Unique Position for Englishman.'
64 Klemesrud, 'Toller Cranston.'
65 Cited in Terry, 'The Ice Man,' 41.
66 Loeser, 'Canadians,' 33.
67 Cited in Stensrude, 'The Path to Excellence,' 38.
68 Keating, 'Figure Skating: Tough Guy Stojko Refuses to Be Upset.'
69 Perkins, 'Stojko in Good Sport to Launch Attack.'
70 Perkins, 'Elvis Dazzles.'
71 Staples, 'Skating Is No Wussy Sport,' 30–40, 90–1.
72 Perkins, 'Elvis Dazzles.'
73 Staples, 'Skating Is No Wussy Sport,' 37.
74 CTV, 'Skate Canada,' 7 November 1992.
75 Chatto, 'Spin Meister,' 48.
76 Stewart, *Perpetual Motion*.
77 Cited in Laine, 'Trendy Twosome,' 23.
78 Burt, *The Male Dancer*, 13.
79 Ibid., 10.
80 Bland and Percival, *Men Dancing*, 10.
81 Ibid., 12–13.
82 Burt, *The Male Dancer*, 12.
83 Ibid., 25.

84 Ibid., 24.
85 Sinfield, *The Wilde Century*.
86 Bristow, *Effeminate England*, 2.
87 Garafola, 'Reconfiguring the Sexes,' 246.
88 Ibid., 246–7.
89 Weeks, *Sex Politics and Society*.
90 Bland and Percival, *Men Dancing*, 103.
91 Studlar, 'Douglas Fairbanks,' 110.
92 See Burt, *The Male Dancer*; and Acocella, 'Real Men Don't Point Their Feet,' 78.
93 Connell, *Masculinities*, 45.
94 'Lysacek Ends Gold Drought for U.S.,' ESPN.Com, *Winter Olympics*, 19 February 2010, http://sports.espn.go.com/olympics/winter/2010/figureskating/news/story?id=4926784.
95 Buffery, 'Stojko Blasts Back at His Critics.'
96 Barnes, 'Stojko Slams the State of Men's Figure Skating.'
97 Ibid.
98 Canadian Broadcasting Corporation, Olympic Games coverage, 25 February 2006.

Chapter 8: Sequins, Soundtracks, and Spirals

1 Dixon Gottschild, 'Whoa! Whiteness in Dance?' 47.
2 Dixon Gottschild, *The Black Dancing Body*, 19.
3 Kestnbaum, *Culture on Ice*, 141.
4 McGarry, 'Passing as a Lady.'
5 In the skating world, some observers consider 2006 Olympic champion Shizuka Arakawa to be big and muscular. They would likely disagree with my classifying her with the other champions. Photos of Arakawa are easily available on the Internet. Readers can take a look and judge for themselves.
6 Longman, 'As Kim Raises the Bar.'
7 For a discussion of the racialization of skiing in the western United States, see Gilbert Coleman, 'The Unbearable Whiteness of Skiing.'
8 Skate Canada, *Sponsor 'Fact Sheet.'* 2002/3.
9 Smith, 'Kim's Rock Star Power.'
10 'Yuna and Mao Put Asian Markets on Ice,' *Reuters.com*, 24 February 2010, http://in.reuters.com/article/idINIndia-46428420100224.
11 Billings, 'Clocking Gender Differences,' 436.
12 Carlisle Duncan and Messner, *Gender in Televised Sports*, 20.

13 Feder, 'A Radiant Smile from the Lovely Lady,' 63.
14 Ibid.
15 For discussions of the construction of gender through media coverage, see Kestnbaum, *Culture on Ice*; McGarry, 'Passing as a Lady'; and Fabos, 'Forcing the Fairytale.'
16 Gross, *Donald Jackson*, 9.
17 Skate Canada, *Official Rulebook* (2002), 18.
18 Weld Blanchard, 'Olympic Skating, 1920 & 1924,' 6.
19 Hampe, *Stilwandel im Eiskunstlauf*, 133.
20 Stevens, 'Figure Skaters Allowed to Wear Tights, Trousers.'
21 Parkinson Speck, 'The Well Dressed Man,' 36.
22 Shumway, 'Clothes Can Help the Man, Too,' 11.
23 Hollander, *Sex and Suits*.
24 Ibid., p. 97.
25 Gill, Henwood, and McLean, 'Body Projects.'
26 Jackson, *On Edge*, 12.
27 Stevenson, *The BBC Book of Skating*, 70.
28 Nevius, 'Men Dump Sequins.'
29 1992 World Figure Skating Championships – Men's Medal Ceremony, http://www.youtube.com/watch?v=Oj54mUon_gY.
30 Cited by Nevius, 'Men Dump Sequins.'
31 Ibid.
32 Cited in Chatto, 'Spin Meister,' 46.
33 Jackson, *On Edge*, 12.
34 Shawn, *Dance We Must*, 121.
35 Skate Music List (an online listing of the music used by competitive figure skaters, http://www.skatemusiclist.com/index.html).
36 Figure Skating Universe, 4 June 2006, www.fsuniverse.net/forum/printthread.php?t=39600&pp=40).
37 CBC Television, Coverage of Winter Olympic Games, 19 February 1992.
38 Hampe, *Stilwandel im Eiskunstlauf*, 112.
39 Ibid., 110.
40 Feder, 'A Radiant Smile from the Lovely Lady,' 68–9.
41 Desmond, 'Embodying Difference,' 30.
42 Ibid., 32.
43 Intersex Society of North America. 'How Common Is Intersex.'
44 Genel, 'Gender Verification No More.'
45 Fausto-Sterling, 'The Bare Bones of Sex,' 1491.
46 Bordo, *The Male Body*, 26.
47 Cited in Hanna, *Dance, Sex and Gender*, 171.

48 Helfrich, 'Three Famous Figures,' 20.

49 'Dressing the Part,' 5.

50 Boeckl, *Willy Boeckl on Figure Skating*, 157.

51 Salchow cited by Hampe, *Stilwandel im Eiskunstlauf*, 83.

52 H.D.J. White, 'The Art of Free Skating,' 2.

53 Gregory, 'So You Want to Figure Skate,' 9.

54 Brunner, 'A New Year, a New You,' 19.

55 Boeckl, *Willy Boeckl on Figure Skating*, 123.

56 Curry cited in Pikula, 'John Curry,' 76.

57 Nolt cited in Kim, 'Beyond Spirals with Jeff Nolt.'

58 For discussion of this question as it relates to athletic bodies, see Butler, 'Athletic Genders.'

59 Shawn, *Dance We Must*, 123.

60 Ibid., 118.

61 Ibid., 119.

62 Tarasov, *Ballet Techniques for Male Dancers*, 68.

63 Shawn, *Dance We Must*, 117.

64 Tobias, 'It's Becoming O.K. in America for Boys to Dance.'

65 Shawn, *Dance We Must*, 119.

66 Patricia Chafe, personal communication, 18 July 2006. It is possible that a woman could win – she would just have to be 20 per cent better than the men with her component scores!

67 Patricia Chafe, personal communication, 25 July 2010. According to Chafe, who is an expert on the new scoring system, recalculating Kim's short program component scores using a factor of 1.0 instead of 0.8 would have increased this portion of her score from 33.8 to 42.25, giving her a short-program score of 86.95 and putting her in fourth place among the men. Doing the same recalculation for the long program would have taken Kim's component scores from 71.76 to 89.70, giving her a long-program score of 168.00 and putting her in first place in the men's long program. Thus, the recalculation of Kim's component scores would have increased her total Olympic score from 228.56 to 254.95 and would have put her in 3rd place overall among the men. Now, had Kim also been able to skate for thirty more seconds and do another jump, as the men do – even a simple well-done double jump – she would have had a total score of 257.85, enough to outscore Evan Lysacek and win the competition. Chafe says that there are many people in the skating world who would argue that had Kim actually been competing against men she would not have received the same Grade of Execution (the quality of an element) or Program Component Scores that she received competing against women. What they mean

by this is that Kim is a good skater – for a girl. Chafe suggests, rightly I think, that such arguments are a good indication of how reluctant some people are to acknowledge that a woman could be the best skater in the world.

Epilogue

1 Doyle, 'There's No Artistry to Blades.'
2 MacDonald, 'It's Hockey Season.'
3 Schwarz, 'Figure Skating Rivalry.'
4 Ewing, 'Chan Fires Back.'

Bibliography

A Skater. *The Art of Skating*. London: Basil Stuart, 1832.

Acocella, Joan. 'Real Men Don't Point Their Feet.' *Village Voice* 23, April 1985.

Adams, Douglas. *Skating*. London: George Bell, 1890.

Adams, Mary Louise. '"Death to the prancing prince": Effeminacy, Sport Discourses and the Salvation of Men's Dancing.' *Body and Society* 11, no. 4 (2005): 63–86.

– 'Freezing Social Relations: Ice, Rinks, and the Development of Figure Skating.' In *Sites of Sport: Space, Place*, ed. Patricia Vertinsky and John Bale, 57–72. London: Routledge, 2004.

– 'The Game of Whose Lives? Gender, Race and Entitlement in Canada's "National" Game.' In *Artificial Ice: Hockey, Culture and Commerce*, ed. David Whitson and Richard Gruneau, 71–84. Peterborough: Broadview Press, 2006.

– 'The Manly History of a Girls' Sport: Gender, Class and the Development of Nineteenth-Century Figure Skating.' *International Journal of the History of Sport* 24, no. 7 (July 2007): 872–93.

– 'To Be an Ordinary Hero: Male Figure Skaters and the Ideology of Gender.' *Avante* 3, no. 3 (1997): 93–110.

– *The Trouble with Normal: Postwar Youth and the Construction of Heterosexuality*. Toronto: University of Toronto Press, 1997.

Advertisement for Saks Fifth Avenue. *Skating*, December 1937.

Albert, W., and D.I. Miller. 'Takeoff Characteristics of Single and Double Axel Figure Skating Jumps.' *Journal of Applied Biomechanics* 12 (1996): 72–87.

Alderson, Evan. 'Ballet as Ideology: *Giselle*, Act 2.' In *Meaning in Motion: New Cultural Studies of Dance*, ed. Janice C. Desmond, 121–32. Durham, NC: Duke University Press, 1997.

Alexander, S.M. 'Stylish Hard Bodies: Branded Masculinity in *Men's Health* Magazine.' *Sociological Perspectives* 46, no. 4 (2003): 535–54.

Allain, Kristi. 'Real Fast and Real Tough: The Construction of Canadian Hockey Masculinity.' *Sociology of Sport Journal* 25, no. 4 (2009): 462–81.

American Psychiatric Association. *Diagnostic and Statistical Manual IV–Text Revision–2000 (DSM–IV–TR–2000)*. http://online.statref.com.proxy.queensu.ca/Document/Document.aspx?FxId=37&DocId=1&SessionId=FC27FFJSICXCSFLJ.

Anderson, Eric. 'Orthodox and Inclusive Masculinity: Competing Masculinities among Heterosexual Men in a Feminized Terrain.' *Sociological Perspectives* 48, no. 3 (2005): 337–55.

Anderson, George ('Cyclos'). *The Art of Skating, with illustrations, diagrams, and plain direction for the acquirement of the most difficult and graceful movements*. 4th ed. London: Horace Cox, 1880.

Baillie, G. *Figure Skating Simplified for Beginners*. London: Selwyn and Blount, 1922.

Barmak, Sarah. 'No Giant Leap for Gays at the Games.' *Toronto Star*, 28 February 2010. http://olympics.thestar.com/2010/article/772679.

Barnes, Dan. 'Stojko Slams the State of Men's Figure Skating.' *Montreal Gazette*, 19 February 2010. http://www.montrealgazette.com/sports/2010wintergames/Stojko+slams+state+figure+skating/2588813/story.html.

Bassett, G.W., and J. Persky. 'Rating Skating.' *Journal of the American Statistical Association* 89, no. 427 (1994): 1075–80.

Beaumont, Kenneth M. 'Some Aspects of Modern International Skating.' *Skating*, January 1929.

Benet, Lorenzo. 'Tanith Belbin and Evan Lysacek: Ice Skating's Hot Couple.' *People.com*, 3 February 2007. http://www.people.com/people/article/0,,20010788,00.html.

Biberhofer, Franz. *Chronik des Wiener Eislaufvereines* [Chronicle of the Vienna Skating Club]. Vienna: Verlag des Wiener Eislaufvereines, 1906.

Billings, Andrew C. 'Clocking Gender Differences: Televised Olympic Clock Time in the 1996–2006 Summer and Winter Olympics.' *Television and New Media* 9, no. 5 (September 2008): 429–41.

Bird, Dennis L. 'Curry in Unique Position for Englishman.' *Times* (London), 2 February 1976.

– *Our Skating Heritage: A Centenary History of the National Skating Association of Great Britain, 1879–1979*. London: National Skating Association of Great Britain, 1979.

Birrell, Susan, and Mary G. McDonald. 'Reading Sport/Articulating Power Lines: An Introduction.' In *Reading Sport: Critical Essays on Power and Representation*, Susan Birrell and Mary McDonald, 3–13. Boston: Northeastern University Press, 2000.

Bizer, Peter. 'Die femininen Herren [The Feminine Gentlemen].' In *Das Goldene Olympiahandbuch* [The Golden Olympia Handbook], ed. Frank Grube and Gerhard Richter. Hamburg: Hoffmann und Campe, 1976.

Blanchard, Theresa Weld. 'Fourth Olympic Winter Games.' *Skating*, April 1936.

Bland, Alexander, and John Percival. *Men Dancing*. London: Weidenfeld and Nicolson, 1984.

Boeckl, Wilhelm R. *Willy Boeckl on Figure Skating*. New York: Self-published, 1937.

Bondy, Filip. 'AIDS-related Deaths Rock the World of Figure Skating.' *Globe and Mail*, 28 November 1992.

– 'Skater Impatient with Reaction to AIDS.' *New York Times*, 7 March 1993.

Bordo, Susan. *The Male Body: A New Look at Men in Public and in Private*. New York: Farrar, Straus and Giroux, 1999.

– 'Reading the Slender Body.' In *Unbearable Weight: Feminism, Western Culture and the Body*, ed. Susan Bordo, 185–212. Berkeley: University of California Press, 1993.

Bourdieu, Pierre. *Distinction: A Social Critique of the Judgment of Taste*. Trans. Richard Nice. Cambridge: Harvard University Press, 1984.

– 'Sport and Social Class.' In *Rethinking Popular Culture: Contemporary Perspectives in Cultural Studies*, ed. Chandra Mukerji and Michael Schudson, 357–73. Berkeley: University of California Press, 1991.

Brailsford, Dennis. *British Sport: A Social History*. Cambridge: Lutterworth, 1992.

Brasseur, Isabelle, and Lloyd Eisler. *Brasseur and Eisler: To Catch a Dream*. With Linda D. Profuse. Toronto: Macmillan, 1997.

Brett, Philip. 'Musicality, Essentialism and the Closet.' In *Queering the Pitch: The New Gay and Lesbian Musicology*, ed. Philip Brett, Elizabeth Wood, and Gary C. Thomas, 9–26. New York: Routledge, 1994.

Bristow, Joseph. *Effeminate England: Homoerotic Writing after 1885*. Buckingham: Open University Press, 1995.

British Olympic Committee. *The Fourth Olympiad: The Official Report of the Olympic Games of 1908*. London, 1908.

Britt, Maj. 'A Swede in Britain.' *The Skater* 1, no. 2 (1949).

Brown, Douglas A. 'Revisiting the Discourses of Art, Beauty and Sport from the 1906 Consultative Conference for the Arts, Literature and Sport.' *Olympika: The International Journal of Olympic Studies* 5 (1996): 1–24.

Brown, Hugh Stowell. 'Manliness: A Lecture.' London: YMCA Lectures, [British Library], 1857–8.

Brown, Nigel. *Ice Skating: A History*. London: Nicholas Kaye, 1959.

– '1968 World Championships.' *Skating*, May 1968.

– 'Whither Skating.' *Skating*, May 1977.

Browne, George H. 'International Skating Union (Again).' *Skating*, February 1925.

– 'Figure Skating.' Unpublished manuscript, ca. 1923. World Figure Skating Museum, Colorado Springs, CO. File: Jackson Haines.
– *A Skating Primer: The New Skating*. Springfield: Barney and Berry, 1912.
Brunner, Melitta. 'A New Year, a New You.' *Skating*, February 1969.
Bryson, Lois. 'Sport and the Maintenance of Masculine Hegemony.' *Women's Studies International Forum* 10, no. 4 (1987): 349–60.
Buffery, Steve. 'Stojko Blasts Back at His Critics.' *Toronto Sun*, 20 February 2010. http://www.torontosun.com/sports/vancouver2010/news/2010/02/20/12963196.html.
Burke, Phyllis. *Gender Shock: Exploding the Myth of Male and Female*. New York: Anchor Books, 1996.
Burstyn, Varda. *The Rites of Men: Manhood, Politics and the Culture of Sport*. Toronto: University of Toronto Press, 1999.
Burt, Ramsay. *The Male Dancer: Bodies, Spectacles, Sexualities*. London: Routledge, 1995.
Butler, Judith. 'Athletic Genders: Hyperbolic Instance and/or the Overcoming of Sexual Binarism.' *Stanford Humanities Review* 6, no. 2 (1998). http://www.stanford.edu/group/SHR/6-2/html/butler.html.
– *Bodies That Matter: On the Discursive Limits of Sex*. New York: Routledge, 1993.
– *Gender Trouble: Feminism and the Subversion of Identity*. New York: Routledge, 1990.
Button, Dick. *Dick Button on Skates*. Englewood Cliffs, NJ: Prentice-Hall, 1955.
– 'Worldscope/1966 World Championships.' *Skating*, May 1966.
Cahn, Susan. *Coming on Strong: Gender and Sexuality in Twentieth-Century Women's Sport*. New York: Free Press, 1994.
Carlisle Duncan, Margaret, and Michael A. Messner. *Gender in Televised Sports: News and Highlights Shows, 1989–2004.* Amateur Athletic Foundation of Los Angeles, 2005.
Carter, Philip. 'An "Effeminate" or "Efficient" Nation? Masculinity and Eighteenth-Century Social Documentary.' *Textual Practice* 11 (1997): 429–43.
CBC Radio. *The Inside Track*. 'The Last Closet.' 16 October 1993.
CBC Radio, Toronto. Sports report on *Metro Morning*. 17 December 1992.
CBC Television. Coverage of 1992 Winter Olympic Games, Albertville, France. 19 February 1992.
Chamberlain, Carl. 'The United States Championships.' *Skating*, June 1949.
Charlotte [Oelschlägel]. *Hippodrome Skating Book*. New York: Hippodrome Skating Club, 1916.
Chatto, James. 'Spin Meister.' *Toronto Life*, February 1994.
Chauncey, George. *Gay New York: Gender, Urban Culture and the Making of the Gay Male World, 1890–1940*. New York: Basic Books, 1994.

Cheetham, L. 'Ladies' Chapter.' In D. Adams, *Skating*. London: George Bell, 1980

Christie, James. 'Helped to Turn Skating into a Performing Art.' *Globe and Mail*, 16 April 1994.

Christie, James, and David Longford. 'Pulling the Strings.' *Globe and Mail*, 5 February 1994.

'City of Athletes.' *Toronto Life*, November 2002.

Clark, Joe. 'Gay Blade.' *Village Voice*, 14 December 1993.

Clarkson, Michael. 'Skating's Spectre.' *Calgary Herald*, 13 December 1992.

Claus, Basil. 'Skating as Dance and Theatre.' *Dance Magazine*, December 1942.

Colledge, Cecilia. 'Which Is It – Art or Sport?' *Skating*, January 1977.

'Comparisons.' *Monthly Freeze*, November 1931.

Connell, R.W. *Masculinities*. Berkeley: University of California Press, 1995.

Connor, Steve. 'New Lad Emerges as Old Style Wimp.' *Independent*, 7 September 1998. http://www.independent.co.uk/news/new-lad-emerges-as-old-style-wimp-1196513.html.

Copley-Graves, Lynn. *Figure Skating History: The Evolution of Dance on Ice*. Columbus, OH: Plataro Press, 1992.

Cox, Yvonne. 'Some Jump, Some Smile.' *Chatelaine*, December 1989.

Craig, Jack. 'CBS Is on Thin Ice with Skating Strategy.' *Boston Globe*, 5 June 1994.

Cronin, Mike. 'Bobsledding.' In *International Encyclopedia of Women's Sports*, vol. 1, ed. Karen Christensen et al. New York, 2001.

CTV Television. Broadcast of men's short program at Canadian championships. 5 February 1993.

– Broadcast of men's long program at Skate Canada. 5 November 1994.

– Broadcast of men's long program at world championships. 30 March 2000.

– Broadcast of men's short program at world championships. 28 March 2000.

Cuddy, Jack. 'Sonja Henie a Sensation Both in Making Pictures and in Public Appearances.' *Globe and Mail*, 22 January 1938.

Curtin, Michael. *Propriety and Position: A Study of Victorian Manners*. New York: Garland, 1987.

Daniels, Dayna B. 'Country Club.' In *Berkshire Encyclopedia of World Sport*, ed. David Levinson and Karen Christiansen, 379–86. Boston: Berkshire Publishing Group, 2005.

– *Polygendered and Ponytailed: The Dilemma of Femininity and the Female Athlete*. Toronto: Women's Press, 2009.

– 'You Throw Like a Girl: Sport and Misogyny on the Silver Screen.' *Film and History* 35, no. 1 (2005): 29–38.

Davis, G. [George]. *Frostiana or A History of the River Thames in a Frozen State*. London: Printed and published on the River Thames, 5 February 1814.

Davis, Laurel R. 'Male Cheerleaders and the Naturalization of Gender.' In

Sport, Men and the Gender Order: Critical Feminist Perspectives, ed. Michael A. Messner and Don Sabo, 153–61. Champaign, IL: Human Kinetics, 1990.

Deacon, James. 'Sex Sells – To a Point.' *Maclean's*, 30 November 1998.

Deakin, J.M., and F. Allard. 'Skilled Memory in Expert Figure Skaters.' *Memory & Cognition* 19, no. 1 (1991): 79–86.

Delistraty, D.A., E.J. Reisman, and M. Snipes. 'A Physiological and Nutritional Profile of Young Female Figure Skaters.' *Journal of Sports Medicine and Physical Fitness* 32, no. 2 (1992): 149–55.

Deney, George. *Traité du patinage*. Paris: Delarue Libraire-éditeur, 1891.

Desmond, Jane C. 'Embodying Difference: Issues in Dance and Cultural Studies.' In *Meaning in Motion: New Cultural Studies of Dance*, ed. Jane C. Desmond, 29–54. Durham, NC: Duke University Press, 1997.

Diamantidi, Demeter, Carl von Korper, and Max Wirth. *Spuren auf dem Eise* [Tracks on the Ice]. Vienna: Alfred Hölder, 1881.

DiManno, Rosie. 'Half-naked Candeloro Fine Ending to Long-Running Skating Soap Opera.' *Toronto Star*, 28 February 1994.

Dixon Gottschild, Brenda. *The Black Dancing Body: A Geography from Coon to Cool*. New York: Palgrave Macmillan, 2003.

– 'Whoa! Whiteness in Dance?' *Dance Magazine*, June 2005.

Donaldson, Mike. 'What Is Hegemonic Masculinity?" *Theory and Society* 22 (1993): 643–57.

Doran, D'Arcy. 'Orser Wanted Palimony Suit Details Hushed.' *Toronto Star*, 19 November 1998.

Douglas, Delia D. 'To Be Young, Gifted, Black and Female: A Meditation on the Cultural Politics at Play in Representations of Venus and Serena Williams.' *Sociology of Sport Online* 5, no. 1 (2002). http://physed.otago.ac.nz/sosol/v5i2/v5i2_3.html.

Doyle, John. 'There's No Artistry to Blades, It's Just an Inelegant Gimmick.' *Globe and Mail*, 6 October 2009.

'Dressing the Part: The Sartorial Side of Skating.' *Monthly Freeze*, March 1931.

Dufek, J.S., and B.T. Bates. 'The Evaluation and Prediction of Impact Forces during Landings.' *Medicine and Science in Sports and Exercise* 22, no. 3 (1991): 370–7.

Dufresne, Todd, and Gary Genosko. 'Jones on Ice: Psychoanalysis and Figure Skating.' *International Journal of Psychoanalysis* 76 (1995): 123–33.

Dufur, Mikaela J. 'Gender and Sport.' In *Handbook of the Sociology of Gender*, ed. Janet Saltzman Chafetz, 583–600. New York: Kluwer Academic/Plenum Publishers, 2006.

Dummitt, Christopher. *The Manly Modern: Masculinity in Postwar Canada*. Vancouver: UBC Press, 2008.

Editorials. *Monthly Freeze*, April 1928, December 1931.

Eichberg, Henning. 'The Enclosure of the Body: The Historical Relativity of "Health," "Nature" and Environment of Sport.' In *Body Cultures: Essays on Sport, Space and Identity*, ed. John Bales and Chris Philo, 47–67. London: Routledge, 1998.

Eichelberger, Brenda. 'Voices on Black Feminism.' *Quest: A Feminist Quarterly* 3, no. 4 [Special issue on Race, Class, and Culture] (Spring 1977): 16–28.

Eisen, George. 'Jewish History and the Ideology of Modern Sport: Approaches and Interpretations.' *Journal of Sport History* 25, no. 3 (Fall 1998): 482–531.

Elliot, M. 'The Edinburgh Skating Club, 1778–1966.' In *The Book of the Old Edinburgh Club*, vol. 33, pt 2. Edinburgh, 1971.

Ewing, Lori. 'Chan Fires Back at French Skater's Criticism over Lack of Quad.' *CTV Olympics*, 23 March 2009. http://www.ctvolympics.ca/figure-skating/news/newsid=7524.html.

Fabos, Bettina. 'Forcing the Fairytale: Narrative Strategies in Figure Skating Competition Coverage.' *Sport in Society* 4, no. 2 (Summer 2001): 185–212.

Fausto-Sterling, Anne. 'The Bare Bones of Sex: Part 1 – Sex and Gender.' *Signs* 30, no. 2 (2005): 1491–528.

– *Sexing the Body: Gender Politics and the Construction of Sexuality*. New York: Basic Books, 2000.

Feder, Abigail M. 'Big Girls Do Cry: Femininity and "Toughness" in the Kerrigan-Harding Affair.' *The Drama Review (TDR)* 38, no. 3 (1994): 17–22.

Feder, Abigail M. '"A Radiant Smile from the Lovely Lady": Overdetermined Femininity in "Ladies" Figure Skating.' *The Drama Review* (TDR) 38, no. 1 (1994): 62–78.

Ferrara, C.M., and E. Hollingsworth. 'Physical Characteristics and Incidence of Injuries in Adult Figure Skaters.' *International Journal of Sports Physiology and Performance* 2, no. 3 (2007): 282–91.

Fillunger, Carl. 'Zur Europa-meisterschaft [European championship],' *Allgemeine Sportzeitung*, 26 February 1893.

Foote, Stephanie. 'Making Sport of Tonya: Class Performance and Social Punishment.' *Journal of Sport and Social Issues* 27, no. 1 (2003): 3–17.

Foucault, Michel. *The History of Sexuality, Volume 1*. New York: Penguin, 1981.

– *Power/Knowledge: Selected Interviews and Other Writing, 1972–1977*. Ed. Colin Gordon. New York: Pantheon, 1980.

Fowler, G. Herbert. *On the Outside Edge: Being Diversions in the History of Skating*. London: Horace Cox, 1897.

Frias, Carlos, and William M. Hartnett. 'Heavy Pressure: NFL Players Struggle with Weight Game.' *Palm Beach Post*, 29 October 2006. http://nflretirees.blogspot.com/2006/10/heavy-pressure-nfl-players-struggle.html.

Galindo, Rudy, with Eric Marcus. *Ice Breaker*. New York: Pocket Books, 1997.

Garafola, Lynn. 'Reconfiguring the Sexes.' In *The Ballet Russes and Its World*, ed. L. Garafola and N. Van Norman Baer. New Haven, CT: Yale University Press, 1999.

Garcin, J. *Le vrai patineur* [The True Skater]. Paris: Gillé Fils, 1813.

Gasner, Cynthia. 'Life Experiences Forge Human Rights Champion.' *Canadian Jewish News*, 3 January 2008. http://www.cjnews.com/index .php?option=com_content&task=view&id=13795&Itemid=86.

Gay, Peter. *Pleasure Wars: The Bourgeois Experience, Victoria to Freud*. New York: W.W. Norton, 1998.

Genel, Myron. 'Gender Verification No More?' Women's Sport Foundation, January 2001. http://www.womenssportsfoundation.org/Issues-And-Research/Equity-Issues/Archive.aspx.

Gerber, Ellen W. 'Chronicle of Participation.' In *The American Woman in Sport*, ed. Ellen W. Gerber, Jan Felshin, Pearl Berlin, and Waneen Wyrick. Reading, MA: Addison-Wesley, 1974.

Gilbert Coleman, Annie. 'The Unbearable Whiteness of Skiing.' In *Sport Matters: Race, Recreation and Culture*, ed. John Bloom and Michael Nevin Willard, 141–67. New York: New York University Press, 2002.

Gill, Edward. *The Skater's Manual: A Complete Guide to the Art of Skating*. Revised ed. New York: Andrew Peck & Co., 1867.

Gill, Rosalind, Karen Henwood, and Carl McLean. 'Body Projects and the Regulation of Normative Masculinity.' *Body and Society* 11, no. 1 (2005), 37–62.

Glantschnig, Helga. *Meine Dreier: Schlittschuhbuch* [My Threes: Skating Book]. Graz: Droschl, 1998.

Gluckman, Amy, and Betsy Reed. 'The Gay Marketing Moment.' In *Homo Economics: Capitalism, Community and Lesbian and Gay Life*, ed. Amy Gluckman and Betsy Reed, 3–10. New York: Routledge, 1997.

Goodfellow, Arthur. 'When the Worlds First Came to America.' *Skating*, March 1981.

Goodwin, H.A.C. 'An Introduction to Figure Skating.' In *Ice Rink and Skating World*. November 1930.

Graves, George W. Letter to Mrs Charles B. Blanchard, 4 January 1932. World Figure Skating Museum and Archives, box: Brunet, Blanchard, College; file: Graves to Blanchard.

Gregory, Norman V.S. 'So You Want to Figure Skate.' *Skating*, March 1961.

Grenfell, Christopher C., and Robert E. Rinehart. 'Skating on Thin Ice: Human Rights in Youth Figure Skating.' *International Review for the Sociology of Sport* 38, no. 1 (2003): 79–97.

Grewal, Shabnam, ed. *Charting the Journey: Writings by Black and Third World Women*. London: Sheba, 1988.

Grimditch, William H., Jr. 'Dynamism.' *Skating*, January 1944.

Gross, George. *Donald Jackson: King of Blades*. Toronto: Queen City Publishing, 1977.

Grossman, Arnold H., Anthony R. D'Augelli, Nicholas P. Salter, and Steven M. Hubbard. 'Comparing Gender Expression, Gender Nonconformity, and Parents' Responses of Female-to-Male and Male-to-Female Transgender Youth.' *Journal of LGBT Issues in Counseling* 1, no. 1 (May 2006): 41–59.

Gruneau, Richard. 'Modernization or Hegemony? Two Views on Sport and Social Development.' In *Not Just a Game: Essays in Canadian Sport Sociology*, ed. Jean Harvey and Hart Cantelon, 9–32. Ottawa: University of Ottawa Press, 1988.

GutsMuths, J.C.F. *Gymnastics for Youth*. Originally published in German in 1793. Trans. C.G. Salzman. London: J. Johnson, 1800 [published in English under Salzman's name].

Guttmann, Allen. 'Olympics.' In *International Encyclopedia of Women and Sports*, vol. 2, ed. Karen Christensen, Allen Guttmann, and Gertrude Pfister. New York: Macmillan Reference, 2001.

Haguenauer, M., P. Fargier, P. Legreneur, A. Dufour, B. Cogerino, M. Begon, and K.M. Monteil. 'Short-term Effects of Using Verbal Instructions and Demonstration at the Beginning of Learning a Complex Skill in Figure Skating.' *Perceptual and Motor Skills* 100, no. 1 (2005): 179–91.

Hall, M. Ann. *The Girl and the Game: A History of Women's Sport in Canada*. Peterborough, ON: Broadview Press, 2002.

Hampe, Matthias. *Stilwandel im Eiskunstlauf: Eine Ästhetik und Kulturgeschichte* [Style Transformation in Figure Skating: An Aesthetic and Cultural History]. Berlin: Peter Lang, 1994.

Hanna, Judith. *Dance, Sex and Gender: Signs of Identity, Dominance, Defiance, and Desire*. Chicago: University of Chicago, 1988.

Hargreaves, Jennifer. *Sporting Females: Critical Issues in the History and Sociology of Women's Sports*. London: Routledge, 1994.

– 'The Victorian Cult of the Family and the Early Years of Female Sport.' In *The Sport Process: A Comparative and Developmental Approach*, ed. Eric G. Dunning, Joseph A. Maguire, and Robert E. Pearton. Champaign, IL: Human Kinetics, 1993.

Harris, Daniel R. 'Effeminacy.' *Michigan Quarterly Review* 30, no. 1 (1991).

Heathcote, J.M., H. Ellington, E. Syers, and M.S. Monier-Williams. *A History of the National Skating Association of Great Britain, 1879–1901*. London: National Skating Association, 1902.

Hedges, Sid G. *Ice-rink Skating: An Easy Way to Waltzes and the Bronze Medal*. London: C. Arthur Pearson, 1932.

Heinlein, Franz. *100 Jahre Wiener Eislauf-Verein* [100 Years of the Vienna Skating Club]. Vienna: Wiener Eislaufverein, 1967.

Helfrich, George. 'Henriette Sontag.' *Skating*, May 1926.

– 'Three Famous Figures.' *Skating*, January 1928.

Henderson, John. 'Changing Perceptions of Skaters.' *Denver Post*, 8 February 2007. http://www.denverpost.com/ci_5181586?source=rss.

Henie, Sonja. *Wings on My Feet*. New York: Prentice-Hall, 1940.

Hennessy, John. 'A Monthly March to Immortality.' *Times* [London], 6 March 1976.

Hill, Darryl B., and Edgardo Menvielle. '"You have to give them a place where they feel protected and safe and loved": The Views of Parents Who Have Gender Variant Children and Adolescents.' *Journal of LGBT Youth* 6 (2009): 243–71.

Hill, George E.B. 'Ladies' Championship.' *Skating*, May 1931.

Hill Collins, Patricia. *Black Feminist Thought: Knowledge, Consciousness and the Politics of Empowerment*. 2nd ed. New York: Routledge, 2000.

Hoffman, Rosetta. 'Sonja Henie – Queen of the Ice.' *Strength and Health*, March 1937. http://www.sonjahenie.net/qoi.htm.

Hollander, Ann. *Sex and Suits: The Evolution of Modern Dress*. New York: Alfred A. Knopf, 1994.

Holt, Richard. *Sport and the British: A Modern History*. Oxford: Clarendon Press, 1989.

Hopkins, Stephen. 'Switch Blades.' *Saturday Night*, December 1989.

Howe, Henry W. 'Report of Special Committee on Judging.' *Skating*, December 1925.

Huggins, Mike. 'Sport and the Upper Classes: Introduction.' *Sport in History* 28, no. 3 (September 2008): 351–63.

Humphreys, Helen. *The Frozen Thames*. Toronto: McClelland and Stewart, 2007.

Hunter, Brad, and Gretchen Drummie. 'Orser in "Shock" over Lover's Suit.' *Toronto Sun*, 19 November 1998.

Hutchinson, Roger. *Empire Games: The British Invention of Twentieth-Century Sport*. London: Mainstream, 1996.

'Ice Skating Goes into Big Figures.' *Skating*, March 1940.

'International Figure Skating.' *Manchester Guardian*, 16 February 1898.

International Skating Union. Regulations, 1961.

International Skating Union, Regulations, 1994–1996.

Intersex Society of North America. 'How Common Is Intersex?' http://www .isna.org/faq/frequency.

Jackson, Jon. 'Frozen in the Closet.' *The Advocate*, 14 February 2006. http://
www.thefreelibrary.com/Frozen+in+the+closet%3a+why+don't+those+
fabulous+Olympic+figure+skaters...-a0141848557.

– *On Edge*. With James Pereira. New York: Thunder's Mouth Press, 2005.

Jakabsson, W. 'Criticism on the Modern Tendencies of Free Skating.' *Skating*,
April 1927.

Jamieson, Katherine M. 'Reading Nancy Lopez: Decoding Representations of
Race, Class and Sexuality.' *Sociology of Sport Journal* 15, no. 4 (1998): 343–58.

Jeffords, Susan. *Hard Bodies: Hollywood Masculinity in the Reagan Era*. New
Brunswick, NJ: Rutgers University Press, 1994.

J.M.L. 'Skating for Ladies. Why Ladies Ought to Skate, and Why They Do Not.'
Godey's Lady's Book, December 1863.

'John Curry.' *Times* (London), 16 April 1994.

Jones, Ernest. *The Elements of Figure Skating*. 2nd. ed. London: George Allen and
Unwin, 1952.

Jones, Robert. *A Treatise on Skating*. London, 1772.

– *A Treatise on Skating*. Revised ed. London, 1823.

Kane, Mary Jo, and Eldon Snyder. 'Sport Typing: The Social "Containment" of
Women in Sport.' *Arena Review* 13, no. 2 (November 1989): 77–96.

Kasser, Katherine V. 'Round Table Talks on Boy Skaters.' *Skating*, December
1945.

Katz, Jonathan Ned. *The Invention of Heterosexuality*. New York: Dutton, 1995.

Kaufman, King. 'So They're All Gay, Right?' *Salon.com*, 22 February 2002.
http://dir.salon.com/story/people/feature/2002/02/22/galindo/index
.html.

Keating, Steve. 'Figure Skating: Tough Guy Stojko Refuses to Be Upset.' Nando.
net news service, 12 February 1998.

Kennedy, Elizabeth Lapovsky, and Madeline D. Davis. *Boots of Leather and Slippers of Gold: The History of a Lesbian Community*. New York: Routledge, 1993.

Kessler, Suzanne J., and Wendy McKenna. *Gender: An Ethnomethodological
Approach*. New York: Wiley, 1978.

Kestnbaum, Ellyn. *Culture on Ice: Figure Skating and Cultural Meaning*. Middle-
town, CT: Wesleyan University Press, 2003.

Kidd, Bruce. *The Struggle for Canadian Sport*. Toronto: University of Toronto
Press, 1996.

Kim, Lorrie. 'Beyond Spirals with Jeff Nolt.' *6.0 Skate*, Spring 2001.

– '"Gayest Sport in America." So How Come No Figure Skaters Are
Out?' *Outsports.com*, 9 February 2006. http://www.outsports.com/
olympics/2006torino/kimfigureskating.htm.

Kimmel, Michael S. 'Consuming Manhood: The Feminization of American Culture and the Recreation of the Male Body, 1832–1920.' In *The Male Body*, ed. Laurence Goldstein, 12–41. Ann Arbor: University of Michigan Press, 1994.

– *Manhood in America: A Cultural History*. 2nd ed. New York: Oxford University Press, 2006.

King, Samantha. 'Consuming Compassion: AIDS, Figure Skating, and Canadian Identity.' *Journal of Sport and Social Issues* 24, no. 2 (May 2000): 148–75.

– 'What's Queer about (Queer) Sport Sociology Now? A Review Essay.' *Sociology of Sport Journal* 25, no 4 (2008): 419–42.

Klemesrud, Judy. 'Toller Cranston: Lonely at the Top.' *New York Times*, 2 June 1977.

Krause, Elizabeth. '"The bead of raw sweat in a field of dainty perspirers": Nationalism, Whiteness, and the Olympic-class ordeal of Tonya Harding.' *Transforming Anthropology* 7, no. 1 (1998): 33–52.

Laberge, Suzanne, and Mathieu Albert. 'Conceptions of Masculinity and Gender Transgressions in Sport among Adolescent Boys: Hegemony, Contestation and the Social Class Dynamic.' In *Masculinities, Gender Relations, and Sport*, ed. Jim McKay, Michael A. Messner, and Donald Sabo, 195–221. Thousand Oaks, CA: Sage, 2000.

Laine, Barry. 'Trendy Twosome.' *Ballet News* 7, no. 2 (1985).

Lambert, Luna. *The American Skating Mania: Ice Skating in the Nineteenth Century* (Washington: National Museum of History and Technology, 1978).

Laurendeau, Jason, and Carly Adams. '"Jumping like a girl": Discursive Silences, Exclusionary Practices and the Controversy over Women's Ski Jumping.' *Sport in Society* 13, no. 3 (2010): 431–47.

Lawton, Christopher. 'Sequins? What Sequins? Canada's New Spin on Triple Loops.' *Wall Street Journal*, 3 April 2009. http://online.wsj.com/article/SB123870938255484175.html.

Lee, Joon Oluchi. 'The Joy of the Castrated Boy.' *Social Text* 84–5, nos. 3–4 (2005).

Leger, Louise. 'Here's Looking at You Kurt.' *Broadcast Week*, 5–11 February 1994.

Lenskyj, Helen. *Out of Bounds: Women, Sport and Sexuality*. Toronto: Women's Press, 1986.

Levine, Martin P., and Michael S. Kimmel. *Gay Macho: The Life and Death of the Homosexual Clone*. New York: New York University Press, 1998.

Lewis, John F. *Skating and the Philadelphia Skating Club*. Philadelphia, 1895.

Lid, Franz. 'Elvis Lives.' *Sports Illustrated* (Canadian edition), 7 February 1994.

Lipetz, J., and R.J. Kruse. 'Injuries and Special Concerns of Female Figure Skaters.' *Clinics in Sports Medicine* 19, no. 2 (2000): 369–80.

Lippe, Gerd von der. 'Sportification Processes: Whose Logic? Whose Rationality?' *Sport History Review* 32 (2001): 42–55.

Loeser, Frank. 'Canadians.' *Skating*, April 1975.

– 'Sport vs. Art.' *Tracings*, no date (ca. mid-1980s). [Available at World Figure Skating Museum, file: Frank Loeser Nowosad.]

Longman, Jere. 'As Kim Raises the Bar, South Korea Delights.' *New York Times*, 26 February 2010.

Lorber, Judith. *The Paradoxes of Gender*. New Haven: Yale University Press, 1994.

Lowerson, John. *Sport and the English Middle Classes, 1870–1914*. Manchester: Manchester University Press, 1993.

MacDonald, Gayle. 'It's Hockey Season, but Wait a Second. Isn't That Tie Domi … Ice Dancing?' *Globe and Mail*, 3 October 2009.

Mangan, J.A. *Athleticism in the Victorian and Edwardian Public School*. Cambridge: Cambridge University Press, 1981.

Mangan, J.A., and James Walvin, eds. *Manliness and Morality: Middle-class Masculinity in Britain and America, 1800–1940*. Manchester: Manchester University Press, 1987.

Matteo, Sherri. 'The Effect of Sex and Gender-schematic Processing on Sport Participation.' *Sex Roles* 15, nos. 7–8 (1986): 417–32.

McClintock, Anne. *Imperial Leather: Race, Gender and Sexuality in the Colonial Contest*. New York: Routledge, 1995.

McCrone, Kathleen E. *Sport and the Physical Emancipation of English Women, 1870–1914*. London: Routledge, 1988.

McDaniel, Roy W. 'As to Figure Skating.' *Skating*, March 1929.

McGarry, Karen. 'Mass Media and Gender Identity in High Performance Canadian Figure Skating.' *The Sport Journal* 8, no. 1 (2005). http://www.thesportjournal.org/article/mass-media-and-gender-identity-high-performance-canadian-figure-skating.

– 'Passing as a Lady: Nationalist Narratives of Femininity, Race, and Class in Elite Canadian Figure Skating.' *Genders* 41 (2005). http://www.genders.org/g41/g41_mcgarry.html.

– 'Performing Nationalisms: Spectacle and Identity in High Performance Canadian Figure Skating.' Unpublished doctoral dissertation. York University, 2003.

McGillivray, David. 'Are Skaters Athletes?' *Canadian Skater*, April 1982.

Meagher, George. *Lessons in Skating*. Toronto: George N. Morang & Company, 1900.

Melody, Tom. 'At Home with the Jenkinses.' *Skating*, May 1966.

Messner, Michael A., Margaret Carlisle Duncan, and Kerry Jensen. 'Separating the Men from the Girls: The Gendered Language of Televised Sports.' *Gender and Society* 7, no. 1 (March 1993): 121–37.

Messner, Michael A., and Donald F. Sabo. *Sex, Violence and Power in Sports*. Freedom, CA: The Crossing Press, 1994.

Metheny, Eleanor. 'Some Differences in Bodily Proportions between American Negro and White Male College Students as Related to Athletic Performance.' *Research Quarterly* 10 (December 1939): 41–53.

– 'Symbolic Forms of Movement: The Feminine Image in Sports.' In *Connotations of Movement in Sport and Dance*, ed. Eleanor Metheny, 43–56. Dubuque, IA: Wm. C. Brown, 1965.

'Miss Weld Wins Laurels.' *New York Times*, 7 February 1918.

Milton, Steve. *Skate: One Hundred Years of Figure Skating*. Toronto: Key Porter, 1996.

Mitchell, Roy. 'How Queer Is Figure Skating?' *Xtra*, 20 November 1997.

Monier-Williams, Montagu S. *Figure-Skating*. London: A.D. Innes, 1898.

Monsma, E.V., and R.M. Malina. 'Correlates of Eating Disorders Risk among Female Figure Skaters: A Profile of Adolescent Competitors.' *Psychology of Sport and Exercise* 5, no. 4 (2004): 447–60.

Montreal Skating Club. *The Constitution of the Montreal Skating Club*. 1860–1.

Moore, Teresa. *Reflections on the CFSA, 1887–1990*. Gloucester, ON: Canadian Figure Skating Association, 1993.

Morrow, Don. 'Sweetheart Sport: Barbara Ann Scott and the Post World War II Image of the Female Athlete in Canada.' *Canadian Journal of the History of Sport* 18, no. 1 (1987): 36–54.

Morse, Margaret. 'Sport on Television: Replay and display.' In *Regarding Television: Critical Approaches – An Anthology*, ed. E.A. Kaplan, 44–66. Los Angeles: American Film Institute, 1983.

Mosse, George L. *The Image of Man: The Creation of Modern Masculinity*. Oxford: Oxford University Press, 1996.

Munns, Tommy. 'Scanning the Field.' *Globe and Mail*, 29 Janaury 1938.

National Museum of History of Technology. 'The American Skating Mania: Ice Skating in the Nineteenth Century.' Washington, 1978.

'The National Skating Association's Commemoration Week.' *The Field* 99 (22 February 1902).

Neale, Steve. 'Masculinity as Spectacle: Reflections on Men and Mainstream Cinema.' *Screen* 24, no. 6 (1983): 2–16.

Negra, Diane. *Off-White Hollywood: American Culture and Ethnic Female Stardom*. New York: Routledge, 2001.

Nevius, C.W. 'Men Dump Sequins, Try More Macho Style.' *San Francisco Chronicle*, 28 March 1992.

Nixon, Sean. *Hard Looks: Masculinities, Spectatorship and Contemporary Consumption*. New York: St Martin's, 1996.

North, Christopher. 'Winter Rhapsody.' *Blackwood's Edinburgh Magazine* 29 (February 1831).

Ohler, Shawn, and Murray Whyte. 'Orser Unmasked by Lawsuit.' *National Post*, 19 November 1998.

'Olympic Skating: An Appreciation and Some Comments.' *Monthly Freeze*, March 1928.

Orser, Brian, with Steve Milton. *Orser: A Skater's Life*. Toronto: Key Porter, 1988.

Parkinson Speck, Elizabeth. 'The Well Dressed Man.' *Skating*, May 1945.

Parks, Carolyn. 'Sex: Male, Profession: Dancer?' *Dance Magazine*, 27 April 1953.

Parks, Roberta J. 'Biological Thought, Athletics and the Formation of a "Man of Character": 1830–1900.' In *Manliness and Morality: Middle-class Masculinity in Britain and America*, ed. J.A. Mangan and James Walvin, 7–34. Manchester: Manchester University Press, 1987.

Pawson Bean, Dawn. 'Swimming, Synchronized.' In *International Encyclopedia of Women and Sports*, vol. 3, ed. Karen Christensen, Allen Guttmann, and Gertrud Pfister, 1145–9. New York: Macmillan Reference, 2001.

Perkins, Dave. 'Elvis Dazzles.' *Toronto Star*, 13 February 1998.

– 'Stojko in Good Spot to Launch Attack.' *Toronto Star*, 13 February 1998.

Perry, Larry. 'Boston Woman Skater Wins Championship.' No date [the competition, as reported in other clippings, was in March 1917]. World Figure Skating Museum, file: Theresa Wells Blanchard, 1911–1918 [78.7.10].

Pikula, Joan. 'John Curry: Scaling Olympia on Arabesques and Ice.' *After Dark*, December 1976.

Poovey, Mary. *Uneven Developments: The Ideological Work of Gender in Mid-Victorian England*. Chicago: University of Chicago Press, 1988.

Pope, Harrison G., Jr, Roberto Olivardia, Amanda Gruber, and John Borowiecki. 'Evolving Ideals of Male Body Image as Seen through Action Toys.' *International Journal of Eating Disorders* 26, no. 1 (May 1999): 65–72.

Porter, E.B., C.C. Young, M.W. Niedfeldt, and L.M. Gottschlich. 'Sport-specific Injuries and Medical Problems of Figure Skaters.' *Wisconsin Medical Journal* 106, no. 6 (2007): 330–4.

Posner, Michael. 'Just as Things Looked Hopeless, Kathy Saved the Day.' *Maclean's*, 23 February 1976.

Pronger, Brian. 'Outta My Endzone: Sport and the Territorial Anus.' *Journal of Sport and Social Issues* 23, no. 4 (1999): 373–89.

Proudfoot, Jim. 'Browning Is a Scrapper,' *Toronto Star*, 10 March 1990.

– 'Dream Team Qualifies as Only True Amateurs.' *Toronto Star*, 9 August 1992.

Purdy, Daniel. 'The Whiteness of Beauty: Weimar Neo-Classicism and the Sculptural Transcendence of Colour.' *Amsterdamer Beiträge zur neueren Germanistik* 56 (2004).

Quintanilla, Michael. 'Mabel Fairbanks, 85; Black Ice Skater.' *Los Angeles Times*, 4 October 2001. http://articles.latimes.com/2001/oct/04/local/me-53367.

Rand, Erica. 'I Wanted Black Skates: Gender, Cash, Pleasure, and the Politics of Criticism.' *Criticism* 50, no. 4 (2008): 555–80.

Reed, Susan. 'Fear on the Ice.' *People*, 25 January 1993.

Renold, Emma. 'Learning the "Hard" Way: Boys, Hegemonic Masculinity and the Negotiation of Learner Identities in the Primary School.' *British Journal of the Sociology of Education* 22, no. 3 (2001): 369–85.

Renwick, Paul. '"Ball up!": Ice Skating in New York's Central Park, 1860–1870.' Unpublished master's paper, Department of History, University of Toronto, no date.

Reuel, Fritz. *Das Eissportbuch* [The Ice Sport Book]. Stuttgart: Dieck, 1928.

Reuters.com. 'Yuna and Mao Put Asian Markets on Ice.' 24 February 2010. http://in.reuters.com/article/idINIndia-46428420100224.

Richards, Christopher. 'Schmockey Night in Canada.' *Xtra*, 30 January 1997.

Richardson, T.D. 'The Master Skater: An Appreciation of Gillis Grafstrom.' *Monthly Freeze*, December 1930.

– *Modern Figure Skating*. 2nd rev. ed. London: Methuen, 1938.

– 'Retrospection.' *Monthly Freeze*, November 1928.

Riemer, Brenda A., and Michelle E. Visio. 'Gender Typing of Sports: An Investigation of Metheny's Classification.' *Research Quarterly for Exercise and Sport* 74 (2003): 193–204.

'Rob McCall Dies after Lengthy Illness.' *Halifax Chronicle Herald*, 16 November 1991.

Rofes, Eric. 'Making Our Schools Safe for Sissies.' In *The Gay Teen: Educational Practice and Theory for Lesbian, Gay and Bisexual Adolescents*, ed. G. Unks, 79–84. London: Routledge, 1995.

Rohanram, Radhika. *Imperial White*. Minneapolis: University of Minnesota Press, 2007.

Rosenzweig, Roy, and Elizabeth Blackmar. *The Park and the People: A History of Central Park*. Ithaca: Cornell University Press, 1992.

Rottnek, Matthew, ed. *Sissies and Tomboys: Gender Nonconformity and Homosexual Childhood*. New York: Routledge, 1999.

Ryan, Joan. *Little Girls in Pretty Boxes: The Making and Breaking of Elite Gymnasts and Figure Skaters*. New York: Doubleday, 1995.

Salzmann, C.G. *Gymnastics for Youth or a Practical Guide to Healthful and Amusing Exercises*. London: J. Johnson, 1800. [Originally published in German in 1793 by Johann Christoph Friedrich Gutsmuths. The English translation was published under translator Salzmann's name.]

Scheurer, Richard A. 'Breaking the Ice: The Mabel Fairbanks Story.' *American Visions*, December–January 1997. http://findarticles.com/p/articles/mi_m1546/is_n6_v12/ai_20084308/.

Schilling, Chris. *The Body and Social Theory*. 2nd ed. London: Sage, 2003.

Schmalz, Dorothy L., and Deborah L. Kerstetter. 'Girlie Girls and Manly Men: Children's Stigma Consciousness of Gender in Sports and Physical Activities.' *Journal of Leisure Research* 38, no. 4 (2006): 536–57.

Schwartz, Larry. 'Billie Jean Won for All Women.' *Espn.com*. http://espn.go.com/sportscentury/features/00016060.html.

Schwarz, Alan. 'Figure Skating Rivalry Pits Athleticism against Artistry.' *New York Times*, 18 March 2008.

Shawn, Ted. *Dance We Must*. New York: Haskell House Publishers, 1974.

Shumway, F. Ritter. 'Clothes Can Help the Man, Too.' *Skating*, January 1954.

Siltanen, Janet, and Andrea Doucet. *Gender Relations in Canada, Intersectionality and Beyond*. Toronto: Oxford University Press, 2008.

Silvera, Makeda, and Nila Gupta, eds. 'Women of Colour.' *Fireweed*, Spring 1983.

Simmons, Steve. 'The Last Word.' *Toronto Sun*, 6 May 1992.

Sinfield, Alan. *The Wilde Century: Effeminacy, Oscar Wilde and the Queer Moment*. New York: Columbia University Press, 1994.

Skate Canada [known as the Canadian Figure Skating Association until 2000]. 'Associate Membership Profile Statistics.' From *Annual Reports*, 1996–2005.

– 'A Message from CEO William Thompson.' http://www.skatecanada.ca/en/news_views/news/2008_2009/may_6.cfm.

– *Official Rulebook*. 2002.

– *Sponsor 'Fact sheet.'* 2002/3.

'The Skating Championships.' *Globe* (London), 17 February 1898.

Skating Club, The. *Historical Sketch of the Club and Description of the Rink and Pavilion*. London, 1909.

Smith, Beverly. *Figure Skating: A Celebration*. Toronto: McClelland and Stewart, 1994.

– 'Helping Buddies through Bad Times.' *Globe and Mail*, 23 November 1992.

– 'He's Soaring over Ice.' *Globe and Mail*, 1 February 1991.

– 'Kim's Rock Star Power.' *CTV Olympics*, 18 December 2009. http://www.ctvolympics.ca/figure-skating/news/newsid=23144.html.

Springs, Sonja. 'Skating's Shadow.' *Montreal Gazette*, 26 January 1993.

Staples, David. 'Skating Is No Wussy Sport.' *Saturday Night*, October 1997.

Stensrude, Curt. 'The Path to Excellence.' *Skating*, October 1983.

Stephenson, Lois, and Richard Stephenson. *A History and Annotated Bibliography of Skating Costume*. Meriden, CT: Bayberry Hill Press, 1970.

Stevens, Neil. 'Figure Skaters Allowed to Wear Tights, Trousers.' *Kingston Whig Standard*, 19 June 2004.

Stevenson, Alexandra. 'International Chit-chat.' *Tracings*. January/February 1993.

Stevenson, Sandra. *The BBC Book of Skating*. London: British Broadcasting Corporation, 1984.

Stewart, Otis. *Perpetual Motion: The Public and Private Lives of Rudolf Nureyev*. New York: Simon and Shuster, 1995.

Strait, Raymond, and Leif Henie. *Queen of Ice, Queen of Shadows: The Unsuspected Life of Sonja Henie*. New York: Scarborough House, 1985.

Stryker, Susan. '(De)Subjugated Knowledges: An Introduction to Transgender Studies.' In *The Transgender Studies Reader*, ed. Susan Stryker and Stephen Whittle, 1–17. New York: Routledge, 2006.

Studlar, Gaylyn. 'Douglas Fairbanks: Thief of the Ballets Russes.' In *Bodies of the Text: Dance as Theory, Literature as Dance*, ed. E.W. Goellner and J.S. Murphy, 107–24. New Brunswick, NJ: Rutgers University Press, 1995.

Sussman, Herbert. *Victorian Masculinities: Manhood and Masculine Poetics in Early Victorian Literature and Art*. Cambridge: Cambridge University Press, 1995.

Swift, E.M. 'Spin City.' *Sports Illustrated*, 23 February 1998.

Swift, Frank, and Marvin R. Clark. *The Skater's Textbook*. New York, 1868.

Syers, Edgar, and Madge Syers, ed. *The Book of Winter Sports*. London: Edward Arnold, 1908.

Sykes, Heather. 'Queering Theories of Sexuality in Sport Studies.' In *Sport, Sexualities and Queer/Theory*, ed. Jayne Caudwell, 13–32. London: Routledge, 2006.

Tagg, Brendan. '"Imagine a man playing netball!": Masculinities and Sport in New Zealand.' *International Review for the Sociology of Sport* 43, no. 4 (2008): 409–30.

Tarasov, Nikolai. *Ballet Techniques for Male Dancers*. Trans. E. Kraft. Garden City, NJ: Doubleday, 1985.

Taylor, Darien. 'Looking Back, Moving Forward: 25 Years of HIV/AIDS in Toronto.' AIDS Committee of Toronto, 29 November 2007. http://www .actoronto.org/home.nsf/pages/act.docs.0599.

Taylor, G.M., and D.M. Ste-Marie. 'Eating Disorders Symptoms in Canadian Female Pair and Dance Figure Skaters.' *International Journal of Sport Psychology* 32, no. 1 (2001): 21–8.

Taylor, Joe. 'Athlete or Artist … Which Direction for Our Skaters?' *Canadian Skater*, November/December 1976.

Terry, Walter. 'The Ice Man.' *Saturday Review* 3, no. 3 (1979).

Theberge, Nancy. 'Toward a Feminist Alternative to Sport as a Male Preserve.' *Quest* 10 (1985): 193–202.

Thomas, Katie. 'College Team Teaches a Lesson in Tolerance.' *New York Times*, 7 May 2010. http://www.nytimes.com/2010/05/09/sports/09oneonta .html?_r=1&src=me.

Thomson, Duncan, and Lynn Gladstone-Millar. *The Skating Minister: The Story behind the Painting*. Edinburgh: National Galleries of Scotland and National Museum of Scotland, 2004.

Tobias, Tobi. 'It's Becoming O.K. in America for Boys to Dance.' *New York Times*, 9 January 1977.

Toronto Curling and Skating Club. *By-laws*. 1875.

Tough Guys: Violence, Media and the Crisis in Masculinity. Produced and directed by Sut Jhally. Media Education Foundation, 1999.

Transgender Law Center. 'Transgender and Gender Non-conforming Youth: Recommendations for Schools.' http://www.transgenderlaw.org/resources/tlcschools.htm.

Trujillo, Nick. 'Hegemonic Masculinity on the Mound: Media Representations of Nolan Ryan and American Sports Culture.' In *Reading Sport: Critical Essays on Power and Representation*, ed. Susan Birrell and Mary G. McDonald, 14–39. Boston: Northeastern University Press, 2000.

Turner, Roger F. 'Sidelights of the 1931 World's Championships.' *Skating*, May 1931.

'Twenty Years of the USFSA.' *Skating*, December 1941.

Vail, George. *L'art du patinage*. Paris, 1886.

Vandervell, H.E., and T. Maxwell Witham. *A System of Figure Skating*. 2nd ed. London: Horace Cox, 1874.

Vertinsky, Patricia. *Eternally Wounded Woman: Women, Doctors and Exercise in the Late Nineteenth Century*. Manchester: Manchester University Press, 1990.

Victoria Skating Club. *Act of Incorporation, By-laws and List of Shareholders of the Victoria Skating Club of St John*. 1870.

Vinson, Maribel Y. *Advanced Figure Skating*. New York, 1940.

– 'Gay Blades.' [Letters to her family] 1933. World Figure Skating Museum. Box: Vinson Diaries.

– 'Gay Blades: Part II.' 1936. World Figure Skating Museum. Box: Vinson Diaries.

Volland Waters, Karen. *The Perfect Gentleman: Masculine Control in Victorian Men's Fiction, 1870–1901*. New York: Peter Lang, 1997.

Wade, A.C.A. *The Skater's Cavalcade: Fifty Years of Skating*. London: Olympic Publications, 1939.

Walvin, James. 'Symbols of Moral Superiority: Slavery, Sport and the Changing World Order, 1800–1950.' In *Manliness and Morality: Middle-class Masculinity in Britain and America*, ed. J.A. Mangan and James Walvin, 242–60. Manchester: Manchester University Press, 1987.

Wayne, June. 'The Male Artist as Stereotypical Female.' *Arts in Society* 2 (1972).

Weeks, Jeffrey. *Sex Politics and Society: The Regulation of Sexuality since 1800*. 2nd ed. London: Longman, 1989.

Weld Blanchard, Theresa. 'The Fourth Olympic Winter Games.' *Skating*, April 1936.
– 'Olympic Skating, 1920 & 1924.' *Skating*, December 1935.
– 'Skating's Part in the War.' *Skating*, January 1942.
Wendl, Ingrid. *Eis mit Stil* [Ice with Style]. Vienna and Munich: Jugend und Volk, 1979.
Wenn, Stephen R. 'Give Me the Keys Please: Avery Brundage, Canadian Journalists, and the Barbara Ann Scott Phaeton Affair.' *Journal of Sport History* 18, no. 2 (1991): 241–54.
West, Candace, and Dan H. Zimmerman. 'Doing Gender.' *Gender & Society* 1, no. 2 (June 1987): 125–51.
Whannel, Garry. *Media Sport Stars: Masculinities and Moralities*. London: Routledge, 2002.
'What Has Happened to Skating All Over the World the Last Two Years.' *Skating*, December 1941.
Whedon, Julia. *The Fine Art of Ice Skating: An Illustrated History and Portfolio of Stars*. New York: Harry N. Abrams, 1988.
White, H.D.J. 'The Art of Free Skating.' *Ice Rink and Skating World* 1, no. 2 (May–June 1930).
White, Patrick. 'Figure Skating Gets Tough.' *Globe and Mail*, 4 February 2009.
Whitson, David. 'Sport in the Social Construction of Masculinity.' In *Sport, Men and the Gender Order: Critical Feminist Perspectives*, ed. Michael Messner and Don Sabo. Champaign, IL: Human Kinetics, 1990.
Wiggins, David. 'Great Speed but Little Stamina': The Historical Debate over Black Athletic Superiority.' *Journal of Sport History* 16 (Summer 1989): 158–85.
Wilkes, Debbi, and Greg Cable. *Ice Time: A Portrait of Figure Skating*. Scarborough, ON: Prentice-Hall, 1994.
Williams, Jean. *A Game for Rough Girls? A History of Women's Football in Britain*. London: Routledge, 2003.
Willis, Paul. 'Women in Sport in Ideology.' In *Sport, Culture and Ideology*, ed. Jennifer Hargreaves, 117–35. London: Routledge and Kegan Paul, 1982.
Windhausen, John D. 'Russia's First Olympic Victor.' *Journal of Sport History* 3, no. 1 (1976): 35–44.
Winzer, Hugo. 'Geschichte des Eiskunstlaufs [History of Figure Skating].' In *Handbuch der Leibesübungen, Band 8: Eissport*, ed. Carl Diem, Artur Mallwitz, and Edmund Neuendorff. Berlin: Weidmann, 1925.
– 'An Outline of Figure Skating.' *Skating*, April 1927.
Witham, T. Maxwell. 'Figure Skating.' In *The Badminton Library of Sports and Pastimes: Skating, Figure Skating, Curling, etc.* London: Longmans, Green, and Co., 1892.

Witt, G.F.C. 'Letter to the Editor.' *Skating*, December 1949.

Wright, Benjamin T. *Skating around the World, 1892–1992: The One Hundredth Anniversary History of the International Skating Union*. Davos: Platz, 1992.

Wright, Richard. 'Blade Spinner.' *Saturday Night*, July 1987.

Wu, S.S., and M.C.K. Yang. 'Evaluation of the Current Decision Rule in Figure Skating and Possible Improvements.' *The American Statistician* 58, no. 1 (2004): 46–69.

Young, David. *The Golden Age of Canadian Figure Skating*. Toronto: Summerhill Press, 1984.

Young, Linda. *Middle-class Culture in the Nineteenth Century*. Houndmills, Basingstoke: Palgrave Macmillan, 2003.

Zell, Alan. 'A Sporting Image.' *Skating*, May 1970.

Ziegler, P., S. Hensley, J.B. Roepke, S.H. Whitaker, B.W. Craig, and A. Drewnowski. 'Eating Attitudes and Energy Intakes of Female Skaters.' *Medicine and Science in Sports and Exercise* 30, no. 4 (1998): 583–6.

Illustration Credits

The Skater by Gilbert Stuart: Board of Trustees, National Gallery of Art, Washington.

'The Combined-Figure' from *Figure Skating* by Montagu S. Monier-Williams (London, A.D. Innes, 1898).

Jackson Haines: *The Art of Skating: Its history and development with practical directions* by Irving Brokaw (London, Letchworth at the Arden Press, 1910).

Skating Rink before the Stubentor by Franz Kollarz: Austrian National Library Photo Archives (ÖNB Wien, 229.413-B).

Madge Syers: World Figure Skating Museum and Hall of Fame.

Nikolai Panin and Henning Grenander: *The Art of Skating: Its history and development with practical directions* by Irving Brokaw (London, Letchworth at the Arden Press, 1910).

Gillis Grafstrom: World Figure Skating Museum and Hall of Fame.

Karl Schäfer: Austrian National Library Photo Archives (ÖNB Wien, Pf 8.751:D(1)).

Sonja Henie: World Figure Skating Museum and Hall of Fame.

Dick Button: World Figure Skating Museum and Hall of Fame.

John Curry: World Figure Skating Museum and Hall of Fame.

Toller Cranston: Skate Canada Archives.

Kurt Browning: scottgrant.photoshelter.com.

Elvis Stojko: Gerry Thomas/Skate Canada Archives.

Jeffrey Buttle: scottgrant.photoshelter.com.

Patrick Chan: scottgrant.photoshelter.com.

Index